leaps & unhorsed the fiend. Bayardo
was of a bay colour
animal. After Rin...
he escaped & could not be caught
again though many attempts were
made to do so & afterwards it was
considered lucky to see the horse.
He is supposed to be still alive,
& the rumour goes that he has
been seen on several occasions
at various parts of the Country,
& that some of the braves of
the inhabitants have combined
together to catch him but have
so far failed; also it is reported
that a 'demon' horseman rides him
now with whom Bayardo seems
quite happy.

BAYARDO

The Life, Times and Legacy of an Edwardian Champion

BAYARDO

The Life, Times and Legacy of an Edwardian Champion

By Peter Corbett

Foreword by Tony Morris

Published in 2010 by Rinaldo Publishing Bury St Edmunds IP29 5HD

A catalogue record for this book is available from the British Library.

ISBN 978-0-9566642-0-4

Produced in association with David Lewis XML Associates Ltd., Bungay, Suffolk
Printed in the UK by CPI William Clowes, Beccles NR34 7TL

In the steady gaze of the horse shines a silent eloquence that speaks of love, loyalty, strength and courage.

L. McGuire

Acknowledgements

Considerable thanks are due to Nigel Pullen for his substantial contribution with regard to all matters relating to the breeding and stud careers of the horses covered in this book and for supplying the breeding statistics in the appendices. In addition I would like to thank him for not only reading and scrutinizing the texts – eliminating many of the author's errors - but for his unstinted enthusiasm, support and advice which he displayed from the moment the project was first discussed with him.

In addition special thanks are due to the following: Tim Cox for all his help in reading the texts, tracking down various items and for granting access to his extensive library and for his help, views and encouragement. Paul Mathieu for his help, encouragement and for supplying his notes compiled when writing *Masters of Manton* and for establishing the authentic history regarding Alfred Cox's life in Australia. In addition Paul's help, support and encouragement were such that without them it is not certain this project would have reached completion. John Berry for reading the texts and making sure some of the more embarrassing grammatical errors did not survive into print, for his professional advice, help and for his encouragement. Grateful thanks to Tony Morris for his kind and excellent foreword and for allowing access to his library, for sources that even Tim's prodigious library, for once, could not produce, and for his encouragement. Greg Way was helpful in supplying books and finding various sources of information. Caroline Bridge helped with some aspects of horse behaviour. To the Sangster family, Brian Meehan and his staff, for allowing access to the original training yard at Manton and for their welcome and help during the time of my visit. Finally, to my wife Brenda for her help with the photographs, designing the jacket and unstinting support, particularly during the exasperating times.

Picture acknowledgements

The author and publisher are grateful to the following for providing the majority of the illustrations in this book and for allowing their copyright photographs to be reproduced:

Rouch Wilmot Thoroughbred Library
Mary Evans Picture Library

Whilst every effort has been made to trace the copyright holders of all the illustrations for this book, it has not been possible in every case. The publishers will be pleased to rectify any omissions whenever possible.

Ratings

The ratings given throughout the book are either *Timeform* ratings, from 1948, *A Century of Champions* prior to that date or the author's calculated with reference to the ratings supplied in both of those publications. Not all ratings are the same and where they differ those concerned are indicated. The individual ratings for each of Bayardo's races are the authors. All ratings are calculated using the same principles used by those two publications: they are designed to be comparable with any horse that ran since the beginning of the Twentieth Century. For example a horse rated 130 in Bayardo's time is considered the equal of a horse rated 130 at any time in the Twentieth Century and up to the present day.

The value of money

Wherever a sum of money is quoted the approximate present day value will be given in brackets. For example a pound in 1909 is worth about 64 pounds today. Britain suffered rapid inflation from 1914 until 1920 and then deflation until the commencement of the Second World War in 1939. For the period Bayardo was at stud and his progeny the multiple used is 35 times. It should be remembered that any true comparison is impossible simply because the retail price index is not measured in the same way today as it was a hundred years ago and money is not spent in the same way or on the same products. Inaccurate it may be but it is all that is available as a means of comparing the value of money with that of a century ago.

Foreword
by Tony Morris

WHEN John Randall and I came to compile a list of the best horses of the Twentieth Century for our book *A Century of Champions*, and to assign ratings for them, we noted a glaring omission from the canon of equine biographies.

There was no doubting Bayardo's greatness. He was a champion in each of his three seasons in training, progressing from outstanding precocious juvenile sprinter to Classic winner at three, then to reveal himself as a magnificent stayer at four, with a Gold Cup performance that was never surpassed.

The rating we gave to Bayardo when he was four in 1910 was 141, an indication of exceptional merit. As we worked forward in making our assessments we found that we could rate no horse more highly until 1933, when we ranked three-year-old Hyperion, a grandson of Bayardo, 1lb higher. And we placed Tudor Minstrel, Hyperion's grandson, on the same mark for his exploits at three in 1947.

Those figures underline Bayardo's importance as an athlete and as a progenitor; his impact on racing and breeding was nothing short of phenomenal. Yet nobody had ever recognized his achievements with a full-scale tribute. There were books on Hyperion, Ribot, Brigadier Gerard, Mill Reef, Nijinsky and most of the other conspicuous greats of the Twentieth Century Turf, while Bayardo remained unacknowledged, in danger of being forgotten.

That threat has at last been averted, and today's generation of race fans need no longer be ignorant of this great horse's deeds and his contribution to the breed. Peter Corbett has done a first-class job in providing an overdue tribute, and I heartily recommend this work to all who love the Thoroughbred and the sport of horseracing.

Tony Morris,
Newmarket, August 2010.

Contents

Prologue 1885

Mount Gipps, New South Wales, Australia. The tension mounts over a card-school as a young Englishman scrutinises the hand he has been dealt. In a best-of-three rubber the score is one-all, the stakes are high and he is resolute that he must prevail. The fierce expression on the features of the Scotsman opposite suggests he is just as determined to win. The cards are played and eventually the young Englishman smiles.

*　　*　　*

Manton, England. A leading trainer is engaged in his daily routine having spent many years building up a top stable in order that his son might eventually succeed him and train the best horses for the wealthiest owners in the land.

*　　*　　*

Hartford, Connecticut, North America. A four year old boy is occupying himself with the normal pastimes that infants of that age are wont to do, totally unaware that his future is to be one of fame and fortune as a rider of thoroughbred race-horses in a faraway land.

*　　*　　*

Ellesmere Stud, Newmarket, England. In residence is a thirteen-year- old stallion, a top-class stayer as a race-horse, who would go on to sire three Derby winners, but whose lasting fame would begin through a horse well below classic standard.

*　　*　　*

Malton, England. A yearling filly who will win two good races as a juvenile but nothing else is being prepared for her life in thoroughbred racing. But it is as a broodmare and her production of a filly which, although she would never race, would in turn foal a filly that would eventually become one of the greatest broodmares of the Twentieth Century.

*　　*　　*

His foaling may have been more than twenty years in the future, but the human and equine ingredients were gradually coming together; the events slowly unfolding that will culminate in the production of one of the greatest race-horses of the Twentieth Century.

CHAPTER 1

Life in Bayardo's time

Nineteen hundred and six was just over half way through the Edwardian age. Queen Victoria had died five years previously, after a reign lasting almost sixty four years, and had been succeeded by her second child and eldest son Edward VII. Nearly all periods of time are described as times of great change but few can match the period from 1901 to 1914. No monarch had had more impact on their subjects' lives than Edward, both prior to and after his ascension to the throne. He was already well known in his capacity as Prince of Wales, a role he filled from the age of one month until the age of sixty.

Although heir apparent he was largely excluded from royal duties, (his mother considered him too unreliable to be trusted with any affairs of state) and thus with nothing worthwhile to occupy him he devoted his time to society. Although responsible for numerous good works, these are not what he is most remembered for in the period up to the end of the nineteenth century. He was known to have an eye for a beautiful woman, was cited in two divorce cases and earned from the author Henry James the nickname of "Edward the Caresser". However, as Prince of Wales he was treated with considerable deference by the newspapers in regard to his amorous pursuits. Whereas the daily exploits and pastimes of his mistresses' Alice Keppel and Lillie Langtry were freely reported the Prince was never mentioned in any connection with them. At his Coronation in 1902 due to the number of his mistresses in attendance a pew was set aside for them to view the ceremony. This was referred to as "the loose box". It should not be construed from the Prince's behaviour that he did not love his wife, the Danish Princess Alexandra, whom he married in 1863: he loved her from the moment he met her until his death. Alexandra was a popular Queen and there is no evidence that Edward ever loved anyone else. He was unfaithful because he had time on his hands and enjoyed fornication, not because he was unhappy with his wife.

He was popular as both Prince of Wales and as king but it seems not everyone liked him. In 1900, when he was still Prince of Wales, and accompanied by the Princess, an anarchist attempted to assassinate him on a train as it left a railway station in Brussels. The would-be assassin stepped on to the footboard of the train and, pointing a gun through the window, fired at least twice. "Fuck it!" exclaimed His Royal Highness, "I have taken a bullet!" It transpired that all the shots had missed. It is

1

imagined that apologies were extended to the Princess for the use of such a profanity!

The Prince's reputation reached a low point during a card cheating scandal which became known as the Tranby Croft Affair or the Baccarat Case in 1890. Sir William Gordon Cumming was accused of cheating and he sued his accusers. The case came to court and the Prince appeared as a witness and was not seen to best advantage. It was a tribute to his resilience that his prestige had been restored by the time he ascended the throne. In fairness it should not be thought that he was remembered entirely for an excessive libido and a taste for fast living. There are many examples of his kindness, generosity and humour. He had no official role and could not take any worthwhile employment so consequently although he had prestige he also had considerable time on his hands with little else to occupy it but pleasure.

In the world of thoroughbred racing he was also a successful and popular owner-breeder, having won the Derby twice with Persimmon and the Triple Crown winner, Diamond Jubilee. He was later to win it for a third time with Minoru. His support and involvement in Racing was not approved of by his mother who had no great affection for the sport and was thought, by the time Edward became involved, to actively dislike it. Queen Victoria had visited Ascot enthusiastically when she was young but never attended again after Prince Albert's death. Either way Her Majesty would seem to have been very ignorant about racing. When Lord Rosebery won his second Derby in successive years she asked him if this feat had been achieved with the same horse!

The Prince of Wales's association with racing during this period helped considerably in spreading its popularity with all classes, and, for the first time, women as well as men. After one of his horses had won the crowd loved to shout "good old Teddy" in appreciation. The Prince despite his enthusiasm for racing was never a good judge of a thoroughbred according to his trainer Richard Marsh. The Prince had perhaps less excuse than most for his inability to recognise a good horse as he owned and bred Diamond Jubilee a horse with a conformation described by Marsh and others as "without fault".

As Edward the Seventh he was a popular monarch during his all too short reign of just nine years. One of the reasons for this lay in his understanding that the British people liked to see their sovereign and he appeared in public more than any of his predecessors since the fall of the Stuarts. He had worked hard as Prince of Wales for the benefit of hospitals, raising considerable sums, and this work was maintained after he became king. Edward reigned over an Empire that covered one third of the globe, he ruled over three hundred million subjects in thirty one countries and his Empire was the envy of the world and upon which, of course, the sun never set.

The Edwardian period, which in many eyes continued, at least in spirit, beyond the Kings death in 1910, until the Great War broke out in 1914, is always recalled as a golden age. Only in retrospect can it be seen that this was not the case. The British Empire, despite appearances, had passed its zenith when Queen Victoria died. Britain's commercial and industrial rivals were steadily overtaking her and scientific inventions were undermining her position as mistress of the seas. However, at the outset of his reign in 1901 there were few clouds on the domestic horizon. The Boer War would soon be over, Home Rule for Ireland was not yet a significant issue and the suffragette movement, formed in 1903 as the Women's Social and Political Union under the formidable leadership of Mrs. Emmeline Pankhurst, was still in its relative infancy.

The year 1906, in which Bayardo was foaled, was an eventful year. The Liberal Party won a landslide victory in the general election with a mandate for reform, although not however from all of His Majesty's subjects as there was not universal suffrage, which was still some twenty two years away. The Liberal party may have had a mandate for reform in many areas but this did not include extending the right to vote beyond its narrow base as this would have granted the vote to all men and more crucially to women, a suggestion that they, and indeed all political parties, considered preposterous. Just how absurd the idea of giving women the vote was thought by those in power was soon demonstrated by the actions of the police and the inaction of the politicians when the suffragette movement became active. Middle and working class women in the movement were subjected to the most horrendous treatment in prison after arrest for public order offences which were designed to highlight their cause. Suffragettes from the aristocracy who were arrested were freed almost immediately in order to prevent the movement gaining publicity. After the 1906 election the Liberals had 399 seats and the Conservatives 156. The Labour party won thirty seats and changed its name from the Labour Representation Committee.

There were considerable differences in income between the peoples of Britain. An agricultural labourer was paid about £47 per annum (£3,008), an unskilled worker about £60 (£3,840) and a professional footballer about £200 (£12,800). At the other extreme the Duke of Westminster's annual income from his London properties alone was approximately £250,000 (£16,000,000) and similarly, the gross rent revenues from Lord Derby's estates amounted to just short of £300,000 (£19,000,000). Domestic servants were relatively inexpensive. A butler earned £60 per annum (£3840) a housekeeper £45 (£2880) a chef £80 (£5120) and a ladies maid £32 (£2048). Various other household staff earned between £12 (£768) and £28 (£1792) per annum. It should be remembered that domestic staff had all their food and shelter provided and had little leisure time to spend any money.

Those fortunate enough to be in possession of wealth had little to fear from the Inland Revenue as the standard rate of Income Tax was no more than one shilling in the pound, or 5%. A gentleman of leisure could survive quite happily in London society, providing he had wealthy friends prepared to entertain him, on £500 (£32,000) per annum, and plenty did. A house in St James's Place could be rented and staffed with a cook, parlour-maid and housemaid for £270 (£17,280) per annum. The annual cost of keeping a racehorse in training was about £110 (£7,200).

As the majority of the population spent at least half of their income on food it would be useful to see how much various items cost. Two pounds of sugar were one and half old pennies (40 new pence) a pound of tea one shilling and four pence (£4-27p) a pound of butter a shilling (£3-20) and a pint of beer 2 old pence (54 new pence). To pay for any of these and other necessities of life most of the working population would need to toil until death as the Old Age Pension, although part of the Liberal Party's agenda for reform, was not introduced until 1908. At the other end of the social scale at either Oxford or Cambridge University a student, it was said, could live on £160 (£10,240) per annum, this, however, did not include holidays, clothes or travelling! Incidentally if today's students are sometimes considered less than industrious it is interesting to note that in 1909 a quarter of students did not take a degree. The master of Magdalen College Oxford was of the opinion that these individuals had attended university just to play sport and enjoy themselves!

Although change was occurring gradually in 1906 Society was strictly ordered and an individual's place clearly defined with little or no opportunity for advancement in class terms no matter how successful an individual may be in whatever field. Different sections of society did not mix unless there was some specific reason for doing so. The only way people could meet in upper class circles was by introduction as it was considered *infra dig* simply to talk to an individual to whom one had not been formally introduced. Many of the aristocracy only mixed socially with other men and their families that they had attended school – that is to say a public school - or university with or whom they knew from their London clubs. Their somewhat narrow view of matters was that if a person had not attended their old school, or college, nor were they members of one of their clubs, they would not want to have any social intercourse with them in any event! No gentleman would speak to a lady unless an introduction had been effected. Even if they had been introduced if unmarried they could under no circumstances be left alone without a suitable chaperone as such an occurrence would have ruined the ladies reputation irrevocably. This would all change after the Great War.

Women, over and above not being able to vote, were second class citizens. They were thought capable of little more than home making, child rearing, and, if from the leisure classes, looking decorative. In no period in history have women looked more beautiful than the Edwardian era. This was achieved with elegant long dresses which reached the floor and some wonderful and sometimes extravagant hats. Their figures were kept trim and alluring by means of tightly laced corsets which on occasions caused them to faint. This beauty and grandeur was not achieved without considerable attention to detail. A society lady would change her attire as often as six times a day! It is a wonder she had time for anything else! A visit to a country house for a weekend house party could require as many as twenty eight different outfits. They may not all be worn but would be needed in order to be enable her to look at her best in any conceivable situation. Women were unable to attend university, (Oxford first made degrees open to them in 1920), or otherwise improve their usually limited or often nonexistent education. Progress in any of the professions was virtually impossible and only the most determined were able to achieve any professional status and were therefore denied the opportunity to carve out careers or to have any direct influence on the nations' affairs. The more able married women, however, sometimes worked diligently behind their prominent husbands', and there are some famous examples of their influence.

The population of England and Wales was just under 36 million (61 million today) of which, in 1901, twenty percent lived in London and all told about three quarters lived in urban districts. London was not just the largest city in Britain it was also the biggest in the world. Longevity was 51 for a male and 54 for a female (75 and 79 respectively today). Some statistics suggest that longevity was, in reality, only about 45. There was a high incidence of childhood mortality, particularly amongst the poor, with one in seven children dying before the age of five. Childbirth was by no means without its dangers and a distressingly high number of women died giving birth, which, with large families of six, seven or more commonplace, was for some mothers a regular ordeal rather than a source of joy. Contraception was crude and often ineffective. It was considered a taboo subject and therefore rarely practised and never discussed. Members of the lower classes who fell ill were reliant on charitable institutions as a National Health Service was still over forty years away.

Not that medicine could do much beyond providing comfort in any event. Surgery was crude by modern standards and usually involved cutting out large sections of the affected area or amputation to prevent the spread of infection. Survival from surgery was largely a matter of an individual's general well being. Most illness's had no effective cure and without antibiotics, which were forty years away, even a mild infection, if ignored, could prove fatal. Although Louis Pasteur had discovered bacteria as long ago as 1867 the knowledge to combat infection and disease was moderate. Treatments for Cholera, Typhoid, Scarlet Fever and Tuberculosis were having a limited impact on such diseases however, they still claimed many lives. Only in retrospect can medical knowledge of the period be seen as relatively ignorant. Many causes of death amongst the poor, (where any cause was formally recorded that is), would be unrecognisable today. Causes of early death amongst poor people were mainly related to poor housing and nutrition together with overwork and ultimately a lack of will to carry on. One area in which women were indispensable was in hospitals, not as doctors or surgeons of course, which were almost the exclusive province of men. However, wards were run by sisters, usually with an iron fist, and virtually all nurses were women who were expected to be totally dedicated to their vocation to the exclusion of any social life: and marriage, of course would have been out of the question.

Life in England during this period, for those fortunate enough to be born to comfort and privilege - and also, to an extent, for the middle classes - was the acme of comfort and well-being. It was, in retrospect and in the imagination, a period of weekend house and shooting parties, endless sunny summer afternoons, (although curiously it saw two of the wettest summers on record 1902 and 1912, August of that year being the worst in three hundred years), an age of elegance and leisure, of opulence and extravagance, often, it has to be said, at the expense of taste. For example shooting parties were on a lavish scale in respect of both the food and drink and the sport provided. On one recorded occasion seven guns, in what seems to have been an orgy of ritual slaughter, accounted for no fewer than 3,937 birds.

Evenings could involve a visit to a West End Theatre, (where, incidentally, smoking was not permitted), or to Covent Garden for an evening of Opera. Alternatively dining could be either simple or, more probably if more formal, consist of as many as nine courses. One famous dinner given in honour of Lord Rosebery in 1902 had an astonishing eleven courses! A lady would of course be unable to indulge herself to any great extent as she was constrained by those corsets! A gentleman could always dine at his club where he would have peace and quiet and, as many saw it, the distinct advantage of being able to mix exclusively with his own gender. The Edwardians would appear to have been determined to justify Oscar Wilde's observation of a decade or so previously that "nothing succeeds like excess"! Life for the upper classes was an endless round of pleasure from the time the maid opened the curtains in the morning (not too early!) and lit the bedroom fire, until the finish of the last after dinner cigar of a long evening.

With the Conservatives in power prior to 1906, the majority of the ruling classes were content to be moral and intellectual passengers with little or no concerns about wider society. Events in Russia, the increasingly aggressive stance of the German Kaiser and the famous Anglo French *entente cordiale* were merely items to be noted in the newspapers over breakfast before more pressing and in the reader's view more important matters regarding the day's social round took their attention. Edwardians were very confident and had a certainty in their role and position in a world whose mood and grandeur are somehow retrospectively encapsulated by the music of Edward Elgar, Frank Bridge, York Bowen, and Frederick Delius.

The suburban middle classes were largely prosperous, contented and self-satisfied, living ordered and conscientious existences. Most lived in comfortable homes and would have had a cook and a parlour maid as their servants. Husbands would have white collar jobs in clerical or managerial capacities, or professions such as physicians, lawyers, clergymen or professors. Wives would be at home managing domestic matters and making sure that they were dressed appropriately and attractively. Respectability was all important: they feared only that they might be guilty of some social *faux pas* resulting in loss of face or that misfortune might threaten their cherished status. Respectability meant of course, not divorcing or separating except in the most extreme circumstances. A wife who left her husband would lose all status and be an outcast from society- including (quite possibly) her own family. Divorce in England that permitted remarriage had only been possible by Act of Parliament until 1857. This act permitted a wife to obtain a divorce if she could prove two of three charges: cruelty, desertion or adultery. A husband, however, was entitled to a divorce on proof of only one charge! A succession of acts between then and 1895 had gradually improved the situation of divorced wives. However, none of these made life exactly easy for an ex-wife. During their hours of leisure the middle classes kept an interested eye on the lives and events of royalty, the upper classes and the leading sportsmen, actors and actresses. Without television and radio, information was gleaned from a plethora of illustrated glossy, weekly magazines which were eagerly read. A large proportion of these publications did not survive the Great War.

In the world of literature George Bernard Shaw was the leading figure. A highly intelligent and brilliant Irishman he was a socialist whose writings were characterised by incisive thoughts and an ability to expose the hypocrisy and cant of the times. Shaw enjoyed revealing the national weaknesses and absurdities of the period and his writings influenced political and social thinking. He was also very witty and cared little for social niceties. Upon receiving what most would have considered a cherished invitation from a prominent member of the aristocracy worded "Lady____ will be at home on Friday next at 11-00 am", Shaw returned the invitation marked "So will George Bernard Shaw!" ++ On the duties of a parent his advice was "If you can't be a good example you will just have to be a horrible warning!" At a formal dinner he was placed next to a leading female actress who thought rather too much of herself and was boring Shaw to death. When a rare lull in her constant inane chatter allowed him to speak he asked her "Would you sleep with a man for a thousand pounds?" (£64,000). She replied in a somewhat coy intimate manner, a trace of a smile playing on her lips, "That would depend if he were handsome". Shaw thought for a moment. "Would you sleep with a man for a pound?" he asked. "Of course not!" She replied with considerable indignation. "What sort of woman do you think I am?" "I thought we had established the sort of woman you are" said Shaw, "We are now haggling over the price!" He was awarded the Nobel Prize for Literature in 1925.

The working classes' were employed in various ways. Some were in domestic service, including charwomen or washerwomen. There were over two million thus employed significantly fewer than the three million that had been so employed thirty years earlier. Over six hundred thousand others were employed as coachmen, drivers, cabmen, porters and on the seas and canals. Their entertainment came from public houses, sport and the music halls where Miss Marie Lloyd, whose third husband, Bayardo's first jockey Bernard Dillon some 17 years her junior, was one of the principal attractions. Life was very hard for those at the bottom of the social scale and girls as young as ten were placed in prostitution often by a member of her own family. Should matters become too unbearable and an individual make an attempt at suicide, if unsuccessful, this could result in prosecution, as suicide was illegal until 1961.

As today, Professional Association Football was very popular, but almost entirely the entertainment of working class men. Entrance to a game in the First Division cost sixpence, (£1-60) with only some FA Cup matches costing more. Even in those days football was quite capable causing surprise when it came to buying and selling players. The sporting world had been shocked when in 1905 Alf Common was transferred for a fee of £1,000 (£64,000). The middle and upper classes preferred Rugby Football. Cricket, which was enjoyed by all classes of society, was governed the world over by the Marylebone Cricket Club based at Lords. It was a class-riddled sport with amateurs and professionals meeting only on the pitch. They changed in separate dressing rooms, entered the playing area by separate gates and, when playing in away matches, stayed

++ Contemporary figures are just as capable of insulting prominent individuals in similar circumstances. When the current Duke and Duchess of York were first married their representative telephoned the late comedian Peter Cook to ask about his availability for a dinner party they were to hold. Cook replied that he would consult his diary. "Ah, sorry no", he said, "I see I am due to watch television that evening".

in separate hotels. Absurd as these arrangements seem today, during Edwardian times it enabled amateurs to play the game for fun and to entertain as there was no pressure on their level of performance. The professionals played the game more dourly as could only be expected from individuals whose livelihood was derived from the game and who often lived in fear that injury would prevent them from playing, or that moderate performances could result in their contracts not being renewed.

The Olympic Games were held in London in 1908 but were unrecognisable from today. The games had been switched to London after Italy withdrew in 1906. Of the 2,022 competitors representing 21 countries only 44 were women. In one instance a competitor left his office during the morning to compete in an event and afterwards returned to his office and was back at his desk by late afternoon! The true amateur tradition indeed! However, the games were not without controversy, were not characterised by the Olympian spirit and degenerated into petty nationalistic squabbles. The Americans complained about everything and considered themselves isolated. There were disputes about which rules some disciplines should be conducted under. As Britain was the host, it was the British versions of rules that took precedence. As the Games progressed a strong anti-American feeling developed as the Americans let it be known that they felt themselves disadvantaged. They may have had a point in some respects: for example all 800 judges were British and were not always considered to be entirely impartial, particularly in regard to the four hundred and forty yards race being declared void for interference after an American had beaten the hot favourite, a Scotsman.

Matters were not helped by the Irish being forced to compete under the British flag which caused considerable resentment to the Irish Americans. The climax occurred after the marathon when the Italian winner Pietri Dorando was disqualified in favour of an American, after they had lodged a protest that the Italian had been assisted to reach the line. Queen Mary was so upset by this that she later persuaded King George V, who inherited King Edward's racing interests, to name a colt after the unfortunate Italian. Sadly Dorando, the horse that is, although able to win races was not particularly talented. Finally King Edward who had been an enthusiastic supporter of the games refused to attend the final ceremony and give out the prizes. The games did, however, introduce one lasting aspect which survives today. The marathon had been run over twenty five miles in previous games. However, because the organisers wanted the race to begin at Windsor Castle and end in front of the Royal Box in the White City Stadium, the distance worked out at precisely twenty six miles and 385 yards. This distance for the Marathon has remained to this day.

These entertainments were of course only for those in the cities. There was little for those who lived in the countryside which was in a state of gradual but relentless decay following the slump in the 1870s. The countryside had been haemorrhaging able bodied men and their families since that time. By 1909, approximately nine out of ten families in the larger centres of population had migrated there from the countryside within three generations. This resulted in huge overcrowding in cities particularly London creating slums. Some families were housed in a single room and it was not unknown for two such families to be crowded together with the consequent rapid spread of disease.

The internal combustion engine was in the process of transforming the way everyone travelled. Gottlieb Daimler had produced his first motor car in 1886 and by 1904 there were approximately 8,450 motor cars and the speed limit was raised from fourteen miles an hour to twenty. By 1910 the number of cars had increased to over 53,000. Initially motor cars were not universally popular, being considered dirty and noisy, and motorists could expect to be verbally insulted and worse occasionally attacked by stones. Car theft was not unknown but this was usually to procure spares. No sensible motorist set off on any journey without a box of spares to cope with the almost inevitable breakdown! At a more egalitarian level the arrival of the motor omnibus meant that ordinary people could travel much longer distances from where they lived. In addition communications had been transformed when Guglielmo Marconi developed the equipment for converting radio waves into electrical signals. In 1895 he first successfully transmitted long-wave radio signals and in 1901 he sent a signal across the Atlantic.

Edwardian confidence in everything British was never better illustrated than in the race to build the fastest and most comfortable form of sea travel via the luxury liner. Plans had begun in 1908 to build a liner even greater than the *Lusitania* and in 1912 the building of the *Titanic* was completed. Weighing an astonishing 46,382 tons she was the largest ship ever built at that time. She was equipped with every conceivable luxury in her first class deck and was very comfortable by almost any standards in the second class areas. Only in steerage was comfort on a grand scale absent. In addition due to her unique design of individual sealed compartments below decks, she was considered by her owner to be unsinkable by any force of nature and, possibly tempting fate, by any act of God. This example of industrial-strength hubris invited disaster, but the magnitude of it, when it occurred, was beyond imagination.

The *Titanic* set sail in April 1912 on her maiden voyage for New York. On the third night the captain changed course to proceed further south after receiving iceberg warnings. With no moon visibility was moderate and the sea so calm it was described as looking like glass. The ship was travelling too fast in the circumstances and an iceberg was spotted too late to prevent a collision. The iceberg that *Titanic* struck was, despite her huge size, incredibly, ten times larger and seven eights below the surface of the water. The "unsinkable" *Titanic* foundered in less than two hours with a horrifying loss of life. Of the 2,367 passengers and crew 1,635 souls were lost, due to the misplaced confidence that *Titanic* was unsinkable, the relatively swift speed at which she sank, the lack of sufficient lifeboats and the fact that the nearest ship, that could be contacted, was four hours away. Because she was considered invulnerable she had not been equipped with enough life boats for more than half of the people she carried. In retrospect this ghastly event just over two years away from a cataclysmic war of epic scale is somehow an indication that the period of the wealthy, indulgently luxuriant lifestyle of the Edwardians was drawing to a close.

Bayardo's time saw many innovations. The War minister Viscount Haldane reorganised the army and with the Reserve Forces Act in 1907 he amalgamated all voluntary military organizations into the Territorial Force intended for home defence only. It was renamed the Territorial Army in 1921. Lord Baden Powell wrote a book called "Scouting for Boys" which became the handbook for the movement which he founded 1908 called "The Boy Scouts". This was followed two years later by the foundation of "The Girl Guides". The concept spread rapidly and soon became a strong moral force worldwide.

Aviation was in its infancy and Sam Cody was the first man in Britain to emulate the Wright brothers' feat of powered flight in an aeroplane. This extravagantly moustached Iowa-born, larger-than-life character ran through an extraordinary variety of occupations – buffalo hunter, horse tamer, gold prospector and Wild West entertainer – before taking to the air. His debut flight in October 1908 was a seat-of-the-pants affair. Flying twenty feet above the ground at thirty miles per hour he remained air-borne for all of twenty seven seconds and covered 1,390 feet (428 meters) before crashing and destroying his plane while trying to avoid some trees.

The *Daily Mail* offered £1,000 (£64,000) as a prize for the first man to fly across the channel. A French engineer Louis Bleriot won the prize beating two other competitors. He set off from France on a very windy morning with poor visibility and rough sea conditions in the channel. Although there was a French warship on standby to help if needed, Bleriot, incredibly, took off without a compass, watch or map! Not surprisingly he lost his way and, with the wind trying hard to bring him down, eventually, and probably by dint of good fortune, he spotted a friend in a field waving the French flag and guided his plane towards it. In attempting to land, he crashed when turning his engine off prematurely ending his thirty seven minute journey in a less than dignified manner. Nonetheless a remarkable achievement had been accomplished and flying distances had been shown to be possible.

In addition in the year of Bayardo's birth, F G Hopkins, later Sir Frederick, discovered vitamins, the suffragette movement became active and the breakfast table saw for the first time that indispensable food source: Kelloggs Corn Flakes. A German hairdresser Karl Nessler invented the permanent wave; despite using cow's urine mixed with water, the "perm" became an instant success. Edith Nesbit wrote *The Railway Children* and gave a century of delight to children and grown-ups alike. Giving similar pleasure, John K Farnell made the first British teddy bear. Unlike earlier bears made in Germany, the British bear had a fatter body, flatter face and shorter arms and legs. Mills and Boon began publishing romantic novels and for a century the hearts of women of all ages have fluttered to stories of demure maidens entwined with strong handsome men. In 1907 Persil was first marketed and ever since housewives have been able to wash "whiter". In the same year a type of plastic comprising also phenol and formaldehyde resin was patented as Bakelite and marketed as having "a thousand uses". In 1905 the Magic Circle was formed and ever since audiences have marvelled at sleight of hand tricks as well as more astonishing illusions. Charles Rolls and Henry Royce founded "Rolls-Royce Limited" and unveiled the "Silver Ghost". Cunard launched *Lusitania*, the world's largest and fastest passenger ship, a title temporarily taken by *Titanic* six years later. She was to be best remembered for being torpedoed by the Germans during the Great War killing 1,198 of the 1,959 people on board including many women and children.

In London the traffic problem was becoming chronic. There were seven hundred buses in service with three hundred more about to follow. Following protests by one hundred prominent people in August 1906 the open-topped buses were hauled off the streets because they were too noisy. In 1906 London buses were involved in 2,448 accidents, many attributed to mechanical failure. The Underground was progressing rapidly and two new lines were built and named the Piccadilly and Bakerloo. These were deeper below the surface and round, hence the name tubes. Previously the underground was built as trenches then filled in.

Abroad there was a Zulu uprising against British rule which was met with a swift and brutal response. San Francisco was destroyed by earthquake and fire. In Russia, where revolution was still eleven years away, there was a general strike and in Italy Mount Vesuvius erupted destroying most of Naples.

In 1906 the unimaginable horrors of the Great War were only eight years away but, such was the confidence of Edwardian England, an occurrence of that magnitude would have seemed light years distant. During the endless summer of 1914, although War had been discussed and had seemed inevitable for some years, the prospect brought no fears and was even welcomed by some as there was an assumption that a quick victory would reinforce England's total superiority. There were few who could have imagined the world of the Edwardians destroyed for ever, the nation on the verge of bankruptcy, a whole generation of its youth slaughtered or maimed, and the spirit of those that remained left permanently scarred, in just four years.

CHAPTER 2

Racing in Bayardo's Time

Thoroughbred horse racing in 1906 reflected society and was essentially the province of the aristocracy and the wealthy. It was governed autocratically by the Jockey Club whose control and rulings were total and without any possibility of contradiction. The Club had gradually strengthened its powers over the period from 1808 until 1870. By that time the limits of the racing season were defined, restrictions placed on the racing of two-year-olds and the minimum distance of five furlongs established for three-year-olds and up. Juveniles were not permitted to race beyond six furlongs before the 1st July and beyond seven until 1st September, after which restrictions were removed. It defies belief but until towards the end of the nineteenth century a race open to all ages was run over the full Cesarewitch course of two miles and two furlongs. The race, the Feather Plate, was run at Newmarket's final meeting, the Houghton, and was nearly always contested by juveniles only, however, three-year-olds and up did take part on occasions. The idea of a two-year-old running over such a distance today would certainly invoke the attentions of the RSPCA. It can only be assumed that the pace was not usually brisk; even so the extended distances would be interesting and it is possible to imagine the unedifying spectacle of exhausted juveniles following each other home like three mile chasers in particularly heavy going.

The Club's influence, although dictatorial, was largely for the good of the sport and it was responsible for racing developing along organised lines. There were far too many racecourses and regulation was essential. All racecourses were required to meet certain criteria and courses had to submit their annual accounts to the Jockey Club. This enabled the Stewards to control the amount of prize money and dividends. Race meetings had to be licensed annually, as did trainers, owners and jockeys. However, a requirement that from 1877 all meetings must provide a minimum of 300 sovereigns (£25,000) in added prize money for each days racing and that each race must be worth at least £100 (£6,400) to the winner, proved devastating to many courses. In addition an edict that

"Neither the programme, nor the result of any flat-race meeting in Great Britain shall be published in the official *Racing Calendar* unless the said meeting is advertised to be subject to the established Rules of Racing as settled by the Jockey Club. If a horse should run in a race at any meeting in Great Britain which is not so advertised he is perpetually

14

disqualified for all races to which these rules apply", ensured that compliance was total.

The Club also organized the collection of owners' fees and forfeits, the payment of prize money and the collection of jockeys' fees. By 1890 the Club had become omnipotent and its control total by a completely new set of Rules of Racing. These remained largely unchanged apart from a few alterations and additions for just over a hundred years until modern changes removed much of the Club's responsibilities a century or so later. Not all the decisions made by the Jockey Club made sense. In 1905 they reintroduced four-furlong races, something that had been considered undesirable when discontinued in 1870, and these continued until 1913.

The leading owners, Lord Derby, Duke of Portland, Lord Carnarvon, Mr Leopold de Rothschild, Sir James Miller, Major Eustace Loder, Mr W Hall Walker (later Lord Wavertree) and Mr Jack and Solly Joel were largely owner-breeders. However, change was about to occur as a different sort of owner began to emerge: industrial barons, commoners and even foreigners, particularly Americans, invested large sums. It was just as well that owners were wealthy because frequently they raced for their own money: racecourses did not always add anything to the stakes they simply on occasions guaranteed that a certain race would have a set amount of prize-money. This often resulted in a surplice with the extra going to the owner of the winner. Only in the most valuable races: some weight-for-age contests and big handicap races would the racecourse executive add any significant money to the owners' stakes. The five classics had added money on occasions but it was not until after the Great War that they always benefited from contributions from the racecourse.

Attendance at races had been confined largely to the upper classes and, as they would have thought, the plebeian section of society. The respectable working class and the middle classes generally ignored racing. This was changed forever when Sandown Park opened in 1875 with its revolutionary (as it seemed at the time) design of an enclosed racecourse with separate areas. Until then race meetings were held on public land with no restriction of access, apart from private stands. Only Newmarket ignored the need for the support of the general public and continued actively to discourage ordinary spectators. The introduction of separate enclosures had made race-going a suitable pastime for women who would be safe from "ruffians" and "undesirables". Until then, women had usually only attended Ascot and Goodwood. The enclosed course was an instant success and was followed three years later by Kempton Park and in the early 1890s by Hurst Park, Lingfield and Gatwick. The introduction of separate enclosures enabled racecourses to charge for admission. Previously the general public had been able to attend free-of-charge unless they had wished to use one of the private stands – assuming that is they would have been allowed admission without the need for a sponsor.

Almost all races of any consequence took place during the week with only very moderate fare offered on Saturdays. Racing on Saturdays was in any event only a relatively recent innovation. For example in 1874 there were only ten Saturday meetings held but by 1910 there were meetings scheduled for each Saturday. Traditionally Saturdays had been used to transport horses back to their stables after racing during the week at whichever meeting they had attended. The meetings at Ascot, or Royal Ascot as it is now known, and Goodwood, Glorious Goodwood today, were the highlights of the racing and social year and the only occasions when racing took place at either venue.

Race-goers setting off for a day at the races would not know for certain which horses would be competing that day as there were no overnight declarations; these were not introduced until 1961. The racing papers (which were also sporting papers) *The Sporting Life*, *The Sporting Chronicle* and *The Sportsman* carried lists of the horses entered in each race with an indication of probable runners. However, decisions about whether or not to run were sometimes made very late and it was usually only about 45 minutes before each race that the final runners were known. When they were known they were not announced over a loud speaker but as with any other information, for example results, they were indicated via a number board. A race-card was of little value being cramped in layout and containing only a list of every horse entered without any information regarding riders, draw – which was made when the final runners were known - or form. There was no race commentary and it is not hard to imagine many race-goers asking each other immediately after race which could have 40 plus runners "Who won?" Touts at each training centre would wait at the local station to see which horses were being loaded on to race trains and, just as important, which were not. A horse sent to the races may not always run, but one not sent definitely will not!

There was no recognisable form published as today. *The Sportsman* had at one time published a weekly paper containing results for the previous week up to the day before. However, this seems to have ceased by 1906. The ordinary race-goer would be unlikely to subscribe to the *Racing Calendar* and, unless he followed racing closely, would have very little idea of detailed form. However, information about the wellbeing of horses was readily available and each newspaper employed tipsters and gallops men to provide tips and guidance to help punters make their selections. More so then than today the betting market provided a useful guide and together with rumour and "inside information", which proliferated, and, if a race-goer listened to everything said to him, it was possible to have a "reliable" tip from the "right sources" for nearly every horse in a race.

One major change during this period occurred when the starting flag was replaced by the starting gate. Races had always been started by flag but the principal problem was one of false starts. Some races could start as much as an hour later than advertised with sometimes a dozen or more false starts not uncommon. Some jockeys deliberately spoiled the start if they felt it would help their mounts. Jockeys openly betted and some were much better riders than they were punters! Frequently jockeys backed other horses in the race with obvious dangers to fair and honest riding and they were forbidden to bet from 1900. The starting gate was first introduced in 1896 but was not universally popular; indeed it seemed that no one had a good word to say for it! However, it was an immediate success and the number of false starts were reduced which meant that races were more likely to start closer to the advertised time.

It would however, be wrong to assume that all was tranquil. At the turn of the century the so called "American Invasion" had introduced a number of undesirable individuals to racing. Thoroughbred racing in America was under threat from puritans and had been made illegal in many states. This resulted in almost all owners, trainers and jockeys heading across the Atlantic, initially to England. Although the importation of jockeys, which transformed riding styles, could be seen, retrospectively at least, as generally a good thing, the practice of doping to win, second nature to almost all American trainers, had threatened to make a mockery of the formbook. Doping was accepted practice in the United States and, after a number of spectacular betting coups, the Jockey Club, who had been slow to understand the threat, outlawed the practice in 1904, having seen at first hand an example, provided by The Hon. George Lambton, of how it was done.

There was considerably less racing than today. In 1906 there were 285 meetings scheduled for the flat – including mixed meetings – compared with 579, on turf, in 2009. In addition in 2009 there were also 324 meetings scheduled for the all-weather tracks. Yet there are still those who persist in the notion that there is not too much racing! However, there were more racecourses. In 1906 there were 47 racecourses that staged flat racing compared to 35 in 2009. There were no watering systems and racing often took place on very firm ground. Races were not graded and there was no Pattern which was not introduced until 1971. The most important races were the five classics and, much more so than now, the big handicaps. Horses were not rated and the weights for each horse in a handicap were allocated on a race by race basis.

The previous twenty years had witnessed a plethora of high-class horses, probably the most concentrated period of excellence in the history of the sport. Since 1884, racing had seen the following:- St. Simon,

Ormonde, Minting, The Bard, Donovan, Orme, La Fleche, Isinglass, Ladas, Persimmon, St Frusquin, Galtee More, Velasquez, Flying Fox, Diamond Jubilee, Ard Patrick, Rock Sand, Sceptre and Pretty Polly. As if this was not enough, the early part of this period saw the greatest jockey of all time, Fred Archer at his zenith before his tragically early death; and possibly racing's greatest trainer, John Porter.

This then was the world into which Bayardo was born when he was foaled at his owner's stud in Newmarket on 31st January 1906.

CHAPTER 3

A Promising colt

Bayardo was a brown colt by Bay Ronald out of Galicia who was by Galopin. The decision to mate Galicia with Bay Ronald would probably not have met with universal approval. Even Bay Ronald's owner Major Leonard Brassy admitted "he could not be described as quite a first class racehorse". He was of the opinion that the hard preparations, thought necessary at that time, for long distance races, took some of the steel out of Bay Ronald, who was not very robust, particularly when immature. In addition his progeny did not seem to be on the upgrade. His first offspring were juveniles in 1902 and despite a good beginning (he sired a colt, Macdonald, in France who was up to classic standard and a very good filly, Rondeau, who was later to be the dam of the top class sire Teddy, in the first three seasons) other results had not been very encouraging. His fee, which had risen to one hundred guineas (£6,720), had been reduced to seventy five (£5,040) by 1905. All in all not the ideal stallion it would seem. Nonetheless, Alfred Cox must have seen something in Bay Ronald and was determined to send Galicia to him. It was to prove an inspired decision.

When selecting a suitable mate for Galicia, some of the best stallions, including sons of St. Simon, who was by Galopin, could not be considered for a daughter of Galopin, due to the resultant close inbreeding. At that time the following stallions, of considerably higher reputation than Bay Ronald, were available: Ayrshire, Carbine, Cyllene (to whom Galicia was sent a year later, a mating which produced the Derby winner Lemberg), Ladas, Melton, and Rightaway. All of these stood at between 100 (£6,720) and 250 (£16,800) guineas. Interestingly Flying Fox, who was closely inbred to Galopin and could, of course, not have been used, was standing for 600 guineas (£40,320). Alfred Cox, who was constrained by neither fashion nor cost, sent Galicia to Bay Ronald for just 75 guineas (£5,040). His insight was to be richly rewarded.

Why did Cox want to use Bay Ronald? On paper at least Hampton's son Bay Ronald appeared a good cross for Galicia. Hampton's sire Lord Clifden was a grandson of the mare Volley, whose full brother Voltigeur featured as the great grandsire of Galicia. Furthermore, Galicia's third dam Blue Light, was by Rataplan out of Borealis, who was by Newminster out of Queen Mary's Derby and Oaks winning daughter Blink Bonny. This mirrored the pedigree pattern found in Hampton, who not only boasted Newminster and Rataplan close up in his pedigree, but also a

19

third dam who was none other than that same influential broodmare Queen Mary. Finally, Bay Ronald's dam Black Duchess was a son of Galopin out of a daughter of Sterling, and with these two stallions featuring close up in Galicia's pedigree it meant that Bayardo was inbred 4x2 Galopin and 4x4 Sterling. Cox may have been attracted to Bay Ronald as a mate for Galicia because the resulting pedigree pattern would closely resemble those of two major winners of 1903: Jean's Folly, winner of two important races in Ireland (the Anglesey and Railway Stakes) and the Oaks winner Our Lassie. It is also possible that Cox simply wanted to use Bay Ronald for Galicia as it would provide a desirable inbreeding to Galopin with two free generations.

Bayardo's great grand-sire Lord Clifden was a high-class performer. As a juvenile Lord Clifden won the Woodcote Stakes at Epsom and the Champagne Stakes at Doncaster. Whilst he was being trained for the Derby the following year, an attempt was made to injure him by digging holes in the gallops and filling them in with flints. This unspeakable plot was thwarted before any harm was done. (It is probably safe to say that the majority of horse lovers in any era would happily have seen the perpetrators forced to run barefoot over broken glass!) Lord Clifden may have been unlucky in the Derby as there were incredibly 34 false starts! The starter was blamed for an over cautious approach and unfortunately Lord Clifden was reported to have covered the most ground after each start. He finished second in the Derby and may have been unlucky in more than one respect as his jockey George Fordham - considered by some at least the equal of Fred Archer - made one of his few mistakes and looked behind him to see if there was any danger. There was and Lord Clifden was beaten a head. However, Lord Clifden made amends in the St. Leger although he missed the break and was still about 50 lengths behind with a mile to go but managed to get up to win by half a length. Fordham did not have the opportunity of repairing his mistake as he had been replaced by John Osborne. Lord Clifden was an exceptionally handsome horse with a tremendous stride and a perfectly docile temperament with only one vice: when he was being inspected he would playfully lash out! Heavens above it is hard to imagine that the local vet enjoyed his visits much! He sired other good horses in addition to Hampton, but his major contribution to the breed was that he was responsible for the line which led to Hyperion, whose influence worldwide was to be immense.

Bayardo's grand-sire Hampton stood barely 15.2 hands high and began his racing career in selling plates and it was some time before his great racing merit was appreciated. He was to win nineteen races on the flat plus one over hurdles, including eleven at two miles or farther. He was sound, tough and durable and a great success at stud where he sired three Derby winners. However, it was through his son Bay Ronald that he achieved lasting fame.

Bayardo was not a very imposing type as a yearling and was between small and medium sized. He was just over 15.3 hands when racing and almost 16 when he went to stud. In other words he did not change much! Assessing a horse's conformation from photographs is not easy and of course he can't be seen moving! However, one observation that requires very little scrutiny concerned his front legs. He was noticeably over at the knees, something that characterised both Bay Ronald and Galopin. This conformation fault became more pronounced as he got older, as it usually does and can be most clearly seen in the portrait of Bay Ronald. Being over at the knee does not in itself usually prevent a horse from standing training; indeed a school of thought amongst older horsemen suggests that a horse that is over at the knee will never get a tendon strain. It is certainly better than the opposite condition: back at the knee or calf knee a condition which often results in problems with soundness, usually in the tendon just behind the knee. Crucially though Bayardo had short, straight cannon bones with, as far as can be seen from photographs, good bone with no sign that he was "tied in": the cannon bone is narrower than it should be just below the back of the knee. Long cannon bones are undesirable as they are more likely to lead to un-soundness. A horse has muscles in the top part of its leg but none below the knee as these continue as tendons in front and behind the cannon bone. It can be readily appreciated that short, strong cannon bones are a distinct asset. In addition he had good hind legs with good-sized sound hocks: able to provide support with no evidence of "sickle hocks" so called because the hocks resemble a sickle. His pasterns would appear to be fine: at the correct angle, possibly a little upright behind, and neither too short or too long.

Bayardo may not have been very big, but from the moment he was broken he was confident in who he was. He had speed as a youngster and was said to be capable of doing everything within himself in company with other horses whether they were just cantering or galloping. He was not by all accounts particularly attractive in his early days, but with familiarity there was a great deal to like about him. Apart from being over at the knee he would not seem to have any other obvious conformation faults. Although he had a rather plain head with lop ears he had a good long neck and a well angled shoulder: not too straight but at an angle of approximately 45%. His withers would seem to have been of a good length and taper nicely into a back which would be described as lengthy but not too much so. He was described as having a "great depth of girth (the circumference of his body behind the withers) and possessing beautifully sprung ribs". In addition he "stood over plenty of ground and was an exceptionally good walker". His stifle would seem to be almost directly under the hip and well forward, he had good, long thighs and, although it is hard to be sure without seeing them from behind, he would seem to have well-developed gaskins, in proportion to his thigh: a little shorter than the thigh, which would have provided good leverage and a long stride plus the power to drive him forward. In short he may not have been an attractive type when compared to others but he was essentially well-made with all working parts in proportion.

When mature he was viewed more positively probably because he was by then a proven top racehorse! He was then described as an attractive, well-proportioned type, not particularly handsome, with the aforementioned plain head and lop ears. This feature, which does not lend attraction to a horse, has the virtue of often belonging to the good and honest equine. In addition to being over at the knee Bayardo had a more serious problem: he suffered from fleshy sensitive feet, particularly his front ones, and although he was to remain sound throughout his racing career, ground conditions were always to be important, not usually to the outcome of a race, but to the level of his performance. This problem was not very evident during his juvenile career and only became serious during the early part of his three year old career and until he retired the following year. This condition was later confirmed as laminitis a potentially fatal condition for which there is no cure and only treatment to alleviate the symptoms. Despite not being a particularly distinguished looking horse he had one outstanding feature: his wonderful action and its ground devouring stride which was constantly remarked upon.

From his pedigree it would not have been assumed the Bayardo would be precocious; however, from the moment he was broken that is exactly what he was. Alec Taylor saw Bayardo's speed and exceptional promise as soon as he began training him. He is unlikely to have inherited much speed from Bay Ronald, who had failed to win as a two-year-old, but there was every chance that he did from Galicia. The possibility of speed from his dam may have been the reason Bayardo was so well entered up for his juvenile season. At this time it was necessary to enter for races sometimes up to two years in advance and the most important and valuable races required entrance six months or more prior to the event.

Bayardo was entered in seventeen early-closing races, the first of which was at Sandown Park on 1st May. In addition he also had an entry at Epsom during the Derby meeting. This was for the Great Surrey Foal Stakes over five furlongs rather than the Woodcote Stakes which was over six. This is interesting because the Great Foal Stakes closed in October 1906, when Bayardo was a foal, as opposed to the Woodcote which closed in October 1907 at which stage he was a yearling. This suggests that at an early stage it was thought that Bayardo might possess speed. There was probably no chance that he would take up his option at Sandown. Although *The Sportsman* had commented on the 27th April that he was well, but he had not been noted as doing any sharp work on the gallops. In addition during the latter days of April heavy snow fell and training was abandoned on at least one day. When it was not snowing heavy rain took its place. The weather during April had been extraordinary. The temperature had been very low during the Craven meeting at Newmarket. By the Thursday the weather was bitterly cold and by the time racing had begun the rain had turned to snow and a "veritable blizzard" swept across the heath.

Bayardo continued to progress and it was considered that he might be good enough to make his debut at Ascot. He would need to have been showing good speed to be considered by Alec Taylor for such prestigious company on his debut. Taylor was not noted for his training of two-year-olds and not given to pushing them at any time so Bayardo himself must have been making it clear that he might be ready. Whether it was Taylor or Alfred Cox who suggested a trial is not clear, but it was normal practice at that time to "try" horses on the gallops under race conditions before they appeared on the racecourse. Also in the trial and owned by Cox were Lady Vista and Highness, both of whom were un-raced at the time of the trial. Like Bayardo they were also to make their debuts at Ascot the following week. In addition Cox also owned Seedcake and Smuggler. Alec Taylor owned Merry Masham. The other horses would have been owned by either Cox or Taylor as Cox refused to allow his horses to be tried and sometimes not even worked with any other owner's horses without his express permission. Cox, whose health was not good, was not well enough to travel to Manton to witness the trial.

On Tuesday 9th June a trial over 5 furlongs was arranged with the result as shown below.

Beating the moderate Seedcake was considered encouraging but no better than that. He actually beat him easily by 52 pounds! Thirty four pounds weight for age, plus 6 lengths, which over 5 furlongs at three pounds a length equates to an additional 18 pounds. At this time Seedcake was a modest maiden who had run three times as a juvenile and also three so far that year. Overall in six seasons Seedcake won only 3 of his 44 starts, two moderate plate races and a selling handicap, carrying

1	Bayardo	c	2 yrs	8st 8lb	Madden
2	Seedcake	c	3 yrs	8st 8lb	Toon
3	Smuggler	c	2 yrs	7st 1lb	Hulse
	Lady Vista	f	2 yrs	8st 5lb	Broadwood
	Cellerette	f	2 yrs	8st 8lb	Hill
	Highness	f	2 yrs	8st 5lb	Baker
	Merry Masham	g	2 yrs	8st 5lb	Clark
	Sibola colt	c	2 yrs	8st 8lb	Trigg

Won easily by 6 lengths : one length second and third.

7stone 10 pounds. However, he would probably be rated in the area 50 to 60. It is possible that Seedcake was a better work companion than his race record would suggest as there was a suspicion that he was something of a "morning glory" and that he did not reproduce his best form on the racecourse.

Smuggler was beaten seven lengths in receipt of 21 pounds. This amounts to a beating of 42 pounds. Smuggler had raced twice at this point without any distinction and finished last of four at Ascot the following week on the same day that Bayardo made his debut. Smuggler was to race a further 5 times that year without winning. At three, he did better, winning two of his seven starts, a valuable stakes race and a plate. At four he failed to win either of his two starts.

Lady Vista ran seven times without winning that year. At three she managed to win just a maiden apprentice plate from 12 starts. At four she won a stakes and a sprint handicap from 11 starts. After which she went to stud. Cellerette never ran in a race.

Highness ran four times that year without winning. At three she won the Newmarket Oaks and the Derby Handicap, a valuable race, from seven starts. At four she won the Liverpool Autumn Cup, a valuable handicap, from seven starts. She too then went to stud. Merry Masham ran seven times in three seasons without winning.

Bayardo was ridden by Otto Madden, then one of the leading jockeys but, it appears, not exactly the sharpest knife in the drawer! Incredibly he failed to notice that he was riding a two-year-old and mistook Bayardo, thinking he was Seedcake, the only three-year-old in the trial. Consequently after he had won the trial easily he concluded that the Manton juveniles were very moderate and consequently he made arrangements to ride Doro in the New Stakes at Ascot.

Alec Taylor did not see Madden again after the trial until before breakfast on the Tuesday morning, the first day of Ascot week. Discussing mounts with him for the week, Taylor spoke in an expectant manner assuming that Madden would be looking forward to riding Bayardo,

"Of course you know what you have to ride?" Taylor asked Madden.

"I am not quite sure" he replied and he pulled out his book in which he recorded his future mounts. Together they looked at the programme for the week. Taylor pointed to Bayardo's name amongst the entries for the New Stakes on Thursday and said;

"There's the horse you have to ride".

"Which horse" rejoined Madden.

"Why Bayardo of course" explained Taylor. "But," said Madden,"I don't ride Bayardo"

"Yes you do. That's the one"

"No I don't. I'm afraid your two-year-olds can't be any good". Said Madden, "That three-year-old I rode murdered them!"

"That wasn't a three-year-old you idiot" exclaimed Taylor, "that was Bayardo!"

The truth then dawned on Madden that he had made an awful mistake and was guilty of stupidity, or, if that seems harsh, certainly a lack of cognisance. Because he had won the trial so easily he believed that, despite Bayardo's size, he had ridden a three-year-old. It can be no surprise that Madden never rode Bayardo again. He had made the most costly mistake of his career.

Incidentally, this story would seem to indicate that Taylor did not speak to Madden before or directly after the trial. It may seem incredible that Taylor did not speak to all the jockeys beforehand to give orders and pass on any useful information about each mount. After the trial was over, it would again seem to defy belief that he did not speak to each jockey to obtain their views. Perhaps he thought that he had seen all that he needed and that Madden and the other jockeys could add nothing of value! However, it is more likely that as the jockeys riding in the trial had to catch the eight o'clock train from Marlborough, to reach Hurst Park for that day's racing, there was insufficient time for any detailed debriefing. Even so, that Taylor seems not to have spoken to Madden at any time afterwards seems remiss, particularly as some of the runners had engagements at Ascot the following week.

There is another possibility. There was often a culture of secrecy surrounding trial gallops and it was possibly felt that it was necessary to keep the jockeys in the dark about which horse each was riding. When a formal trial was held each jockey would be weighed out on scales that concealed from him the weight he had been given by the trainer. It is possible that a jockey engaged in a trial would be riding a horse whose name and weight he did not know. In addition trials were conducted at daybreak in order that the touts would not witness anything. If Alfred Cox was hoping to have a sizable bet on Bayardo at Ascot, he would not have been pleased if reports of the trial were spread to all and sundry. It is significant that, whereas gallop reports appeared each day in the sporting and racing papers, this particular trial was not reported and it was quite likely held in Manton's valley under cover of strict secrecy. Despite this, it is clear that Taylor had expected Madden to know that he had been riding Bayardo, or at the very least a juvenile, in the trial. In any event both Taylor and Cox were furious that Madden had undertaken to ride Doro at Ascot. Fortunately Bernard Dillon was at that time riding well and was available.

Bayardo was engaged in both the Coventry and New Stakes at Ascot. The New Stakes was worth about £100 (£6,400) more to the winner than the Coventry Stakes. However, they had similar conditions and were both over five furlongs, but the New Stakes had attracted more entries. The only other difference was that the New Stakes closed on

November 5th 1907 and the Coventry on 7th January 1908. These were the only races for which Bayardo was entered at the meeting.

On the Saturday before Ascot Bayardo went five furlongs which would, it was hoped, put him spot on for his debut. However, he did not impress everyone. *The Sportsman's* reporter on the Manton gallops, who of course had not witnessed the trial, did not tip him to win at Ascot. He was more enthusiastic about the chances of an un-raced and un-named filly out of Sceptre, her first foal. She did not appear at Ascot, but did win before the season finished. She was not named until the following year but, as Maid of the Mist, she won the Nassau Stakes plus a smaller stakes event.

Bayardo travelled to Ascot on the Wednesday before the race. His racing career was about to begin.

CHAPTER 4

Ascot debut

Royal Ascot today means five days of the very best flat racing unparalleled anywhere in the world and an important social occasion with fashion very much to the fore. It was the same in 1908 except that it was of four days' duration and the only occasion when racing took place at the venue all year. It was a major social occasion, possibly even more so then than today, and the racing was of more importance. With international competition and ease of world travel a horse can miss several targets nowadays and still find an important race with big prize money as a target. In Bayardo's time this was the major meeting to aim for and it was not unusual for a horse to race twice during the four days. The big problem at Ascot for many years had been the state of the ground which was usually firm or hard and in addition uneven. Horses frequently returned from the meeting injured or jarred up as a result of the ground. There were, of course, no watering facilities during that period.

As today the Royal Enclosure was by invitation only. However, unlike today, such an invitation would only be forthcoming to the elite of society: the upper classes. After he had ascended the throne in 1901, Edward ruled that an invitation for admission to the Royal Enclosure would only be extended to those who were also eligible to receive invitations to court. The number was limited to 1,200. He did relax one rule. Access to the enclosure was at that time denied to actors and actresses. The King had been annoyed that the actor Charles Hawtrey had been denied access. He took it upon himself to issue a badge personally much to the disgust of his representative Viscount Churchill who considered it his duty to be on guard for anyone in the enclosure who, in his opinion at least, should not be there. He personally vetted all applications and placed them in three baskets marked "certainly", "perhaps" and "certainly not".

Queen Victoria had been an enthusiastic attendee in her youth, although only on Tuesdays and Thursdays when the procession took place. The Royal procession did not take place on each day until 1920 and the practice has continued to the present. However, after Prince Albert's death in 1861 Victoria never attended Ascot races again. The Prince of Wales first attended in 1863 and from 1866 was there each day, much to his mother's chagrin as she felt he should only attend on Tuesday and Thursday. Had the Queen's wishes prevailed it is not certain that the Royal meeting would have survived in the same format as today.

The Prince was responsible for elevating its popularity to new heights and restoring its pageantry.

Bayardo cantered on the course during the morning of his race and *The Sporting Times* special correspondent recalled some years later what he saw. Four horses were noted exercising up the back stretch the reverse way from Swinley Bottom. Bayardo had been partly hidden from view by one of his work companions but when he emerged the observer noted the horse's great freedom of action and the ease with which he tucked his hocks under him after he had passed by. After working Bayardo was walked round and the observer was impressed with the amount of ground he stood over and yet he was so admirably put together as almost to give the impression of being a short-coupled colt. He went on to note that almost all great horses are good walkers and Bayardo was exceptional in this respect. The colt took a long stride yet took it quickly which made him a particularly smart walker. Another peculiarity he noted was his great depth of girth and beautifully sprung ribs. Later at the races the observer noted his pedigree and was disappointed to find he was by Bay Ronald.

Whatever the reports of Bayardo's form and well being, something encouraging about him must have been circulated by the quidnuncs at Ascot for him to be prominent in the betting for his debut. The New Stakes (known since 1973 as the Norfolk Stakes, Group 3,) was often used, as it was now by Taylor and Cox, at that time for promising debutants. This looked a particularly strong renewal and before the race most observers thought it was between Perola and Perdiccas who were renewing rivalry after the former had won the Woodcote Stakes at Epsom beating the latter in receipt of ten pounds. Sunflower, who like Bayardo was making his debut and was marginally preferred to him in the betting, was reported to be doing particularly well at home. Bayardo's level of performance on the gallops was not commented on as of course only his general work had been witnessed by the touts and gallops men. *The Times* reported that the weather was fine with plenty of sunshine. In the paddock Bayardo was described as "nice, lengthy bay, with a white streak, and a little streak of white on the coronets of his off fore and hind feet". *The Sportsman's* man on the spot described him as a "very handsome colt".

The ground was good after rain on the Wednesday. It had been very fast on the first day. The time compares favourably with others at the meeting. On the Tuesday an identical time was recorded in a juvenile race on faster ground. On the Wednesday after the rain a similar time was recorded by three-year-olds. The state of the ground at Ascot had improved drastically since the turn of the century. It defies belief now but until that time the crowd had been permitted to walk on the course without restriction. The famous promenade of the great and the good

Ascot Heath Thursday 18th June 1908 Going : Good

New Stakes for two year olds over 5 furlongs. £10 (£640) each with £1000 (£64,000) added of which the second received 10 per cent and the third 5 per cent. 115 entries Value to the winner £1817-10 shillings (£116,320)

1	Bayardo	8st 10lb	B Dillon	114++
2	Perdiccas	8st 10lb	W Higgs	108
3	Perola	9st	D Maher	111+
4	Sunflower II	8st 10lb	W Griggs	106
5	Blankney II	8st 10 lb	H Jones	105
6	Vivid	8st 7b	L Lyne	
7	Corinnus	8st 10 lb	C Leader	
8	f by St Maclou-Great Dame	8st 7 lb	W Broadwood	
	Pernambuco	8st 10 lb	F Wootton	
	Turban	8st 7 lb	W Halsey	
	Doro	8st 7 lb	O Madden	
	f by St Maclou-Ramondia	8st 7 lb	W Saxby	
	Blue Cap	8st 7 lb	H Randall	

Betting 6-4 Perola, 5-1 Perdiccas, 6-1 Sunflower II 7-1 Bayardo 10-1 Doro 100-8 Blankney

Won by one and half lengths ; neck second and third. Unofficially the distances afterwards were a neck and a head.

Time : 1 min 3. 4/5 sec

Sporting Life race analysis;-

"Pernambuco was fractious and Perola, Turban and Ramondia filly were slowly off. The running was made by Vivid from Blankney. Bayardo on the far side of the course heading Perdiccas, in the centre; then after an interval came Sunflower II, Blue Cap and Doro, Corinnus being the most prominent of the remainder. Half way Bayardo assumed command from Perdiccas, Sunflower II and Perola, the latter of whom made up a lot of ground in the last furlong, but could not reach Bayardo".

took place on the course itself and this considerable human traffic often resulting in some dreadful surfaces on the track for what might be considered, at least by some, the most important part of the show, the horses. The promenade was then sacrificed in the interests of the ground and that together with better turf management resulted in improved going by the time Bayardo raced on it. The promenade from that time on took place in the paddock. This period certainly saw plenty of change. The stands were demolished in September 1901 and completely rebuilt by May 1902. In addition, 1908 saw the construction of the "Five Shilling Stand", the precursor to the modern Silver Ring. This was the idea of the King as he felt that not enough was done for the ordinary public.

The race was never in doubt and has been described as a canter by the writer Theodore Felstead. It should be borne in mind that many easy wins were described as "canters" during that period. Today a victorious horse is described as winning in a canter only on the rare occasions that the jockey is not required to move appreciably, sit lower in the saddle or ask the horse for any perceptible effort. *The Times* said he won very easily and with what turned out to be splendid example of understatement observed that "he is such a useful looking sort and should certainly be heard of again"!

This was an impressive performance by a debutant, after which he was promptly acclaimed the best two-year-old so far and Alec Taylor was delighted. Alfred Watson writing as "Rapier" in *The Illustrated Sporting and Dramatic News* commented "It soon became evident that Manton shelters the best colt of the season so far. Mr Fairie has had some horses of high class and he tells me he thinks this is undoubtedly the best he has owned". It is amazing how little has changed. Similar remarks are made with considerable frequency these days, usually by a jockey or trainer with a view to increasing potential stallion value! At least on this occasion the words were proved to be accurate. *The Sportsman's* view was that he showed no greenness and that after his saddle was removed there were no marks to be seen.

Perdiccas was a good horse to have beaten on Bayardo's debut. He had raced four times and won twice. He was to race a total of nine times that year winning once more, the Molecomb Stakes at Goodwood. He met Bayardo only once more that year, in his next race.

The Persimmon filly Perola, who was the short-priced favourite, had made an impressive debut at Epsom. She was unlucky here in that she was slowly away, jumped the road which caused her to lose her stride, then made up considerable ground and was beaten only just over a length and a half. As Bayardo won, at the very least, comfortably, Perola's poor start probably made no difference to the result. However, had she got away on terms he would certainly have been required to exert himself a little more.

The opinion that Bayardo would have won in any event was challenged by Newmarket's *Sportsman* reporter who said he was fortunate that Perola was slowly away as she would have won if she had got away on terms. An un-named reporter from this paper had taken an immediate dislike to Bayardo and took every opportunity to write in unfavourable terms about him. It is an assumption but it is probably the same individual on each occasion. This reporter's jaundiced view regarding Bayardo will be noted again. However, on a more positive note the *Diamond Racing Journal* noted that he had been highly tried in the race and that "this is a fine colt and a stayer".

Perola was to race a total of seven times as a juvenile winning three more times, the Exeter Stakes at Newmarket, Rous Memorial Stakes at Goodwood and, easily, the Hardwicke Stakes at Stockton. She was to meet Bayardo once more in the Dewhurst Plate. The following year she was to win the Oaks.

Sunflower II, also making his debut, raced once more winning the Lavant Stakes at Goodwood. Of the others Blankney won the Gimcrack Stakes at York. He was to meet Bayardo once more. Vivid won the Imperial Produce Stakes at Kempton and The Prince of Wales Plate at York. She was to be beaten another three times by Bayardo. None of the rest won a race of any kind that year.

Bayardo had made a most impressive start to his racing career. He had displayed speed and the necessary temperament to produce his best form in an environment that would have been totally alien to him. A racehorse's first experience of a racecourse is crucially important. If he enjoys himself together with the atmosphere and competitive environment then a successful career with the horse fulfilling his potential beckons. Conversely an unpleasant incident of any kind may lead the horse to think that going racing means a repetition of his bad experience and it may be some time before he can be persuaded that it is not some kind of punishment. After Ascot connections of Bayardo could look forward to a successful career.

CHAPTER 5

Sandown Triumph and Glorious Goodwood

Bayardo missed his next three engagements, all over five furlongs, including the July Stakes at Newmarket's First July meeting, paradoxically run that year on 30th June! It had looked as if he would have little opposition should he accept for the race. He was impressing all at Manton and Alfred Cox would certainly have wished for him to run. However, Bayardo was coughing although when this started or when he recovered is unclear. It is a pity that he could not have run at Newmarket because he would have met Minoru. In the event they were not to meet at all that year. The result - Minoru was second to Battle-axe - suggested that Bayardo would have won with some comfort. Instead for his second race Bayardo headed to Sandown for the National Breeder's Produce Stakes, one of the most important and certainly the most valuable two year old race of the season at the time. Its value was well over one and a half times greater than the next valuable race which was the Middle Park Plate.

Entry for the National Breeders' Produce Stakes for 1908 closed on 1st August 1905, BEFORE any of the participants had even been foaled. The race conditions – given away possibly by its title - required that only produce of mares covered in 1905 were eligible, which of course restricted the race to two-year-olds. There were 285 entries originally and these had been whittled down to 19 by the day of the race. The race conditions, which were complicated to put it mildly, also allowed Bayardo three pounds because Bay Ronald covered at less than 100 guineas. This was more than negated by the nine pound penalty imposed for his win at Ascot. Today the race is the National Stakes and is nothing like as important as it was, is run before Ascot at the end of May and has only Listed status.

There was some suggestion that, because he had been coughing, Bayardo would not be fit enough for the race. However, Taylor would not have run Bayardo at Sandown if he thought he was not fit and well. He had done some sharp work over five furlongs on the 11th July which would have established his readiness for the race. He then worked six furlongs "sharply" with Cellaret colt (later named Moscato) and Sceptre filly (later to be named Maid of the Mist) on Wednesday 15th which would have brought him to racing pitch. Alfred Watson wrote about

Bayardo "If he runs I expect him to win and that it will be no surprise if Excellenza colt beats Louviers".

The weather was described by *The Sporting Life* as "not so muggy as the previous day, but more like January, than July, with April showers thrown in". It further noted that the King was present and "was greeted by brilliant company in the pretty paddock, the umbrageous shelter of which was very welcome to the fair sex, whose dainty toilettes otherwise would have suffered". It is difficult to imagine any modern day writers – Alastair Down of the *Racing Post* for example - describing a day at the races in a similar fashion! Only by reading the passage at least twice does its meaning become clear! The "*Life*" concluded, "The attendance all round was again a large one and the executive can be congratulated on the success achieved".

The field of fourteen was large by the standards of the race and had been exceeded only once in the previous eighteen years. This was a strong renewal with most of the best of the season's juveniles to date taking part. Clearly, although Bayardo was an impressive winner of his only race, he was considered far from unbeatable and it did not deter the opposition. There were only five withdrawals from the nineteen listed on the race card.

The going has been described as both fair and heavy. Judging by the times for other races over the two days of the meeting the ground was probably nearer heavy than soft. Bayardo's time was the fastest over the distance of the four races run. One race, a seller, did not have a recorded time. *The Sporting Chronicle* observed that Bayardo was an "elegant bay who shows such fine scope and quality with legs remarkable for those short cannon bones which spell strength and endurance". *The Sporting Life* noted that "he possessed the best qualities of his sire without any of the waywardness". Oh dear, why did this observer not keep his thoughts to himself? Talk about tempting fate!

The significance of this race was that this was the first time he had been ridden by Danny Maher. Thus began a partnership which was to be nearly as controversial as it was successful. It is also interesting to note that Maher was happy to jump off and make all the running with Bayardo, apparently, a willing partner in these tactics. Maher was never to repeat front running in any race that was more than a match until almost the end of Bayardo's career. It was certainly not possible to ask Bayardo if he was happy to making the running or not! However, it is hard to imagine that he could have won such an important race on only his second racecourse appearance in this fashion if he had not been happy to be in front. Maher reported to Alfred Cox that Bayardo "did not need to exert himself". Alfred Watson expressed the view that "There can be no doubt about Bayardo for there were unquestionably smart animals behind him. In fact to win as he did was an achievement which causes

Sandown Park Saturday 18th July 1908 Going : Fair/Heavy

National Breeders' Produce Stakes of £5,000, of which nominator of winner received £300, nominator and owner of the second each £200, and nominator and owner of the third each £100 by subscription of £1 each ; if left in after January 1st 1907 a further £5 ; if left in after October 8th 1907 a further £16 ; and if left in after March 31st 1908 a further £21 ; with £437 added ; for two year olds. Five furlongs 268 entrants, viz. 71 at £43, 43 at £22, 82 at £6, and 72 at £1 value to the winner £4357 (£278,848)

1	Bayardo	9st 2lb	D Maher	122+
2	Excellenza colt	9st 1lb	H Randall	117+
3	Vivid	8st 7lb	L Lyne	107
4	Perdiccas	9st 1lb	W Higgs	
5	Louviers	9st 5lb	H Jones	
6	William the Fourth	8st 10lb	Wm Griggs	
7	The Jabberwock	8st 10lb	B Dillon	
8	Sweet Story colt	8st 0lb	Walter Griggs	
9	Diospyros	8s 10lb	J H Martin	
10	Dinnet	8st 8lb	O Madden	
11	Hamerton	8st 10lb	W Halsey	
12	Balnacoil	9st 2lb	W Saxby	
	Kilmein	8st 7lb	F Wootton	
	Tantonie Belle	8st 0lb	C Trigg	

Betting 7-4 Bayardo, 5-1 Excellenza colt, 10-1 Sweet Story colt, 100-9 The Jabberwock, 100-8 Kilmein, 100-7 Perdiccas, 100-6 any other

Won by a length; half a length second and third. The fourth and fifth were some distance behind.

Time:1 min 4. 4/5 sec

Sporting Life race analysis;-

"The Jabberwock and the Excellenza colt were a trifle on their toes at the start, but the delay was not a particularly long one. When the signal was given Kilmein half whipped round and was left, whilst Diospyros, William the Fourth and Tantonie Belle began very slowly. As soon as they got fairly going Bayardo, towards the centre, cut out the work from Vivid, the Excellenza colt and Louviers these being followed at a considerable gap by The Jabberwock, Perdiccas (who did not jump off as smartly as those in front of him), Hamerton, Balnacoil and the Sweet Story colt, the rear being brought up by William the Fourth and Tantonie Belle. There was little or no change in this order for more than half the journey when the Excellenza colt got his head in front of Vivid, but Bayardo was still commanding them for speed and the issue was placed beyond doubt before the distance was reached. Bayardo, making all the running, and winning in smashing style".

Bayardo to stand out by himself. It is highly improbable, if all goes well with him, that he will be beaten this season by anything seen out so far".

The Excellenza colt was by Gallinule, and later named Glasgerion. He had won convincingly on his debut and this was his only defeat at two. He won his two subsequent starts as a juvenile both valuable stakes races. Vivid had run in the New Stakes. Louviers came into the race unbeaten, having won a plate and then the Coventry Stakes. He did not win again that year in top two-year-old races. He ran a total of seven times and did not meet Bayardo again, *The Sporting Life* noted that he would improve, like all progeny of Gallinule, and probably more than Bayardo, it concluded.

Balnacoil won a minor stakes race from five races. This was his only race against Bayardo. Perdiccas had run in the New Stakes. The Jabberwock won a plate race from his eight starts. He did not meet Bayardo again. None of the others won a race of any kind that year.

Bayardo was an impressive winner by any standards. However, *The Sportsman's* man, presumably the same individual who thought he was lucky to win at Ascot was not impressed. This myopic individual felt on the evidence of two races, both won comfortably, confident enough to say, without equivocation, that Bayardo would not achieve much and nothing to compare with Pretty Polly or Cyllene. It has to be wondered what he had seen to make him form such a moderate opinion of Bayardo on so little evidence. It is one of racing's oldest clichés that no horse is judged without prejudice. However, it is seldom that so blatant an example occurs as this.

Bayardo's rate of progress must have been impressing Alec Taylor and for his next race he was sent to Goodwood just ten days later. He had an alternative engagement at Liverpool over five and a half furlongs which was worth slightly more but instead he was upped in distance to six furlongs for the Richmond Stakes. The race was probably of similar importance then as today, currently classified as Group 2. It was not the most valuable juvenile race of the meeting, or the most important, however, although there were six early-closing two-year-old races at the meeting, it was the only one for which he had been entered. The race had a strong history of distinguished winners; however, apart from Vivid, who has already been mentioned, the other two runners, Oakmere and Sister Betty, both ran well enough at times but neither won a race of any sort. Despite its rich history the value of the race was modest by the standards of the time and compared with other juvenile races.

Glorious Goodwood, as it is always known, celebrated two hundred years of racing in 2002. It differs from Ascot in just one respect: formality. The racing is generally top-class over five days although there is a feeling that there are now too many of those unfathomable handicaps so beloved by bookmakers and that the quality of the meeting rather tails off and would probably be better over four days rather than five. Notwithstanding this, due to the lack of formality, the atmosphere is more relaxed than Ascot and was described many years ago by Edward VII as "a garden party with racing attached". As one approaches Goodwood for the first time, it seems inconceivable that a racecourse exists. From the grandstand the panoramic views in one direction across the downs are breathtaking and in the other the sight of the Solent is almost its equal. On a lovely

English summer afternoon there is no place quite like it. In 1908 Goodwood, like Ascot a four-day meeting, was held at the end of July. Until after the Second World War Goodwood only held this one meeting each year.

Bayardo was led six furlongs "sharply" by Moscato in preparation on the Saturday before the race.

"He had considerably enhanced his reputation by the style of his win after he had endangered his chance by getting badly away", noted *The Sporting Life*. It further observed that Maher did not bustle him, allowing him to get fairly into his stride, before calling on him for a serious effort with the result that Bayardo had the issue safe a quarter of a mile from home, eventually winning in a canter. "The opinion grows that Mr Fairie owns the best two year old seen out so far this season", it concluded without, it has to be said, sticking its neck out to any great extent! *The Sportsman*, described him as "Powerful, low, lengthy and old fashioned but in very bloodlike way". It must have been a comfort to know that someone at that paper had formed a favourable view of Bayardo!

Bayardo was slowly away, he had been noted as "fidgety at the gate" by the *Sporting Chronicle*. The Goodwood six-furlong course is uphill for a furlong then downhill for about another furlong then slightly downhill to the finishing line. Had Maher asked Bayardo to make up the lost ground too quickly he would have risked unbalancing him coming down the decline and that may have cost him the race. This is a good example of Maher's skill and understanding of the requirements of an inexperienced juvenile and the result was that Bayardo was not in any way inconvenienced by his tardy start. Alfred Cox, who in the

---

Goodwood Tuesday 28th July 1908 Going : Good

Richmond Stakes of £25 each, 10 ft for acceptors, with £500 added, of which second received £200 and third £100; for two year olds. Entrance £3, only ft. if declared. T.Y.C. Six furlongs. 73 entrants ft. declared for 31 value to the winner £652 (£41,728)

1	Bayardo	9st 8lb	D Maher	120++
2	Vivid	8st 7lb	L Lyne	96
3	Oakmere	8st 10lb	H Jones	91
	Sister Betty	8st 7lb	W Halsey	

Betting 1-3 Bayardo 4-1 Vivid 20-1 any other
Won by three lengths; two lengths second and third
Time: 1 min 14. 3/5 sec

Sporting Life race analysis;-

"Sister Betty dashed away with a commanding lead of Oakmere and Vivid, with Bayardo, who got very badly away, some distance in the rear. Oakmere was the first to cry content and Vivid then pressed Sister Betty, who when beaten at the distance, was not ridden clean out, and Bayardo, gradually closing on Vivid, won easily with his ears pricked".

circumstances must have been very confident beforehand, was quoted as saying "I had no fear at any moment and I am as nervous as a kitten when I see a chance of being beaten".

The going was given as good and described as "beautiful" by the *Diamond Racing Journal*. Considering that Bayardo was slowly away and won easily, his time, which was only a second slower than that for the Stewards Cup, was very good. In addition it is worth noting Bayardo carried 9 stone 8 pounds whereas none of the first nine to finish in the Stewards Cup carried more than 7 stone 12 pounds. A second is generally taken as five lengths and therefore it is not unreasonable to conclude that Bayardo could have finished five lengths behind the winner of that great handicap, which only carried 7 stone, giving him 36 pounds. A two year old should be receiving 18 pounds from an older horse in July and therefore Bayardo could be said to have given away 54 pounds and been beaten 15! This may seem somewhat tenuous but it does indicate that he was now progressing rapidly.

It was clear that unless a juvenile of outstanding merit appeared, Bayardo would be unlikely to be beaten that season.

CHAPTER 6

The Middle Park and Dewhurst

After three easy victories Bayardo was given a rest until the end of September. The *Diamond Racing Journal* reported that he had been "on the easy list" after Goodwood although whether this was due to an injury or other malady is not clear. The *Winning Post* reported that he had been coughing. Whatever the problem it meant that he was unable to take up his entries for the Champagne Stakes at Doncaster, which then, as now, was an important and valuable race, and also at Manchester where he had been nominated for the Autumn Breeders' Foal Plate. Instead he headed to Newmarket's First October meeting for the Buckenham Stakes. This was a very valuable five and a half furlong race at that time, but is no longer staged. The race conditions seem strange now. They required "Each subscriber to name three mares and to bring the produce of one to the post". There were twelve subscribers therefore the maximum number of runners could only ever have been twelve. The raced closed on 2nd January 1906 before Bayardo and the rest of the field had been foaled.

Newmarket is universally acknowledged as the "Headquarters of Racing". However for many years it was a daunting and unwelcome place for strangers. It consists of vast almost unbroken expanses of the Heath most of which has been owned by the Jockey Club from about the middle of the nineteenth century. However, it did not initially own the most famous of the gallops on the Limekilns which in those days it leased. The first recorded race was in 1622 and after various highs and lows it reached its nadir during the period from about 1830 until a revival began with the success in the 1863 Derby of Macaroni, who defeated Bayardo's great grandsire Lord Clifden by a head. Macaroni was trained at Newmarket by Jem Godding and he proved that horses could be successfully trained there. During the previous thirty years or so, a conviction had formulated that horses could not be successfully trained at headquarters, due to the adamantine condition of the gallops. Macaroni's triumph began a revival of the town's fortunes and during the late Victorian and early Edwardian period Newmarket reached its zenith with great horses, personalities and a few villains just to add colour.

The Jockey Club, at that time, regarded the racecourses and gallops as its own private fiefdom and for many years it did not encourage visitors.

This is something of an understatement. When a railway company organised a cheap train service during the 1860s Admiral Rous vindictively responded by making visitors very unwelcome. He arranged that all the races should start and finish at different places! Racing at Newmarket could be uncomfortable and complicated with different courses and winning posts at various points. This made a day's racing difficult, or impossible, for those spectators not on horseback. There were as many as five different winning posts but only one judge's box! This was on wheels, and during the course of the afternoon it was drawn from post to post as required by a donkey.

There was no grandstand worthy of the name, only a derelict structure which had been condemned as unsafe. This was cramped and uncomfortable and no one was allowed to use the upper part of it, which was the only place a decent view of the races could be obtained. A new grandstand was built in 1876 at a cost of £20,000 (£1,500,000). This had been opposed by the members of the Jockey Club as too expensive. However the real problem was their rooted objection to something that they considered so drastically innovative! The grandstand subsequently paid for itself many times over. In 1873 all trainers at Newmarket had to obtain a licence from the Jockey Club to train on the Heath and it was by no means a formality that one would be forthcoming. From 1905 all trainers, wherever they trained, were required to be licensed.

By Bayardo's time, matters at Headquarters were not much better. However, the old Cambridge course, which ran at an angle to the Rowley mile across the top of the incline and parallel to the Cambridge Road finishing near to the Hamilton Road where the entrance to the course is today, had closed in 1905. Since then the advent of the motor car has made Newmarket more accessible to visitors. Although it suffered a downturn in its fortunes for a few years after the Second World War, today it is thriving and there are over 2,500 horses trained on the Heath making it comfortably the largest centre catering for thoroughbreds.

Newmarket is loved for what it is and those who possess an undying affection would not have it any other way. Others consider it bleak and featureless and in the view of one visitor it was "acre upon acre of bugger all". Certainly if the weather is not kind it can seem cheerless during the spring or autumn meetings, but during the summer on a fine day the July course with its unchanging charm is everything the true lover of thoroughbreds and horse racing could desire.

The only work Bayardo had been noted doing for some time had not been particularly exerting. He was led by Seedcake on the 16th September over six furlongs and then six furlongs again by Seedcake at a "useful pace" on Monday 21st. On the 23rd he again worked six furlongs led by Seedcake and finally on the 26th Seedcake led Bayardo in company with Sceptre filly and Lady Vista six furlongs "sharply" as his final preparation for the Buckenham Stakes. In their edition on the 26th the *Diamond Racing Journal* reported that Bayardo was "all right again after a slight indisposition". On Monday 28th he left on the long journey for Newmarket.

After three races and three convincing wins Bayardo was considered amongst the best, if not the best, of the season's juveniles and it was not surprising that, with only a possible maximum of eleven opponents, just two took him on.

The distance of the race, which is no longer used, is unusual.

This really was a very moderate race. "M'Call's Racing Chronicle" described the win as a "common canter". Bonnie Lassie had been out six times without winning and was to win only a nursery from ten starts. This race was Vivario's only start that year. It was probably as well that the race was so uncompetitive. *The Sportsman* noted that Bayardo was "sweating profusely after the race as he had been short of work because he had been off colour". This would seem to confirm that he was short of his best which is not surprising as he had not done enough work to be fully fit.

Alfred Watson waiting in the Birdcage for Bayardo to return after the race came across the trainer William Waugh who lamented that Vivario was very slow, that this was Bonnie Lassie's seventh unsuccessful race, that Bayardo had had nothing to beat and that he would have nothing to beat on Friday in the Rous Memorial. He concluded that he would also have little to beat in the Middle Park or Dewhurst either! That was that then! So much for the juveniles of 1908!

At this stage Danny Maher was concerned to establish his position as Bayardo's rider for the following year, a clear indication of his regard for him. Whatever Maher's worries, it was unlikely he would have been replaced in any event. He may not have been aware of it but Alfred Cox was just as keen that Maher should remain Bayardo's jockey!

Newmarket Tuesday 29th September 1908 Going : good
Buckenham (post produce) Stakes of £300 each h. ft. ; for two year olds. T.Y.C. Five furlongs 134 yards 12 subs value to the winner £1500 (£96,000)

1	Bayardo	9st 0lb	D Maher	82++
2	Bonnie Lassie	8st 11lb	H Randall	76
3	Vivario	8st 11lb	W Earl	64

Betting 1-25 Bayardo 40 Bonnie Lassie and Vivario
Won by three quarters of a length ; four lengths second and third.
Time : not taken

Sporting Life race analysis;-
  "Bonnie Lassie led on sufferance for three furlongs where Bayardo joined issue the three then racing in close company till a quarter of a mile from home where Bayardo drew away and won in a canter".

The Buckenham Stakes was run over the two-year-old course which at that time started about nine furlongs from where the winning post is today. The finishing line was therefore halfway down the course, about three and a half furlongs from the current winning post. This course is no longer used. The reason for this seemingly strange arrangement was to spare the need for juveniles to have to negotiate the dip and the incline which is steeper than it appears up to the winning post in front of the stands. From a spectators' point of view this was not such a problem in the past when the majority of attendees at Newmarket were on hacks. However, as more general race-goers went racing on foot, walking almost half a mile to the winning post and the same distance back was not an enticing prospect for what amounted to little more than a walk-over. It was reported that as the winning post was so far from the grandstand some spectators did not bother to walk down to see the race. Possibly the only surprise was that any did at all!

Despite his lack of peak fitness, Bayardo's exertions could not have amounted to much as he was brought out again three days later for the Rous Memorial Stakes. William Waugh was right: there was no opposition to speak of. This is a little surprising as he had clearly not been at his best in the Buckenham Stakes and while the race would bring him on it would not have brought him to fever pitch. The Rous Memorial Stakes is no longer run. It was rumoured that Bayardo had gone home after the Buckenham Stakes which must have pleased connections of the sixteen horses entered for the race that were present on the course. However, when their hopes were dashed, and it was clear he was going to run again, only one horse opposed him and prevented a walk-over. Perola had been an intended runner and she would have ensured that Bayardo would have been made at least to gallop, rather than canter, the entire trip. However, she was unable to run. This mass withdrawal by connections, although understandable to a degree, speaks far louder with regard to the level of Bayardo's domination than anything written or spoken.

Opposed only by Auceps, who had won a maiden at long odds just three days earlier and did not race again that year, Bayardo had a very simple task. The only surprise was Bayardo's price. In the circumstances a return of 5% on an investment with very little risk looks quite attractive! This race was run over the Rous course, the start of which was five furlongs from the winning post in front of the stands. At least for this race spectators were not troubled to walk far to see the finish of a race which could hardly be described as entertaining!

Alfred Watson lamented that the public had yet to see Bayardo really gallop. He also noted that neither had Alfred Cox or Alec Taylor! This is because although he had been asked questions at home, he had managed to answer them without the need to exert himself.

Newmarket Friday 2nd October Going : Good

Rous Memorial Stakes of £15 each, 10 ft. for acceptors, with £400 added for owner and £100 for the nominator of winner ; for two year olds ; second received £50 out of the stakes ; entrance £5 only ft. if declared. Rous Course, 5 furlongs. 50 entrants, ft declared for 21 value to the winner £730 (£46,720)

1	Bayardo	9st 0lb	D Maher	100++
2	Auceps	8st 7lb	B Lynham	87

Betting 1-20 Bayardo
Won by one and a half lengths.
Time : 1 min 4 4/5 sec

Sporting Life race analysis
 "Bayardo cantered in front all the way"

At this stage it was obvious that Bayardo was the best juvenile to have raced so far. However, *The Sporting Life* was by no means sure that he had the most potential. The following appeared on Saturday 3rd October after Newmarket's First October meeting had concluded.

"The racing we have seen this week at Newmarket cannot be said to have appreciably advanced our knowledge concerning the merits of the front rank two year olds. Bayardo stands where he did, easily first, and in all probability he will maintain that position to the end of the season. Whether his superiority will be as pronounced next year is, however, another matter. He is a medium sized colt, and already has rather a set appearance. There does not seem the scope for development about him which is to be found in some of his opponents. I know one or two good judges who seeing him for the first time last Tuesday, declared themselves disappointed. Nevertheless, the fact remains that so far he has proved himself a brilliant performer, and as there is no reason to suppose that he will fail in any of his remaining engagements, this Autumn, we may look forward to finding him installed a good winter favourite for the Derby. Glasgerion, winner of the Hopeful Stakes, is a colt of quite a different stamp. He is a big lengthy fellow, who is hardly likely to come to maturity until next summer. The hypercritical among the cognoscenti find fault with his long back. Perhaps he is at a disadvantage there, but I am, nevertheless, pretty confident that with ordinary luck, he will grow into a magnificent three year old".

It would seem that Bayardo was fighting prejudice from more than one quarter! Some of this was almost certainly because many breeding experts could not bring themselves to believe that Bay Ronald could sire a really good horse and preferred to look elsewhere for the juvenile with most potential. In addition there were plenty who considered that he was not the most physically impressive and that a better looking sort must appear eventually.

It was time to step up in class again, this time to the Middle Park Plate. This was a more important race at that time than today, although it is a Group One. It was the second most valuable juvenile race of the year, after the National Breeders' Produce Stakes, won earlier by Bayardo. It is not usually realised today that the top two-year-old race at Newmarket during this time was not the Dewhurst, but the Middle Park - and it was far more valuable. In Bayardo's time their respective values were, the Middle Park £2505 and the Dewhurst £1477. Over the years the value of the races gradually came together until during the nineteen eighties when the value of the Dewhurst gradually increased in real terms and the Middle Park reduced. Today the Dewhurst is worth half as much again, about £150,000 against £100,000. A top juvenile today would automatically run in the Dewhurst and only sprint-bred types tend to run in the Middle Park.

It was inaugurated in 1866 when William Blenkiron, founder of the Middle Park Stud, a large commercial operation, offered the Jockey Club £1,000 (£70,000) to augment a sweepstakes for a new race to be run at Newmarket in October. This offer was accepted. However, the race was an instant success and, after Mr Blenkiron's money had been accepted for a few years, the Jockey Club assumed responsibility for the added money. The money was reduced by half and on one occasion a number of breeders contributed towards the prize. The Middle Park became a stakes race in 1921.

There is a difference between a plate race and a stakes races, although in Bayardo's time the distinction would seem marginal. In 1908 "a "plate" was a race to be run for money or other prize without any stake being made by the owners of the horses engaged". There was a set formula for the allocation of any surplus between those horses that finished second and third. "A "sweepstakes" was a race in which stakes are made by the owners of three or more horses engaged, to be paid to the winner or other horses placed, and any such race is still a sweepstakes when money or other prize is added". The Middle Park Plate was a race of 500 sovereigns guaranteed which was supposed to be added to the entrance and forfeit stakes. However, in 1908 the owners contributed 100% of the prize money. When it became a stakes race 1000 sovereigns were added to the entrance and forfeit stakes. The problem with British racing at this time, as now, was prize money. Overall owners contributed over 62% of the money they competed for. This compared badly with France, Australia, New Zealand and Argentina where owners contributed between 18 and 25% of stakes. In response to this and other problems the Jockey Club in November 1919 proposed some drastic, for the Club that is, changes including the abolition of plate races. When in 1920 The

Jockey Club revised the definitions, plate races were to continue, probably as a result of pressure from Racecourse Executives, but the definitions were clarified and the distinctions between them became clearer. Not it has to be said to the advantage of owners.

The Middle Park immediately became established as the principal race for juveniles. However, in its early years it seemed that the winner was doomed to fail in the following year's classics. It was not until 1885 when Melton won the Derby that the spell was broken. In the next nine years four Middle Park winners won the Derby but, at the time Bayardo contested the race, none had done so since Galtee More in 1897.

In the early years double-figure fields were the norm, usually fifteen at least with one running contested by no fewer than thirty. The average field for the first thirty two renewals had been fourteen. However for the last ten years the average had been just under eight. There had been sixteen single-figure fields, the smallest being five for the 1897 renewal won by Galtee More who went on to win the Triple Crown the following year. However there had never been either a match or a walk-over, which was now the likelihood. Even in 1885 when the highly regarded Minting was the winner the number of runners was nine.

Of the original nominations 28 were present on the course at Newmarket or were trained at Headquarters. There seemed to be a possibility that Edmond Blanc would send his colt Fils du Vent, whose brother Jardy had won the Middle Park in 1904, from France. However, he had been third and fourth in his last two races and did not look good enough. William Cooper had not been convinced that Bayardo was superior to his filly Perola on the basis of their running at Ascot. Bayardo had won of course, but had been in receipt of four pounds. This meant that the filly had been seven pounds "wrong" at the weights. In addition Perola had missed the break and jumped the path. Doro and Phaleron had been expected to run in the Middle Park but again their connections thought better of it.

Shortly before the race, Sir Daniel Cooper commented to Alfred Watson regarding his filly Vivid, who had just won the Imperial Produce Stakes at Kempton, "My little brown filly is wonderfully well". Watson replied, "But you surely can't have any chance of beating Bayardo?" Sir Daniel thought musingly, "No, I suppose not." He was however doubtless thinking that strange things happen in racing. Certainly if an upset was to occur the best chance a horse has would be when she is at her best, as Vivid seemed to be at the time. It seemed that only Blankney was likely to oppose Bayardo. In the event Vivid and the severely overmatched Shikaree were allowed to run. Quite simply, as far as the connections of all the top juveniles of 1908 were concerned, Bayardo was best avoided.

In preparation for the race on a dull morning Thursday 8th Bayardo was led five furlongs "sharply" by Seedcake, two days later on Saturday he was led for a "sharp" six furlongs by Seedcake in the company of another juvenile and the same trio went six furlongs on the following Monday. On Wednesday Bayardo left for Newmarket.

The Sporting Life reported that the weather was splendid with plenty of sunshine.

The Middle Park Stakes today is worth 72% of its' 1908 value.

The going was given as hard. If this was the case then plenty of those who raced over the four days of the meeting did not seem to relish it, as the times were slow. On many occasions in the past it has been shown that the firmer the ground, the slower the times will be compared with, for example, good to firm. This is because horses will not stretch out completely if the ground is uncomfortably firm.

Bayardo's time was about the median for the period from1900 until the Great War and about two and a half seconds faster than for the period from 1887 until 1900 and the "American invasion". The weather during October 1908 had been abnormally warm and dry in parts of the north and east. On the 3rd the temperature in Whitby, Yorkshire, had reached 29c (84f). The ground, of course, would not in any way have suited Bayardo. Vivid was fresh from winning the Imperial Produce Stakes and Blankney had just won the Gimcrack. Shikaree failed to win any of his five races.

As the betting indicated, Bayardo was expected to win easily. He won, but it was his least impressive performance of the year. Alec Taylor had

---

Newmarket Friday 16th October. Going : Hard

Middle Park Plate of £500, added to a Sweepstakes of £30 each, £20 ft., of which the second received £200 and the third £100 ; for two year olds ; entrance £5 ; of the surplus, viz. £75, second received two-thirds and the third the remainder. Bretby Stakes Course, 6 furlongs. 115 entrants £2,505 (£160,320)

1	Bayardo	9st 3lb	D Maher	119
2	Vivid	9st 0lb	O Madden	112
3	Blankney II	9st 0lb	W Higgs	100
	Shikaree	8st 10lb	B Dillon	

Betting 1-6 Bayardo 10-1 Vivid 100-6 Blankney II 100-1 Shikaree
Won by a length ; four lengths second and third.
Time 1 min 15 4/5 sec

Sporting Life race analysis;-

"The paddock inspection occupied little time and Mr E Willoughby had no trouble at the post with his four charges and he dispatched them on their journey to a perfect start. It was not before a furlong had been covered that the line was broken then Shikaree fell back half a length and Bayardo took a very slight lead of Vivid, Blankney II in the centre being at the latter's quarters. After leaving the bushes Blankney II began to feel the pace and began to lose ground and Bayardo always having the measure of Vivid stretched away up the hill to win very comfortably".

noticed that his charge was uncharacteristically listless and lethargic in the morning but was unable to find anything wrong with him. It may have been that he was still suffering from some residue of the malady that had laid him low the previous month. Taylor decided there was no reason why he should not run. In any event it was probably unlikely that Alfred Cox would have agreed to scratch unless Bayardo had been unsound or sick. The lassitude had passed by the evening. In the circumstances this was a very creditable performance to win when perhaps a little under the weather and on unsuitably fast ground.

The race was run over the Bretby course which is a furlong longer than the Rous course and finishes at the same place. Kettledrum of the *Sporting Chronicle* was not impressed and thought he "detected a rolling eye" and noted that Bayardo had not impressed physically as much as he had done in the summer. *The Sporting Life* was also unimpressed and the following appeared under its "Sporting Intelligence" column

"The Middle Park Plate, the event of the day, brought out four competitors, and ended as had seemed inevitable, in the victory of Mr Fairie's Bayardo. Notwithstanding, however, that the result was never really in doubt, the colt cannot be said to have done his work quite in the fashion which was expected of him. According to his running in the Richmond Stakes at Goodwood, Bayardo should have readily cantered away from Sir Daniel Cooper's Vivid, who here was able to make something of a race. It seemed, indeed, as if a very few pounds would have turned the scale. Sir Daniel Cooper told his friends that his daughter of St. Frusquin and Glare was particularly well; but so was Bayardo. The two met at weight for sex - that is to say, the filly received 3 lb, and she decidedly forced Bayardo to gallop - which he did with his mouth open and his ears back, usually symptoms of either distress or of an ungenerous disposition. He won by a length. At Goodwood Bayardo gave Vivid 15lb. and beat her in a canter by three lengths. The contrast between the two performances was remarkable; and an impression has arisen that very likely too high an opinion had been formed of the son of Bay Ronald and Galicia. The other two starters were Mr Raphael's Blankney II and Mr L Neumann's Shikaree; but, though the former had won the Gimcrack Stakes it is impossible to rank him with the best of his age, and Shikaree had run twice without getting into the first half dozen. Whether Bayardo will run in the Dewhurst Plate a fortnight hence will depend on the state of the ground. If rain comes and it is softer, he is to start, according to present plans; if the course continues to be hard, he will not be sent to incur the risk of being jarred. Whatever may happen this autumn, however, there are those who gravely doubt whether he will prove himself a really good three-year-old".

This would seem to have been written before it was known that Bayardo was perhaps not at his best. However, it already seems clear that he would be better with some give in the ground. Whether racing with his mouth open was due to any ungenerous tendencies, because the ground was too quick or a reflection that all is not well, it seems that a reputation for, at best, quirkiness or, at worst, possible unreliability was taking shape. Notwithstanding all of this, clearly Vivid improved and Bayardo was below his best juvenile form.

It is also seems apparent that the writer was exasperated by the lack of serious opposition to Bayardo in this most important race. Apart from him there were another twenty seven juveniles presumably most of them fit, well and able to race, yet only three took him on and the other twenty four simply spent the day occupying their stables on the racecourse or where they were trained. It is understandable that, for the neutral, an uncompetitive race which leaves nobody the wiser is frustrating when there is a desire to see a challenging contest. The connections of these horses can hardly be blamed. If they considered Bayardo unbeatable then they would feel that he would take the £2,505 prize for winning and the rest of the field would be competing for the considerably lesser total sum of £300 that was available to the second and third. Understandably they preferred to wait for a race they might be able to win. Of course, had Bayardo been beaten because he was off colour then some serious questions might well have been asked, particularly regarding the old adage that one should never be scared of one horse!

According to Alfred Watson, the race was never in doubt. Yet in his view Bayardo's performance destroyed the impression he had given of doing everything well within himself. Some observers had claimed that for a few strides Vivid had held Bayardo, something with which Watson did not agree. In his view Bayardo had readily left Vivid and won decisively. However, what had not impressed him was the way in which Bayardo, when going about his business, had not only put his ears back (something he had not done before) but had also opened his mouth, and he felt that he had not performed his task at all handsomely. Watson was waiting for Bayardo to return to unsaddle and asked the jockey Sam Loates what he thought of the race. "I think that with four or five pounds more on his back the colt would have been beaten," he replied. Loates was considered a shrewd and competent observer and his views are pertinent.

The hard ground was given as a reason and that Bayardo had "had about enough of it for the season." However, he had not really been so heavily raced. This was his sixth race and in two of them he had done little more than canter and although he may not have been altogether at his best had enjoyed a break during August and September. Alfred Cox was anxious to run in the Dewhurst and banish any thought that Bayardo was anything but comfortably the best juvenile of the year, which some were inclined to doubt.

The intelligentsia again remarked about Bayardo's lack of scope and the feeling persisted that he would not progress and improve at three. Some observers lamented the lack of opposition to him in the Middle Park Plate in which they pointed out he had been unimpressive. Others wished that Holiday House, who had shown such promise and at that stage had won four of his five races, could have taken him on. They felt that Bayardo would have been put in his place by such a meeting. However, Holiday House had not been nominated for any of the valuable end-of-season races. In any event this assumes that his connections would have been any more likely to want to race than those of the other twenty four possible opponents who clearly did not. Holiday House won four successive races in the north but did not beat any of the leading two-year-olds. He then finished second in a valuable stakes race at Derby, beaten a short head but giving the winner sixteen pounds, but he finished the year unplaced in the Free Handicap for which he had started favourite. He did not race again and did not stand training as a three-year-old, where incidentally he could not have run in either the in Guineas or the Derby as he had not been nominated although he had for the St Leger.

The Sportsman's writer, very likely the same nescient individual who had doubted that Bayardo would achieve anything much, stated that he should run in the Dewhurst Plate as he was in the form of his life and would not improve next year. Clearly his myopia was no better!

Bayardo accepted for the Dewhurst Plate. This was a valuable race but less important than the Middle Park and, of course, much less significant than today: the most prestigious juvenile race over seven furlongs. It was inaugurated in 1875 because it was felt that a more severe test was required over a longer distance. Both the Middle Park and the Dewhurst had been won by the same horse six times by 1908.

One week before the race on Thursday 22nd Bayardo was led by Seedcake at a "good pace" for seven furlongs and two days later on Saturday he was led seven furlongs by Seedcake in company with another which would have kept him ticking over nicely. On Wednesday 28th he left for Newmarket.

Alfred Cox was eager for the fray in the Dewhurst. He was keen to show Bayardo's critics that he was the horse that all at Manton and others had thought from the beginning of the season. William Cooper was to run Perola as he was also of the view that his filly had been maligned. The *Sporting Chronicle's* Newmarket columnist was certain that a locally trained horse would beat Bayardo as in the writers view he had shown an "apparent disinclination for his work in the Middle Park Plate". He also noted that he thought Bayardo had had enough for the year.

At Newmarket the *Sporting Life* noted that the weather had struck a rich vein of sunny conditions that would have done credit to the summer and, but for the carpet of autumn leaves, it was possible to imagine that racing was taking place on the July course. There were twenty-five of the original entries at the course and five stood their ground against Bayardo. In the paddock Perola was noted as charming and furthermore "she stripped a far better filly than when running in the Cheveley Park Stakes". She did, however, swish her tail on the way to post. The *Diamond Racing Journal* noted that Bayardo "showed plenty of temper before the race" and was observed by the *Sporting Life* going to post "short and scrappy". Kettledrum of the *Sporting Chronicle* reported that the bookmakers were happy to stand Bayardo to any money at odds-on for as much as any punter wanted. However, it further noted that not many big backers seemed to want to support him! The conditions of the race required the winner of the Middle Park or any other race which had a value of 1,500 sovereigns to carry a ten pound penalty.

The Dewhurst Stakes today is worth almost twice as much in real terms as in 1908.

The ground was given as good. This is probably accurate. Bayardo's time was about a second and a quarter faster than the median from 1900 until the Great War and about four seconds faster than the period from 1886 until 1900. The Dewhurst Stakes was one of only two races run over seven furlongs over the four days. No time was taken for the other race. *The Sporting Life* noted that Perola showed her true form but she

---

Newmarket Thursday 29th October Going : Good
Dewhurst Plate of £300, added to a sweepstake of £25 each, 15ft., of which the second received £100 ; for two year olds ; entrance £3. Last 7 furlongs of RM 83 entrants £1477 (£94,528)

1	Bayardo	9st 5lb	D Maher	131+
2	Perola	9st 0lb	O Madden	118
3	Lucina colt	8st 9lb	H Jones	105
4	Great Peter	8st 9lb	W Bullock	
5	Carrousel	8st 9lb	H Randall	
6	Carbineer	8st 9lb	W Saxby	

Betting 20-75 Bayardo, 10-1 Carrousel, 100-8 Perola
Won by three lengths ; same second and third
Time : 1 min 29.1/5 sec

Sporting Life race analysis;-
"The competitors were sent off to a capital start, Perola immediately taking command from Bayardo, the latter racing on a tight rein in advance of Great Peter and Carbineer with Carrousel upsides whipping in. Leaving the bushes behind Bayardo drew to Perola's girths and the pair descended into the dip neck and neck, but the favourite took the measure of Perola and drawing away at his leisure won in smooth style".

was only able to "lay along side the favourite, but only as long as Maher pleased, as the Manton "crack" showed no signs of the staleness which had characterised his victory over Vivid at the last meeting, but cantering well within himself, came away at pleasure out of the Dip".

Although the big hitters had not wanted to play the betting again suggested that Bayardo had a simple task. He was back to his sparkling best and beat Perola with the greatest of ease. She, of course, had already been beaten by Bayardo and was to win the Oaks the following year. However, this time there had been a turnaround in the weights of nine pounds, Perola now in receipt of five pounds whereas she had given four pounds at Ascot. This was an outstanding performance, one which would probably have won most renewals in the twentieth century. Not many winners of the race have given a future classic winner almost a stone beating and done it with ease. The Lucina colt was later named Specimen but he raced only once at three, nine times at four and once at five without success. The nearest he came was to be beaten a neck in a maiden and a handicap. He was sent to South Africa. None of the others won a race of any kind that year. Bayardo had now won both the Middle Park and Dewhurst, a double achieved by Lemberg the following year, but not again until Diesis in 1982. The race was run over the last seven furlongs of the Rowley mile. This is the same course that the Dewhurst Stakes is run over today.

The larger field for this race compared with the Middle Park was probably occasioned by the unconvincing manner of Bayardo's victory in that race. The prize money available for the second was less and there was no third prize. Clearly some thought it possible he could be beaten. The grounds for this may have lain in the distance of the race. This was the first time Bayardo had raced over seven furlongs and, as he had so much speed, the hope may have been that he would not see out the trip.

On a note of caution the *Diamond Racing Journal,* who had noted that Bayardo had shown "plenty of temper prior to the race, observed that he did the same afterwards. The tendency to display "temper" as they put it "may prove a formidable obstacle to his success later on" it further opined. More positive was the view of Alfred Watson who felt that Bayardo's reputation had been entirely vindicated. Nothing could have been smoother than this performance, particularly as Perola had stuck to her work well. Danny Maher was aware that the filly might cause him problems. "I came away rather soon for she goes a great pace and I did not want to leave it too long and let her get at me just at the finish" he said discussing the race afterwards.

CHAPTER 7

Champion Juvenile

Bayardo was of course champion juvenile and much had been written and said about him, not all of it to his credit! However, the *Sportsman's* special commissioner, probably William Allison, wrote the following on the Thursday evening after the Dewhurst.

"Then as to the racing there was practically nothing of serious importance except to see Bayardo do another gallop and Radium win another Cup. I should never have committed myself so strongly in Bayardo's favour after the Middle Park Plate had I not been perfectly sure of my ground and after today I suppose all the doubting Thomases of that week will be once more gathered into the fold of believers. I have written from the first that it is long that I have seen a colt I like as well as Bayardo. There is nothing flashy nothing of the flat-catcher about him but every point is good and he is quite of the old-fashioned business-like sort such as we see in Herring's pictures. He is low but he is very lengthy with enormous heart-room and perfect forehand. He is equally good to follow and he is balanced to a nicety in every movement. He will never be a big one but he has ample range and scope and when fairly extended he is as fine a mover as ever was seen". He continues "It is generally considered that Bayardo is a slovenly mover in his slow paces, but this I fancy is mainly due to Maher's prudent habit of never giving the ring much of a show in the canter down. Anyhow, Bayardo is a worthy descendent even of Blink Bonny. He retires unbeaten and with ordinary luck he will maintain his supremacy throughout next year. Already one cannot help thinking what an ideal sire he will be for mares of Blair Athol blood such as those of the Paraffin family. He has done quite enough racing for one year but there will now be a well deserved long holiday".

The view had been expressed by contemporary reporters that Bayardo was "set" and lacked scope by one and by another as lengthy and having scope! Which was true? It is fair to say that, looking at photographs of Bayardo and his half brother Lemberg as juveniles, the latter would seem to have more scope. However, although it is difficult to make considered judgements from photographs, it is hard to see evidence that Bayardo was "set" and would not change as he matured. It is probably true that whilst he had some scope he gave the impression that others would improve more. The *Winning Post* certainly thought he was an impressive juvenile judging by their comments written in December when reviewing the year; "Bayardo, a symmetrically moulded dark bay with excellent shoulders, supporting stout neck, a strong back good to follow behind the saddle, his only fault being his not quite perfect head". What was definitely true for all to see was that in maturity he was a fine specimen, as shown by the picture taken as a ten-year-old the year before he died.

A more worrying area seemed to be that Bayardo might have a temperament problem. Kettledrum of the *Sporting Chronicle* reminded his readers that he had always been a supporter of Bayardo's talent and did not think he was temperamental. However, some of his acquaintances were not so enthusiastic. He quoted one as saying "wait until he is fairly tackled and he will try to crawl down the nearest hole". It seems safe to say that he was not an admirer! The bookmakers, however, seemed sure that he was the most likely top three-year-old as Bayardo was offered at only 7-2 for the Derby in early November and he had shortened to 11-4 by the end of the year.

How good were the juveniles of 1908? It would be an exaggeration to say they were a vintage bunch. They were in truth just average with only Bayardo worthy of a rating above 120, using the *Timeform* scale. According to a *Century of Champions* Bayardo's rating of 131 would have been enough to have made him leading juvenile in all but five years of the twentieth century. He finished the year unbeaten in seven starts and, with the exception of the Middle Park, had yet to be extended. He did of course win more prize money than any other juvenile. He was second in terms of overall prize-money won, behind a three-year-old Your Majesty.

Bayardo was lucky in some respects; for example Lord Derby the leading owner-breeder had some mainly disappointing juveniles and the *Sporting Chronicle's* Newmarket correspondent thought the horses in training at Headquarters were the worst he had seen for some time. Over the season Bayardo had improved in appearance and it was now thought that he stood out in looks. This view was not shared by the *Sporting Life* correspondent who was such a fan of Glasgerion and thought Bayardo looked set at two and lacked scope! Perhaps a case of handsome is as handsome does!

There follows a list of the most valuable races for two-year-olds open to colts with the winner and the races' value to the winner.

Bayardo annexed three of the top four and five of the top ten races in terms of value. He had not been nominated for the Imperial Produce Plate at Kempton or the Prince of Wales Stakes at Goodwood. He would in any event not have run in the latter as he ran in the Richmond Stakes. In addition he was not nominated for the Great Lancashire Breeders Produce Stakes. Of the other races he missed the Champagne because he

National Breeders Produce Stakes	Bayardo	4,357 (278,848)
Imperial Produce Plate	Vivid	2,569 (164,416)
Middle Park Plate	Bayardo	2,505 (160,320)
New Stakes	Bayardo	1,817 (116,288)
Prince of Wales' Stakes	Attic Salt	1,800 (115,200)
Champagne Stakes	Duke Michael	1,720 (110,080)
Coventry Stakes	Louviers	1,715 (109,760)
Great Lancashire Breeders Prod St	Duke Michael	1,614 (103,296)
Buckenham (post produce) Stakes	Bayardo	1,500 (96,000)
Dewhurst Plate	Bayardo	1,477 (94,528)

was under the weather and he ran in the New Stakes rather than the Coventry at Ascot.

The following ratings are calculated by using, as far as possible, collateral form. They are designed to be comparable with *Timeform* ratings that are produced for their *Racehorses* annual: Holiday House rated 119 would be comparable with a juvenile of any other year with the same rating. The main problem with producing ratings from this period is that only the first three finishers were officially placed in most races. A horse whose best performance was a close-up fourth may not have that effort taken into account. The ratings are not comparable with those which might have been produced by a handicapper using methods and theory which is applicable to handicapping for race purposes. In such circumstances a handicapper might allot Bayardo 9 stone 7 pounds, but might consider that he would need to concede more than 13 pounds to Perola or 19 pounds to Vivid in order that a race between them would be competitive. The reason for using *Timeform's* rating method and not the *Racing Post's* or the International Classifications is simply that *Timeform's* ratings started over sixty years ago and have an admirable record of consistency, compared to the *Racing Post* which only started in 1987 and the International Classifications which although of longer standing began only in 1986 in their current form. Prior to that date ratings had been calculated on a 0-100 scale instead of 0-140 as at present. In addition there is evidence that the International Classifications are not always consistent and some ratings suggest "political" interference.

It is important to distinguish between a ratings service such as those provided by *Timeform, & Raceform Racing Post* ratings and the official handicapper. A rating by *Timeform* is an expression in the form of a figure of a horse's merit. A *Timeform* rating is usually about 3-4 pounds higher than those allocated by the *Racing Post* in their ratings and about 5-7 pounds higher than those supplied by the official handicapper today. However, it is important to remember that the official handicapper is not a ratings service and should not be regarded as such. He has only one objective: to ensure as much as possible competitive handicap racing. Handicapping is said to be an art and not a science. But that relates to the days when a handicapper would draw up weights for a specific race with the intention of giving every horse a theoretically equal chance. Only the Grand National is treated in this manner now. The element of handicapping that is an art form is discounted as the rating is largely based on form except where a once-raced horse that won is entered for a handicap. In these circumstances the handicapper is required to guess the horse's level of ability, a situation which can astonish a relative newcomer

Bayardo	c	131+	7
Holiday House	c	119	6
Perola	f	118	7
Electra	f	116	8
Perdiccas	c	113	9
Glenesky++	c	113?	5
Louviers	c	112	7
Vivid	f	112	9
Duke Michael	c	112	5
Strickland	c	112	11
The Whirlpool	c	112+	4
Glasgerion	c	112+	4
Battle-axe	c	111	9
Blankney	c	110	7
Harmonica	f	109+	1
Minoru	c	109	6
Temnos	c	109	7
The Jabberwock	c	108	8
Verderer	c	107+	3
Princesse de Galles	f	107	6
Third Trick	f	107	5
Eudorus	c	106	7
Basil	c	106	6
Eddystone	f	106	6
Telbedde	g	106	8
Lucina colt	c	106?	2
Attic Salt	f	105	7
Sunflower II	c	105+	2
Genny	f	105	7
Mulvaney	c	105	6
Mother in Law	f	105	9
Bonny Bay	f	104	3
Phaleron	c	104	4
Canonite	c	104	7
Gutfreund	c	104	2
Oakmere	c	104	7
Queen Mother	f	103+	2
Blackstone	c	103	8

++ Trained in Ireland

Bayardo – From a painting by A C Havell

Alec Taylor senior "Grim old Alec"

The Duchess of Montrose "Carrie Red"

Alec Taylor junior "Young Alec"

Manton House

The Manton Stables

On the Manton Downs

Alfred Cox "Mr Fairie"

Cox's house on the Severals at Newmarket

The Wizard of Manton

The Paddock at Ascot during Bayardo's time

An aerial view of the Bandstand at Ascot

as a dapper well-dressed man

Danny Maher as a top jockey and . . . .

to racing that a horse's chances in a race can be based on somebody's guesswork, however educated.

Notwithstanding this, reference has been made to the weights for the Free Handicap which was run on 30th October 1908. Bayardo's rating is taken form *A Century of Champions* and used as a starting point. The number following is the number of races each horse took part in as a juvenile. Compare these with the number of appearances of modern leading juveniles.

The most likely of these to improve was probably The Whirlpool who, although he had won only one of his three races, had made his debut later in the season, and Glasgerion, who had won three of his four races and, as our Newmarket man noted, had plenty of scope! His only defeat was by Bayardo in the National Breeders' Produce Stakes. In addition Holiday House had plenty of supporters who thought that he was one to back in any future meeting with Bayardo.

A moderate collection of juveniles or not, Bayardo's superiority was unquestioned and overwhelming even by those who doubted he could sustain his advantage. Unless something improved significantly, or Bayardo failed to progress or regressed, few would have argued that the Triple Crown of 1909 looked to be at his mercy.

CHAPTER 8

Classic failure

Bayardo's classic season did not begin well. The weather during the early months of 1909 was dry and bitterly cold. Throughout February and March persistent winds blew from the north and east. Bayardo, like many thoroughbreds, liked warmth and sun and loathed the cold, and he was unable to thrive in these conditions. The searing east winds parched the Manton gallops. The journalist Sidney Galtrey recalled in his memoirs the chilling conditions that prevailed during the early part of 1909: "winter that year lingered long on the lap of spring, and there was much malice and hate in the long prevalence of northerly and easterly winds". As a result of this the new grass did not grow and even the best gallops became very hard. These unfriendly conditions caused considerable discomfort to Bayardo's fleshy, sensitive feet. In addition he also had trouble with his teeth which in turn gave him problems with his digestive organs. As if this was not enough, he slipped one frosty morning when fooling about at exercise and lamed himself temporarily. There is a story which suggests that what actually happened was Bayardo, on a cold morning with plenty of ice on the ground, was giving his usual trouble by refusing to return to his box after working. Three or four lads were attempting to man-handle him when he slipped and badly strained his quarters. When his trainer discovered the problem at evening stables it was obvious that Manton's champion would remain in his box for some time. Very probably the lads concerned were also subjected to considerable admonishment as to their future care of the stables' star!

Alec Taylor was a master at preparing a horse for a race but these trials would have tested even the most patient practitioner and few, if any, were more patient than he. Taylor must have been very worried that, unless matters improved soon, the best juvenile he had so far trained would not be ready for the first classic. When it is considered that Bayardo was the warmest ever winter favourite for the Derby, with the exception of Friar's Balsam in 1888, the pressure on Taylor can be readily imagined.

In early January the betting for the Derby was as shown on the next page.

These were appalling odds for an event nearly five months away. Even if the bookmakers thought Bayardo the most likely winner and that there was little in the way of serious opposition, it does not explain the excessively ungenerous odds offered about the rest of the possible runners. It can only be assumed that for some reason they were not keen to bet.

11-4	Bayardo
5-1	Glasgerion
10-1	Mat o' the Mint
10-1	Fils du Vent
12-1	Valens
12-1	Whirlpool
12-1	Golden Flight
16-1	Duke Michael
16-1	Diamond Stud
16-1	Grimmet
20-1	bar

With this in mind it would seem to be a pity from "Robin Goodfellow's" point of view that there were no exchanges in 1909. Alfred Watson, who wrote as "Rapier" in *The Illustrated Sporting and Dramatic News*, and had championed Bayardo as a juvenile, had an annual contest with "Robin Goodfellow" who wrote for the *Daily Mail*. Each chose twelve horses to follow. Watson of course included Bayardo in his twelve. However, "Robin Goodfellow", clearly one of those not convinced that Bayardo would train on, did not. Had there been exchanges he would surely have jumped at the chance to lay Bayardo at about 3-1! This is an indication of how, despite his total superiority over his contemporaries, there were plenty who did not feel that he was the genuine article.

In late January *The Winning Post* reporter Robert Le Diable (Robert Sievier) wrote that Bayardo had been seen, not he recorded with Alfred Cox's permission, and that the son of the late Bay Ronald had not only gone the right way but had done better than even his most ardent admirers could have anticipated. He further opined that Bayardo had furnished all round and that no man could now fault him. There was more in a similar vein but no mention of any problems so clearly all was well at that time! However by March matters were very different.

Bayardo was now having a difficult time with the unpleasant weather and hard gallops, even so he was very much the stable star and, it would seem, was perfectly well aware of this! Sidney Galtrey, in his memoirs, recalls an incident when visiting Manton at about this time. He noted that it was a morning of fleeting shafts of pale winter sunshine, but with plenty of bite in the wind.

"Let me begin by relating an incident I personally witnessed which gave me an insight into the unusual character of a very unusual horse. Outstanding horses, usually fillies, have almost invariably some curious characteristic or another. The horses that cold morning in March 1909 had just filed through the covered entrance into the stable yard on their return from exercise. All but one had dutifully gone to their respective boxes. The exception was the great horse himself. There he was, standing as stubbornly as a mule, just standing and anxious, evidently, to make the minimum (sic) fuss about it and un-wishful of annoying anyone. They could not get him into his box. Every now and then he had the mood to be thus obstinate and mulish.

What was to be done? Why, nothing but wait. Wait until Bayardo thought the moment had arrived to enter. Until it had done so, he would pay no heed to any amount of coaxing. He blinked contemptuously at the offering of a wisp of grass which he knew would be held in advance of him until the stable door had closed on him. He seemed to know that they would not be rough with him. After all he was the favourite for the Derby with outstanding prospects of winning the Triple Crown of Two Thousand Guineas, Derby and St Leger".

This incident induces the thought that Bayardo must have had quite a dislike of his stable if he did not wish to at least get out of the biting wind!

It is interesting to look at a typical day in the life of Bayardo at this time. Assuming the day was a routine one and did not involve a trial or serious work it would begin at five o'clock when he would be fed with corn, beans and chaff. Sometimes it might be anything which suited his appetite! A mental picture of Bayardo leaving a note of his breakfast requirements on his stable door comes to mind! At six he would leave his stable for the gallops where he was exercised over whatever distance was best suited to his next race. At eight he would be back in his stable – assuming he had consented to return to it that is, if not, probably sometime between eight-thirty and nine - and after being brushed he was fed and watered the feed this time consisting of more corn, beans and green chaff, which is cut up grass. He is then left on his own until four o'clock when he was walked out for half an hour and afterwards he is "done": dressing, watering and feeding. At five-thirty he was given feed consisting of corn. At seven he would be made comfortable for the night. Firstly his lad would have brushed and hand-rubbed him, a form of massage which was intended to help muscular development, and after this vital operation was completed he is fed again and left for the night. In Bayardo's case at least an anxious trainer or his head lad might look in on him at about ten o'clock taking care not to disturb the great horse.

News of Bayardo's problems were beginning to emerge and on 13th March the *Diamond Racing Journal's* Manton man reported that Bayardo had "met with a slight setback and had been given a dose of physic". The exact nature of the medication is not specified and it is hard to imagine that anyone at Manton would have divulged the information. The *Sporting World* reported that he had suffered some problems with his teeth. It never rains but it pours!

Despite these difficulties the bookmakers still considered Bayardo to be the most likely winner of the Two Thousand Guineas. These were the odds available on the 20th March;-

Bayardo	9-4
Glasgerion	6-1
Sir Martin	6-1
Duke Michael	6-1
	12-1 bar

Due to the condition of Bayardo's feet, which were constantly worrying Alec Taylor, together with other problems the utmost care was taken with him and following his lameness he was on the easy list for some time. During the second half of March Bayardo did no more than canter and when he was back in stronger work he was not impressive. Between the 31st March and the 8th April Bayardo worked over distances ranging from six to twelve furlongs but only at "steady" and "half speed" with only one piece of work described as "useful". He did not seem to be thriving and, with the Two Thousand Guineas less than three weeks away, his prospects were not encouraging. In the circumstances it was becoming clear that Taylor was unable to give Bayardo the thorough preparation he would have needed for the 2000 Guineas. With his habitual patience and restraint Taylor, who would of course never have rushed any aspect of Bayardo's training, found it was going to be impossible to get him to his liking in time for the first Classic. Alec Taylor's first consideration was always for the horse's welfare and, however tempting it must have been to press on, he realized that time was not on his side. It must, therefore, have been with considerable sadness that he advised Alfred Cox to scratch him from the race.

This would have been a bitter disappointment to Taylor. History would show that he was to win twenty one classics including the Two Thousand Guineas four times. However, at this stage of his career he had won just one classic, the St Leger in 1905, and Bayardo was by some way the best two-year-old he had trained and his best chance of winning the first classic. Bayardo had been a very fast juvenile and, despite his breeding, the Two Thousand Guineas looked his best chance of winning a classic. Horses that mature quickly and show their best form at two often fail to train on and stay middle distances. It was entirely possible that Bayardo would not have been able to stay the Derby and St Leger distances. Taylor could not be certain that other chances would come his way and, in any event, it was unlikely he would ever again have a juvenile the equal of Bayardo; and, as things turned out, he didn't.

It should also be remembered that the Two Thousand Guineas, although very important today and a Classic, was much more so in

Bayardo's time. Today if a horse is too backward to be ready for the Two Thousand Guineas connections can wait for the Irish equivalent or the St. James's Palace Stakes. The two latter races do not carry the same monitory value as the Two Thousand Guineas, but both are Group One and confer similar status as far as breeding value is concerned. However, in Bayardo's time there was no Irish equivalent - it was not inaugurated until 1921 - and the St James's Palace Stakes was worth only 40% in monitory terms and considerably less in status. Without a Pattern system as today the Classics were the most important races and if a horse lacked the stamina for the Derby missing the Two Thousand Guineas was a serious matter. In the circumstances it can be readily appreciated that Alec Taylor would not have taken the decision to advise Cox to withdraw Bayardo lightly.

Alfred Cox, however, insisted that he should run. As with all his horses, he mapped out Bayardo's races and, short of him actually breaking down, he expected him to run where engaged. It seemed irrelevant that his colt was unbeaten and that this would be the greatest test of his career to date. In fairness to Cox, and trying to look at matters from his point of view, he probably felt that, based on Bayardo's considerable superiority as a juvenile, he could win the 2000 Guineas when short of peak fitness. In addition, despite his overtly confident manner, he too may have harboured doubts about Bayardo's stamina and possibly felt that the Guineas represented his best chance of securing a classic. At this time Cox had won only one classic, the One Thousand Guineas in 1895 with Galeottia. It would have caused him considerable annoyance to withdraw from the race and leave it to be won by a horse that Bayardo could have, as racing men might say, "picked up and carried" at his best. Cox was not the most patient or tolerant of men and it was more than likely that no force or persuasion on earth could have resulted in him withdrawing Bayardo.

Alec Taylor was left with no option but to proceed with Bayardo's preparation for the race. It would be interesting to know what his thoughts were at this time. He was a meticulous man who was proud of the way he prepared a horse for a race and took considerable pains to ensure that all was well. In all probability Taylor was disgusted by Cox's lack of concern for Bayardo's welfare, something Taylor would always have considered a priority. The likelihood was that he simply decided he would carry on as he had been, but was ever conscious that he would not be able to press Bayardo at any stage, for fear that the whole season could be compromised at any moment.

Alfred Cox visited Manton on Thursday 8th April and witnessed Bayardo's work. He went ten furlongs at a "good gallop" led by his usual work companion Seedcake. This would have been the fastest work Bayardo had done for over a week. The distance is interesting. Bayardo was being trained for a mile race which would normally entail six and seven furlong canters or gallops. However, it seems likely that with Bayardo's delicate feet and the firm training gallops, Taylor considered that work over longer distances, which would be at a slower pace, would be more beneficial in bringing him to race fitness, whilst limiting any damage to his feet. There seems little doubt that this piece of work was important in ascertaining Bayardo's level of readiness for the Guineas and Alec Taylor was evidently not happy.

Over Easter on Friday 9th April "Augur" of the *Sporting Life* wrote an article speculating on the Derby prospects. The Craven meeting was imminent and he noted that it was unlikely that Bayardo would appear until the 2000 Guineas, in which there would be every prospect of a clash between Glasgerion and Bayardo. While noting that Bayardo had beaten Glasgerion easily on the only occasion they had met as juveniles in the National Stakes, and conceding that Bayardo was head and shoulders above his contemporaries, he suggested that all this may be turned over in the coming weeks. He stated that he was not alone in considering that Glasgerion would prove himself better than Bayardo this year. This is because he was considerably bigger and that "a good big 'un will always beat a good little 'un". Glasgerion was already 16 hands, a height Bayardo might never attain. In addition, reports from Newmarket suggested that his well being was satisfactory, something that could not be said about Bayardo. As it turned out, Glasgerion was beaten in the Craven Stakes and was subsequently dropped in distance, where he became a successful, if not outstanding sprinter. It is, however, notable that Bayardo, despite his undoubted supremacy as a juvenile, still had plenty of doubters with regard to his ability to sustain his status during his classic year.

Bayardo had been nominated for two races at Newmarket's Craven meeting, the Biennial Stakes and the Column Produce Stakes, both over a mile. There was, of course, no possibility that he would take up either option. Ironically the Craven Stakes was not the most valuable race for three year olds over a mile at the Craven meeting. Indeed it was not even the second! The Biennial was worth £662 (£42,300) the Column Produce £1058 (£67,700) and the Craven £525 (£33,600).

Bayardo worked a mile at "good speed" with Seedcake on Wednesday 14th. However, it was necessary to establish exactly where he stood in terms of fitness and a trial was arranged over a mile on 21st April. The trial was not held in secret and was reported in the sporting papers. The result was as shown on the next page.

Seedcake had been used in Bayardo's juvenile trial. Here he was beaten 43 pounds: twenty pounds weight-for-age he should have received, plus twenty one pounds he was conceding, plus two pounds for a length beating. Maid of the Mist, who was Sceptre's first foal, received only a

Bayardo	3 yrs	9st5lb
Seedcake	4 yrs	7st 12lb
Maid of the Mist	3 yrs	9st2lb
Moscato	3 yrs	8st5lb

Won easily by a length; a head between second and third.

sex allowance from Bayardo. She had failed to win any of her three races at two and, after this trial, she won two of her five races that year, a minor stakes race at Newmarket and the Nassau Stakes at Goodwood. She was retired at the end of the season and eventually earned fame as a foundation mare at the Astor's Cliveden stud. Moscato had been beaten in his only race as a juvenile and won two of his ten races as a three-year-old. He lost all seven of his races at four.

The trial was obviously not a disaster. Seedcake had been disposed of easily enough but Maid of the Mist was only beaten six pounds and it convinced Alec Taylor that Bayardo was some way below his best. It must be assumed that Cox was fully aware of the situation but, probably still, overtly in any event, confident that a partly fit Bayardo could prevail, insisted on having his way. The *Diamond Racing Journal's* view was that the trial proved nothing as it seemed to have been contested by horses short of full fitness. Bayardo therefore was due to reappear in the 2000 Guineas with an interrupted preparation, without a race and with his trainer unhappy that he was anywhere near peak condition. It was not to be a recipe for success.

However, remembering how far ahead of his peers Bayardo had been the previous year it would seem that the connections of his opponents were not very confident they could beat him. Richard Marsh, Minoru's trainer, wrote in his memoirs *A Trainer to Two Kings,* "It seemed absurd, I suppose, that we could think of beating this high-class two-year-old (Bayardo). Marsh had however heard about Bayardo's vicissitudes for he wrote, "Various conflicting reports were in circulation about him. Some said he had not grown or done well, others that trouble had been experienced with his rather shelly feet. I told my friends that Minoru could not possibly be better, but if Bayardo were at his best then we should never be able to beat him". Marsh's confidence in Minoru followed an impressive win in the Greenham Stakes at Newbury giving weight to Valens. There was a suggestion that all could not be well with Bayardo and that he must be well short of his best, because Taylor had chosen to run him in a trial at home against modest horses he could beat easily. A race at Newmarket would have tested him more of course, but would have had the advantage of bringing him nearer to peak fitness than a trial.

Alfred Watson, writing just before the race, was not at all sure who would win. He noted that Bayardo would be the favourite, and odds on at that, but that on current form the best horse was probably Minoru. However, he had been rated 20 pounds behind Bayardo as a juvenile and it was hard to imagine that he had improved 20 pounds over the winter. But perhaps his most surprising observation was that Bayardo might not stay a mile. Again the view was being advanced that such was the brilliant speed displayed by him at two that there were plenty who thought he could not have stamina to match.

On the 24th April on a fine morning Bayardo worked six furlongs "usefully" with Seedcake and his final work prior to the Guineas was seven furlongs at "half speed" on Monday 26th and he left for Newmarket the next day. *The Sportsman's* Manton correspondent was confident that he would prevail, as was the *Sporting Life's* man. Such confidence must have been based on his juvenile form rather than his current state of well-being.

The Two Thousand Guineas was the fourth of the five classics to be inaugurated. It was thirty three years after the St Leger and twenty nine years after the Derby that in 1809 a sweepstakes of 100 guineas each (half forfeit) for three year old colts and fillies was added by the Jockey Club to Newmarket's First Spring Meeting. The race was run over, and still is, the Rowley Mile. For the first running there were 23 subscribers and eight starters. The One Thousand Guineas was added in 1814 in order that a race exclusively for fillies could be included. Originally the 1000 Guineas was run over the Ditch Mile which is level and less exacting than the Rowley Mile, starting as it did at the ten furlong start (across the flat) and finishing before the dip. The race was not switched to the Rowley Mile until the 1870's.

Early in the nineteenth century many races were decided by heats and some were tests over as long as four miles. However, the practice of settling races over heats was decreasing as was the distances over which races were conducted. At Newmarket races were mostly matches or sweepstakes decided by a single contest. By introducing the St Leger, Oaks and Derby the originators were following the trend not only for a single contest but also for deciding the outcome over a distance which was reasonably within the compass of a three-year-old. It also demanded that the winners of such races combined speed in addition to abundant stamina. A three year old thoroughbred is not a mature horse but his physical development normally advances steadily throughout the season. Therefore a test over fourteen furlongs in September is considered a suitable test but races over lesser distances were thought fairer in the early part of the season for underdeveloped horses. The five "Classic" races formed a progression from a mile to fourteen furlongs as the season developed with tests over separate courses of different conformation.

"The Two Thousand Guineas Day at Newmarket will long be remembered by visitors to headquarters, for perfect conditions prevailed, while the enthusiastic scene which followed His Majesty's victory in the big race has probably never been equalled at Newmarket. As usual there was a greatly increased company for the second stage of the meeting and perhaps there has never been a bigger gathering of motor cars at Newmarket than was seen yesterday afternoon on the Heath. Fortunately for the visitors the weather proved finer than on the opening day but the heavy showers greatly benefited the track and the famous Rowley Mile was looking at its best". These were the observations of *The Sporting Life*. In the Birdcage Bayardo's box was besieged by people trying to see him. Most concluded that he was "on the big side" and this increased confidence in Minoru who looked very fit and was walking round quietly. Minoru's Royal owner, Edward VII was present. *The Sportsman's* representative was in no doubt about Bayardo's condition: he was not racing fit. The *Diamond Racing Journal* reported that Bayardo "did not look fit and had not grown". Kettledrum of the *Sporting Chronicle* also noted that he had not grown but had thickened out. He further observed that Bayardo did not look comfortable walking round the Bird Cage prior to being mounted. Someone noted that he had not grown to which another responded "The beggar's grown all right but he's grown ugly"! Alfred Cox could not have been too confident of victory as he asked his bookmaker if he would lay him £10,000 to £5,000 (£640,000 to £320,000) against Bayardo being placed. He was not accommodated something the bookmaker probably later regretted.

The Two Thousand Guineas today is worth only 68% of its' 1909 value.

The going was given as good and, based on time, it was at least that, possibly good to firm or even firm. The time was a record for the Two Thousand Guineas at that time. It was about three and a half seconds faster than the median from 1900 until the Great War and about eight seconds faster than the median from 1889 to 1900. It was almost certainly the fastest ground Bayardo had ever raced on and he would not have appreciated it even had he been in the peak of condition.

Bayardo's reputation was such that he started at odds on. It would seem that the general public, while aware that he might not have been completely ready (there had been persistent public rumours in circulation throughout April, and it was no secret that all was not well), were seemingly unaware of just how troubled his preparation had been. His defeat was greeted with widespread amazement, tempered by joy at a Royal victory.

Odds layers knew their fate passing the bushes as Bayardo ran without any dash and Maher did not ride him out. He was boxed in at the dip and denied a clear run but this made no difference to the result. Maher

Newmarket Wednesday 28th April 1909 Going: good

Two Thousand Guineas Stakes of £100 each, h ft., for entire colts and fillies foaled in 1906 ; colts 9 st fillies 8st 9 lb ; second received £400 and third £200 out of stakes. RM (900 entrants --£5,000) (£320,000)

1	Minoru	9st 0lb	H Jones	127+
2	Phaleron	9st 0lb	W Earl	122
3	Louviers	9st 0lb	G Stern	119
4	Bayardo	9st 0lb	D Maher	116
5	Fidelio	9st 0lb	B Dillon	
6	Diamond Stud	9st 0lb	W Halsey	
7	Blankney	9st 0lb	W Higgs	
8	Sealed Orders	9st 0lb	F Wootton	
9	Orange Bud	9st 0lb	B Lynham	
	Grimmet	9st 0lb	Wm Griggs	
	Fop	9st 0lb	O Madden	

Betting 8-13 Bayardo, 4-1 Minoru, 100-7 Louviers, 20-1 Diamond Stud, 25-1 Fop

Won by two lengths; a length and a half second and third. Unofficially there was a length and a half between third and fourth.

Time:1 min 37 4/5 sec

Sporting Life race analysis;-

"Orange Bud was the first to leave the Birdcage and he was followed by Fidelio, Louviers, and Diamond Stud, the last to go down being Sealed Orders. Bayardo moved with the smoothest action on the way to the post, but arriving there he was a trifle restless. There was little delay, however, and almost at the first attempt the signal was given to a good start some ten minutes after the set time. Louviers wide on the stand side swerved and shut out Sealed Orders and he quickly stretched away with a clear command of Fidelio, Phaleron, and Blankney the latter pair on the top ground heading Bayardo and Minoru, the rear being brought up by Orange Bud. The first to drop out of the front rank was Fidelio after they had traversed a quarter of a mile whereupon Phaleron became the nearest attendant on Louviers the pair being clear of Blankney and Bayardo with Minoru at the favourites heels. Before reaching the bushes Blankney was beaten and Bayardo and Minoru took closer order to the two leaders of whom Louviers was beginning to tire and Phaleron got to his girths down the hill. At that point Maher drew his whip on Bayardo and Minoru dashing up between Phaleron and Louviers before the Abingdon Mile Winner Post was reached shot clear and amid tremendous excitement the King's horse had the verdict safe in a few strides and he had only to be kept going to win in handsome style".

reported that from beginning to end Bayardo was constantly changing his legs. While there was no doubt that Minoru was fitter and in better shape, Bayardo should not have been that far behind, at least judging from paddock appearance. However, the combination of a lack of hard condition and the fast ground gave Bayardo little chance. Another jockey in the race when asked about Bayardo's behaviour said he gave no trouble at the start but was "in a lather" before they had travelled two furlongs. All things considered it is probably safe to conclude that

Bayardo was not a happy horse: his feet had been troubling him, he had endured a miserable winter and now he was being asked to race on firm ground. It is hardly surprising he did not stride round the paddock, then sweated up and constantly changed his legs during the race.

There was much sympathy extended to Alec Taylor and Alfred Cox and they bore what must have been a devastating blow stoically. Having witnessed their horse easily dispose of all opposition the previous year, their feelings on seeing at the bushes that Bayardo was in dire trouble can well be imagined. Cox was probably more surprised than Taylor. After all, he was the one who had insisted on running and it therefore follows that he had expected Bayardo to overcome the difficulties. Taylor, who of course understood much better the size of the task, had probably prepared himself for the possibility of such an outcome.

There was a suspicion amongst some observers that he had not trained on. Minoru, whose name is Japanese for "success", had been rated 20 pounds below Bayardo in the two-year-old handicap. He had won just one of his six juvenile races and had been beaten in two nurseries. He had never opposed Bayardo at two, at which age he was never considered a classic prospect. He was though reported to have thrived over the winter and had won the Greenham Stakes at Newbury in the spring. He was to win five of his six races at three.

At two Phaleron had shown some form but failed to win any of his four starts. He did better at three winning five of his eleven starts. He was to meet Bayardo again in the Derby but never again after that. Had connections of Phaleron believed that the Guineas form was an accurate reflection of the two horses merits they had four more opportunities after the Derby, including the St Leger, to confirm it. They elected to take none of them.

Louviers had been beaten by Bayardo in the National Stakes at two. At three he won four of his six races and was to meet Bayardo twice more. He was to finish in front of Bayardo again in the Derby, before Bayardo was able to demonstrate his superiority beyond doubt. Diamond Stud won one of his ten races. He met Bayardo once more in the Derby. None of the others achieved much of note in top company.

Alfred Watson, a strong, if on one occasion a wavering, supporter of Bayardo as a juvenile, was now of the view that he was not the horse he had looked the previous year. He had never been keen on Bay Ronald as a sire and could not see him as a sire of classic winners. Notwithstanding Alec Taylor's opinion (something Watson respected) and Danny Maher's anxiety to keep the ride, he had thought Bayardo the likely winner of the Guineas due more to the weakness of the opposition than any qualities possessed by him. Alfred Cox had expressed his confidence and apparently his intimate friends had all plunged on. That Minoru was fitter was not in doubt, but Bayardo had certainly been fit enough to have run better than he did. Some observers noted that Maher eased him when beaten, but Watson's view was that the horse eased himself, possibly because he was un-genuine. This would seem to be harsh as Bayardo had repeatedly changed legs, something which would hardly have given Maher any confidence that he could win. Maher would not have wanted to punish Bayardo unnecessarily and it is almost certainly safe to conclude – in the light of future events - that he did ease him. In addition as *The Winning Post* noted Bayardo was certainly not wound up and that after the race he had "blown like a March wind".

It was probably no more than an average 2000 Guineas and a fit and well Bayardo, at his best, would surely have won. Throughout its history racing has never been short of stories of ill luck. There will always be those who make excuses for beaten horses and express regrets of what might have been, all of which provide mostly pointless introspection. The fact remains that Minoru was the best colt on the day, under the prevailing conditions and circumstances, and it would be churlish to say otherwise. It was time to re-gather and attempt to get Bayardo fit and ready in time for the Derby. Immediately after the Guineas he did only light work but in preparation for his next race – probably the Newmarket Stakes - he worked six furlongs "usefully" in company with Seedcake on 8th May and on 10th twelve furlongs at a "good pace".

Bayardo now slipped from favouritism for the Epsom Classic. This is something of an understatement: he was offered at 20-1! This was despite Alfred Cox saying he was perfectly well and coming back to his best. This price, not surprisingly, was taken fairly quickly. His odds contracted to 10-1 then 5-1. There were suggestions that he was not a stayer and would not have the stamina for the Derby. It is not difficult to understand this view. Although he was bred to stay at least twelve furlongs, with stamina on both sides of his pedigree, such was the speed he had shown as a juvenile that it was conceivable that he would turn out to be a sprinter/miler. This is despite his physique which was the antithesis of that of a sprinter. It is worth remembering that apart from the Middle Park, when he had been slightly under the weather but still won comfortably, all his wins had been very easy and achieved without any need for Bayardo to exert himself.

Bayardo's lifeless performance in the Guineas, combined with the glowing reports from Newmarket of the manner in which Minoru was thriving, tilted the balance in favour of the Royal colt. In addition from turf headquarters news of another formidable rival in the shape of Sir Martin suggested that Bayardo might not even be the second favourite. Sir Martin had won a moderate handicap at Newmarket on his only appearance so far that year. However, as an indication of the impression he had made at headquarters he was promoted to favouritism over Minoru for the big race.

Bayardo's only entry between the Guineas and the Derby was for the Newmarket Stakes at the Second Spring meeting. Today the biggest test for the Derby, apart from the Two Thousand Guineas, is the Dante Stakes which is run at York but of course was not inaugurated until after the Second World War. In Bayardo's time the Newmarket Stakes was a valuable race worth £2,140 (£137,000) and the most important trial for the Derby, after the Guineas. His participation would thus have been an interesting guide to his progress. Surely if he had been only just below his best in the Guineas this would have been an ideal opportunity for him to advance his level of fitness to a point that is essential to win the Derby. Alfred Cox liked his horses to fulfil their engagements and it would have been entirely in character for him to have run Bayardo. That he did not do so speaks eloquently about Bayardo's state of readiness. Instead of running at Newmarket on the 11th May, the day before the Newmarket Stakes, Taylor decided to work Bayardo in company with Seedcake and Moscato over twelve furlongs. They went "a good striding pace" but instead of Bayardo having a good work-out Maher was obliged to ease him down and the work was "won" by Moscato. When news of this became known the unease about Bayardo's welfare became yet more acute.

In Bayardo's absence the Newmarket Stakes was won by Louviers who comfortably beat Electra with Carrousel well beaten in third. The more observant readers may have noticed an apparent contradiction in terms in the above. The Newmarket Stakes was run at the Second Spring meeting, although it was the third meeting held that spring! The first meeting was known as the Craven meeting and the second meeting was called the First Spring Meeting. That's clear then!

Despite working moderately Bayardo was gradually improving and only one question remained. Was the Derby coming too soon? The big day was only about a fortnight away when Bayardo at last began to please Taylor enough for him to be hopeful that the colt might be regaining his form. However, although matters were improving, in his heart of hearts he knew that time was too short and that Bayardo, if he were to win, would have to do so when still short of his best.

His work schedule in the run up to the Derby is interesting. Following his disappointing work on the 11th he did nothing of consequence until Sunday 16th when he went a mile "at good pace" with Seedcake. The following day - Monday 17th - he worked twelve furlongs at half speed. Bayardo was not however, pleasing everybody. *The Sportsman's* Manton gallops observer noted that he did not like what he saw of Bayardo, who was not extending himself on the gallops. On the 18th and 19th he went six furlongs and then on Thursday 20th with the sun shining Alfred Cox was present to see him cover twelve furlongs in company with Smuggler. There is no suggestion that this was in any way a full trial and in any event as it was not held in secret it was almost certainly normal work over the full Derby distance. On a foggy morning 22nd Seedcake led him six furlongs "sharply". On Sunday 23rd Alfred Cox was present when Seedcake led Bayardo twelve furlongs in a "rousing good gallop" with Bayardo noted as moving "freely and well". Finally on Monday 24th he went six furlongs. The Manton gallops man thought that Bayardo had done well but the firm ground would be all against him. Bayardo left Manton on the following day for Epsom. Alec Taylor had done all he could; it was now up to the horse. It would be interesting to know just what his thoughts were as he watched his charge being loaded onto the train bound for Epsom. There is a story which suggests that Taylor was still not happy enough with Bayardo to run him in the Derby. It seems that Cox might have been persuaded to withdraw from the race in the best interests of the horse. However, Mr Washington Singer was committed with some large anti-post wagers on Bayardo and that he did all he could to induced Cox to run. This story may well be authentic but it is hard to believe that Cox's decision to run, bearing in mind all that is known about him, was heavily influenced by the state of someone else's betting book.

Bayardo must have improved considerably with regard to his condition since the Guineas, as indicated by the observations of Richard Marsh in the paddock before the Derby. Minoru's trainer, looking at Bayardo, noticed a difference. He wrote in his memoirs, "I must say I was impressed with the very marked improvement in him. He looked a different horse and the sight of him really set my anxieties alight again". Earlier in the day Marsh had noticed Bayardo out at exercise and had been shocked by his improvement. After the Two Thousand Guineas he had not considered Bayardo a threat in the Derby due to his moderate run which was at such variance to his towering juvenile form. Marsh noted that there was a vast improvement and reflected afterwards that had the Derby been a fortnight later history might have been written differently.

Derby Day! It is some time since those two words quickened the nation's pulse. For many years it was the last Wednesday in May or the first Wednesday in June and for Londoners it meant a day out when they could enjoy themselves as on no other occasion. The day was even of such significance that Parliament rose for the day. On Derby Day itself the country would talk of little else and indulge in small wagers or take part in sweepstakes, and interest, which had been growing day by day since the Two Thousand Guineas, reached its climax. It was racing's big day and it was shared with no other event. The Downs would be filled to capacity, with as many as a million people at the height of the race's popularity, enjoying a plethora of entertainments of every imaginable kind. Many would not see the race itself but to be on the Downs on Derby Day was to be part of a great tradition. It had drama, romance, triumph, tragedy, joy and anguish. However, whatever the result of the race itself, the vast majority who visited simply had a tremendously enjoyable day. All of society was on display: the aristocracy in the main grandstand, gentlemen in morning dress and ladies in fashionable outfits; the middle classes in the grandstand attired in their best clothes and the working classes massed on the downs, a teeming sea of humanity. It was a peculiarly English occasion that brought out the best and, it has to be said, the worst aspects of national character. Truly a mix of the patrician and the plebeian! By 1909 the Derby had a rich history and had for some years been known as "The Blue Riband of the Turf". It was the ambition of every owner to own a Derby winner, every trainer to train one and every jockey to ride one. The previous one hundred and twenty nine renewals had provided a rich tapestry of drama, triumphs and disasters and the race would provide many more in the following years. Quite simply, as far as thoroughbred racing in England and the rest of the racing world was concerned, at that time there was no other racing day to be compared with it.

From a purist racing point of view it is hard to see why the Derby and not the St Leger should have been racing's big day. Epsom has never been considered an ideal track for any horse and it is totally unsuitable for many. It is almost entirely on an upwards or downwards gradient, has an awkward corner running into the straight and, assuming a horse has managed to overcome these difficulties, the course then slopes alarmingly from right to left. Horse and jockey must then somehow contrive to maintain their balance and produce their fastest effort for just over three furlongs until the finishing post is reached. As if all this was not enough the soil is largely of clay and drains quickly providing some very firm going and sometimes rough ground for the big race. Ground conditions were not helped by hack-riders thoughtlessly using the track. When the Clerk of the Course "dolled off" part of the course he was accused of interfering with the public rights of local equestrians! It was not until well after the Great War that the going at Epsom was at all kind to any horse with a requirement for comfort under foot.

Compare that to the Town Moor at Doncaster where the track is almost entirely level, apart from Rose Hill which is some way from home. In addition the bends are sweeping and the straight is nearly five furlongs long and very wide giving every opportunity for horse and rider to find their stride and position. Finally the turf is wonderful and usually provides a fair surface, perfect for almost every horse of any make and shape. Horses frequently return from Epsom with injuries but rarely from Doncaster as a result of the track.

Notwithstanding this, and the fact that the St Leger is the older race and frequently had a higher value to the winner, it was Epsom and the Derby which captured the hearts and minds of the people of England probably because London is the hub of our small island even today and definitely in Bayardo's time. Both classics provide a great day but The Derby (or Grand National) would be the race most non-racing people would have mentioned if asked during Bayardo's time to name a horse race.

With this magnificent history and tradition it is a great sadness to many lovers of racing that the position of the Derby is now so reduced in importance, and has been for the last twenty or so years. It may still be the ambition of many owners, trainers and jockeys to win the race but the yearning is not on the same scale as in the past. It still provides a great day, but in importance it has declined. Moving the race to a Saturday was a grave mistake. In recent years there has been an obsession to hold as many significant races as possible on Saturdays as opposed to midweek. Why? Racing is in competition with other sports and activities on Saturday. The Derby now shares the day with other race meetings, sometimes as many as six, and all manner of other sporting and leisure events, not to mention weddings, garden fetes, and even the weekly supermarket shopping etc. It has suffered the humiliation of having the off-time changed to coincide with half time of a football match and the management claiming the move was a great success! The sporting sections of the Saturday newspapers, with plenty of demand from other sports, do not automatically lead with the race. Only those with a vested interest in promoting the race commercially would argue that the race and the day continue to maintain its prestige. Another indicator of the race's decline came in 2009 when the panel responsible for recommending which sporting events should be protected and always shown on "free-to-air" channels decided that the Derby was no longer important enough to be so protected. The status of the race reduces a little each year and only strong measures can revive it. The race needs promoting properly. Why do modern racecourse management's seem to think that promoting racing requires loud tuneless music and for footballers, "pop" stars and numerous "celebrities" to be pushed repeatedly down our throats? The lead up to the Derby should feature all the trials on terrestrial television and a few days after each race various stables could be visited for interviews with the wellbeing of the horses as the centre-piece. That way by Derby day each runner will be well known to the viewers who can form attachments to them. In addition the race should be restored to the first Wednesday in June, or even Friday, where it can be the highlight of the day, on which the nation can stop for about three minutes at around three-forty-five in the afternoon and racing can once again have its day which it would share it with no other event.

The Derby today is worth over twice as much as 1909. In spite of this few would argue that in importance the ratio is almost exactly reversed.

Epsom Wednesday 26th May 1909 Going: good

One Hundred and Thirtieth Renewal of the Derby Stakes of £6,500 (including £500 for nominator of winner) with £400 for second and £200 for third, by subscription of £50 each, h. ft., or £5 if declared, with £1,250 added ; for three year old entire colts and fillies; colts 9st fillies 8 st 9 lb. About a mile and a half. (299 entrants, viz. 15 at £150, 184 at £25, and 100 at £5 ----- £6,450) (£412,800)

1	Minoru	9st	H Jones	126
2	Louviers	9st	G Stern	125
3	William the Fourth	9st	W Higgs	124
4	Valens	9st	F Wootton	123
5	Bayardo	9st	D Maher	114+
6	Electric Boy	9st	W Bray	
7	Strickland	9st	Wm Griggs	
8	The Story	9st	Wal Griggs	
9	Sandbath	9st	R Keeble	
10	Phaleron	9st	W Earl	
11	Diamond Stud	9st	W Halsey	
12	Prester Jack	9st	W Saxby	
13	St Ninian	9st	C Trigg	
14	Brooklands	9st	D Blackburn	
	Sir Martin	9st	J H Martin	

Betting 3-1 Sir Martin, 7-2 Minoru, 9-2 Bayardo, 8-1 Valens 9-1 Louviers, 20-1 Phaleron and William the Fourth, 40-1 The Story, 50-1 Diamond Stud and Strickland 66-1 Electric Boy, Sandbath, St. Ninian and Prester Jack
Won by a short head; half a length second and third. Unofficially the distances thereafter were half a length and about five lengths.
Time: 2 min 42 2/5 sec

Sporting Life race analysis;-

"Paddock critics were denied a view of Bayardo who did not enter the enclosure until the horses were being marshalled for the preliminaries which were afterwards carried out in the order of the card. In the canter nothing moved with greater freedom than Bayardo, Minoru, Phaleron and William the Fourth. Electric Boy was the last to reach the starting point and, but for the backing from the tapes of Bayardo, they would have been despatched at the first time of asking. Sandbath dashed under the tapes without breaking them and on their being lined up again Sir Martin, Prester Jack and Strickland became a trifle fractious. Nevertheless the delay was not a very long one and six minutes after the advertised time the lever was handled to a magnificent start. Nearly a furlong was covered before the line was broken by Brooklands, the pacemaker for Louviers, who stretched out with a two lengths lead of his stable companion the pair being followed by Sir Martin, Diamond Stud on the outside St Ninian and Electric Boy, the latter just ahead of Bayardo and Minoru, the King's horse being allowed to get nicely into his stride before increasing his pace while The Story and Valens were racing side by side at Minoru's heels in front of Strickland the two whippers-in being Sandbath and William the Fourth. Passing under the City and Suburban starting-gate Diamond Stud and Electric Boy were racing upsides at an interval of two lengths behind the two leaders, Sir Martin, towards the right and Minoru on the left now being followed by Phaleron and Valens. Bayardo and Strickland, who were running with plenty of fire, improving their position before The Story with St Ninian now

falling a long way in the ruck. As soon as the mile post was left behind the pacemaker had fulfilled his mission and Louviers deprived him of the lead, Sir Martin going on third, Minoru fourth, Phaleron Valens and Electric Boy being in a cluster next with Bayardo Strickland and The Story the most conspicuous of the others. At the top of the hill Brooklands began to fall back and Strickland dashed up to with a length of Louviers, Electric Boy and Minoru being handy while William the Fourth, Valens, Sir Martin and Bayardo were in a group next with Sandbath at their quarters. Halfway down the hill Sir Martin was crowded in upon and, losing his balance, pecked so badly as to shoot his jockey from the saddle. Louviers came round the bend at the head of his field, but, unable to get a fair grip of the ground, he slithered a trifle out towards the right and Jones sensing the opportunity whipped Minoru up on the inside, Electric Boy being their nearest attendant as the line for home was entered, with Valens and William the Fourth the next pair, the latter having to come round the outside owing to the mishap to Sir Martin whilst Bayardo was the most conspicuous of the remainder. Although Minoru had appropriated the lead in the straight he was immediately steadied, and, running on a tight rein permitted Louviers to resume the lead in three furlongs from home. From this point a long running tussle commenced between the pair who were about two lengths clear of Valens and William the Fourth the two leaders fighting it out stride for stride twenty yards from the Bell, Minoru got his head in front, and, although both were tiring perceptibly they displayed the utmost gameness and His Majesty's gallant colt, battling off the challenge of Louviers won a great race amid unparalleled enthusiasm by a short head half a length was the margin between second and third. Scarcely a head away Valens was officially placed fourth, Bayardo a moderate fifth, then after an interval came Electric Boy (ran well), sixth Strickland (not disgraced) seventh The Story (baulked) eighth Sandbath ninth Phaleron tenth Diamond Stud (beaten after six furlongs) eleventh Prester Jack twelfth and last Brooklands.

The going was given as good and that is probably accurate. The time for the Derby was moderate, almost five seconds slower than for the Coronation Cup over the same distance, run the following day. It was about one and a quarter seconds slower than the median from 1900 until the Great War and about three and a quarter seconds quicker than for the period from 1889 until 1900.

Bayardo's starting price indicates that the betting public did not believe he was back to his best. It may also have been an indication that some thought he had not trained on or that he would not stay twelve furlongs. On his juvenile form 9-2 would have been very generous. Those admirers who had not lost faith backed him for the Derby at a price which would have been scarcely imaginable when the season began. Interestingly, not everyone thought that having Danny Maher riding Bayardo was to his advantage. Although he had won the Derby twice, he was considered by some to have a modest record at Epsom. His post-race comments seem to confirm that he did not have Bayardo in the best position, or at least in one he wished, when disaster struck.

The morning had been grey, wet and unpleasant until about eleven o'clock, but the weather gradually improved up to the off-time. Bayardo was late coming into the paddock and, whilst the rain would have eased the ground for him, his supporters would not have been encouraged when Maher was seen to take him tenderly to post. This would almost certainly have been no more than a precaution, and was probably not the case all the way down, bearing in mind that The *Sporting Life's* race analysis man asserted that he went to post freely. He was reported to be fractious at the start.

The crowd was rewarded with what plenty of them had come to see, a Royal victory. Apart from providing, from the general public's point of view, a very popular outcome, the race was unsatisfactory. Louviers was leading the favourite Sir Martin down the hill when the latter stumbled. Bayardo was tracking him, and giving every indication that he was going well enough, when Maher, along with several other jockeys, was forced to swerve and/or snatch up. Reports suggest that he lost about six lengths. Maher was to claim that he lost sixteen! How on earth he arrived at that calculation can only be guessed at. However, what is clear is that Bayardo lost any chance and Maher did not persevere and was noted standing up in his stirrups approaching the post, where he finished fifth. There are at least two pictures of the finish, a head-on photograph and one taken from higher up. Maher can clearly be seen easing Bayardo behind the quartet of hard ridden horses in front of him and yet he is beaten only about five lengths. Minoru was fortunate to escape the carnage completely. He fought out a desperate finish with Louviers to hold on by a short head. Minoru was all out to win and Louviers was in front just after the line. There is some evidence that Minoru did not truly stay and more will be said of this in due course.

The question as to whether Bayardo would have won cannot be adequately answered. The incident was too far out for any certainty. In addition, as Taylor did not think he was at his best, he may not have been fit enough to have prevailed in what was an all out driving finish. However, it is not out of the question that without interference, and had Maher managed to get him into contention, he could have out-speeded the four horses in front of him inside the final furlong. He was beaten less than six lengths despite being eased, and the interference (which *The Sporting Life's* analysis man missed) must have cost him about that distance. It is not even certain that Sir Martin stumbling was the major cause of Bayardo's problems, there is evidence to suggest that it merely exacerbated them. Kettledrum of the *Sporting Chronicle* noted that Bayardo suffered interference before Sir Martin fell observing that Bayardo had been on the heels of Minoru before the incident during which Maher could be seen standing up in his irons. Afterwards Bayardo was seen to be behind. This being the case Bayardo had lost touch with

Minoru before Sir Martin's stumble. The jockey's post-race comments certainly confirm that Sir Martin's misfortune was not the first problem he had encountered. It hardly seems important. Whatever the cause of Bayardo's woes had endured a rough race and matters had not worked out.

Had he benefitted from better fortune in running the evidence of subsequent races suggest that Bayardo could have out-speeded those four horses that finished in front of him. However, Maher's thoughtfulness in not giving Bayardo a hard race would have helped considerably in making sure he was able to see out a long season. He was to race a further eleven times and a hard race at Epsom may have ruined him for the foreseeable future.

Would Bayardo have had a better chance if he had not run in the 2000 Guineas? Did running when not fully fit on firm ground take too much out of him and set him back? If he had missed the Guineas would he have been able to run in the Newmarket Stakes and therefore had a better preparation for the Derby? There are clearly more questions than answers. What seems clear is that Alec Taylor's masterful training had overcome possible disaster and somehow kept Bayardo roughly on track.

Minoru's trainer Richard Marsh was generous enough to concede that had the race taken place a fortnight later Bayardo might have won. He wrote "When once Alec Taylor got Bayardo right as a three-year-old his excellence was undeniable. Fortunately for us this did not happen until after Minoru had won the Derby." A crestfallen Maher's post race comment to Taylor and Cox was "Twice I had been foiled of an opening and had waited too long until Sir Martin fell (sic) right in front of me." What Taylor had to say in response is not recorded. He and Maher were to have many an argument about the right way to ride Bayardo. It is impossible to be certain but it seems that Maher was probably in error in not taking Bayardo closer to the leaders rather than waiting towards the rear. Theodore Felstead, reflecting on the Derby many years later, wrote that "the King had won with the moderate Minoru, a result hardly believable with a horse like Bayardo in the field".

The form of the Derby proved to be no better than average as the season progressed. Minoru won the St James's Palace Stakes and the Sussex Stakes before losing in the St. Leger. He then won the Free Handicap in a desperate finish by a short head. Louviers, who had run Minoru to a short head in the Derby, ran in three stakes races afterwards. He won two but in the other was easily beaten by Bayardo. He ran once at four in the Coronation Cup where he finished third. William the Fourth won the Ascot Derby before finishing, appropriately, fourth in the Grand Prix de Paris on his only other race that year. At four he ran twice and was beaten on both occasions by Bayardo.

Phaleron raced eight more times after the Derby, winning four. His wins included the Jockey Club Stakes. He did not meet Bayardo again either that year or the following year. At four he benefited from a walkover to record his only win from six races. Valens ran ten times winning a plate, a Cup race and two walkovers. He twice finished second, in the Duchess of York Stakes and the St. Leger, and on both occasions he was beaten easily. At four he won the Newbury Spring Cup from two outings. Sir Martin won two of his five races after the Derby that season, the Challenge Stakes and a valuable handicap. He did not meet Bayardo again until the Ascot Gold Cup the following year. Before Ascot he had won the Coronation Cup. The other eight horses ran a total of 49 times that season winning only a handicap and six plate races.

It seems inevitable that *The Sportsman's* nameless, correspondent, almost certainly the same writer who was so certain that Bayardo would achieve little, should have something to say following the Derby. This fustian individual, whose comments continued to suggest that he was not exactly Argus-eyed, wrote portentously "I will be surprised if Bayardo wins another race of any importance". Heavens above! Did being proved wrong about Bayardo the previous year teach him nothing about making perfunctory remarks? His statement suggests that he did not speak to either Maher or Taylor, or, if he did, he was so determined to denounce Bayardo, that he was not going to let a little thing like interference, however crucial, affect his views!

George Lambton believed that Sir Martin would have won had he not stumbled. He is entitled to his view and coming from such a distinguished source deserves close consideration. However, it seems strange that he did not consider the effect on Bayardo's prospects of Sir Martin's antics in front of him. Even if he had not given the matter any thought on the day, with hindsight he might have wondered if Bayardo could have won. It is possible, of course, that Lambton considered Sir Martin superior to Bayardo, which would be an eccentric view in the light of subsequent events. Lambton was writing in 1923, having had plenty of time to consider the matter. Some horses always seem to be overrated with their supporters unwilling to concede that they could be mistaken. Such a horse was Sir Martin. He was bred in America, sold, and sent to England to compete in the Derby. He won a handicap before the Derby but had been entered in only two early-closing races afterwards and had not been entered for the St Leger. He did run in France at Deauville on 15th August in the Grand Prix de Trouville-Deauville a race worth £4,000 (£256,000) where he finished second. One of the races for which he had been entered in England was the Champion Stakes, and if connections had thought they could beat Bayardo, their horse was fit and well when the race was run. However, they preferred to run in and win the Challenge Stakes, worth one third of the value of the Champion Stakes, and then run in the

Cambridgeshire where he finished third. This is not surprising, if they did not think their horse could beat Bayardo, as second prize in the Champion Stakes was £150 (£9,600) whereas the Cambridgeshire had a first prize of £1,370 (£87,600).

Lambton's view may have been based on his form aged four when he won the Coronation Cup at Epsom. It was certainly better than anything he achieved at three, but would not have enabled him to beat Bayardo at his best at either age three or four. Although clearly improved at four, nothing Sir Martin ever achieved at aged three suggested he was better than Minoru never mind Bayardo. Sir Martin may have been close in the Derby if he had not fallen but was not certain to have prevailed. It is readily conceded that Sir Martin was a better horse than Minoru at four but, to state the obvious, the Derby is a three-year-old race, *res ipsa loquitur!* George Lambton did not give the impression of having any special enthusiasm for Bayardo, despite the fact that he was the grand-sire of the best horse Lambton ever trained – Hyperion - and mentions him only once in his outstanding and entertaining autobiography *Men and Horses I have known.* By any yardstick Bayardo would certainly have been in the top ten horses he ever saw and it is strange that all he can think of to write about him was an observation that his half-brother Lemberg was a better looking horse! Perhaps too much is being made of this as it is entirely possible that Lambton simply had no worthwhile recollections of Bayardo. After all he only mentioned Phalaris once in his book and he was a horse that, although short of greatness as a runner, still won fourteen races while Lambton was training him. It is conceded that he would not have known at the time of writing that Phalaris would turn out to be a great sire!

The Guineas and Derby were gone and Bayardo had failed to gain even a place in either race. It seemed scarcely believable after his total dominance as a juvenile that he could have done so moderately. The obvious answer was simple: he had not trained on, just as some had predicted. In the circumstances those who took this view could hardly have been surprised by events. Many considered that he had been physically unimpressive as a juvenile and had lacked size and scope. Bayardo had simply been overtaken by better sorts and this had happened before and would again. The form of both races looked consistent with Minoru and Louviers finishing in front of him on both occasions. The only concession came from some who, while certain that his lack of scope meant that he was not progressing, admitted that he retained his superb action. Alec Taylor and Alfred Cox could only keep their counsel and belief in Bayardo and that although twice beaten, and convincingly as well to the casual observer, he was only *vulneratus non victus* and not as some had assumed a spent force. They had little choice but to take their horse, and his by now battered reputation, back to Manton and resolve to give him a chance to prove the doubters wrong and to give his supporters something to cheer. There was one voice who pointed out something that seemed to have been overlooked by those quick to denounce Bayardo: he was not the only horse at Manton who had been out of form that year. The cold spring had put back all the inmates, and winners were in short supply. When the stable returned to form, if Bayardo could still not win, then that would be the time to write him off.

CHAPTER 9

Ascot again and the Eclipse

Bayardo must have been not that far short of full fitness in the Derby because, after only a short period to recover from Epsom, his work schedule was stepped up with a view to running at Ascot. After light exercise for a few days he galloped a mile with Seedcake and an unnamed colt out of Lily Surefoot on 3rd June. On Thursday 10th June he was led by another horse over twelve furlongs. The following day he went "a sharp" six furlongs and the day after, Saturday, he covered fourteen furlongs in company. This was better work and pleasing Alec Taylor enough to convince him that Bayardo, who must have been showing a considerable improvement in his well being, could run at Ascot. On the 14th he left for the Royal meeting.

By now Alec Taylor, at last, had Bayardo near to his liking. It was time for Bayardo to repay all his trainer's patience and skill by showing what sort of horse he really was. There was also the matter of silencing the doubters, rebuilding his tarnished reputation and confronting the critics who held the view that he had not only failed to train on, but was possibly not a genuine either. The *Diamond Racing Journal's* Manton man reported Bayardo going "great guns" between Epsom and Ascot and noted that he was also entered for the Grand Prix de Paris. This race for three-year-olds was due to be run on 27th June over fifteen furlongs and was worth £14,027 (£897,750) to the winner. With no "Arc" at this time (it was inaugurated in 1920) the Grand Prix de Paris was the most valuable race in France worth almost twice as much as the French Derby. William the Fourth and Valens both ran from England the former finished, appropriately fourth, and beaten, with equally pleasing symmetry, just under four lengths but the latter was unplaced. Bayardo was about a stone better than William the Fourth by the end of the season and while it is difficult to be certain it would appear that Bayardo could have won the Grand Prix de Paris if he had run.

At Ascot his race was to be the Prince of Wales' Stakes run on the first day. The race is different from the one of the same name today. Until 1939 it was a race for three-year-olds only. After the war it was discontinued and not reinstated (in a revised form) until 1968. There is no comparable race at the Royal meeting today and the distance of a mile and five furlongs is no longer used. It would be impossible today as the start would need to be either on a bend or from inside number one car park! It would seem that Taylor and Cox had no doubts about

Bayardo's stamina as they selected a race over thirteen furlongs rather than a mile. However, it seems that many thought he would also run in the St James's Palace Stakes held at that time on the Thursday.

The going was given as good. It is difficult to be sure about this based on time as the course was reconstructed in 1955 and some of the distances are different. In addition the early pace was slow. Bayardo won easily but although he finished "with his ears pricked" he was also noted as changing his legs towards the finish.

Bayardo's starting price was generous based on his juvenile form and he won more comfortably than the distance suggests. Cattaro had won the Biennial Stakes at Newmarket and although he afterwards collected only a walkover in a total of twelve races he ran was fairly consistent. Verne had finished third in the Oaks but did nothing for the form subsequently and did not win at all that year from five starts. Via won a stakes race at Liverpool from eight starts. King Charming won three moderate plate races from nine starts. Bayardo had won, but he still could not please everyone. *The Sportsman's* correspondent – our friend again probably - adhering doggedly to his opinion regarding Bayardo, noted that he was fortunate to win and owed his victory to the slow early gallop which resulted in the race not being a true test of stamina. Good grief! It really was going to take something special to alter his stubborn view and persuade him to acknowledge any good in Bayardo! Assuming it really is the same individual he certainly seemed to be affected by a permanent *cacoethes carpendi* (an obsession with finding fault) where

---

Ascot Heath Tuesday 15th June 1909 Going : Good

The Prince of Wales' Stakes of £50 each, h. ft., with £1,000 added, of which second received £300 and the Third £200 ; for three year olds. New Course, about one mile five furlongs. (63 entrants £2,150) (£137,600)

1	Bayardo	9st 5lb	D Maher	122+
2	Cattaro	8st 13lb	W Earl	115
3	Verne	7st 12lb	Wal Griggs	92
4	King Charming	8st 3lb	O Madden	
5	Via	8st 8lb	B Lynham	

Betting 4-6 Bayardo, 7-2 Verne, 100-12 Cattaro,
Won by three quarters of a length : five lengths second and third.
Time : 2 min 55. 2/5 sec

Sporting Life race analysis;-

"Cattero showed the way to Verne and Bayardo with Via whipping in for five furlongs when Bayardo took up the running from Verne and King Charming. Bayardo was steadied at the junction of the courses and King Charming drew out from the favourite and Verne the latter of which was in difficulties at the entrance to the straight where Bayardo was cantering at King Charming's heels and immediately afterwards Bayardo took measure of his opponents and, stalling off the challenge of Cattero, won easily".

our hero was concerned! Notwithstanding this the nightmare interregnum was over and he was back on track. It was time to demonstrate that he was still the Champion!

Bayardo stayed at Ascot until at least Thursday so presumably Alfred Cox gave thought to letting him take up his entry in the St James's Palace Stakes. If he had done so he would have again met Minoru. However, Cox uncharacteristically decided not to accept the challenge. It was suggested that Cox was not sure that Bayardo was the force he was and wished to avoid Minoru. That may have been true, but a more likely reason was that the race would have come too soon as it was just two days later. Horses at that time frequently raced twice during the Royal meeting and Cox thought nothing of racing his horses without a break, but a race against Minoru in these circumstances, when Bayardo had only just regained his form, would probably not have been wise. It is also possible that Cox did not want to run Bayardo over a mile. He was never to return to that distance, over which he never won. In Bayardo's absence in the St James's Palace Stakes Minoru beat two opponents easily.

Nonetheless Bayardo was in action just ten days later. However, as stated earlier he was not to be Paris bound but off to Sandown instead. Despite his win at Ascot it was an indication of how far he had slipped in public regard that he did not start favourite for the Sandringham Foal Stakes, a race which is no longer run. He was presumably fully fit by now and in preparation he went seven furlongs on the 22nd and he then worked a "sharp" mile on the 24th the day before the race.

Sandown Park was opened in 1875 and was the first of the "modern enclosed courses". It differed from the old-fashioned country course in that it was enclosed and everyone paid to enter separate enclosures. A country course would be on open land and it was only necessary to pay to enter the private stands. To create Sandown Park some enterprising individuals secured the park and built the stands and after obtaining the necessary licence began to hold race meetings. This venture was purely a sporting one with the object of providing good racing near London and not to make large profits. It was an immediate success despite the course not meeting universal approval. The five-furlong course was not popular then and it is not with many today. Six-furlong races were originally held but as the start was on the bend into the straight that could hardly have been satisfactory either. The starts must have been entertaining with all the riders trying to obtain a good spot on the inside! However, viewing, then, as now, was outstanding. Ladies were happy to attend after being encouraged by the introduction of the club system and it was soon a fashionable haunt for wealthy Londoners. By Bayardo's time the course was well established and very popular.

Sadly today Sandown is principally a National Hunt course that happens to stage the Eclipse Stakes. Eclipse day itself is not too bad although the card could do with a re-think but most of the meetings held there on the flat are mundane and in need of revitalising. The management should be aiming to stage more Pattern racing and upgrading the racing currently staged. "Whitbread Day", as it will probably always be known, should cease staging flat racing and concentrate on a suitable finale to the jumps season. They could then stage an outstanding two-day early season flat meeting. The size of the crowd on "Whitbread Day" would not be affected but the numbers for the two flat days would increase markedly.

The weather was unseasonably wet and miserable, not very pleasant for race-goers but ideal for Bayardo! *The Sporting Life* reported that "few people were attracted to the paddock where they would needed to have braved a pitiless drizzle to view the horses which were close-sheeted against the weather". The rugs and mackintoshes were only removed when it was time to mount. It further noted that conditions were "more in keeping with the Manchester November Handicap because in addition to the rain a mist which was detrimental to colour had set in and spoilt the view of the racing. The course, despite all the rain, was not heavy by any means, the hoofs just cutting an impression here and there. The showers had left the track beautifully fresh and green and it was a pity that the bad weather quite spoiled the attendance. As it was the muster which included many leading patrons of the national sport was a good one, the enclosures being well filled while the enlargements and improvements in the public ring came to fill a long felt want". It has to be said that writers at that time sometimes had what seems, by today's standards, an odd way of expressing themselves!

Speculation prior to the race was centred on Bayardo's participation which had been in doubt. It is hard to believe that it was the going which caused any problem and it is possible that Cox might have considered the weight concession too great as he was not yet back to his best. Certainly the considerable weight concession which both Bayardo and Louviers had to give away made them vulnerable to the lightweights.

The going description of heavy was probably correct, notwithstanding the *Sporting Life's* observation that it was not. Bayardo's race was the only one over ten furlongs run during the two day meeting. It was noticed that Maher kept Bayardo held up until the last possible moment and got into difficulties. A sign of things to come …

This was a tremendous effort with the weight concession. *The Sportsman's* correspondent (far more likely to be the writer of his juvenile eulogy than the author of so much to his detriment!) described it as the best performance by a three-year-old of the season so far. Kettledrum of the *Sporting Chronicle*, who had always expressed both the hope and opinion that Bayardo would come good at some stage during the year, was very enthusiastic. He wrote "seldom in the history of racing has a

Sandown Friday 25th June Going : Heavy

Sandringham Foal Stakes of £2000, viz. £1,500 for owner and £250 for nominator of winner, £100 for owner and £50 for nominator of second £75 for owner and £ 25 for nominator of third ; for three year olds ; entrance £26, £11 if declared by January 5 1909, or £1 if declared by October 8 1907. One mile and a quarter. (123 entrants, viz. 32 at £26, 51 at £11, 40 at £1 £1724) (110,336)

1	Bayardo	9st 10lb	D Maher	138+
2	Verney	7st 0lb	J Plant	97
3	Oakmere	8st 2lb	Walt Griggs	109
4	Chanteur	7st 3 lb	J Howard	
5	Louviers	9st 10lb	G Stern	
6	Baillet Latour	8st 3lb	W Earl	
7	Fizzer	7st 4lb	F Fox	
8	Habana	7st 0lb	G Ringstead	
	Venti	8st 3lb	J Thompson	
	Druce	8st 0lb	E Houlihan	

Betting 2-1 Louviers, 4-1 Bayardo, 4-1 Verney, 6-1 Chanteur, 100-8 Oakmere, Won by one and a half lengths ; two lengths second and third.
Time 2 min 15. 4/5 sec

Sporting Life race analysis;-

"The field was out in good time, but a long delay occurred at the post. Chanteur, Fizzer, and Venti taking a lot of getting into line. Taking them at a happy moment, all but Druce got well away. Baillet Latour, Venti and Chanteur were off in close company followed by Habana with Fizzer, Verney and Bayardo next and Druce settling down last. The three leaders kept close company for half a mile and then Chanteur took a slight lead of Baillett Latour this pair being a matter of two lengths in front of Fizzer. Then came Habana, Verney, Louviers and Bayardo, with Venti now last except Druce. With little change they ran till a quarter of a mile from home, where Louviers took second place to Chanteur, Fizzer and Habana giving way and Verney and Baillet Latour became third and fourth in front of Bayardo who directly afterwards was a bit hampered by Verney. Below the distance Chanteur gave way to Verney and Bayardo with Oakmere and Louviers at their heels; but the King's horse was at the end of his tether and Bayardo getting out of difficulties was pulled to the outside 150 yards from home, where Louviers shut up ; and quickly settling Verney's account, Bayardo came out and won in a canter".

dethroned and reviled Champion thoroughbred so completely vindicated himself or so assertively replied to his critics". He considered the performance very meritorious particularly in the circumstances. The light-weights had sort to exploit their weight concession by making it a "cracking pace" in heavy going and equally heavy rain. The weight Bayardo had given away was 38 pounds to the second, 22 to the third and 35 to the fourth. That he won in a canter was a considerable achievement. It is not easy assessing such performances accurately after such a long period. However, it is hard not to conclude that not only had Bayardo returned to his best, but that he had proved it with a performance that would have won a much better race. In addition the claims that he was not genuine foundered on this race. Bayardo could hardly be considered un-genuine if he was prepared to give his best in appalling conditions and conceding up to nearly three stones. If he was the type of horse likely to "duck the issue" this was as good a time as any.

Hindsight is a wonderful thing, but surely 4-1 was a generous price and represented tremendous value! Probably punters did not consider that Bayardo had been all that unlucky at Epsom. Louviers was made favourite on the strength of his third in the Two Thousand Guineas, his win in the Newmarket Stakes and his short head defeat by Minoru in the Derby. He had also won the Triennial Stakes at Ascot at long odds on to demonstrate that he was in form. The punters' view was understandable. Louviers' form was better than Bayardo's and he had finished in front of him twice. Louviers raced only once more that year winning a minor stakes at Goodwood at long odds on. Louviers was trounced here which only increased the sense of frustration that with any luck Bayardo could have won the Derby.

Verney, to whom Bayardo conceded 38 pounds, won a minor stakes and two plate races from eight starts. Oakmere won just a handicap from nine starts. Chanteur won a minor stakes and a plate from nine starts. The others won just a maiden and a handicap between them. With the exception of Louviers who carried the same weight, Bayardo conceded at least 21 pounds to all the other runners. He was hampered but still won very easily. The ground would have been more to his liking and the race completed his redemption and fully restored his reputation.

This must have been a wonderful moment for Alec Taylor and Alfred Cox! They had suffered the agonies of his depressing efforts in the Guineas and Derby but now, with his wins here and at Ascot, he had completely recovered his form. Bayardo was not only as good as he was as a juvenile but, more excitingly, he was giving every indication that he was better. The *Diamond Racing Journal's* Manton man thought Mr Fairie was probably sorry now that he had scratched from the Grand Prix de Paris. Hindsight really is wonderful!

The first two classics were lost for ever as far as Bayardo was concerned and nothing could bring them back; however, there were still some big races left to aim at. Bayardo's critics would need to accustom themselves to the taste of humble pie! It would not have been so bad for them if they had contented themselves with mild comments. But Bayardo had polarised opinion. Now, where was that correspondent from *The Sportsman* and Kettledrum's friend who had suggested Bayardo might crawl into a hole? What did they have to say after Bayardo's last two races? The racing public were now aware that he was as good as ever, and that he was over his earlier problems. Never again would he run without being made favourite. *The Sporting Life* considered that Bayardo's chance as he approached the final furlong did not look great, but at that point he put in "some grand work".

Alfred Watson conceded that he had been wrong about Bayardo. He was impressed by the way he settled matters in a half a dozen strides when Maher asked him. In his opinion only good animals are capable of this. Watson's prejudice against Bayardo, formed after the Two Thousand Guineas, was dissipated by his performance at Sandown in which he won, in Watson's opinion, with at least seven pounds in hand. This was Watson's second and final *volte-face* with regard to Bayardo. He was never again to doubt his ability. It has not been possible to find any record of *The Sportsman's* correspondent being so gracious.

For Bayardo's next race there was a choice between the Duchess of York Plate at Hurst Park on 24th July or the Eclipse Stakes at Sandown eight days earlier. Alec Taylor and Alfred Cox must have been very happy with Bayardo by now as the decision was taken to oppose older horses in the Eclipse. Views differ about when it is best for three-year-olds to take on their elders. Despite the weight concession, most feel that doing so in April, May and June, particularly over distances above a mile, is unfair to the younger generation. By July however, the balance begins to shift in favour of three-year-olds and from August onwards there are some who feel that they get too great a weight concession. July 16th would seem to be about the right time for a three-year-old to race against older horses for the first time over ten furlongs.

The Eclipse Stakes is a very important race today and carries Group One status. However, in 1909 it was more than that: it was the richest race of the season, worth more than each of the five classic races. This supremacy in terms of prize money continued until the Great War. Afterwards the prize money was comparable to the classics until the Second World War, after which it began to slip behind. Today the Eclipse is worth just over a third of the value of the Derby. It was instigated in 1886 and named after the most famous racehorse of all with the idea of guaranteeing a £10,000 (£640,000) prize fund. The race was not run in 1887 because 300 entries were not received (the minimum number stipulated in the race conditions) or 1890 because the necessary funds for a £10,000 (£604,000) prize could not be raised. At that time the Derby was worth £4,700 (£300,800). By 1909 the Eclipse Stakes was well established and had provided some memorable renewals. Today it is worth less than half of its 1909 value in real terms.

Bayardo was by now fully fit and in preparation he went a "sharp" six furlongs on both 8th and 10th July. *The Sporting Life* published a list of probable runners on the 10th July. Of the 16 runners given eight were three-year-olds. On the 13th he covered ten furlongs with Moscato at "good striding gallop" and the same pair on 14th worked six furlongs "sharply" and on the 15th a mile "at good pace". These works would have kept him ticking over nicely for what would be quite a challenge taking on his elders.

In the event no three-year-old was declared against him. None of those who had been nominated and left in at the last forfeit stage would have stood any chance and unfortunately all those who might have run well had been either withdrawn or had not been entered. His chance to avenge those who had beaten him in two classics would have to wait. However, this represented an outstanding chance to confirm his status to even the most purblind of his critics and silence those and others who had been so quick to proclaim that he had not trained on. He had only three opponents. It seems remarkable that only three horses took him on for the most valuable race of the season. There had been only four runners on one previous occasion when St Frusquin won in 1896. Of the original entrants nineteen remained after the final forfeit stage. However, only the four eventual runners were present on the course and there was little prospect that anything else travelling on the day.

The King was in attendance and there were hopes that the Queen would accompany him. However, it was not to be, due to the muggy weather which threatened rain. This also resulted in a crowd smaller than anticipated by many, particularly the railway company which found that it had arranged too many special trains. The paddock was crowded with race-goers eager to see the four runners. Bayardo was noted as having flop (sic) ears and drooping quarters! In addition his walk was complimented and he was said to have power behind the saddle and, though quiet, was evidently wound up for the task ahead. He was noted going to post as having a daisy-cutting action.

Early betting laid odds of five to four against Bayardo. However, at the off the ring was asking for odds of eighty five to forty to be laid on.

Bayardo won easily. However, Maher nearly suffered the indignity of being shut in with only four runners. His finish was described by *The Sporting Life* as "steam-engine-like" after Maher had switched him. *The Life* continued "He sailed past Royal Realm and Santo Strato as if they were standing still and amidst a perfect roar of relieved suspense won in smashing style. It was a magnificent performance which made the regrets of those who backed him for the Derby more poignant", it concluded.

Danny Maher did not ride a great race. It is true to say that he was on the best horse and, while he was probably well aware of what he had underneath him, it was noted by *The Sporting Life* that "the crisis came some furlong from home, where Bayardo taking closer order - appeared to be shut in behind the two leaders". "Danny" it concluded, "evidently knew more than the onlookers, but he gave them a rare fright, though with the race in hand; but accidents will happen and it would have been much plainer sailing to have taken the outside in such a small field and reduced the risk of not getting through to a minimum".

Sandown Park Friday 16th July 1909 Going : Heavy

Twenty-second renewal of the Eclipse Stakes of £10,000 (£640,000) of which the owner of the second received £800, of the third £115, nominator of winner £500, and of second £100 ; by subscription of £5 each for three year olds if declared by October 8 1907, or £10 for four year olds if declared by March 26 1907 ; if left in after those dates a further £21 each ; if left in after March 31 1908, a further £24 for three year olds or £32 for four year olds ; and if left in after January 5 1909 a further £55 for three year olds or £52 for four year olds ; with £2,501 added. Eclipse Stakes Course , one mile and a quarter. (167 entrants, viz 29 at £115, 15 at £63 26 at £60 42 at £31 22 at £26 14 at £10 and 19 at £5----- (8,870) (£567,680)

1	Bayardo	3 yrs 9st 2lb	D Maher	136++
2	Royal Realm	4 yrs 9st 8lb	Wm Griggs	126
3	Santo Strato	4 yrs 9st 11lb	O Madden	127
4	Your Majesty	4yrs 10st 0lb	Walt Griggs	128

Betting 40-85 Bayardo, 100-30 Your Majesty, 100-9 Santo Strato, 100-6 Royal Realm

Won by two lengths ; length between second and third. Unofficially the distance between the third and fourth was a length.

Time : 2 min 18. 4/5 sec.

Sporting Life race analysis;-

"Santo Strato was first away, but after going a furlong Royal Realm stretched out with a four lengths lead of Santo Strato who in turn had daylight between himself and Your Majesty (Bayardo in rear). Into the straight they came in Indian file, Royal Realm having a clear advantage of Santa Strato, Bayardo still racing on a tight rein on Your Majesty's heels. The latter made his effort below the distance and drew into second place but shortly afterwards he was beaten and Bayardo brought with one run from the rails to the outside challenged and with an electric spurt quickly put paid to Royal Realm and won easily".

The going has been given as soft and heavy. The lack of times over the two-day meeting makes assessment difficult. The time for the Eclipse was very slow, approximately twelve seconds slower than the standard time over the same course today. It was about eight seconds slower than the median for the period from 1900 until the Great War and about five seconds slower than for the period 1888 until 1900. There were only four runners and *The Sporting Life* race analysis suggests that the pace was not quick and its observer noted the slow early pace which he felt had played into Bayardo's hands. However, taking all the evidence the going was probably nearly, if not exactly, heavy.

This was Bayardo's first race against older horses and as the odds suggested, he was expected to win easily. Royal Realm contested good races all year but won only a plate race from ten starts. As a three-year-old he had finished third in the Jockey Club Stakes. Santo Strato had successfully carried top weight in the Chester Cup and competed in three other top races that year. As a three-year-old he had won the Prince of

Wales Stakes at Newmarket and finished second in both the Hardwicke
and Eclipse Stakes and third in the St Leger. However, this was his last
run this year. He was sent to France. Your Majesty was the previous
year's top prize money winner when he was victorious in the Eclipse
Stakes and St. Leger. However, he contested three top races this year
without success. He was the disappointment of the race and it was
considered that he was not the force he had been the previous year. This
was a good if not outstanding renewal and it is a measure of Bayardo's
now restored stature that he was expected to win easily.

Maher was generally but not universally condemned for his riding.
The jockey Mornington Cannon was among some who expressed the
opinion that he rode an excellent race. To most observers it looked as if
Maher was hoping to stay on the rails and get up on Royal Realm's
inside. However, that idea seemed futile as Royal Realm hung on and no
gap between him and Santo Strato appeared. Only then did Maher,
having waited until it seemed almost too late, switch to come round the
outside. It seems incredible that having almost been boxed in during the
Sandringham Foal Stakes on the same course he should now find himself
in an almost identical position. In fact, there had also been another
instance at Sandown on a horse called Hayden when Maher had been
forced to use the whip vigorously to get up and win a race which, but for
being boxed in, he would have won comfortably.

Notwithstanding Cannon's view, which seemed to suggest that going
up the inside was the best route, surely in a four-runner-race attempting
to come up the inside is arrogance bordering on stupidity when by
switching outside an unimpeded passage without surrendering any
ground is assured. It is hard for individuals who have never ridden in a
flat race to be entirely sure when criticizing a jockey's ride, particularly
when they have not even seen the race! However, in the absence of any
reason for Cannon suggesting that Maher had ridden an excellent race,
one can only conjecture. Was he saying that switching was risky because
the horse would give away some, if not much, ground, or because the
horse may have become unbalanced? It would have been interesting to
have heard more of Cannon's views. All was well this time and Bayardo
was spared a hard race to win. In future matters might not work out so
fortunately.

Bayardo's reputation was now fully restored. However, he was not
allowed to rest long in his stable at Manton and just eight days later he
appeared in the race at Hurst Park which had looked an alternative to
the Eclipse but now it was to be in addition to it! Surprisingly Bayardo
had not been nominated for any early-closing races at Goodwood. There
was therefore no prospect of him meeting Minoru in the Sussex Stakes a
race which was nowhere near as important then as now and was not
even as valuable as the plate race Bayardo ran in at Hurst Park. The

respective values were £617 (£39,000) as against £979 (£62,656). Even so this is a great pity, not least because by now both horses were at their peak. Had it been possible for them to have met in the Sussex Stakes, it would at least have settled any argument about who was better at a mile. As it turned out, Minoru had little trouble in beating his only opponents, Prester Jack and Verney. On the other hand Minoru had been nominated and could have run against Bayardo at Hurst Park. Then it would have shown which horse was better over ten furlongs! Was Richard Marsh avoiding Bayardo or was it that the King wanted to win at Goodwood? In his autobiography Marsh stated that he was opposed to running a St Leger prospect at Goodwood unless he had good limbs and feet, which Minoru did not have. In view of this, why run over a mile at Goodwood in preparation for the St Leger rather than ten furlongs plus? Was the decision taken out of his hands? He observes that Bayardo did not run at Goodwood but fails to note that he was not entered in any early-closing races. It is speculation but Marsh would have been aware that Bayardo had regained his best form and may have felt that there was no point in meeting trouble halfway. The St Leger was soon enough to test Minoru against Bayardo again. One thing seems certain. Bearing in mind what Marsh had said it would probably have been better to run Minoru at Hurst Park on a flatter course over ten furlongs as preparation for the St Leger than over a mile on Goodwood's uneven terrain. However, running at Hurst Park meant opposing Bayardo!

In preparation Bayardo "cantered" six furlongs with Seedcake on the 21st and then worked a mile at a "good pace" with Moscato on the 23rd.

The day at Hurst Park, which was to close in 1962, was windy with clouds "scudding" across the sky bringing several drenching storms which alternated with rain and sunshine in conditions more reminiscent of April. The brisk breeze soon dried the ground and the going was perfect. The race was always likely to be a three-runner race as only three horses were present on the course. In the paddock Bayardo had a companion – the only time in his career that he was reported to have been accompanied - and *The Sporting Life* noted that, "Bayardo showed more, make, shape and quality than Valens, who has furnished into a powerful, well balanced colt. Perola, the Oaks winner, is a grand filly with a head like a colt. Notwithstanding his companion Bayardo was a bit excited by the big crowd assembled to see the start and took some coaxing to line up behind the tapes. However, the three runners got off together".

The Sporting Life reporter noted that Perola was swishing her tail in an ominous manner and that a quarter of a mile from home Valens looked to be going well enough for a "desperate finish". But Maher was motionless on Bayardo and suddenly Wootton was hard at work on Valens and it was all over. It was the reporter's view "that if Mr Fairie's

Hurst Park Saturday 24th July Going : Good
Duchess of York Plate of £1,300, viz. £1,000 for winner, £200 for second, and £100 for third ; for three year olds ; entrance £21, £11 if declared by March 30 1909, or £1 if declared March 31 1908. One mile and a quarter. (71 entrants, viz. 21 at £21, 37 at £11 and 13 at £1----£979 (£62,656)

1	Bayardo	9st 10lb	D Maher	131++
2	Valens	9st 10lb	F Wootton	126
3	Perola	9st 7lb	B Dillon	

Betting 2-11 Bayardo, 9-1 Valens,
Won by two lengths and a bad third
Time 2 min 8. 0/0 sec

Sporting Life race analysis;-

"Bayardo was evidently nervous amidst the big crowd that lined the rails on both sides of the starting post and his excitability delayed the start eight minutes. The trio got evenly away, and Perola forcing the pace soon had three lengths lead of Bayardo which she maintained until well into the straight where the other pair began to draw up, Valens being on the outside. They caught Perola a quarter of a mile from home and soon Wootton afterwards was uneasy on Valens while Bayardo was going well within himself, Danny riding with elbows out and without being bustled the favourite won by two lengths".

colt continues improving at the same rate the St Leger is a foregone conclusion".

The ground description is difficult to verify as there are no standard times for the course, which is now closed. The average time for the distance was two minutes twelve seconds. Bayardo's race was the only one run over ten furlongs over the two-day meeting.

Bayardo was long odds on for a race in which he was not expected to be troubled. He won comfortably. It was in retrospect a better race than it might have looked beforehand. Valens, who by the end of the season was rated the fourth best three-year-old, was to benefit from two walkovers that year but had competed in some top races including the Derby. Perola had won the Oaks and had been beaten by Bayardo before. It would seem that she set a fast pace and was eased when beaten and did not run again this year. It really would have been a cracking race if Minoru had run!

There was only one aspect of this victory that was unsatisfactory, and that only in hindsight. Bayardo displayed signs prior to the race that he did not like the crowds at the start. This tendency not to like crowds would bring trouble later. As it was, on this occasion he delayed the start for a short while.

Nonetheless he was back in form and Messrs Taylor, Cox and Maher could look forward to Bayardo completing his redemption with every chance of winning the one remaining classic, the St Leger.

CHAPTER 10

Classic success

With six weeks to go before the St. Leger, Bayardo was given only light work to keep him ticking over. He was noted only cantering or doing "healthy exercise" for the first half of August. He had only one entry in any case and that was for a race at Derby which was only seven days before the St Leger. Alec Taylor was quite capable of producing Bayardo on the day without any need for a preparatory race, although Manton had been subjected to some malady which had affected a few of its inhabitants. Bayardo was apparently due to run at Derby as a prep race and in all probability did not run due to the illness in the stables. However, Bayardo's preparation seemed unaffected and his work schedule suggested all was well. The first strong work after his break was on the 21st August when he went fourteen furlongs at a "good striding gallop" with Moscato. On 24th he went a mile at a "good pace" with Moscato and on a stormy morning the following day the 25th Moscato led Bayardo and Laomedia two miles at a "good striding gallop" with Benwhat – a modest sprinter but good enough to run in the Stewards Cup - jumping in for the last six furlongs, presumably to ensure there was no slacking! The following day he went a mile at "a good pace" in company and on Saturday 28th August he went ten furlongs at a "nice pace".

The general feeling now was that Bayardo was the best three-year-old and this was reflected in the betting for the St Leger. On 20th August these were the odds:-

Bayardo	5-4	was 6-4
Minoru	7-2	was 3-1
Louviers	8-1	
Bachelors Double	100-8	
The Story	25-1	

It was time for Alfred Cox to view his horse's preparation for the final classic. On Monday 30th he was present to see Bayardo go fourteen furlongs in company with four others at what was described by one observer as "a good striding gallop" and another as "a rattling good gallop"! Either way it can be safely assumed they did not dawdle! After "good half-speed" work for the next two days and six furlongs at "useful pace" on Thursday he concluded his St Leger preparations on Saturday by going two miles "exercise only" in company. The *Diamond Racing Journal* said he was doing "wonderfully well" in his preparation for the St Leger. Bayardo left Manton on Monday 6th September with confidence high and *The Sportsman's* Manton correspondent confidently forecasting victory.

The St Leger is the oldest classic. First run in 1776 it predates the Derby and Oaks by four and three years respectively and the Two and One Thousand Guineas by thirty three and forty years respectively. Its beginnings were as a humble sweepstakes over two miles and a field of five competed in the inaugural running and one of ten for the second, both being run at the old course at Cantley Common. In 1778 the race name and venue were changed to the St Leger and Town Moor respectively. The race was named after a popular local sportsman Lt-Gen Anthony St Leger of Park Hill. The race distance was shortened to one mile six furlongs and 193 yards in 1813 and to the present distance on one mile six furlongs and 132 yards in 1826.

It is true to say that the value and importance of the St Leger was at least equal to that of the Derby during the nineteenth century and up until just after the Second World War. Only from then onwards has the St Leger not been an automatic objective of the Derby winner. For the greater part of this period a horse was considered more valuable and not less for proving himself over staying distances and would be expected to race at four and attempt to win the Ascot Gold Cup over two and a half miles. Sadly no winner of the Derby today would run in the St Leger and an owner would be thought insane if he nominated the Ascot Gold Cup as his principal objective the following year. Connections are more likely to try to win the Eclipse or the International Stakes at York, both run over ten furlongs, in order to satisfy fashion-conscious breeders who are terrified that proven stamina somehow indicates that a horse can't also possess speed. Some sympathy is due to commercial breeders as they need to sell their stock, and bloodstock agents will shun horses presented at the sales that are considered to possess too much stamina and too little speed; and there are too few private owner/breeders today who can breed and not consider any commercial aspects.

The St Leger has been under unnecessary pressure for some years. The Irish and French versions of the St Leger have been opened to older horses and are now no longer classic races in the accepted sense and have become simply all-aged staying races. Certain individuals in the media, some with enough experience and sense to know better, have advocated either following the Irish and French examples, which defies belief, or worse still if this is possible, reducing the distance to ten furlongs. Why, for heavens sake? What is definitely not needed is another ten-furlong Group 1 race for three-year-olds. The St Leger should be celebrated for what it is: a championship staying race for three-year-olds. It is a race with as fine a tradition as any in England and a good deal better than most. Nevertheless, because some in racing, whose opinions carry perhaps to much weight, feel staying races are against modern thinking it is quite in order to discard two hundred-plus years of memorable history. Luckily the executive at Doncaster has held out against these idiotic ideas and has maintained the race in it historical form. The size of the crowds which flock to the Town Moor on St Leger day is its reward.

Stamina is important to the thoroughbred something that is becoming clearer. American racing has become largely a spectacle of pure speed and, in the view of some, ruined by the practice of breeding out all stamina in order to concentrate on speed - much soundness has also been sacrificed on the altar of speed - and American breeders now find it almost impossible to produce a top class horse who can truly stay a mile and a half, never mind the St Leger distance. Yet it is less than forty years since they produced possibly the greatest racehorse of all time: Secretariat, whose performance in the mile and a half Belmont Stakes was arguably the greatest single performance by any racehorse at any time, anywhere. If this seems an ambitious statement it is worth remembering that he ran seemingly insane fractions, completed the first ten furlongs in less than two minutes and twelve in two minutes twenty four seconds flat. The second horse was as much as thirty one lengths behind! However, that was then and American racing has now reached the stage where they describe a race over a mile and a half as a "Marathon", for goodness sake! Even extending the race, run at the Breeders Cup, to one mile and six furlongs does not deserve the description "marathon" as it is still a mile short of what Europeans would consider an extreme staying distance. Incredible as it now seems, America proudly staged the prestigious Jockey Club Gold Cup over a distance of two miles until 1975. It is now run over ten furlongs. The introduction of artificial surfaces, or "synthetics" as the locals call them, will change North American racing in future and in the view of many certainly for the better. All-out speed may be replaced with races run at a more European tempo.

The great years of American racing (i e 1930 -1980, few would argue that the sport has been in decline since that time not least because race-day medication is permitted) were partly built on breeding to European stallions who possessed abundant stamina, and the pedigrees of top American horses, up until about twenty years ago, contained plenty of stamina. It was when American breeders became obsessed with speed that stamina began to drain away. Few would argue that British and European bloodstock is again pre-eminent throughout the world. This pre-eminence was built on the progeny of great sires who excelled over a variety of distances, not just 8-10 furlongs which seems to be the mania today.

In Europe the position is nowhere near as bad although there are signs that stamina is not encouraged. For example it appears to be acceptable to win a Group One race over twelve furlongs, but it becomes a crime if the same horse does not win a Group One over ten or shorter; and he signs his death warrant in a metaphorical sense if he then wins over farther than twelve furlongs. It would be a tragedy if in twenty or thirty years' time European racing is also lamenting the lack of top-class stamina in our leading horses.

Today the St Leger is still a great occasion but those who attempt to convince themselves that it is competed for by the cream of middle distance three-year-olds are capable of remarkable self-deception. Anyone who disputes this has only to check how many St Leger winners in recent years were superior to the Derby winner. The horses that finished behind the winner of the Derby nowadays are often considered non-stayers and consequently are asked to revert to shorter distances. Only those who lack the speed to win over shorter distances are aimed at the St Leger and the winner's stud prospects today are most likely to be that of a provider of National Hunt horses. Unfortunately this has resulted in the quality of horse competing in the St Leger and other staying races deteriorating in the last few years. Even the standard of Derby winner has declined. Apart from the 2008 winner Conduit, who it was hoped would help reverse the races decline, the last winner of St Leger capable of running to a Timeform rating of 130 was Snurge in 1990. Since then in eighteen renewals the average rating of the winner has been 122. The average rating of the Derby winner in the same period has been 127. The average rating of the Derby and St Leger winner in the twenty years before 1990 was 131 for the Derby and 127 for the St Leger. It is unlikely that any horse capable of running to a rating of 130 will ever try to win the St Leger again unless we are blessed with an owner with more sense of history than stud value.

Conduit presented a welcome change. He was the best winner since Reference Point twenty one years previously and quite capable of winning at Group One level over twelve furlongs something he demonstrated by winning the Breeders Cup Turf in successive years. However, in 2009 it is significant that his first two races were over ten furlongs where he was unable to reproduce his best form before his convincing win over twelve in the "King George". He will not however, be returning to staying trips! There was a terrific opportunity in 2009 to enhance a horse's reputation along with that of the St Leger if only Sea The Stars had been aimed at the race. Not surprisingly the horse's connections elected for another race over ten furlongs. It is said that there is no such thing as a racing certainty. However, it is as certain as it can be that no dual Two Thousand Guineas/Derby winner will ever again run in the St Leger. The sport is much the poorer for knowing it.

In 1909 the opposition to Bayardo would be the Guineas and Derby winner Minoru whose trainer, Richard Marsh, was convinced that he had never had him better and fully expected him to win and claim the Triple Crown. Marsh said "I know I have good one to beat in Bayardo, but he has a good one to meet in Minoru!" Sadly, apart from Minoru, of those others that had finished in front of Bayardo in the Guineas and Derby only Valens re-opposed. The connections of Phaleron preferred to wait until the Jockey Club Stakes where they were certain to avoid Bayardo as he had not been nominated for that race. He had finished in front of Bayardo in the Guineas but behind him in the Derby. The only conclusion that can be made is that they did not think that Phaleron could win the St Leger. Louviers had been trounced by Bayardo in the Sandringham Foal Stakes and William the Fourth was to suffer a similar fate the following year. Bachelor's Double had easily won the Irish Derby and a plate in a canter. It was not easy to assess his chances at this level.

By this stage there was little doubt in most observers' eyes that Bayardo was the best three-year-old. However, apart from his win in the Eclipse against older horses, and two stakes wins plus one in a plate against his own age group, the fact had to be faced that he had failed to gain even a place in the first two classics. Supporters of Bayardo could claim that lack of condition contributed to his failure at Newmarket in the Guineas and bad luck had caused his failure in the Derby. After all, Epsom with its undulations can upset many horses and luck often plays a significant part there. However, Doncaster was one of the fairest tracks in the country with plenty of time to find a position along the five furlong straight. The straight in Bayardo's time was slightly different than today. It had a gentle curve about halfway but nothing that would affect any horse's chance. If he were beaten here there could be no excuse. The distance should not prove a problem. Bayardo had already won over a mile and five furlongs, albeit in a slowly run race, and, although neither his sire or dam proved very effective over staying distances, his grandsire Hampton had won eleven times over two miles or beyond. In the circumstances, an extra furlong and a half was probably within his compass. The going should also not prove any concern. He had demonstrated the he acted on any surface, although any give would be in his favour.

Alfred Watson felt that the Leger was a match between Bayardo and Minoru and he expected "A great fight between the two with Bayardo getting just the better of it", he wrote before the race. Richard Marsh, however, would have none of this. He firmly believed that Minoru would win, indeed must win. It was his belief that he had never had the King's Two Thousand Guineas and Derby winner as well as he did now. The colt had not suffered any setbacks in his training or been sick for even a day. He was certain that Minoru would prevail. *The Sporting Life's* correspondent in his assessment of the day's racing predicted that, in a close race, Minoru, who he pointed out had beaten Bayardo twice, would prevail. The field was probably settled the day before as only seven horses of the original entry were present on the course and all were scheduled to run. The measure of Bayardo's rehabilitation as the season's best three-year-old can be gauged by the fact that he was made favourite over Minoru and was backed at 11-8 on the day before the race. The paddock was packed as race-goers and professionals studied the runners. *The Times* noted that:-

"No horse could possibly have looked better than did his Majesty's Minoru in the paddock before the start of the St Leger. Every mark and muscle which is found in the perfectly trained thoroughbred was conspicuous; and Richard Marsh may well have been satisfied with the colt's condition, as indeed he was. His confidence could not have been greater and therefore it unfortunately follows that no possible excuse can be made for the failure of the Derby winner. Minoru and Bayardo were equally centres of attention, the crowd round the son of Bay Ronald and Galicia being so dense when he was being saddled that Mr Fairie was unable to get near enough to inspect his colt; but he was fully aware of his well being, and the experts who obtained a good view, including Darling the Beckhampton trainer, were forcibly impressed by Bayardo's appearance. He like Minoru was at the height of condition and the ailment which had affected his stable companion and half brother Lemberg and other occupants of the Manton stable had scarcely touched Bayardo".

The *Sporting Chronicle* noted that Bayardo did not enjoy the crowds and "resolutely declined" to enter a saddling box and it was necessary for Taylor to remove him away to a far corner to saddle him. At least Bayardo was not prejudiced against his box at Manton. He disliked any saddling box and was not going to discriminate one against another!

The King, Edward VII, missed few if any renewals of the St Leger and he was again in attendance to see his colt attempt to become the eleventh horse to complete the Triple Crown. It was to be his last St Leger as he would be dead within a year.

The St. Leger today is worth only 75% of its' 1909 value.

The going has been described as both very firm and soft! Based on time the ground was probably good or possibly marginally on the soft side of good. Bayardo's time was about one and a half seconds slower than the median for the period from 1900 until the Great War and about seven and a half seconds quicker than the median for the period from 1889 until 1900. From 1840 until 1880 the average time for the St. Leger was about three minutes twenty seconds. From then until 1900 the average was about six or seven seconds quicker. From then until the Great War the times were about a further seven or eight seconds faster. From then

---

Doncaster Wednesday 8th September 1909 Going : Good

St Leger Stakes of £6,500 for winner, £400 for second, and £200 for third, by subscription of £50 each h ft. or £5 if declared, with £1,755 added ; for three-olds ; entire colts 9s and fillies 8st 11lb. ; nominator of winner received £500 out of stakes. Old St. Leger Course, about one mile six furlongs 132 yards. (310 entrants, viz. 7 at £50, 174 at £25 and 129 at £5 ---- £6,450) (£412,800)

1	Bayardo	9st	D Maher	130++
2	Valens	9st	F Wootton	126
3	Mirador	9st	B Dillon	124
4	Minoru	9st	H Jones	118
5	The Story	9st	Walt Griggs	113
6	Carrousel	9st	C Trigg	
7	Bachelors Double	9st	J Thompson	

Betting 11-10 Bayardo, 7-4 Minoru, 100-8 Valens, 100-6 Bachelors Double, 33-1 The Story, 40-1 Mirador

Won by one and a half lengths ; half a length second and third. Unofficially the distances thereafter were four lengths and three.

Time ; 3 min 8. 3/5 sec

Sporting Life race analysis;-

"Mr W C Manning had the seven runners weighed out in excellent time, and when the parade had taken place in the order of the card, a slight wait occurred at the post. Minoru was on his toes eager for the fray and moving up to the tapes. At the second attempt Mr Willoughby pulled the lever to a good start. Mirador stretched out with a clear advantage with Bachelor's Double, Minoru, The Story and Bayardo in a group next. Valens steadied into last place. Though Carrousel was the last to get into his stride when they had covered the quarter mile he had improved his position, and before going over the hill out of sight he rose to the front with a two lengths lead of Bachelor's Double and Mirador, with Bayardo and Minoru side by side clear of The Story. They raced thus to the Red House, where Carrousel and Bachelor's Double both showed signs of distress. At the five furlong post Minoru appeared to be in difficulties. The Story drew level with Mirador at the intake turn, where Valens headed the pair, and going into the line for home had a full length advantage. But his supremacy was short lived, as Bayardo came upon him with one rush and, taking his measure at the distance, Mr Fairie's colt won very comfortably and was pulling up at the finish".

---

until the present day the times have varied very little and the standard time at present is three minutes five seconds. Similarly in the Derby covering the same periods the average times were about two minutes fifty seconds, two minutes forty four and two minutes thirty nine. The standard time today is two minutes thirty eight.

The thoroughbred has almost certainly improved in the last one hundred and seventy years, although possibly not all that much if at all since Bayardo's time. Training methods have certainly changed, although it is difficult to be sure, if, and if so, just how much fitter racehorses on the flat are today compared with one hundred years ago. In addition the introduction of watering systems has virtually eliminated very firm ground. However, the most likely contributor to the faster times has been the riding styles and methods which did change significantly, particularly over the period 1900-1914 during the so called "American invasion". Races were generally run at a faster pace and the fitting of much lighter racing plates, another American innovation, helped considerably. In the opinion of North American trainer John Huggins the lighter plates improved a horse's performance by four lengths.

In the event Bayardo won easily and would have won by further if Maher had not begun pulling him up as soon as he had the race won. *The Times* reported "Bayardo nicely balanced for his final effort, and so extraordinary is the colt's speed that the issue was effectively settled in three or four strides. Those strides were taken, when a mile and three quarters had been covered". The *Diamond Racing Journal* said he won "easily" and that it was "difficult to say how much he had in hand". Minoru ran unaccountably badly. He was the victim of a bump which would not have helped, but at no stage did he look like winning. Richard Marsh thought that as a result of the bump Minoru sulked; however, whatever the reason, he was never a factor. Indeed for much of the straight it seemed that the race would be between Valens and Mirador. However, Maher was just biding his time on Bayardo and in a matter of strides the race was over. Richard Marsh considered that Bayardo was a brilliant winner and even at his best and without interference, Minoru would have been second at best. There is no denying there was considerable disappointment amongst the crowd and professional observers. They had badly wanted a Royal victory but could not have been confident that Minoru would prevail; one observer was quoted as saying that he had hoped against hope that His Majesty would win the Triple Crown and he was very disappointed for the King.

Minoru won one more race, the Free Handicap, at odds of 1-2 struggling home by a neck, under Danny Maher, but he was never the same again, racing only once at four. In Minoru's defence Richard Marsh felt that Maher did not ride him well, waiting with him until near the line before trying to win with one burst of speed. Minoru was more suited to being allowed to use his stride. It is perhaps pointing out the obvious, but should not Marsh have mentioned this in the paddock before the race? Particularly so in view of the fact that Maher invariably held his mounts up and came with one late run. Perhaps he did but Maher simply ignored him!

It is the most unsatisfactory aspect of Bayardo's rivalry with Minoru that they never met when both were able to produce their best. Minoru raced seven times as a three-year-old and the St Leger was his only defeat and the only race in which he ran significantly below form. With regard to their head-to-head, it must be conceded that Minoru, with the 2000 Guineas and Derby against Bayardo's St Leger, came out on top. Yet it has never been suggested that Minoru was anything but considerably inferior to Bayardo. Opinion, even that of Minoru's trainer Richard Marsh, and all form lines point to Bayardo's undoubted superiority. J B Robertson, writing some years later, said "He (Bayardo) was superior in every way to the Derby winner Minoru". Yet to be fair to Minoru there is some evidence that he was not a true stayer. His most impressive performances were over a mile in the 2000 Guineas, where he was an easy winner of a competitive race, and the Greenham, St James's Palace and Sussex Stakes. He was all-out to win the Derby and struggled to win a ten-furlong race after his moderate run in the St Leger. This may be simplistic and it is possible that Minoru deteriorated as the year went on. However, his trainer and other observers were convinced that he was in top form for the St Leger, but he ran below form. It should be recorded that, although he appeared to have him in the peak of condition, Minoru's trainer did write that he was not entirely happy with his colt's action on the day of the race, due he felt to the very hard ground! However, he did not expect it to stop him from winning. Richard Marsh lamented that Minoru had been unlucky to have had to meet a horse like Bayardo in the St Leger. He noted that Minoru was therefore not as great as Persimmon and that Diamond Jubilee was inferior to Persimmon and had beaten a moderate field. In saying this Marsh is guilty of a *non sequitur* because, even without Bayardo in the Leger field, Minoru would still not have won. In addition Bayardo's supporters could be forgiven for thinking that Marsh might also have reflected that in a year with milder weather during the spring, Minoru may not have won a classic at all!

It may have been considered that Bayardo had done enough for the year. His reputation was restored and he had raced seven times and won five. To general surprise Cox announced that Bayardo would continue to race. He had a further six engagements and he fulfilled them all. Bayardo was entered for eighteen races as a three-year-old and he ran in thirteen. Of the five he missed, two were before the Guineas and one was between the Guineas and the Derby. A further one was at Ascot where he ran in another race and the last was just before the St Leger. Therefore, once he was fit and well he ran at almost every opportunity. Imagine the reaction today if the winner of the St. Leger appeared even three more times the same year, never mind six! This would almost certainly have been Cox's decision rather than Alec Taylor's. This was in line with his view that his horses fulfilled their engagements where possible. He followed the same policy with Bayardo's half brother, the Derby winner Lemberg, who won 17 of his 24 races and ran, and won, many of the same races as Bayardo.

It is also worth remembering that racehorses during this period raced with considerably more frequency than today. The leading horses would appear up to a dozen times. Some would appear in the top handicaps as well as the many stakes races, although it is true to say that this practice was gradually dying out and is, of course, unheard of today. It is difficult not to conclude that thoroughbreds were considerably tougher during this period and connections more willing to race them. Notwithstanding this, Charles Richardson in his book *The English Turf* (published in 1900) laments that the modern thoroughbred was not as tough and durable as his counterpart forty or so years previously. *Plus ca change* etc! However, it is worth remembering that, as races were generally faster run in Bayardo's time than fifty years previously, more strain was being placed on horses and that may have led to some unsoundness. In addition, in defence of the modern thoroughbred it must be said that some races in Bayardo's time were not very competitive. It is also fair to say that the Pattern system, introduced in 1971, has supplied identifiable targets for top horses and has signalled the end of any horse above a certain level of ability running in handicaps. Winning pattern races demonstrates a level of class, thus enabling breeders to assess ability, and it was no longer necessary or desirable to ask a good horse to prove his ability by conceding lumps of weight to inferiors.

Bayardo remained at Doncaster after the St Leger and, as he was perfectly well and the race had not taken anything out of him, Cox and Taylor thought that it would do no harm for him to canter round for the prize offered for the Doncaster Stakes two days later in a race worth less than 10% of the St Leger.

The going was described as good in one place and soft in another. However, judging by the time, the ground would appear to have dried out a little since the St. Leger, and was probably good ground. The hand-

---

Doncaster Friday 10th September 1909 Going : Good

Doncaster Stakes of £10 each starter, with £500 added of which nominator of winner received £50 and owner and nominator of second each £25 ; for three year olds ; entrance £5. One mile and a half over Old Course. 64 entants, 3 of which were withdrawn on payment of a fine under rule 108------ - £475 (£30,400)

1	Bayardo	9st 5 lb	D Maher	130++
2	Verney	7st 9lb	F Wootton	103
3	Great Peter	8st 7lb	W Bullock	109
	Duke Michael	8st 9lb	W Higgs	

Betting 1-7 Bayardo, 10-1 Verney, 100-7 Duke Michael
Won by a length ; four lengths second and third.
Time 2 min 32. 3/5 sec

Sporting Life race analysis;-

"Verney settled down from Great Peter and Bayardo, but after passing the new Rifle Butts Duke Michael raced up on the outside, and the St Leger winner was eased, falling back two lengths in the rear. Half a mile from home Duke Michael was beaten, and Verney was closely followed by Great Peter and Bayardo the latter of whom attempted to come through between them, but, being baulked had to pull up. Nevertheless, Maher soon got the favourite going again and won in the commonest of canters".

icap ratings appear to suggest that Bayardo's performance in winning this race was almost equal to his win the St. Leger. This is because The St. Leger was a level weights race whereas the Doncaster Stakes involved penalties of between ten and twenty two pounds. It is hard not to conclude that Bayardo could have won the St. Leger just as easily with a seven to ten pound penalty and his performance in the race can be rated much higher. This was a simple task but even so Maher came close to creating a drama. The *Sporting Chronicle* noted that he came between Verney and Great Peter which was unnecessary as he could just as easily have gone round them. He risked one of them closing the gap and sure enough Verney swerved and knocked Bayardo into Great Peter. Bayardo had to be checked and in doing so lost two to three lengths.

Bayardo's rehabilitation as the leading three-year-old was complete in the only way possible: he had won the final classic and done so in a manner which was beyond any argument. No one could now dispute his status as the best of the classic generation: he was now utterly vindicated and even the most fervent doubter had to concede that he was not only the best three-year-old but a horse to rate with the best of any era.

CHAPTER 11

The Champion Stakes and beyond

About this time a rumour began that Alfred Cox was prepared to sell Bayardo to Sir William Bass. The idea of this was described as "grotesquely improbable". Cox was a wealthy man not in need of money. He had always wanted to own a horse of the highest class and now he had one. In the circumstances selling was hardly likely.

After the St Leger meeting Bayardo did little apart from canter and half-speed work until the beginning of October when he worked over longer distances usually in company with Moscato. The most significant work was on the 10th October when he worked fourteen furlongs with Seedcake and Highness with Benwhat jumping in for the final five furlongs. On the 11th he left for Newmarket for the second October meeting with his first objective being the Champion Stakes which, at that time, despite its name, was nowhere near as valuable as today when it is a very important race carrying Group 1 status. It was inaugurated in 1877 and run across the flat which is ten furlongs. However, for three years, 1901, 1902 and 1903, it was run over the last mile and three quarters of the Cesarewitch course. It is interesting to note that the Eclipse Stakes was worth almost ten times the Champion Stakes in 1909 and clearly has greater claims to being regarded as the Championship race over ten furlongs. Until the Second World War the Champion Stakes was often uncompetitive. From 1882 until 1929 the largest field was six with many renewals of two, three or four runners and one walkover. The first double figure renewal was 1944 with seventeen and after the war, the first peacetime one nineteen in 1951. Since then the race has been a highlight of the end-of-season programme with undoubtedly its pinnacle being when Brigadier Gerard won it in consecutive years. The emotion generated when the Brigadier hit the front on the second occasion, and the crowd knew that his final race was to end in triumph, was at an almost unbearable level. Such moments are worth treasuring for a lifetime.

Sadly the race is in steady decline as it has been compromised by being run between the Arc and the Breeders Cup. The management at Newmarket have not helped matters by allowing the value of the race to decline steadily in the last few years so that it is now worth less in actual terms than it was fifteen years ago and unbelievably it is now worth less than the July Cup! As this is being written there is a suggestion that the race be switched to Ascot! This bizarre idea, not exactly opposed it has to be said by the Newmarket management, seems to have come about because Newmarket can't attract enough race-goers for its "Champions" day. However, Ascot with its huge capacity might with an end-of-season spectacular to challenge Breeders Cup day or Arc de Triomphe weekend; fat chance! Ascot quite rightly attracts large crowds for the Royal meeting which is pre-eminent but has never done so in the autumn and it is hard to see how they might now. It is enough to make a traditionalist despair. Where do these lunatic ideas originate? What price history and thoroughbred racing in Britain when it is governed by the sort of individuals who think this type of idea represents progress.

In 1909 Bayardo faced only two rivals. Although thirteen of the original entrants were on the course it seemed that most were waiting to see if Bayardo was running or not. However, the two runners that stood their ground were good horses. One of them was the grand old gelding Dean Swift who by this time although aged 8 was as good as ever. He was tremendously popular with the public and one of Charles Morton's, his trainer, all time favourites. Long, lean, hungry and ragged looking, he possessed hairy heels and had a habit which seems scarcely believable. He sometimes greeted admirers by rearing up and playfully putting his forelegs round their neck! On one occasion at Epsom to his intense astonishment he did this to Lord Lonsdale, the "Yellow Earl". How it was possible to remain upright with approximately twelve hundred pounds, (540 kilos), of racehorse leaning on one's shoulders is hard to imagine! It can only be assumed that the lad in charge had a firm hold of Dean Swift's lead reign in order to prevent him demolishing innocent bystanders in the paddock! ++ To describe him as just a handicapper would be a gross injustice. With his level of ability he would race almost exclusively in Group One and Two company today. He ran in the City and Suburban handicap at Epsom eight years in succession, during its great days, winning twice and being four times placed. He was beaten in the Lincoln by inches after he was left many lengths at the start and was often asked to give away huge amounts of weight. He had won the Coronation Cup at Epsom earlier in the year a race which is today rated as Group One.

Making his debut as a juvenile in 1903, Dean Swift raced a total of 62 times winning 12. The handicapper has no feelings or sentiment and has only one duty: to work out weights that provide competitive racing. However, Dean Swift was an easy target for the handicapper. He never gave less than his best and he was placed on many occasions when giving

++ Unbelievable it may seem, yet on page 70 of Charles Morton's memoirs "My Sixty Years of The Turf" he describes just such a habit.

away considerable weight. That he came so close so often to defying his burdens is ample proof of his inexhaustible courage and will to win. There have been a few better handicappers, not many, in racings history but none had more determination and courage. He finished his career at the age of ten by winning the Chesterfield Cup at Goodwood, an occasion which reduced many of the more emotional race-goers to tears. As he got older the bookmakers called him "Been Swift" and chalked him up at generous prices and frequently had to pay for their temerity.

In the Coronation Cup he beat White Eagle who was the only other runner in the Champion Stakes. He was rated 131 in *A Century of Champions*. Truth, it is often said, is stranger than fiction and the life and racing career of Dean Swift would not be credible in a novel and he must have been the most tremendous character. He had the most agreeable temperament and had a wonderful relationship with his trainer. There were times when Charles Morton was almost able to talk to Dean Swift, for example before a race after saddling him he would tap him on the quarters and the old horse would incline his head in acknowledgment as if to say "yes I know what I have to do!" Race-goers would crowd round to see him being saddled much to the pleasure of the horse who enjoyed the attention. It is hardly surprising that he was regarded with such affection. For many years the Dean Swift Handicap was run at Epsom's spring meeting. Sadly that three day meeting is now just one day event and not even important enough to be described as a shadow of its former self and the Dean Swift Handicap long gone.

White Eagle was himself a top performer who won three of his ten races that year including the City and Suburban handicap, beating Dean Swift a length and a half in receipt of nine pounds, a valuable stakes race and a walk over. As a three year old he had won five of his twelve races including the Sussex Stakes and four other stakes races. He was also second in the St Leger. He had been a leading juvenile having won the National Breeders Produce Stakes.

On the previous night rain had fallen in torrents and the night was described as "black as pitch". However, the morning produced glorious sunshine and the course was very full. The King was unable to be present but the Birdcage was described by *The Sporting Life* as occupied by "a strong muster of rank and fashion, which included most of the principal patrons of the Turf". There was a keen wind to accompany the sunshine. Bayardo should have received nine pounds weight for age from both of his opponents. However, with penalties and Maher's overweight he received only six.

The most interesting aspect of this race, and the most alarming, was Bayardo's refusal to canter to post in front of the stands. Bayardo, who had been described as looking very fit and well, was indulged, and allowed to proceed to the start behind the stands, via a route behind the

Newmarket Tuesday 12th October Going : Soft/heavy

Champion Stakes of £50 each, 20 ft. (to fund), with £1,000 added, of which second received £150 and third £50 ; for three year olds and upwards. AF One mile and a quarter. 42 entrants-----£900 (£57,600)

1	Bayardo	3yrs	8st 7 lb (carried 8st 8lb)	D Maher	136+
2	Dean Swift	aged	9st	Walt Griggs	131
3	White Eagle	4yrs	9st	W Saxby	129

Betting 4-9 Bayardo, 5-1 Dean Swift, 11-2 White Eagle
Won by a neck ; a length second and third.
Time : 2 min 16. 3/5 sec

Sporting Life race analysis;-

"Bayardo refused to face the crowd and could not be induced to canter down, and he had to be taken to the back of the stands and lead by a hack to the post, where he and Dean Swift both gave trouble. However, at the start both moved away smarter than White Eagle. Dean Swift having a slight advantage of the favourite, and the pair at a very slow pace came across the flat, and although they alternatively had their heads in front up to the bushes, it was there that Bayardo shot away from his opponents and from that point had the verdict in safe keeping, winning comfortably".

Cottage. When asked after the race if these antics were of any concern to him Alfred Cox replied, pointing to the winning post "It is what he does there that counts, not what he does elsewhere".

The ground was almost certainly between soft and heavy based on times over the four days of the meeting. Due to the moderate pace the time for the Champion Stakes was slow. On this occasion Bayardo was asked to exert himself but was not in any danger of defeat. Some measure of Bayardo's achievement can be understood when Charles Morton writing in his autobiography some years later observed that in his opinion Dean Swift's performance was the best of his career. Bayardo's performance in winning easily was outstanding particularly as he was three pounds "wrong" at the weights.

Kettledrum of the *Sporting Chronicle* lamented the slow pace for such an important contest. He noted that Bayardo and Dean Swift had exchanged the lead until three furlongs from home at which point Maher asked Bayardo to move ahead. From that point to the line he considered that Maher had merely "amused" himself by doing just enough to keep ahead of Dean Swift and White Eagle. These tactics by Maher seem unfair to a brave and willing horse like Dean Swift who would have tried all the way to the line and deserved better than to be toyed with in this manner. Maher would have been more usefully occupied had he gone on and won handsomely instead of indulging himself at the expense of honest competitors.

Bayardo's exertions were not considerable and he reappeared two days later in the Lowther Stakes. There were fourteen horses still engaged in the race at the course but again the connections of most of those seemed only to be waiting to see if Bayardo was going home. In the event only two took him on. He again met White Eagle whose chance, on worse terms, looked even more hopeless. Due to the longer distance of the race he was required to concede thirteen pounds weight for age. Bayardo was therefore only a pound "worse" at the weights. Although White Eagle was a top horse his owner Col. Hall Walker's decision to run him is hard to understand. What did he hope to gain? Bayardo looked a certainty for the first prize of £470. It is hard to believe he was in need of the £50 for second prize. Perhaps he took the very understandable view that if Bayardo were not at his best he would win and if he was then White Eagle might not have too hard a race in a fruitless pursuit as he would definitely finish second. However, he should not be criticised too much as he prevented what would have been a mismatch. Although Rousay was a good handicapper and had been given 8st 2lbs in the Ebor when the top weight had been 8st 8lbs he stood no chance at all against Bayardo.

Bayardo again refused to canter to post. *The Sporting Life* wrote "As the other day, Bayardo did not seem to relish the prospect of a race, no attempt was made to take him down the course past the stands, but instead of going round behind the buildings, Maher trotted him across the Heath and along the Ditch side of the race track. As I have said the son of Bay Ronald did not seem to be at all happy, but he created no bother, and, after all, the main consideration is that when it came to racing he behaved like a Christian". Indeed he was described as being as quiet as a lamb at the start.

It certainly was not the weather or the crowd that Bayardo objected to because as *The Sporting Life* noted "Nearly all the holiday-makers were absent from Newmarket yesterday, and they missed a glorious day, with a July sky, while the wind having dropped after a hard white frost – not the first this season by the way – the temperature was mild enough for summer costume. After Wednesday's crush and excitement, the comparative quietude was all the more welcome".

The time was very slow. The standard time today for the distance is two minutes fifty six seconds. It is not clear from the *Sporting Life* analysis which horse made the running. However, the *Diamond Racing Journal* noted that Bayardo was at a disadvantage because he had been forced to make his own running.

It was at about this time that Bayardo's quirks of character began to become more pronounced. Although entirely free from vice he had always displayed some strange traits. For example he hated having his ears covered, probably because of his habit, when walking, of constantly moving them backwards and forwards in unison with his stride. This characteristic was shared by his half brother Eastern. Another idiosyn-

Newmarket Thursday 14th October Going : Good

Lowther Stakes of £20 each, h ft. (to fund), with £500 added, of which second received £50, third saved stake ; for three year olds and upwards. Last one mile and three-quarters of Cesarewitch Coourse 37 entrants---- £470 (£30,080)

1	Bayardo	3ys	9st 7lb	D Maher	133++
2	White Eagle	4yrs	10st 5lb	W Saxby	129
3	Rousay	5yrs	8st 13lb	R Keeble	

Betting 9-100 Bayardo, 100-8 White Eagle, 33-1 Rousay.
Won by one and a half lengths ; bad third
Time : 3 min 29. 4/5 sec

Sporting Life race analysis;-

"The three ran in close company till half way across the flat, where White Eagle pulling double, took a slight lead of the favourite. Rousay dropping away beaten at the bushes, Bayardo drew out and won in a canter".

crasy, which alarmed newcomers to the yard at Manton, was his habit of knocking noisily on his manger with his chin. This was known in the stable as "Bayardo's drum". He did the same thing when travelling and as a result developed what was described as "quite a hard scale on his chin". He continued on occasions, after returning from exercise, to stand stock-still in the middle of the yard at Manton, staring into the distance. In these circumstances nothing would induce him to move and enter his box until he was so inclined.

From the time of the Champion Stakes he had developed a strong aversion to cantering past the stands on the Rowley Mile. The moment he turned the corner after leaving the Birdcage and saw the straight one and a quarter miles stretching away in front of him, he dug his toes in and refused to budge. Danny Maher was a beautiful horseman with wonderful hands, but all his powers of persuasion proved hopeless. The Jockey Club ruled that all runners must pass the grandstand on their way to the start. Permission had to be obtained from the Stewards to allow him to be taken down behind the stands. This required Maher to weave his way between the coaches, cars and carriages in the car park. Bayardo, perhaps sensing that he had got his own way, was perfectly happy with this arrangement and under these conditions would proceed to the start without further difficulty. Sidney Galtrey was of the view that this amused him as if causing concern was his intention! Bayardo would have known Maher well enough to know that he would not set about him with his whip.

Unfortunately, the result of all this was that his critics, particularly those who had earlier considered him not to have trained on, while now readily acknowledging his brilliance, condemned Bayardo. There was now a new metaphorical stick for his critics to beat him with and it was seized gratefully. The more charitable described him as "tricky" others were more direct and called him un-genuine. Bayardo's supporters found these accusations difficult to refute and the critics' views were strengthened by the tactics of Danny Maher who declared that Bayardo hated to be in front and therefore whenever possible he kept him covered up until the last possible moment. These tactics suggested a horse that disliked racing and could only be persuaded to do his best if kept on the bridle for as long as possible. Maher sometimes overdid these tactics taking them, on occasions, to extreme levels. Alec Taylor tried to persuade Maher that these tactics were unnecessary and would lead to disaster one day, but the jockey, who could be as obstinate as Bayardo himself, would not listen.

How Maher could be so certain that Bayardo hated to be in front is difficult to understand. On the only occasion Maher had ridden him and set the pace Bayardo had won comfortably in the National Breeders Produce Stakes as a two year old. Had he repeated the tactic, and Bayardo proved un-cooperative, Maher's view would have been understandable. Apart from a race at the later stages of his four year old career the only occasions when he did make the running were very uncompetitive races or match races with his opponent outclassed and Bayardo only required to canter back from the start at probably about the same pace most horses go when moving to post. In both the Champion and Lowther stakes Bayardo had been prominent and had been in front for at least part of each race. Did Maher feel on these occasions that Bayardo had been disinclined to exert himself when he was not tracking another horse? It is significant that Maher made the running on Bayardo as a deliberate tactic once more but that was the following year after Ascot. For whatever reason Maher seemed to have got it into his head that Bayardo would not exert himself and gallop to his full extent when clear of other horses. Maher may well have suspected that Bayardo disliked being in front and his aversion to cantering to the start of the Rowley mile possibly reinforced his view that he did not like to see too much in front of him. Perhaps Maher thought Bayardo suffered from some kind of equine agoraphobia! This would have been strange as his dislike of entering stable boxes would more likely suggest equine claustrophobia!

Just a week later he turned out for the Sandown Foal Stakes. The weather was very pleasant with little wind and the temperature described as being as hot as July. Bayardo was by now effectively unbeatable, that is as long as he could be induced to go to the start! This race looked very uncompetitive and in view of the poor returns for the second and third and with no return at all for the fourth the only surprise was that it was not a walkover.

Bayardo returned to Manton but was on his travels again soon enough as his next engagement was just five days later at Headquarters. On the

Sandown Park Thursday 21st October Going : Heavy

Sandown Foal Stakes of £2000, viz. £1,500 for owner and £250 for nominator of winner, £100 for owner and £50 nominator of second, and £75 for owner and £25 and nominator of third, for three year olds ; entrants £26, £11 if declared by January 5 1909, or £1 if declared by October 8 1907 ; of surplus viz. £119, second received two-thirds and third the remainder ; Eclipse Stakes Course one mile and a quarter. (184 entrants, viz. 51 at £26, 66 at £11, and 67 at £1----£1,724 (£110,336))

1	Bayardo	9st 7lb	D Maher	119++
2	Shikaree	7st 9lb	F Wootton	90
3	Legatee	7st	S Wootton	78
	King Charming	8st 3lb	O Madden	

Betting 7-100 Bayardo, 20-1 Shikaree, 25-1 King Charming 66-1 Legatee
Won by a length ; one and a half lengths second and third.
Time : 2 min 24. 4/5 sec

Sporting Life race analysis;-

"Little time was wasted at the post. Shikaree moving off in close company with King Charming, the favourite being slightly last, some three lengths covering the quartet; but after going about a quarter of a mile, King Charming shot out clear of Shikaree, Legatee and Bayardo. King Charming increased his lead along the railway side and came into the straight three lengths clear of Shikaree who resigned second place a quarter of a mile from home to Bayardo while Legatee was in distress. In a few strides Bayardo, going well within himself, was in front, with the race in hand, and at the half-distance Shikaree passed King Charming, running on stoutly for second place behind the favourite who won as he pleased".

25th October he headed to the Newmarket Houghton meeting for the Limekiln Stakes. This was his fourth race in fifteen days. There was very nearly a walk over. It seems that Succour was an intended runner and when that did not materialize it was decided to run Perseus for the one hundred pounds which was going begging for second place. Both Succour and Perseus were very decent handicappers and although neither would have been able to trouble Bayardo at his best they should have provided some opposition. Perseus had won three races that year and had run in the most valuable handicaps including the Royal Hunt Cup at Ascot where he was good enough to be allocated 7st 13lbs. The top weight that year was 8st 10lbs so he would be rated by a modern handicapper at about 105.

Although there were still twenty entries left in, and as many as eleven of them were stabled at the course, most felt Bayardo was unbeatable and connections preferred to run where they had a chance of winning. One of the problems was the distribution of prize money. For this race the winner would receive over four times the second and the third would save their stake, hardly an inducement to run if there were two horses in the race which were better than yours, and none at all if there were three! Today the winner would typically receive two and half times the second and the third would receive half the second and the fourth half the third. Prize money down to sixth place is of course a regular feature of prize money today.

Sadly for admirers of this wonderful horse some less than complementary things were being said of him. *The Sporting Life* wrote of Bayardo, "by the way, he was in his now customary mulish mood when he emerged from the paddock. An effort was made to induce him to go to the post by the orthodox route but he would not budge an inch, so, making a virtue of necessity, Maher, as on other occasions lately, took him round by the back of the stand". Few great horses are ever described as mulish, which with great respect to that noble animal, is not a word any owner or trainer likes to hear in connection with a thoroughbred racehorse. There was clearly much work to do in repairing his reputation, not in terms of his ability, which was beyond dispute, but with regard to his temperament. If he was to be an attractive proposition at stud then a reputation for being un-genuine and eccentric would not look well on his CV!

Again Bayardo indicated that he was tired of the Rowley Mile. He didn't seem to understand that only the simplest of tasks lay before him! Perseus seemed to run well below form and at his best he should not have been beaten so easily. It is hard to avoid the suspicion that he was not asked for much of an effort.

Even now Bayardo's work for the season was not over. As if by some afterthought he was sent to Liverpool for his final engagement, in a race which has long since been dispensed with. Today only National Hunt racing is conducted at Aintree. However, for many years it staged flat racing and was considered by Lord Derby, whose family home Knowsley Hall was nearby, to be his local course. He was usually well represented at all meetings and always enjoyed having a winner there. The number

---

Newmarket Tuesday 26th October Going : Heavy

Limekiln Stakes of £25 each, 10ft (to fund), with £500 added, of which the second received £100 ; for three olds and upwards. AF. One mile and a quarter. (42 entrants---£425) (£27,200)

| 1 | Bayardo | 3yrs | 9st 8lb | D Maher | 132++ |
| 2 | Perseus III | 3ys | 8st 13lb | JH Martin | 93 |

Betting 1-33 Bayardo
Distance : won by 15 lengths.
Time : 2 min 19. 0/0 sec

Sporting Life race analysis;-

"Owing to Bayardo's dislike to facing the crowd lining the track he was again taken round past the cottages at the back. When the lever was released the Manton colt was quickly in advance of Perseus II and though only cantering drew further away as they came along and won easing up".

of meetings declined until eventually flat racing only took place at the Grand National meeting and finally after the 1976 meeting flat racing ceased altogether.

It is impossible to think that connections today of the leading three year old and a classic winner would bother to run in a race to win the equivalent £40,000 particularly as it was by now almost the middle of November when their charge had already raced twelve times that year! However, under Cox's control, Bayardo had no choice but to soldier on.

Alec Taylor made sure that Bayardo remained in peak condition for his final race of the year. On the 3rd November he went ten furlongs described as "good work" and again ten furlongs described as "useful work" on the 5th with Benwhat again joining in for the final five furlongs. On the 8th he was led alternately by Seedcake and Benedict for fourteen furlongs. He left on the long journey to Liverpool the following day.

Although seven of the original thirty two entries for the race had been left in, as Bayardo and King Amyntas – who was unraced and did not run again - were the only two that had arrived at the course this was only ever going to be a match, or to be more accurate a miss-match. Bayardo was again reluctant to go to post. He was led to within twenty yards of the starting line but then he stopped, and it looked as if there would be some difficulty persuading him to go any further. By a happy inspiration, however, Maher instructed the boy holding the leading rein to loose the horse's head and turning Bayardo round with his hindquarters towards the gate, backed him over the starting line! Perhaps Bayardo was simply trying to say that he had had a long season and as far as he was concerned he had done enough! No sooner had the tapes been lowered than they were released.

Apart from Bayardo not wanting to line up and being bumped at the start the only drama occurred at the first turn when King Amyntas

---

Liverpool Wednesday 10th November Going : Soft

Liverpool St Leger of £700 of which second received £50 ; for three year olds. Entrance £20 ; £13 if declared by January 5 1909 or £3 if declared by March 31 1908. One mile and a half. (32 entrants, viz. 16 at £20, 10 at £13, and 6 at £3----£630 (£40,320)

1	Bayardo	10st	D Maher	112++
2	King Amyntas	8st 4lb	W Higgs	86

Betting 1-66 Bayardo,
Distances won by half a length.
Time not known

Sporting Life race analysis;-

"The pair collided as the tapes flew up they ran in close company until the straight, where King Amyntas was allowed to lead Bayardo on sufferance as the latter, drawing away shortly after won in a common hack canter".

sprawled right and Maher only just avoided a collision. Such was his fame by this stage that many Liverpool factory workers played truant to see the greatest horse of the era run. Proof of a conviction shared by many, that lovers of thoroughbreds will go racing to see a good horse. They certainly did not turn up with any expectation of seeing either an exciting race or of having a hefty bet!

Finally Bayardo's peregrinations for his classic season were over. He had finished his three-year-old career with his eleventh straight win. The last seven had come in just 64 days! Even when consideration is given to the uncompetitive nature of some of the races, taking into account all the travel, which was of course by rail at that time, it is a remarkable achievement. Travelling was time consuming and could test a horse's patience. For Bayardo to travel by train from Manton's nearest station which was Marlborough to Newmarket via Oxford and Cambridge would take eight hours, plus the time from his stable to Marlborough and Newmarket to the course. His total journey time to Liverpool for his final race of the season would have been between nine and ten hours! A horse today could be sent more comfortably by jet aeroplane to the USA in that time and to Dubai in not much more. Credit must go to Alec Taylor for maintaining his condition and to Danny Maher who by settling him so well in his races and asking only what was required kept him fresh and enthusiastic. However, Taylor was unhappy with the way Maher was riding Bayardo. "You cut it too fine" he grumbled. "One of these fine days you'll make an expensive mistake." "I know what I am doing" was Maher's invariable retort.

Bayardo's rating for his three-year-old career in *A Century of Champions* is 139. However, it is felt that this may be a shade below his just deserts and a rating of 140 is probably a more accurate assessment of his ability. In calculating this rating the four races to concentrate on are the Sandringham Foal, Eclipse, St Leger and Champion Stakes. The first was won in a canter the next two were won easily and the last comfortably. The Sandringham Foal Stakes was a tremendous performance with the weight concession and was worth a rating of 138. The Eclipse was won easily in spite of his not having a clear run initially. This race was worth 136 but he could surely have found another two lengths which would give him the extra four pounds. The St Leger was won even more easily with Maher easing Bayardo down once he had struck the front. This effort earned a rating of only 130 but how much more he could have found is anybody's guess. The Champion Stakes was won comfortably and earned a figure of 136. However, it is less clear how much more he had in hand. Therefore it is on the Sandringham Foal and Eclipse Stakes performances that his end of season rating can best be based. It seems reasonable to assume that he could have won by further on both occasions and Bayardo should certainly have been able to achieve a figure of 140 on the evidence of these two races if he had been asked for maximum effort all the way to the line.

The prize money won by Bayardo made sure that Alfred Cox was leading owner and breeder with total prize money of £37,719 (£2,414,01-6) nearly £14,000 ahead of his nearest rival. Alec Taylor was top trainer with £47,165 (£3,018,560) he was £23,000 ahead of his nearest rival. Bayardo himself was leading horse with £24,797 (£1,587,008) nearly £10,000 ahead of the second horse, his old rival, Minoru.

By any standards Bayardo's classic season had been a tremendous success. With of course the obvious proviso that it was in the first two classics that he suffered his only defeats of the year. Perhaps he was demonstrating the old adage that "the fittest horse wins the Guineas, the luckiest the Derby and the best the St Leger". His reputation was of a very talented colt, almost impossible to get off the bit, with a wonderful turn of foot. Pretty bombproof it would seem! Also unfortunately, he had a growing reputation as a difficult individual who liked his own way and was also, possibly, un-genuine. Even Bayardo's most fervent admirers had to concede that there was a case, of at least eccentricity if no more, to answer. Had Alfred Cox decided to retire him now, his reputation would have been tarnished for ever. Cox had turned down an offer of £50,000 (3,200,000) for Bayardo from the Austrian Government evidence indeed of his affection for his champion.

There follows a list of the most valuable races open to three year old colts with the winner and the value of the race to the winner.

Bayardo had not been entered for the Jockey Club Stakes which was over fourteen furlongs and run at the First October meeting, although it is run at the Guineas meeting today. He was also not entered for the Ascot Gold Cup or the Hardwicke Stakes at Ascot which were both open to three year olds at that time.

The most valuable handicaps were the Great Jubilee Handicap at Kempton worth to the winner £2,650 (£169,000), the Manchester Cup £2,570 (£164,480), Royal Hunt Cup £2,160 (£138,240) and the Chester Cup £2,030 (£129,920).

Eclipse Stakes	Bayardo	8,870	(567,680)
Jockey Club Stakes	Phaleron	7,440	(476,160)
Derby	Minoru	6,450	(412,800)
St Leger	Bayardo	6,450	(412,800)
2000 Guineas	Minoru	5,000	(320,000)
Ascot Gold Cup	Bomba	3,430	(219,520)
Hardwicke Stakes	Prima	2,463	(157,632)
The Prince of Wales' Stakes	Bayardo	2,150	(137,600)
Newmarket Stakes	Louviers	2,140	(136,960)

The racing year of 1909 saw in England two of the best North American racehorses attempt to show in Europe the form they had in their native land. Both were four-year-olds, Fair Play, who at stud sired the immortal Man o' War, raced six times but not only did he fail to reproduce his best form but became increasingly vicious. His sire, Hastings, had possessed a vile temper which Fair Play, to an extent, inherited. Man o' War, who as a yearling was to prove almost impossible to break, did not have a similarly unpleasant disposition. Colin, who raced and won fifteen times in North America, was not a sound horse and he unfortunately broke down after he arrived in England and did not race here.

The following ratings have been calculated in the same manner as for 1908. Reference has again been made to the Free Handicap run on 28th October. In addition the weights for the big end-of-season handicaps have been used as a basis for some horses that did not run in conditions stakes and plate races.

It can be seen from these ratings that although there were plenty of three-year-olds rated 120 – 129, however, apart from Bayardo, there was not one rated above 130. Most years the top three-year-old would be rated about 128 – 135 thus giving some hope to those rated just below that the leading horse could be beaten. However, in 1909 once Bayardo's overwhelming superiority had been established few of the connections of those rated below were interested in running against him. One horse Bachelor's Double, who easily won the Irish Derby and two stakes races both at long odds-on, ran his only bad race from four starts against Bayardo in the St Leger.

Three year olds

Bayardo	c	140
Minoru	c	129
Sir Martin	c	128
Louviers	c	127
Valens	c	126
Mirador	c	124
Amadis	c	124
William the Fourth	c	124
Mediant	f	124
Phaleron	c	123
Bachelor's Double	c	122?
Symonds Pride	f	121
Bomba	c	121
Temnos	c	119
Electra	f	118
The Whirlpool	c	115
Perseus	c	115
Diamond Stud	c	117
Perola	f	116
Cattaro	g	116
Glasgerion	c	116
St Victrix	c	115
Balnacoil	f	115
Princesse de Galles	f	114

Four year olds and up

Dean Swift	g	131
White Eagle	c	129
Your Majesty	c	128
Ballot	h	128
Santo Strato	c	127
Royal Realm	c	126
Galvani	h	126
Dibs	c	125
Dark Ronald	c	125
Roi Herode	h	124
Succour	g	124
Primer	c	124
Lagos	c	124
Llangwm	c	124?
Admiral Togo	g	123
Cargil	h	122
Land League	h	122
Priscillian	g	121
Lafayette	h	120
Hallaton	g	119?
Fair Play	c	116?

CHAPTER 12

Ascot Gold Cup Glory

Bayardo remained in training as a four year old with his principal objective the Ascot Gold Cup. During Bayardo's time a top three year old with enough speed to win a Classic race, particularly the Derby and St Leger, was expected to stay in training as a four year old and prove that he had stamina, durability and courage without which a horse could not prevail over Ascot's gruelling two and a half mile course. It was considered important that a horse like Bayardo, who would have been considered a good stallion prospect, could display high class stamina in addition to his speed. Alec Taylor could not have been certain that Bayardo possessed the necessary stamina for a race over this distance. After all, his sire Bay Ronald had finished distressed when he ran in the 1898 renewal. However, his grandsire Hampton stayed two and half miles well and Bayardo had shown that he could stay fourteen furlongs by winning the St Leger.

Bayardo enjoyed a much better winter and came to hand early enough to reappear at the Craven meeting at Newmarket. The race was the Biennial Stakes, the first race of the year for which he had an engagement. There is no comparable race today.

Bayardo returned to the Rowley Mile and it would seem that headquarters held little more attraction to him than it had the previous autumn! The stewards again indulged him and Maher was allowed to take him to the start via the back of the grandstand.

The Sporting Life observed, "In the 50th Biennial Stakes Bayardo was the cynosure of all eyes, and had evidently wintered well, his coat shining like satin. Most of the visitors were content to look on instead of laying the long price of 100 to 9 asked for, and the son of Bay Ronald had an easy task to beat Great Peter". The *Diamond Racing Journal* noted that but for the interference Bayardo would have won more easily.

Despite the winning distance he won as easily as the odds suggest with Maher asking only the minimum required. They were a moderate trio in opposition and failed to win any of the thirteen races they contested between them that year. Cattaro ran well below his three-year-old form. The time for good ground was very slow and the pace was probably moderate.

Bayardo had a choice of engagements for his next race; the March Stakes at Newmarket's First Spring meeting or the Chester Vase at the May meeting, or to be precise, it's only meeting of the year. In making a

Newmarket Thursday 14th April 1910 Going : Good

Second Year of Fiftieth Newmarket Biennial Stakes of £25 each, 10 ft. for acceptors, with £500 added, of which second received 10 per cent and the third 5 per cent ; for four year olds ; entrance £5, only ft, if declared ; last one mile and a half of Cesarewitch Course. 22 entrants, ft. declared for 7---- (£573, 10s.) (36,704)

1	Bayardo	10st	D Maher	127++
2	Great Peter	9st	B Dillon	109
3	Cattaro	9st	W Earl	98
	Tocher	8st	J H Martin	

Betting 9-100 Bayardo, 100-7 Cattaro
Won by three quarters of a length ; six lengths second and third.
Time : 2 min 41. 4/5 sec

Sporting Life race analysis;-

"Tocher settled down from Cattero with Bayardo last for halfway Across the Flat where Great Peter became second, in front of Bayardo. Reaching the Bushes Tocher was done with and Great Peter then drew into the lead by reason of Bayardo being baulked but the favourite challenged down the Bushes Hill and keeping Great Peter at bay won by three parts of a length".

decision between which of these races to contest Bayardo's apparent dislike of the Rowley Mile was possibly a deciding factor. In addition the Chester course is unique in British racing as the only one that is almost entirely on the turn with a very short run in of less than two furlongs. If Danny Maher was right about Bayardo disliking open spaces then Chester would be ideal. Unless he made the running which was extremely unlikely he would not see daylight until the straight. Chester it was and he was Roodeye bound for the fourth running of the Vase. This is not the same race as today which, since 1959, has been confined to three year olds. Before that time it was open to four year olds as well, which must have been to the younger generations considerable disadvantage, particularly in 1910!

By way of preparation on 30th April Bayardo galloped ten furlongs and to ensure that he was kept up to his work a colt Orphah, a decent four year old sprinter, joined him for the last six furlongs. Orphah had been fit for the gallop as he ran just over a week later. Clearly Alec Taylor wanted Bayardo tuned up for his visit to the Roodeye!

Chester is amongst the most attractive of racecourses with its city walls, compact track, all of which can comfortably be seen from the stands without the aid of race-glasses, and an atmosphere in which the spectator feels close to the action. For many years the only really valuable race at the Chester meeting was the Cup a valuable handicap over a distance in excess of two miles and worth twice as much as any other race during the three days. The race is still run today and is still the most valuable race at the meeting. In 1907 the Chester Vase was inaugurated and was an immediate success and by 1910 the Vase was worth 80% of the value of the Cup. Today the Chester Cup is again worth nearly twice as much as the next most valuable race.

The weather however, was not kind with *The Sporting Life* commenting "There were few May-like attributes about the weather yesterday, the sky being lined with grey clouds, while the wind had a wintry edge that made a great coat acceptable and prospects of fine weather were by no means assured. A fairly large company had barely found its strength on the course before a drizzling rain set in and continued without ceasing all afternoon, throwing a wet blanket over what should have been a joyous occasion". It further noted that "the members' stand was brilliant with the rank, fashion, talent, and beauty of the county, a number of house parties from the neighbourhood helping to swell the muster that met the distinguished party from Eaton Hall". The course had "rarely been in better order". The *Winning Post* noted that Bayardo's "depth of girth was remarkable".

The weather would have pleased Bayardo's connections as the going was certain to be on the easy side and kind to his delicate feet!

The ground may have been just on the soft side of good after all the rain.

This should have been easy, however, Maher overdid the waiting tactics and on a sharp course like Chester that is always asking for trouble. He contrived to provide an exciting spectacle of a contest which should have been a formality and it was only in the final stride that Bayardo was in front. Judging by the time on good ground, this must have been a slowly run race, which could only have made Bayardo's task more difficult.

The Times under its "Sporting Intelligence" column wrote the following "Never was the inauguration of a weight for age race of two thousand sovereigns more fully justified than by to-day's race for the Chester Vase; not alone because Bayardo, who never looked better, was a competitor, nor because William the Fourth emerged from the retirement that had extended since he ran in the Grand Prix de Paris over ten months ago. It was Maher's riding of Bayardo that made, while it nearly marred, to-day's race, the finish of which provoked thrills' and palpitations not aroused even by the battle between Neil Gow and Lemberg in the Two Thousand Guineas. In the Guineas the artistry of Maher and Dillon was an elevating feature; today it was a case of Maher leading what looked like a forlorn hope successfully".

"He was so well away on Bayardo that, close to the rails, he made the first bend and entered the straight for the first time almost along side William the Fourth, in the lead. When the short straight was covered and the second bend came Bayardo suddenly dropped back, but only to the

Hampton

Lord Clifden

Galicia

Bay Ronald

Bayardo wins the Richmond Stakes easily

Alfred Cox has plenty to smile about after Bayardo's win

The start of the Middle Park Plate. Bayardo is hidden

Bayardo and the second Vivid after the Middle Park Plate

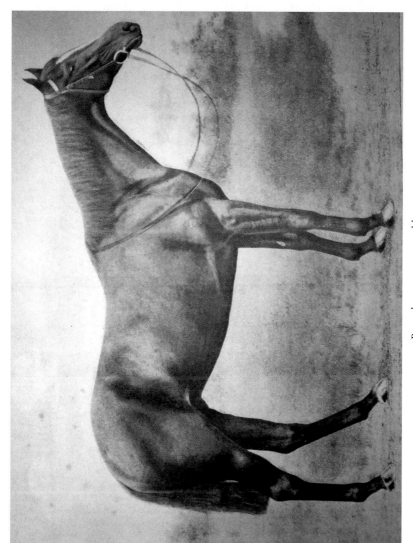

Bayardo as a two-year-old

The Grandstand at Sandown on Eclipse day

Taylor, Cox & Maher before the Eclipse Stakes. They did not always agree!

After interference Bayardo powers home . . . .

but Maher has him back on the bridle by the line

Bayardo enjoys a pick of grass after his win in the Eclipse

The legendary Dean Swift

Chester Tuesday 3rd May 1910 Going: Good

Chester Vase of £2,000 (a Vase value £100 and the remainder in specie), of which owner of second received £200 and of third £100 ; nominator of winner £125, of second £50 and of third £25 ; by subscription of £1 for three year olds or £2 for four year olds ; if left in after October 13 1908 a further £10 for three year olds ; if left in after March 31 1908, a further £10 for four year olds ; if left in after March 30 1909, a further £10 for each ; and if left in after January 4 1910, a further £8 for each ; with £293 added. One mile and a half. (149 entrants, viz. 12 at £30, 10 at £29, 12 at £22, 12 at £21, 26 at £12 12 at £11, 32 at £2, and 33 at £1--- £1595((£102,080)

1	Bayardo	4 yrs	9 st 9lb	D Maher	127+
2	William the Fourth	4 yrs	9 st 7lb	B Dillon	124
3	Malpas	3 yrs	6 st 13 lb	J Evans	106
4	Santa Fina	3 yrs	7st 6lb	H Watts	95
5	Duke Michael	4 yrs	8 st 4 lb	W Higgs	
6	Kalvemor	3 yrs	7 st 4 lb	F Fox	

Betting 1-5 Bayardo, 10-1 William the Fourth, 100-6 Santa Fina,
Won by a head ; three quarters of a length second and third. Unofficially the fourth was ten lengths further away.
Time : 2 min 43. 3/5 sec

Sporting Life race analysis;-

"Malpas jumped off sideways, and Santa Fina showed the way to William the Fourth, Duke Michael and Bayardo, with Malpas bringing up the rear, but approaching the stands William the Fourth took up the running from Bayardo, Malpas and Santa Fina, Kalvemor now dropping back last. Making for the Dee side, William the Fourth was two lengths clear of Malpas, Santa Fina now depriving Bayardo of third place. At the Grosvenor Bridge turn Malpas joined William the Fourth, the pair just being in advance of Santa Fina and Bayardo, and in the straight Malpas headed William the Fourth, but edged towards the right at the distance where Bayardo commenced his run. This gave William the Fourth the advantage, but Bayardo coming with a great burst of speed got up on the post to win by a head".

extent that Malpas deprived him of second place; but when half a mile remained to be covered Bayardo was still in arrears, being several lengths behind Santa Fina, in advance of whom were William the Fourth and Malpas fighting for the command. When the straight was reached for the finish Santa Fina faded out of the foreground and left Bayardo third, but with something like six lengths to bridge in a quarter of a mile. During the first half of that distance he did not improve his position materially, and when the final burst began it appeared that he would finish only third".

"Then, however, Bayardo and Maher began to accomplish almost demoniacal work, and they and William the Fourth reached the judge while the spectators were gasping with excitement. With them it was not so much a question as to whether Bayardo had won, as whether Maher had retrieved the stupefying effect caused when Bayardo apparently dropped out at the crucial period of the contest. Bayardo beat William the Fourth by a head, and sighs of relief were followed by heated discussion, the point of contention being was Maher's jockeyship that of a master or did he nearly throw away a race he ought to have won with fair ease".

The Sporting Life wrote; "The presence of Bayardo doubtless accounted for the smallness of the field for the Chester Vase, but those who laid 5 to 1 on him little expected an exciting race and the lucky narrow verdict that saved their outlay. Bayardo, to look at, never suggests the smasher he is, but at the same time is, perhaps not a spring horse". He was led to post as were all the runners except Malpas. It further commentated on the race from the distance "His (Bayardo's) chance looked gone as Malpas was edging out for the centre, but with a great piece of work on the part of horse and jockey while backers held their breath, the favourite closed up the gap and snatched the verdict right on the post. So near a thing was it that not till No. 1 went up on the board did a triumphant shout peal forth. Had Bayardo being given a clear run he would indubitably have scored pretty easily. Bayardo, in easing up, seemed to slither at the grass covered crossing but righted himself in the next stride".

Not everyone blamed Maher's tactics. The *Winning Post* noted that when he asked Bayardo to close the gap the horse seemed unable to respond resulting in his finding trouble. It further noted that Bayardo seemed not to be able to act on the course was not happy and had his ears laid back.

William the Fourth had been third in Minoru's Derby. He ran only once more, in the Ascot Gold Cup, before he was sent to Hungary. Malpas was one of the unfortunate three year olds. He won just the Sandringham Foal Stakes from eleven starts that year. Duke Michael won an apprentice plate and a handicap from eleven outings. Santa Fina won a handicap from ten starts. Kalvemor failed to win any of his three starts.

Bayardo had therefore won both his races so far that season. In neither race should he have had any trouble winning. However, the combined winning distance was no more than a length! Danny Maher, in keeping with his view that Bayardo hated being in front, and therefore must never see any light, was leaving matters very late. It almost cost him the Chester Vase, but he was not prepared to change his tactics. Alec Taylor did not agree with them, but he would not have been in a difficult position had he wished to order Maher, who it should not be forgotten was the leading rider at that time, to change. Alfred Cox, like almost everyone in racing, had a very high opinion of Maher as a jockey and was paying £2,000 (£128,000) this season for a second option on his services. It would therefore have been surprising if Cox had allowed Taylor to dictate tactics to the man considered the best rider in England at that time. What is not known is exactly what Cox thought about Maher's view about the way to ride Bayardo. It can only be presumed that Taylor and Cox must have discussed riding tactics at some time and the only conclusion is that Cox must have been happy and did not agree with Taylor otherwise Maher would have had to change his tactics or resign as Bayardo's jockey something that he was unlikely to do. It seems safe to assume that Maher had Cox's blessing for his riding tactics.

Three days after Bayardo's win at Chester The King, Edward VII, died peacefully in his bed at the age of sixty eight. It has pleased followers of racing ever since that the last thing he was told, that he is thought to have understood that is, was when The Prince of Wales informed him that his two-year-old filly Witch of the Air had won the 4-15 race at Kempton. His Majesty replied "I am very glad". They were that last coherent words he spoke.

Bayardo's next target as a warm up for the Ascot Gold Cup was to be the Coronation Cup over Epsom's twelve furlong Derby course. Instigated in 1902 it was a good race well worth winning, but not so important then as now with its Group One status, and was worth £1,650 (£105,600) to the winner, good money, but, for example, the Eclipse was worth £8,770 (£561,280). Following his Chester win Bayardo went a mile at a "good brisk gallop" on the 19th fourteen furlongs at a "good striding gallop on the 23rd twelve furlongs "readily" on 25th. On the 29th Alfred Cox was present to see him gallop twelve furlongs presumably in order to satisfy himself that Bayardo was in good shape. On the 31st Bayardo left for Epsom with the *Sporting Life's* gallops man of the view that he was short of peak condition.

Bayardo was one of nine horses from the original entry stabled on the downs. However, on Thursday 2nd June the day of the race he was not declared to run. This was unusual. Alfred Cox's horses kept their engagements whenever possible and as he had only Bayardo left in the race it meant he did not have a runner. It can only be assumed that Cox and Alec Taylor shared the gallops man's view that he was not at his best. Another possible reason for his withdrawal may have been the ground which, although given as good, may have been considered too fast for Bayardo. It is possible that Maher had formed the impression that Bayardo had not enjoyed the track during the Derby. Certainly running at Epsom may have jarred him up or damaged his delicate feet and that would have meant there would not have been enough time for him to recover before Ascot. Cox would have wanted to run at Epsom because the race was at his mercy. However, if he had been in any way off colour then the stress of the race may well have left its mark with disastrous consequences for Ascot. The Coronation Cup was not the objective and after the Two Thousand Guineas and Derby Cox would have had painful memories of what happens when you run a horse that is not considered at its peak.

In the event the race was won well by Sir Martin from Bachelor's Double and Louviers. It must have "stuck in Cox's throat" to see Sir Martin win at the same venue as the previous year when, by stumbling, he had effectively eliminated Bayardo from the Derby. It would have appealed to Cox to have beaten Sir Martin in these circumstances and he must have looked longingly forward to Ascot. Cox, however, did not have too much to complain about. He had won the Derby the previous day with Bayardo's half brother Lemberg!

Epsom had gone and now everything was centred on the build up to the Ascot Gold Cup. It was about this time that Alfred Cox was offered £56,000 (£3,584,000) for Bayardo. Cox however, despite his reputation, had a very real affection for the horse and would never have parted with him. It was said that he liked Bayardo, possibly more than any other horse, due to his 'funny little ways'. In any event as Cox rarely sold his horses it is hard to imagine him changing his habits and suddenly selling a horse which had an outstanding chance to win one of the season's highlights.

Whatever the problem which resulted in him missing Epsom Bayardo's work was gradually increased. He went fourteen furlongs at half speed on the 6th with a mile at a "nice pace" the following day and another "half speed" piece of work also over a mile the day after. This was followed on the 10th with a mile gallop "sharply" in company with Lemberg, fresh from his triumph in the Derby and on course for a successful tilt at the St James's Palace Stakes at Ascot. His final work was a mile at "half speed" on the 13th and a five furlong canter the following day. On the 15th he departed for Ascot with high hopes of sealing his career with a triumph in the Royal meetings showcase race.

Alfred Watson in his preview of the race wondered if Bayardo was quite as good this year as last. His impression from his race at Chester was that he was probably not. However, he thought that Bayardo would beat all the English horses in the event that he turned up. Watson saying this seems to suggest that he might not. However, once he had passed on the Coronation Cup, and he would not have improved his reputation by much had he won that race, unless he was injured, and there was nothing to suggest anything was amiss, the Gold Cup was the only possible objective. By missing the race at Epsom Taylor and Cox must have felt confident that he could stay two and a half miles or it would be better to stay in his box at Manton. Winning the Ascot Gold Cup was considered a huge achievement. However, defeat might well tell against him more than a victory would in his favour. Watson feared that the French runners would be very dangerous. However, as he had been kept in training specifically for the Ascot Cup there seemed to be little point in prevaricating.

The Ascot Gold Cup was the highlight of the Royal meeting from its inception in 1807 until about the mid nineteen eighties and in most years – but not all – it carried the highest prize money. However, between the wars fewer and fewer classic horses were aimed at the Cup and after the Second World War it was rare that a Derby winner would ever be considered for a race which many considered unimportant from the breeding standpoint, something of greater importance, to some, than the status of winning the Cup. The last Derby winner to win the Ascot Gold Cup was Ocean Swell in 1945 and the last one to run in the race was Blakeney who finished second in 1970. In recent years the prize money has declined in real terms so that now it is worth less than both sprint races. The Ascot Gold Cup is now worth just 55% of the Cork and Orrery! Oh dear, very sorry, The Golden Jubilee Stakes. That is bad enough but it is also worth less than the Kings Stand! It is sad that the authorities now consider twenty horses stampeding to be of more visual excitement or importance than a horse showing the courage to race over two and half miles and still have the determination to win. They should however, consider this; the roar that greeted Yeats's triumphant gallop up the straight when he secured his fourth Gold Cup win was of greater intensity and joy than anything that will ever greet the finish of a sprint race even if some of the competitors have travelled halfway round the world.

The Royal meeting of 1910 will forever be known as "Black Ascot". The King, Edward VII, had died on 6 May. On the first day of the meeting *The Times* Court Circular carried the solemn reminder "Lord Churchill wishes to remind Ladies and Gentleman attending Ascot races in the Royal Enclosure that they should wear black as the period of full mourning has not yet expired." Even the race cards were edged in black. *The Daily Mirror* wrote of the opening day

> "Strange and striking were the contrasts at Ascot. The most splendid fete of the year usually had now its dominant note of mourning. No member of royalty was present, the King's pavilion had drawn blinds and closed doors and the occupants of the Royal Enclosure were in black, unrelieved save where ladies wore white flowers or had strings of pearls as the only ornament".

Bayardo was the biggest attraction of the meeting. He had of course won twice there in previous years, The New Stakes as a juvenile and the Prince Of Wales Stakes the previous year. Despite some doubters with regard to his resolution, Bayardo had a tremendous reputation and had shown his form in both outings this year. However, this did not scare away the opposition and one of the largest fields ever lined up for the race. Until

1998 thirteen runners had accepted on only three occasions. Indeed by 1910, since The Gold Cup was inaugurated in 1807, only twice has the field reached double figures, in 1867 and 1902. The reasons are not hard to understand. Because so few horses have any pretensions of winning, it was considered unwise to subject a horse to the severe preparation, considered necessary at that time, to win over such a distance, for a race they could not hope to win. There was speculation and Alfred Watson was not alone in thinking Bayardo might not run. He had not run at Epsom, presumably because he was not in good shape and his possible lack of stamina was a concern.

The elements were kind *The Sporting Life* wrote "The important question of the weather was early set at rest, a dull morning quickly developing into a brilliant afternoon, and the beauty of the day helped to swell the attendance, which especially in the Royal Enclosure, showed a considerable increase. Some relief to the funereal aspect of the scene was afforded by the straw hats in the Tattersall's Ring. Down to the junction of the courses the stands old and new were packed, while the paying division were faced by the battalions of holiday makers, who wandered at will admiring the neat turnouts of the coaching and other clubs which keep up old traditions. Brilliant weather and good going - the last important item secured by the sensible measure of keeping the trampling crowd off the course between the races – conduced to the pleasures of a most charming Cup day shorn of one of its most brilliant features, the Royal Procession".

The paddock was crowded as the field was walked round. Bayardo, was described as "looking as clean and fit as possible". "He is by no means a big horse, and his coat shone over the supple muscles working beneath like satin". *The Times* noted that "Bayardo evoked universal admiration in the paddock". *The Sporting Life* continued "Sea Sick II is a big boned upstanding bay, while Aveu is a common-looking dark bay or brown, and appeared like a hack beside Sea Sick II. Bachelors Double seemed none the worse for his previous day's exertions, which after all were no more severe than a mile winding-up gallop in preparation for this event. The field presented a pretty sight as they paraded before the stand, the bright sunshine being reflected from the horses shining coats and accentuating the bright jackets of the riders".

Alfred Watson was discussing Bayardo in the paddock with an un-named associate; "I didn't quite like the style in which he won at Newmarket" opined his friend. "Why, surely he beat Great Peter easily enough" retorted Watson; the friend hesitated before replying "Yes – I suppose he did". Clearly not everyone was expecting Bayardo to triumph!

The Ascot Gold Cup today is worth only 65% of its' 1910 value.

Ascot Heath Thursday 16th June 1910 Going : Good

Gold Cup, value £500, with £3,500 in specie, added to a sweepstakes of £20 each, h ft., of which the second received £700 and third £300 ; for entire colts and fillies, three years old and upwards. Two miles and a half, starting at the Cup Post and going once round. (59 entrants ---- £3700) (£236,800)

1	Bayardo	4 yrs	9st	D Maher	140+
2	Sea Sick II	5 yrs	9st 4lb	F O'Neill	132
3	Bachelor's Double	4yrs	9st	H Randall	131
4	Royal Realm	5 yrs	9st 4lb	Wm Griggs	128
5	Apache	3 yrs	7st 7lb (car7st 8lb)	C Trigg	121
6	Aveu	4ys	9st	C Childs	
7	Pure Gem	6yrs	9st 4lb	Walt. Griggs	
8	Southannan	6yrs	9st 4lb	H Stokes	
9	Bronzino	3yrs	7st 7lb	F Fox	
	Buckwheat	4yrs	9st	W Saxby	
	Carrousel	4yrs	9st	H Jones	
	William the Fourth	4yrs	9st	B Dillon	
	Sir Martin	4yrs	9st	J H Martin	

Betting 7-4 Bayardo, 9-2 Sir Martin, 6-1 Sea Sick II, 7-1 Bachelor's Double, 100-9 William the Fourth, 100-7 Buckwheat, 100-6 Aveu, 25-1 each Apache and Bronzino

Won by four lengths ; head second and third. Unofficially there was about two lengths between third and fourth and about the same between fourth and fifth.

Time : 4 min 23. 2/5 sec

Sporting Life race analysis;-

"Sea Sick II and Sir Martin were the first mounted in the paddock, but the parade and canter was carried out in the order the horse's names appeared on the card. What little delay occurred at the post was caused by Bayardo, Buckwheat and Pure Gem, but a good start was affected, Southannan dashing away with a four lengths' lead of Sea Sick II, Sir Martin and Bronzino, then came Pure Gem, William the Fourth, Aveu, and Buckwheat, with Carrousel at their heels in front of Royal Realm and Bayardo and Apache whipping in.

In this order they turned out of the straight, when Southannan increased his advantage over Sea Sick II to half a dozen lengths these being followed at an interval of two lengths by Aveu then in close company came Bronzino and Sir Martin while after another gap William the Fourth headed Royal Realm and Buckwheat and next in a group came Pure Gem, Carrousel and Bayardo with Apache still acting as whipper in.

Bayardo travelled on a tight rein in the ruck until seven furlongs from home where Maher let him have his head; and the favourite then drew up quickly on the outside. Before reaching the Brick Kilns, Bayardo raced up and headed Southannan the pair being attended by Sea Sick II, Pure Gem, Aveu, and Buckwheat, with Bachelor's Double coming through rapidly, while Sir Martin dropped back and joined Carrousel in the rear.

Bayardo came into the line for home with the race well won, having as attendants Sea Sick II and Bachelor's Double, the latter of whom was second at the Spagnoletti board, but let the Frenchman pass him again close home. Neither, however, could stretch the favourite at the finish, Mr Fairie's horse winning in a canter by four lengths".

The official distance of four lengths would seem to be an underestimate. There are two photographs of the finish and both seem to suggest that the distance was nearer six.

The above report indicates that Maher let Bayardo have his head. However, there is strong evidence that he did no such thing and that the decision to move quickly to the front seven furlongs out was made by Bayardo. This will be discussed in detail later.

Bayardo's time was very fast about a fifth of a second outside the course record. It was about seven and a half seconds faster than the median for the period from 1900 until the Great War and about thirteen seconds faster than for the period from 1889 until 1900. A fast time in itself means no more than that the race was truly run and the going fast. However, what this does prove beyond any doubt was that Bayardo was required to truly stay the distance. Some renewals of the Ascot Gold Cup in the past had been run in much slower times. Persimmon, a great horse, won in four minutes and thirty four seconds and Isinglass, equally as great, sauntered round in four minutes and fifty nine seconds! This is not to claim that Bayardo was a better Cup winner than those two mentioned. That opinion is for those who saw all the renewals of the period. However, it is clear that Bayardo could not have won the Cup unless he possessed high class stamina.

Bayardo's starting price reflected the opinion of many that a horse with such brilliant speed would not stay two and a half miles. His potential lack of stamina also probably accounts for the large field. The presence of a brilliant and strongly fancied French stayer would also have had its effect on his price.

Alec Taylor, like his father before him, had an outstanding record in staying races and could not have been more confident. Bayardo was in prime condition and cut an impressive figure in the paddock, where, as contemporary reports indicate, judges considered that he looked outstanding. It is unlikely that Taylor ever had him in better shape. Clearly the problems relating to his absence at Epsom could not have been all that serious. He even showed his well being and high spirits by dropping Maher at the start. This was not to be the only indignity Bayardo inflicted on his jockey that afternoon.

The *Sporting Life* race analysis tells only part of the story. Other observations help in understanding the events of a race which was the pinnacle of Bayardo's career.

When the race was underway, Maher as usual kept Bayardo well back in the early stages. At halfway he was still nearer last than first but, importantly, he was still on the bit. He improved his position a little, and then, with six furlongs to go Bayardo was seen to make his decisive move. However, there is considerable evidence that far from Maher giving him his head it was Bayardo who took the decision and, suddenly taking hold of his bit, and with Maher powerless to prevent him, he produced a sensational burst of speed which powered him to the front. The race was as good as over, providing of course Bayardo could stay the trip. He swept majestically round the final bend into the straight clear of his pursuers and although the admirable Sea Sick at no stage gave in, Bayardo galloped resolutely up the straight, eventually easing down and cantering over the line, to a triumphant and emphatic victory. His time was a fifth of a second outside the course record. There is little doubt that had he been in any way pressed in the final furlong he would have broken it. One observer noted "His space-devouring stride at the finish had in it not the slightest indication that he had galloped this long and tiring course". The *Sporting World* in its Turf Notes by *Semper Vigilans* (always vigilant) was of the view that the "Gold Cup distance could have been doubled".

The Times noted that Bayardo "Passed the others simply at his leisure. When the turn into the straight for home was made the bearer of Mr Fairie's white, orange sleeves and cap was galloping comfortably in front, and, sweeping on without a semblance of effort, won by four lengths, a distance which might have been very considerably increased had it been necessary".

This was Bayardo's greatest moment in many respects. He demonstrated incontrovertibly that he possessed not just a brilliant turn of foot, after all, that had not been in dispute even by those most critical of him, but of his will to win. This was truly a great horse deserving of his place amongst the very best, with not just ability, speed and stamina but, crucially, also courage. There can be little doubt that had he not run in the Gold Cup he would have retired to stud with his reputation impaired, with no little thanks to Danny Maher. Far from hating to be in front he demonstrated exactly the opposite. By taking matters into his own hands and racing, with obvious enthusiasm, for the last six furlongs in front and alone, Bayardo gave every indication that, as far as he was concerned, this was a very pleasant way to spend a sunny summer afternoon!

This was Bayardo's triumph more so than it was Maher's and it was in all probability not without some embarrassment for him. It was well known that it was Maher, who had propagated the idea that Bayardo hated being in front, and that it was therefore essential that he was held up and not shown any daylight until the last possible moment. His antics on the Rowley Mile gave rise to a theory that he disliked seeing a clear open expanse in front of him. In the circumstances when Bayardo, it seems, metaphorically raising the fingers of scorn to his rider, burst to the front, he was making a clear statement that he thought he knew more about how he should be ridden than his famous jockey. There seems no doubt that it was Bayardo who took the decision to make so dramatic a move and it was astonishing that Maher did not learn his lesson and his attempt to answer criticism, and justify his obdurate opinion in a future race, was to bring future opprobrium.

Why did Bayardo suddenly make his move as he did? Without getting into the realms of anthropomorphism, it can only be speculation. One possible explanation lies in Bayardo's level of fitness. It would seem that Alec Taylor had produced him on the day to perfection. He had demonstrated his well being and high spirits by dropping Maher at the start. It is worth bearing in mind that this was the first time he had run in a race longer than a mile and six furlongs. It seems possible that a combination of the slower pace of an extreme staying race combined with him feeling so well resulted in Bayardo becoming bored and simply feeling that he had to go quicker. That he chose to go considerably faster only indicates how good he was and confirms that he had a mind of his own. In other words it was simply *"Joie de vivre"*!

The opposition was strong. Even in those days the French had a good record in the race. The unfortunately named five year old Sea Sick II, whose sire Elf II had won the Gold Cup in 1898, was considered by his connections to be unbeatable. He had won the French Derby in a dead-heat in 1908. The previous year, amongst six wins from nine races, he was unbeaten in races from two miles to three miles seven furlongs. His wins included Prix de Longchamps, Prix de Chantilly and the Prix Gladiateur. In addition he was second in the Prix du President de la Republique, over twelve furlongs, which was worth almost £5,000 (£320,000). He was already a winner over two and a half miles this year, guaranteed to stay and clearly a very worthy adversary and he would have been an outstanding challenger in any year. However, it was evident to all before the race that Sea Sick would have no chance of out-speeding Bayardo. However, it was beyond doubt that if Bayardo had lacked stamina, Sea Sick II would have ruthlessly exposed any such limitations.

Bachelors Double's three races so far that year had been the City and Suburban handicap, which he won, the Coronation Cup where he was second, both at Epsom and remarkably the Royal Hunt Cup the previous day which he won! It is hardly surprising horses in the past are considered more durable than today, such a thing would be thought insane nowadays. Running a horse on successive days is nothing exceptional. However, running a horse over a mile one day and two and a half the next most certainly is! It could only be more reckless if the races had been the other way round. Afterwards he won a valuable stakes race at Liverpool from three more starts. He had easily won the Irish Derby the previous year.

Pure Gem failed to win any of his seven races that year and was sent to Russia. Southannan, who was used as a pacemaker for William the Fourth, won two handicaps out of nine races. Royal Realm won a handicap and a plate from thirteen races. The French horse Aveu won two races. Buckwheat won a handicap and a plate from five starts. Carrousel won a moderate handicap from four starts. William the Fourth, who broke down, had run in the Chester Vase.

It would have been no surprise if Bayardo had given Sir Martin a wide berth having nearly fallen over him in the Derby the previous year! Perhaps Bayardo sudden burst of speed was due to him noticing Sir Martin and feeling that he should get away from him as soon as possible! Sir Martin raced only once, apart from Ascot, when winning the Coronation Cup at Epsom a win that to some extent redeemed his reputation which always seemed to be just that bit higher than his ability. He was not bred to stay, found the distance too far, and was eased down. It was thought that his exertions in the Gold Cup were as such that he never recovered. Apache won a minor Stakes and a Handicap from eleven races. Bronzino, did not give his running. He had won two of his eight races, the Greenham Stakes at Newbury and the Doncaster Cup. In addition he finished third in the Grand Prix de Paris and second in the St Leger.

It is interesting to read the contemporary views of Alfred Watson. His observations made about a week after the race make fascinating reading.

"I am inclined to fancy that Bayardo astonished everybody last week. Of course, Mr Fairie has always had a tremendous opinion of the horse, and Alec Taylor has seen him every day for years past. They must have known something like what he was; but nothing that happens on a horse's own training ground can demonstrate just what he will do in the course of a race for the Ascot Cup against a good representative field. That is the point – the "good representative field". At home perhaps the cup horse gallops with a couple of others, and there is something to jump in and lead him for the last mile. You never get the conditions in private that you get in public, and that is why I doubt whether anybody could be confident Bayardo had it in him to give the electrifying exhibition which will make his victory memorable. Why Maher has ridden him in the style with which we were familiar before Ascot, it is utterly impossible to guess. On the morning of the cup day an owner who is among the very best judges of horses and racing that I have ever met, and who, moreover, happens to be particularly well acquainted with the Manton stable, replied to my question whether he intended to back Bayardo with an unhesitating negative, and he added, "I will never back a horse that is not genuine for an Ascot Cup!"

That was the impression of Bayardo that he entertained. It may be that all Maher's wins on Bayardo have been miracles of unexampled genius in the way of jockeyship. The effect they have had is that just indicated. He has always striven to keep the colt behind others, and the well-nigh universally accepted explanation was that he "Did not want to let Bayardo see what he had to do". There can be no sort of doubt that if any accident had prevented Bayardo from running for the Cup, he would have left the Turf under a strong suspicion of being a rogue, or at least of having a decided tendency to roguishness, and this because of the way in which Maher has been pleased to ride him.

Now we all know how utterly unjust such a suspicion would be. No horse that ever trod on racing plates could have given a more gallant and impressive exhibition. The days have long since passed when French horses were lightly esteemed, and a particularly accomplished trainer's opinion with regard to Sea Sick II was that he would prove invincible. He stays, he has speed, he had never been so well in his life. He was genuine, and in France they knew, or thought they knew, all about Bayardo's suspected inclination to turn it up if he saw a long stretch of galloping ground in front of him. It has now been proved that he has not this inclination; but why on earth has Maher apparently been so careful to persuade us that he has had? I am quite certain that the suspicion would have influenced his stud prospects".

"Maher had been much nearer last than first for half the journey, and it was not until about a mile from home that somebody near me remarked "Bayardo is going up a bit." He had improved his position and was fifth or sixth then, some six furlongs from home, Bayardo shot out in a fashion which can only be described as phenomenal. Maher had won in half a dozen strides. Of course, there was a good distance still to go, but practically the race was over. Bayardo led round the bend, sweeping on with effortless ease. Sea Sick was by no means done with. He still galloped steadily on without the least sign of flagging; Bachelor's Double evoked profound amazement by sticking resolutely to the Frenchman.

But their endeavours to live with Bayardo were really absurd. It had been asked whether he could stay. Here he was, after going over two miles in time which misses the cup record by the fraction of a second, striding out as freely and freshly as if the race were just beginning. But oh, why has Maher done such cruel injustice to the horse and allowed such a totally false view of him to gain currency? His refusals to go the post at Newmarket, more than once obliging his jockey to take him round by the back of the stands, were put down to an idea that he "did not like racing". Last year we saw how Maher jammed him into the heels of other horses. He looked so magnificent at Ascot that it seems folly to back anything else to beat him, and I had previously expressed a conviction that he would win for reasons which I gave – a defeat would do him much more harm than a victory". He concludes "Everyone will now most readily accord Bayardo a place among the very best known in the history of the turf".

It is clear Watson had no doubt it was Bayardo who took the decision to quicken when he did. Alec Taylor who knew the horse and his quirks better than anyone, Maher included, also had no doubt and said as much after the Goodwood Cup the following month. Taylor was a very relieved man after the race. He was asked if he felt very proud. He replied "I do, but I am glad it is all over". Taylor had been under a tremendous strain over the previous two months. First Lemberg was beaten in the Two Thousand Guineas then Taylor won the Derby and Oaks with Lemberg and Rosedrop respectively, before preparing Bayardo for the Ascot Gold Cup, a task which almost certainly caused him the greatest strain. After the race Alfred Cox led Bayardo into the winning enclosure and after patting the horse on the neck he smote Alec Taylor affectionately on the back. This uncharacteristic display of emotion was a gesture which spoke more eloquently than any words. He knew only too well the debt he owed to his trainer who had brought his champion to a peak for the greatest challenge and triumph of certainly Bayardo's career and also Taylor's at that time in his career and in retrospect very possibly the greatest of his whole career. Taylor like his father before him was outstanding in staying races and that year in addition to the Gold Cup he trained the winners of the Chester Cup, Ascot Stakes and Northumberland Plate

Theodore Felstead writing some years later, with reference to Taylor's frequent arguments with Maher over the riding of Bayardo, suggests that Maher was responding to yet another request not to hold him up. This is possible, but very unlikely. This was the twenty second time Maher had ridden Bayardo in a race. Alec Taylor was always worried about Bayardo's sensitive feet and was at pains to tell Maher to look after him particularly if the going was fast. However, he had also often asked him not to leave matters until the last moment and he had always refused to change his tactics. Why would Maher, after ignoring all previous requests, suddenly accede and choose to give Bayardo his head in the Ascot Gold Cup, over two and a half miles, on fast ground he was considered not to relish and when he was a potentially doubtful stayer? It should not be forgotten his sire Bay Ronald had finished distressed after the race. This was surely the one race when he SHOULD have held him up to ensure he stayed the trip and was not inconvenienced by the ground before trying to out speed Sea Sick. It is inconceivable that Maher would change the habits of a lifetime and suddenly decide seven furlongs from the finish to make a move and rush from mid division to the front. It would have been entirely out of character in any circumstances, but particularly so in view of the uncertainty about Bayardo staying the trip. If left to himself, Maher would surely have tracked Sea Sick and tried to out-speed him inside the final furlong.

After his juvenile career Bayardo raced eighteen times. However, in reality only five of these were of crucial importance to his place in history. These were the 2000 Guineas, Derby, Eclipse Stakes and St Leger as a three year old and the Ascot Gold Cup as a four year old. He was beaten in the first two and won the next two. The only point in keeping Bayardo in training as a four year old was to win the Ascot Cup. If he had been defeated his status would have been considerably diminished. Maher would have been perfectly aware of this. Had he decided to rush Bayardo to the front and he had proved a non-stayer and Sea Sick II outstayed him it is not difficult to imagine the embarrassment this would have caused him particularly as he had always maintained that the way to ride Bayardo was to hold him up to the last possible moment so that crucially he did not see any daylight. There is little point in labouring the matter any further as the evidence that Bayardo had been in control and not Maher is overwhelming and that he had acted *ex mero motu*.

There can be little argument that Bayardo's performance was not just one of the best but probably the best performance ever in the Gold Cup. Had Bayardo not run in the race then Sea Sick, who was confidently expected by connections to win, would have been heralded as, at the very least, an above average winner. His record was as good as many previous winners and better than most yet Bayardo easily out speeded and then out stayed him to win easing down! Over the years many Gold Cups have been won by horses that stayed well but often they beat horses that did not have the stamina for such a long race. This was certainly not the case in Bayardo's year as Sea Sick had demonstrated that he stayed and could win over distances exceeding three miles. The notable turf writer William Allison was in no doubt when he wrote some years later "Bayardo was one of the best horses of all time. No Ascot Gold Cup was ever – in my time - won quite so easily as was Bayardo's." Allison's experience covered racing from the 1860's until the 1920's and it is a considerable complement for him to say that and suggest that Bayardo was at the very least the equal and possibly superior, at staying distances, to past winners of the calibre of Gladiateur, Isonomy, who won it twice, St Simon, Isinglass and Persimmon. Bayardo's performance was impressive indeed if Allison considered it superior to that of St Simon a great horse, some consider possibly the greatest, and, one who was never beaten.

The rating given to Bayardo's performance in the Cup is 140. However, In *A Century of Champions* his rating is given as 141. This rating was almost certainly given for his performance in the Ascot Gold Cup and probably relies to a degree on an estimate of how far he would have won if he had not been eased and that he probably won by more than the judge decreed. Over a distance of two and a half miles a length equates to not much more than a pound. It is not stretching matters too far to imagine that if asked he may have extended his superiority from an official four lengths, probably between five and six in actuality, to possibly eight lengths, one observer felt the winning distance could have been doubled, which would give him a rating of between 140 and 143. Whilst in the circumstances a rating of 141 seems fair enough, it is not unreasonable to argue that he could have been rated higher and a rating of 142 has been allocated on the basis that he could have won by about two more lengths further if pushed out rather than eased.

Many thought this would have been a good time to retire Bayardo. However, Alfred Cox was never one to allow his horses to idle and further triumphs were planned. With the Gold Cup won it was no surprise that he was withdrawn from the Hardwicke Stakes the following day. Bayardo may have enjoyed his triumph at Ascot but if he had imagined a life of ease from now on he was soon to be disillusioned!

CHAPTER 13

Inglorious Goodwood

Bayardo had not been entered for the Eclipse Stakes, as that was a race Alfred Cox would have wanted to win with Bayardo's half brother Lemberg (he dead heated for first place). In the event, as part of his preparation for the Goodwood Cup he took up an entry for a modest race at Newmarket on the July course.

After a short break Bayardo was back in work. On the 4th July he went fourteen furlongs solo and on the 7th "a good striding gallop" over twelve furlongs. On the 10th he went twelve furlongs at a "good pace" and for good measure he was led the last six furlongs by Avico, who was moderate enough not to have tested Bayardo too much!

Newmarket on the July course at the height of summer is a wonderful place to be! It is one of the few racecourses that people from Bayardo's time could revisit today and have no difficulty in knowing where they are. The unchanging aspects of the July course make it the place it is. Even the introduction of the egregious Friday night concerts that take place after racing can't spoil the beauty although the concerts do not provide a restful atmosphere on those evenings. The area to the rear of the grandstands has undergone a considerable facelift in recent years and the management must be congratulated on the sympathetic way in which the course has been modernised without destroying the atmosphere. Partly paid for, it has to be said, by the said concerts. However, it would astound a race-goer from Bayardo's time to see the view of the course from the members stand partly obscured by the trappings of the concert platform. They would ask - as do members today - which is more important the racing or the concerts? A reply from the management is still awaited! The racing is not consistently top class and indeed some meetings are unworthy of a grade one course. However, the main meeting held in the first half of July is always up to standard apart from the inclusion of too many high-value, ferociously competitive handicaps which race-course executives and bookmakers seem to be obsessed with. Despite there being nine handicaps in three days Newmarket is by no means the worst perpetuator of this.

Bayardo won very comfortably, a canter according to McCalls. This was a very good performance but just how good is hard to judge. How close to his best was Royal Realm? If he was anywhere near then this could be rated in handicap terms as Bayardo's finest performance of his entire career. The Spaniard raced only three times that year failing to win

Newmarket Tuesday 12th July Going : Good

Dullingham Plate of £1,000, of which the second received £100 and the third £50 ; by subscription of £20, or £5 if declared, with £515 added ; for three year olds and upwards. Suffolk Stakes Course, one mile and a half. (37entrants, viz. 20 at £20 and 17 at £5---- £850.) (£54,400)

1	Bayardo	4yrs	10st 8lb	D Maher	134++
2	The Spaniard	3yrs	7st 12lb	C Trigg	106
3	Royal Realm	5yrs	10st 1lb	Wm Griggs	115
4	Gog	3yrs	8st 1lb	F Wells	
5	Buckwheat	4 yrs	10 st 4lb	W Saxby	
6	Lagos	5yrs	10st 6lb	B Dillon	

Betting 1-8 Bayardo, 100-6 Royal Realm, 20-1 The Spaniard, 50-1 each Lagos and Buckwheat, 500-1 Gog

Won by a length ; five lengths second and third.

Time : 2 min 37. 4/5 sec

Sporting Life race analysis;-

"Bayardo cut out the work with a two length lead of Royal Realm and The Spaniard, Buckwheat being some half a dozen lengths in the rear of Gog. The last named moved up ahead of Lagos when they entered the line for home and though The Spaniard deprived Royal Realm of second place in the last furlong he had no chance of overhauling Bayardo who made all the running and won by a length".

and achieving little apart from this, his final race of the year. Bayardo was conceding twenty three pounds more than weight for age to The Spaniard and he beat him as he should have done. In the absence of any extended distances it is probably best to assume that Royal Realm was below his best. Even making allowance for that beating him easily by six lengths giving him seven pounds amounts to a seventeen pounds beating.

However, the biggest surprise is that Maher made all the running, in a race with more than three runners, for the first time since Bayardo was a juvenile. Had he realised that he did not need holding up and was quite happy to make the pace? Did Alec Taylor point out that after Ascot it was unnecessary to use extreme waiting tactics? Either way, Maher must have thought Bayardo was happy on the July course and he was either confident enough to make the running or felt he was in no position after Ascot to employ extreme waiting tactics. Again either way Alec Taylor must have viewed this with some relief knowing that Maher could not get into any trouble. One thing was now beyond dispute. However many races Bayardo would contest in future Maher could no longer claim that he must be held up and come with a late run. What was now obvious to everyone was that Bayardo was happy to be in front either from the start of taking the lead some way out.

This was Bayardo's only appearance on the July course and unlike the Rowley Mile he would not seem to have felt any great dislike for it!

Perhaps the beauty of the July course and more relaxed atmosphere was more top his liking!

It is almost certain that Bayardo's next race at glorious Goodwood was not going to be his last race. In addition to Goodwood he held an entry for the Atlantic Stakes at Liverpool the week before the Glorious meeting. Ironically it was decided not to take up this option even though the first prize was twice that for the winner of the Goodwood Cup. The Atlantic Stakes was won easily by Bachelor's Double who had of course been easily beaten by Bayardo in the Ascot Gold Cup. It may have been that Cox preferred to race Bayardo at the picturesque Sussex Downs course rather than Liverpool which for all its history could not be compared to the aesthetic charms of Goodwood.

The signs were not good on the day of the race and a possible disaster might have been foreseen. Bayardo's feet were again giving trouble and on the morning Joe Lawson took him for a canter on the Downs. He went tenderly and on returning to the stables he said to Alec Taylor; "This horse is not fit to run. It's just asking for trouble". Taylor's reply was "He's got to run, even if he only has one leg". Evidently Cox had made up his mind to run and Taylor felt that he must be obeyed. It was equally ominous that Bayardo was sweating in the paddock and clearly not on good terms with either himself, or the rest of the world, and he refused to pass the judge during the parade and Maher dismounted and led him by. As Bayardo had refused to walk or canter in the right direction someone suggested that in future it would be better to point him in the opposite direction to the one required and then perhaps he would obligingly turn to the correct one! Oh dear, our old hero did not help himself on occasions!

Bayardo's final race was therefore a tragedy and a fiasco and should have been little more than light exercise for him, even allowing for the state of his tender feet. The time was very fast. It was about five seconds faster than the median from the period from 1900 until the Great War and about seventeen seconds faster than the median for the period 1888 until 1900.

The three year old colt Magic was un-raced as a juvenile and at the time of this race he had finished second in the Wood Ditton at Newmarket and unplaced at Ascot in the Vase. Afterwards he failed to win any of his three races, including the Cesarewitch where he was unplaced, and was then retired. This therefore was his only win. However, he should not be underrated as he finished second in a good stakes race and the handicapper was sufficiently impressed by his Goodwood Cup win to allocate him 7 stone 10 lbs as a three-year-old for the Cesarewitch. The top weight that year was 8 stone 13 lbs allocated to a four-year-old and as a three-year-old should have received thirteen pounds then Magic carried just four pounds off top weight. It can therefore be readily seen that as the race

Goodwood Thursday 28th July Going : Good

Goodwood Cup of £1,000 (50 gns. of which is in plate) with a sweepstakes of £50 each, h ft., (to fund) ; second received £200 and the third £100 out of the stakes ; for three year olds and upwards. Two and a half miles. (33 entrants------£740) (£47,360) By permission of the Stewards of the Jockey Club the starting gate has been dispensed with for this race.

1	Magic	3yrs	7st 2lb	F Rickaby, jun.	115
2	Bayardo	4yrs	9st 10lb	D Maher	132
3	Bud	3yrs	7st 4lb	F Fox	

Betting 1-20 Bayardo, 20-1 Magic
Won by a neck ; bad third
Time : 4 min 54. 4/5 sec

Sporting life race analysis;-

"On leaving the paddock Bayardo showed temper and had to be dismounted and led in the parade. Maher got on him opposite the ring and rode him on a short preliminary to the post. There was no further delay and Magic went away at a steady pace from Bud, Bayardo being some three lengths behind the pair. Out of the straight the three went in indian file there being some three lengths between them. Approaching the loop the outsiders went away some ten lengths from Bayardo who on reappearing in sight had closed on Bud. Into the straight Bayardo got within two lengths of Magic and a quarter of mile out just headed him but Magic stayed on well with amazing stamina held the favourite at bay".

turned out Bayardo would need to have been close to his best to have won the Goodwood Cup. His performance was not far below his best and with a better ride he should have prevailed despite the poor condition of his feet and his obvious ill-temper. Bud, a three year old filly, had won one of her six races as a juvenile. At three, she had before the race, won an apprentice plate from five outings. She did not race again afterwards and was sent to France.

Magic had been given a strong and thorough preparation. In the race Fred Rickary, junior, perhaps encouraged by the owner and trainer who thought he had a chance and backed him accordingly, made the running. Setting a strong pace he intelligently gave him a breather whenever they met rising ground. In spite of Ascot and Newmarket on his latest run, or perhaps because of it, Maher, possibly and correctly deciding that the pace set by Magic was fast enough, reverted to his old tactics and held Bayardo up. However, with the distance between him and the leader put conservatively at about half a furlong by some and sixteen lengths by a *Sporting Life* observer, he was guilty of lying too far out of his ground, if that does not sound something of an understatement. Incredibly, Maher made no attempt to close the gap and as Magic came down the straight Bayardo had a seemingly impossible task ahead of him. He was giving away thirty six pounds, including twenty pounds weight for age, plus the distance. It is one of racings timeless aphorisms that you can "give away weight but not distance". Yet here was Maher apparently happy to surrender both without any obvious sign of concern! When finally he woke up to the danger Bayardo made a gallant and heroic effort to close the gap. He produced a wonderful burst of speed which took him level with Magic and possibly a short head in front, but the effort took its toll and he was unable to hold his advantage until the line, and, as they passed the judge's box he was a neck down.

Alec Taylor who was not known for his criticism of jockeys blamed Maher unequivocally "Maher let Magic get a furlong in front and never attempted to close the tremendous gap until reaching the comparatively short straight, and he was giving away all that weight too" he said. Alfred Cox, who it must be remembered was a great supporter of Maher, was also very unimpressed. This was probably the beginning of the disintegration of their relationship. It was finally severed after the St. Leger when Maher rode what Cox considered an injudicious race on Bayardo's half brother, the Derby winner, Lemberg.

After the Goodwood Cup a disconsolate Maher said "I expected him (Magic) to stop. Who would have thought it?" It is a pity that Bayardo's association with Maher ended on such a sad note. On the whole Maher served Bayardo well for most of his two and three year old career. However, in his final year Bayardo raced five times and on balance Maher did not ride him well. In three of them he gave Bayardo two much to do and on two occasions he was fortunate to win. At Newmarket after interference and at Chester when he was shuffled back and at Goodwood he was beaten after Maher's dreadfully injudicious ride. On the July course Maher made all, a sensible option when on the best horse in a moderate race. At Ascot of course Bayardo took the vital decisions with regard to tactics himself! By way of conclusion the manner of Maher's riding at Goodwood seems to offer further confirmation that he was not responsible for initiating Bayardo's burst of speed at Ascot. If he had been he would not have held Bayardo up so far behind at Goodwood. He would have taken the lead some way out knowing that Bayardo was happy to be in front, something he knew from his previous race at Newmarket. The inevitable conclusion is that it would appear that Maher was trying to prove he was right after all and the consequences were there for all to see.

Criticizing jockeys is a popular pastime for all race-goers and punters. If an individual has invested hard earned money and the jockey has looked to have displayed poor judgement then the punter is within his rights to complain and express his view. However, mindless abuse is irritating and contemptible. A jockey weighs about 110 to 120 pounds (50-54 kg) whereas the horse weighs about 1,200 pounds (544 kg). Any misjudgement however minor can't be rectified in an instant and jockeys are frequently required to make split second decisions and he will not always make the right one. If they make a wrong choice there may not be time to correct his horse and place it where he wishes.

Punters should remember this. However, the one mistake which most punters will not forgive is laying too far off the pace. Usually this is because the horse is possibly a non-stayer and the jockey wants to make sure the horse stays the trip. This is hard to understand. Surely the best tactics in these circumstances are to ride the horse working on the assumption that it does stay and if it doesn't at least something is learnt. Sometimes it is because the horse "needs holding up". That is fine, but why at the rear? Why not mid-division? In any event the most important aspect of riding a horse is to ensure that it settles into a rhythm and does not waste energy fighting its rider. Coming fast at the finish from way off the pace and being beaten narrowly is exasperating. Maher did this at Chester and was fortunate that Bayardo's turn of foot rescued him.

Some jockeys on occasions have not enjoyed such good fortune. Greville Starkey was an outstanding jockey. Unfortunately he is sometimes best remembered for losing the Derby on Dancing Brave because he held him up at the rear and came with a late run which failed. Lester Piggott would never have ridden any horse in the Derby in that fashion and Walter Swinburn, who rode the perfect race, won on the inferior Shahrastani. This was a travesty because Dancing Brave was a great horse who should never have been beaten. Unfortunately there was no second chance and Starkey's reward was to be replaced as jockey.

Maher rode an absurd race because he badly misjudged the pace of the race. With Magic setting a fast pace there would have been no reason to make the running himself. But surely he could have sat in second place no more than four or five lengths behind. From his comments he obviously thought Magic was setting too fast a pace and that it was unsustainable. Had he realized that Magic was not running flat out but taking a breather on the uphill sections he would surely have had Bayardo closer. It seems that Maher was caught napping and he was forced to use up all of Bayardo's speed and energy just to close the gap. He made the error for which most racing observers agree that jockeys are fully deserving of execration, particularly on a 1-20 chance.

Trying to look at matters from Maher's point of view he was unlucky. In almost any other race he would have got away with his ride, however injudicious, in the Goodwood Cup. However, it seems clear that Bayardo was not in the best of moods possibly because his feet were troubling him and was clearly not in the same form he had been at Ascot and may simply have been indicating that either he was not happy because he was uncomfortable or that he no longer enjoyed racing. Maher, who, lest it be forgotten in this frenzy of criticism, was a wonderful rider with beautiful hands, may have sensed this and as Taylor had probably told him about the morning gallop Maher may have been trying to conserve

Bayardo as much as possible. As he had been fractious and sweating in the preliminaries it must have looked obvious that as all was not well. However, even when allowance is made for all possibilities there can be few if any observers that do not feel that Maher should have had Bayardo nearer Magic well before the straight.

The distance of the Goodwood Cup is given as two and a half miles. This is because that was the official distance. However, observers noted that it always took about fifteen to twenty seconds longer to run the same distance at Goodwood than at Ascot. Eventually the authorities at Goodwood were persuaded to re-measure the Cup course and discovered that it was two miles five and half furlongs. From then on it was described as about two miles five furlongs.

Reflecting on Bayardo when he had retired to stud, Alec Taylor said, "He was a horse of moods, he could be very different some days to others. But he would always run his race out. I think the greatest performance I ever saw a horse do was put up by Bayardo on one occasion. Maher had him lengths behind, and it looked impossible for him to win. Even then he had to be brought up wide on the outside and be given a hard finish to win a head when he could have won by many lengths". (This race was probably the Chester Vase). "I always told Maher the day would come when something awful would happen through overdoing the waiting and waiting." But Maher would always reply "But I know the horse too well. He doesn't like to be in front." Taylor went on "The reply to that was what happened in the race for the Gold Cup at Ascot. Bayardo just carried him to the front, and the more he got to the front the more he won by. That upset Maher's theory once and for all, but he had forgotten the lesson when we got to Goodwood later in the summer." Note that Taylor said Bayardo carried Maher to the front at Ascot. Here is further confirmation that Bayardo was in charge during the Ascot Gold Cup.

The Goodwood Cup was sad but did no harm to Bayardo's reputation. However, the same can't be said for Danny Maher. The way he rode the race suggested that he was keen to answer his critics and prove that he was right about the best way to ride Bayardo, despite making all the running in his previous race. Bayardo, though was so far behind Magic he would not have been able to see him and must have thought he was in front! Had Maher managed to get Bayardo's head in front on the line it would have been a considerable triumph for him. As it was he was made to look foolish as the jockey who messed up on a 1-20 chance in a three runner race.

It may appear strange that Alfred Cox having decided that Bayardo should continue after the Ascot Gold Cup did not race him again after Goodwood in order to retire him on a high note. Unfortunately he had only two engagements left, both at Newmarket during the autumn, in the Champion and Limekiln Stakes. Bayardo had won both races the previous year and as Cox would have wanted to win the former with Lemberg (he did) it would have meant keeping Bayardo in training for a further three months for what would at best have been a pointless mismatch or an anticlimactic walkover, or worse still possibly witnessing Bayardo complete his career by refusing to race! He had not been left in the Jockey Club Stakes which was a £10,000 (£640,000) race over one mile and six furlongs. This may have had something to do with his dislike of the Rowley mile. Perhaps even Alfred Cox had decided his nerves could only take so much! He could have been entered for the Doncaster Cup which would have been an appropriate finale, at the scene of his St Leger triumph, assuming of course that any opposition had stood its ground. Similarly he could have been entered for the Jockey Club Cup. However, this would have posed the same problem as running in the Limekiln Stakes, keeping him in training for either a mismatch or a walkover.

It is almost certain though that Cox did not decide immediately after Goodwood to retire Bayardo. He was back in work and went a mile at "half speed" on the 3rd August and ten furlongs at a "good pace" on the 7th and twelve furlongs at a "good striding gallop" on the 8th. This schedule would not suggest he had been retired and was winding down! However, that was the last strong work he was noted doing and afterwards he was seen taking only "walking" exercise. It can only be conjecture but Bayardo's mood before the Goodwood Cup together with his problematic feet, which turned out to be laminitis don't forget, may have influenced matters and the decision to retire him was probably not taken until the end of September.

Bayardo retired with, in theory, nothing left to prove. However, it would have been interesting if he could have raced against better three year olds in his final season. The ones he met were beaten easily with the obvious exception of Magic and with the weight and distance concession he was obviously considerably superior to him. Alfred Cox would never have permitted him to race against Lemberg and, although there can be little doubt that Bayardo was better, not by all that much. Curiously had there been no Lemberg, Bayardo would probably have won more races as a four year old. Bayardo was entered for both the Eclipse and Champion Stakes and whilst he would have needed to be at his best to win the Eclipse he would have had only Dean Swift to beat in the Champion Stakes. Cox allowed Lemberg to run in these races as a four year old and in similar circumstances would probably have done the same with Bayardo. The best three year olds of 1910 were Lemberg, Neil Gow and Swynford. Although all form lines, admittedly some rather tenuous, indicate that Bayardo was superior to each of them, it would have removed any doubt it they could have met. Bayardo could have raced against Lemberg and Neil Gow in the Eclipse but Swynford did not run in any race where he could have met Bayardo.

The saddest aspect of his final race was that Bayardo had to retire from racing on a note of anticlimax. However, any doubters had been silenced by his brilliant performance in the Ascot Gold Cup and he went to stud with his reputation high, as a racehorse of superlative merit, courage and character.

CHAPTER 14

Retirement

So there ended the racing career of a great if somewhat complex horse. It was governed by three individuals all with strong determined characters. Throw in Bayardo's not exactly straight forward traits and in the circumstances it is probably a little surprising that, with the potential for disagreement, in the end he managed to win twenty two of his twenty five races. There seems little doubt that his training was controlled by Alec Taylor and as such he can take credit for preparing him so well for each race. However, Alfred Cox would seem to have been in control of where and when he ran and Taylor would have had to adapt his training schedule to accommodate his demands. In his races tactics would seem to have been left entirely to Danny Maher, no shrinking violet and quite capable of defending his corner with a stubborn streak thrown in for good measure. It is a matter of speculation but nonetheless irresistible to wonder about the conversations between the various parties over each issue. There was probably very little argument during his juvenile career which was a succession of triumphs. Only during the early part of his three year old career would there have been any grounds for discord.

There can be little doubt that given total control Taylor would not have attempted to prepare Bayardo for the Two Thousand Guineas after his various setbacks once it became obvious that he was too backward and not progressing quickly enough. The decision to run was unquestionably Cox's. Unconstrained by Cox, Taylor would then have had more time to prepare for the Derby which was undoubtedly the more important race. History may have been different as even Minoru's trainer Richard Marsh conceded. Marsh himself in conjunction with the then Prince of Wales and his advisors were faced with a similar problem in 1896 when Persimmon was backward and unlikely to be ready for the Guineas. They had taken the sensible decision to bypass the Guineas for the Derby which they won together with the St Leger. Had Cox listened to Taylor and Bayardo been able to produce his best on Derby day he would automatically be considered at least the equal, not physically it is conceded, Persimmon was an outstanding example of the thoroughbred, but in terms of ability with that great horse. Had Bayardo won the Derby and the St. Leger he would have automatically joined the greats and his status in the elite strata secure. It is also certain that left to Taylor Bayardo would not have run in the Goodwood Cup.

Alfred Cox was very fond of Bayardo, however, his view that he could ignore the advice of one of the greatest trainers of all time almost certainly cost Bayardo the chance of an unbeaten career something achieved by barely a handful of champions. It is hard not to conclude that had Cox simply enjoyed owning a great horse and Maher allowed himself to be guided by Taylor with regard to riding tactics, Bayardo's career would have been viewed differently. Taylor never felt that there was any justification for Maher holding up Bayardo in the manner he did. Taylor only concern was that Maher looked after Bayardo's feet. Had Taylor been left with the responsibility for making all the important decisions in his career Bayardo's would have been undoubtedly better for it. The inevitable conclusion is that of the four Bayardo and Taylor emerge with unspoilt reputations while Cox and Maher have cases to answer.

Maher's tactics also beg the question about the path Bayardo's career may have taken if he had been ridden differently on occasions. No possible criticism can be directed at Maher during Bayardo's juvenile career. He looked after him well and used his speed sparingly as befits an immature colt. His riding in the Two Thousand Guineas was again beyond reproach. No jockey would have won on a horse short of condition on ground he would have hated even if in peak condition. His riding in the Derby is open to more speculation. He was in a position he was unhappy with and had attempted to extract himself from on two occasions. There was to be no third chance after Sir Martin stumbled in front of him. However, Maher was intelligent enough not to punish Bayardo once his chance had gone and he was eased some way from home.

Maher's failure to obtain a good position is less forgivable on Bayardo, who had the speed to be put anywhere in a race, than on lesser horses that may have lacked the pace to go where its jockey wished. Some individuals were of the opinion that Maher did not ride Epsom as well as he did other tracks. He professed a dislike for the course and considered Tattenham Corner on a wet day to be dangerous. It is a course where some jockeys shine whilst others suffer nightmares. Certainly history has shown that those jockeys that ride Epsom best are nearly always found to be in the best position at all points in a race. In modern times the outstanding example of the art of riding Epsom came most often from Lester Piggott and he was never better than on Derby day when even on a horse that had little chance (an infrequent occurrence it is conceded) he was seldom seen in the wrong position. In modern times only Steve Cauthen, who rode two Derby winners in three years making all the running on both occasions, can be regarded as Piggott's equal at Epsom. Walter Swinburn and Kieren Fallon, of recent jockeys, were not far behind in their mastery of Epsom. Cauthen's judgment of pace on this most difficult of racing terrains remain marvels of modern riding that are unlikely to be equalled. If anyone doubts this, ask how many jockeys on the Derby favourite would set out boldly in front and invite anyone, who thinks they can, to pass him, not once but twice in three years.

Throughout the rest of his classic season Maher did little wrong although he might have allowed Bayardo more of an opportunity to go clear in some of his easier races if only to see what happened. It was unlikely he could have been beaten under any circumstances (only if the opposition is given a furlong start!) and letting him go would at least have told him once and for all if he really did hate to be in front. He won the Limekiln Stakes by fifteen lengths from his only opponent who stood little chance. Maher must have known as he was going clear whether or not Bayardo was happy. The only conclusion can be that he did not think the horse was enjoying himself as he returned to extreme hold-up tactics afterwards. Alec Taylor was always concerned about Bayardo's feet and caution, on fast going, would have been sensible on Maher's part. However, when there was any give in the ground it surely could not have done any harm just to give Bayardo the opportunity of showing just how good he was. The answer to this was shown during the Ascot Gold Cup, run on fast ground, and, without Maher having any say in the matter, Bayardo sprinted to the front and came to no harm.

Returning to Maher's riding of Bayardo as a three year old, in the Eclipse he would seem to have been simply unintelligent. In a four runner race he seemed obsessed with coming up the inside. Luckily he was still able to come round the field and all was well. He did cut things fine in the Champion Stakes which may have been unwise as Dean Swift although out-speeded was a fighter and would battle all the way to the line. As already discussed Maher's riding in Bayardo's final year was over confident. Had he made the running at Chester for example, it is possible Bayardo would have been spared a hard race something that was hardly ideal at the start of the season. In conclusion it seems safe to say that if given more opportunity Bayardo could have given more pleasure and enjoyed a better reputation before the Ascot Cup if he had been allowed to stride away on occasions. A jockey trying to look clever and win by a short head on a horse that has pounds in hand has been a feature of racing since it began and there are not many riders in the history of the sport who can't look back on races where they had more confidence than judgement and were made to look foolish. If any jockeys have forgotten such occasions they have only to ask an average punter and they will remind them of a few instances!

How intelligent was Bayardo? This is a much more difficult area. When humans discuss intelligence in an animal they are almost always guilty of anthropomorphism. The span of intelligence found in man is enormous. There are individuals so intelligent they can understand and explain the latest European Union treaty, in several languages of the community, and successfully complete the Times crossword in under a quarter of an hour, and at the other end of the scale there are others that possess an IQ equal to their shoe size and have the attention span of a flash bulb.

Despite this vast variance of intellectual capacity in man animals are not thought to have quite such a wide range. As a general rule horses - who are herbivores - are not thought to be as intelligent as domestic cats and dogs and other wild creatures that are carnivorous. This may be historical as during the period when all these creatures lived in the wild carnivorous animals were required to hunt and kill to survive whereas herbivorous animals did not. A carnivorous animal needed to employ its brains and develop the skills and cunning required to hunt successfully, more so than the herbivorous animal that did not, as it requires very little mental effort to find and eat grass or nibble the foliage from the odd bush. The horse's ancestors did not employ much intelligence to escape their enemies either. The horse is a flight rather than a fight animal and will run off at full speed at the first sign of surprise or danger, usually without any thought or regard for its immediate environment. The horse gives no heed to the circumstances only that it feels it is in danger and will run, or if confined, attempt to jump any obstacle in its way, without the first thought about its chances of doing so successfully. This behaviour can be suicidal. Nobody that has been close to a horse that has been surprised or frightened will need to be told the truth of this. In addition thoroughbreds can often be nervous creatures which can only exacerbate a tendency to react swiftly. The trainer Sir Mark Prescott once said racehorses spent 100% of their time trying to injure themselves. He also added that 90% of the time the lads were aiding and abetting them! The effect of being trained by man has not contributed much towards improving a horse's intelligence. On the contrary man has tried to make the horse obedient in every way and to depend on him for everything and never to be required to think for himself.

The strongest mental attribute a horse has is his memory. They almost never forget a place they have visited and, if frightened by something along a path or road it will remember both the incident and the spot until the end of his life. They also have a good memory for people and other horses. A horse never forgets anyone that ill treats them. Fred Archer, who like other jockeys of his time occasionally wore spurs, gave a horse called Muley Idris some fearful beatings during races. One day after Archer had ridden work on him one morning on Newmarket Heath, he dismounted and Muley Idris, spotting his chance, grabbed his arm with his teeth and, lifting the jockey off the ground dragged him away before dropping him. Muley Idris then fell to his knees and began savaging Archer. In the event he was lucky that the horse slipped and help was at hand almost certainly saving Archer's life. The horse also remembers individuals that were kind to them. Hyperion never forgot George Lambton and, although he had not seen him for a year, on Ascot Gold Cup day he caught sight of him in his wheelchair at the entrance to the paddock. The horse stopped by Lambton and the lad in charge had some difficulty in persuading Hyperion to leave his old friend. The Derby winner Captain Cuttle was a placid, friendly horse with an unusual dog-like devotion to his trainer Fred Darling. On one occasion when the horse got free and had started to gallop away Darling bellowed after him and Captain Cuttle, recognising his master's voice, stopped immediately and returned as quietly as any well-trained canine.

Horses understand quickly whenever they are in danger or the person they know and trust is not there. In 1745 a Scottish Major killed an English Colonel of the Cavalry took his horse and mounted. The horse reacted by immediately galloping home to its regiment despite all the efforts of the Major to persuade him to go in the opposite direction. The Scottish Major was, of course, arrested. A rare if not unique instance of a horse affecting capture of the enemy! Some racehorses have an affinity with some jockeys and definitely seem to run better for some than others. Horses also remember some racecourses and run better at some than others. One of racings oldest clichés is "horses for courses". Horses also remember other horses they have raced against. Many jockeys and trainers are certain that if a horse they have trained/ridden meets the same horse time and again and, despite its best efforts, can't pass the horse when asked, it will become dispirited. Conversely if the horse has dominance it will confidently display it when asked to exert superiority and sometimes when not!

Many thoroughbred horses are perfectly aware of what is required of them and know when something is different or wrong. The great American horse Native Dancer won 21 of his 22 races. His only defeat came in the Kentucky Derby when he suffered interference and passed the winner a fraction after the line. Native Dancer could not understand why he was immediately led away after the race. He had done what was expected, which was to pass all the other runners, and he knew that after he had raced he was taken to the winner's enclosure where everyone made a fuss of him. He kept looking back at the enclosure baffled about why he was being led away and nobody was taking any interest in him!

In North America the trainer Joe Palmer became convinced that some racehorses not only know what is required of them but are even aware that they need to be in front at the winning post. He trained a horse called Sands of Pleasure who was involved in a close finish in the days before there was a photo-finish camera. Most observers thought Sands of Pleasure had won but the judge thought otherwise and placed him second. The jockey seeing his number placed second steered his mount to the rail away from the winner's circle (in North America only the winner goes into the circle not the placed horses as in Europe). Sands of Pleasure became agitated, reared and kicked at anyone and anything. However, as a son of Fair Play who could be headstrong and passed on this trait to some of his progeny this was not considered particularly unusual. However, to prove his theory Palmer next ran Sands of Pleasure in a race he could not win and afterwards when well beaten he pulled up quietly without even a glance at the winner's circle. Now Palmer placed him in an easy race and asked the jockey, in the event of him winning, to take the horse away and not to the winner's circle. Sands of Pleasure won easily and as the jockey attempted to lead him to the outside rail the horse taking hold of his bit turned determinedly towards the winner's circle.

Horses are very susceptible to voice: they may not understand what is being said to them, in the strictest sense of the word, but the meaning gets through to them. Some years ago there was a trainer with a horse that came over from France that would not thrive. He stood miserably in his box, left most of his food and took no interest in his work. One day the trainer hit on the idea of putting a French lad to do him and as luck would have it there was one in a nearby stable. As soon as the horse heard French spoken to him he took on a new lease of life and began to eat and work heartily.

Horses are normally sociable and enjoy company. Put two horses in adjoining paddocks and they will usually end up standing together often nuzzling each other and sometimes they will groom each other. They are usually only obstinate if badly handled in early life and are inherently courageous. However, the superiority of man over the horse is imaginary. The man may weigh between 130 and 200 pounds (59 and 90 kilos) but the horse weighs about 1200 pounds (540 k). The horse can't be forced and therefore has to be persuaded and that is achieved because man's mind is superior. The skill in training a horse lies in persuading him to enjoy what it is doing, combined with never letting him think he has had his own way. Once the horse has done what he wants to do, against man's wishes in any situation, his naturally superior size will mean that man has lost not only that aspect of training, but his chance of maintaining the upper hand, as the horse then realizes that he is stronger and can't be forced to do anything.

It has been said that it is better, from the point of view of education and training, that a thoroughbred is slightly less, rather than more, inclined towards equine intelligence. This argument is hard to understand. The reasoning seems to be that a less intelligent horse will do as they are told without question, and therefore be easier to train, whereas a more intelligent one will soon realize that it will still be fed and watered whether or not they do as instructed. There is some element of truth, however slight, in this. However, it is hard to find any record of a jockey or trainer describing any horse with ability as lacking intelligence. On the contrary ask any of the connections about a horse that has achieved anything of note and they will tell you that the horse is "very intelligent". Well the owner at least definitely will! This may simply be proof of the old adage that "handsome is as handsome does". The horse has plenty of ability therefore it follows that is intelligent. Very often a horse is simply reacting to the treatment it has received from its handlers. Most trainers can identify a good horse fairly early and will treat them accordingly. Conversely a slow horse is sold as quickly as possible and may change hands often as its lack of ability and speed become evident. If he ends up in unsympathetic hands it may be neglected and not receive the best care and may even be abused. The horse reacts accordingly and is then considered both slow and stupid and also possibly vicious as well. Much of this is stating the obvious and may also be guilty of being simplistic particularly when considering such a complex and varied animal as the thoroughbred. When a man like the American Hall of Fame trainer D Wayne Lukas says that after a lifetime with horses and aged over seventy he learns something new from each horse he trains it should caution anyone who has not trained horses not to make shoddy generalisations.

This began as a discussion about Bayardo's intelligence and it is hoped that the forgoing has not impinged on the patience of the reader by falling into the error of prolixity. Some may view the previous passage in a less charitable light and feel it should be condemned in more forcible terms: *satis eloquentiae, sapientiae parum*, (roughly translated – too many words, too little wisdom!). However, a book about a race-horse should not be afraid of discussing the activity, or lack of it, in the organ between his ears! Alec Taylor said he was a horse of moods, but this did not stop him responding in a race each time he was asked. Bayardo certainly had some strange ways but it can't be concluded from these what level of intelligence he possessed. One man who could have given an incisive view was Danny Maher who rode him twenty four times. Maher was an intelligent man if on occasions an obstinate one. He felt he knew Bayardo well and held the strong view that in his races he needed holding up until the last possible moment, but was then proved wrong in the Ascot Gold Cup. Was there any significance in Bayardo dropping Maher at the start, for the only time, and can any connection be made between this and Bayardo's sudden burst of speed in the race? Maher possessed wonderful balance and Bayardo, who knew Maher very well by then and could have been sure he would never have ill treated him, must have been very restless to have managed to deposit his jockey on the ground.

Most pictures of Bayardo racing show that he was equipped with a running martingale. These are rarely seen on racehorses that run on the flat nowadays but are still used in training and in different guises on polo ponies and by the majority of cross-country three day event riders and horses used for hunting. The martingale gives the rider more control and prevents the horse lifting his head to high. There may not be any significance in the fact that Bayardo was usually equipped with one, Lemberg for example was also fitted with one, it may simply have been the fashion and there is no evidence that Bayardo was in any way difficult to control. If Maher had failed to fully understand Bayardo there seems little hope for anyone else a hundred years distant. The only other individual whose view would have been enlightening was his lad and it has not been possible to find any opinion offered by him. It is probably unlikely that his views were ever canvassed. It seems certain that Bayardo understood what was required of him as much as the next horse and that, as his performance in the Ascot Gold Cup demonstrated he could perform his duties in a spectacular manner, on this occasion before he had been asked, and give every indication that he was enjoying it.

His habits and ways are hard to explain. It may have been that he would have preferred to be kept occupied more. After work his habit of refusing to return to his stable may have been no more than an indication that he was bored there with nothing to occupy him. He even refused to return to the saddling box after the Ascot Gold Cup. Was it just that he disliked being in a box? As Bayardo was such a valuable asset to the stable would some different individual attention have helped? For example would experimenting by leaving him out in a paddock at night, during the summer months, occasionally have helped? Would that have been considered too risky with the possibility of him hurting himself? Was it simply that Alec Taylor was determined to treat him like any other horse and ignore his idiosyncrasies? When in his box he would bang his chin in the door, the famous Bayardo's drum, another possible sign of ennui.

Racehorses spend about twenty to twenty one hours a day in their stable. Some may be happy with this feeling secure knowing that they are fed and cared for. However, as all horses are not the same, there must be some for whom this is like incarceration. A good trainer will always train a horse according to its needs. No trainer would work all his string by galloping them the same distance on the same gallop day after day. The work would be varied with the object of preparing a horse for a certain race and also to keep him interested. Horses are frequently taken to the racecourse to work as a change of routine can persuade the horse to work a little better and bring him to a satisfactory level of fitness quicker. However, it is rare that a stable would keep its horses in any other manner than in individual almost identical stables and kept inside for about eighty five percent of its time.

Bayardo's refusal to canter past the stands of the Rowley Mile is harder to understand. Nine of his twenty five races were on the Rowley Mile and it may be that he found the course featureless and without enough variety to keep him interested. A very experienced horseman once remarked that most horse's needs are simple, that they do not need too much attention and as long as they were well treated, fed, watered and comfortable not much bothered them. They were untroubled by the ills of the world and knew only security, comfort, fear and pain. In addition they understood excitement. He did not include boredom in his list. He noted that some had a poor attention span and were easily distracted while others learnt quickly, just like a nursery full of children. Furthermore the old horseman concluded that it should be remembered that inside that large head was housed a remarkably small brain! Whilst he was perhaps a little cynical, and guilty of not treating horses as individuals, there remains a grain of truth in what he says.

In addition to his frequent refusals to enter his stable at Manton Bayardo also proved troublesome in loading onto race-trains. It required considerable patience and often the only way to get him in would be to turn him round and load him backwards. Once safely in he was as quite as a sheep. Other racehorses have also been very difficult to load. For example Persimmon was very truculent when it came to loading him up for his journey to Epsom for the Derby. Two trains departed without him and there was only one left when eventually as a last resort he was man-handled bodily by twelve men into the truck. Once inside he then walked happily over to his feed and began munching contentedly. But Persimmon was a most genuine horse and must have been aware that loading onto a race train meant he was going racing. Railway journeys were tedious for horses often involving delays. It was not unknown for a train conveying horses to the races to be shunted into sidings in order not to delay passenger trains.

When all things are considered, it seems likely that, in equine terms, Bayardo, who had been a good learner as a yearling, was probably more than averagely intelligent than otherwise. It is interesting to note that his grandson Hyperion was considered very intelligent and took an interest in everything that was happening around him, often, unusually for a horse, in the skies with birds and planes of particular interest. Hyperion also inherited from Bayardo the habit of often refusing to enter is box. Sadly no more definite conclusion can be drawn from what has been said by those close to him and there the matter will have to rest.

Bayardo retired to the Red Post stud where initially he had problems: he suffered some kidney trouble and was sometimes found in his box dripping in sweat and he had some difficulty with his mares. With treatment matters improved and he was eventually a notable success and details of his stud career can be found in the appendices. Unfortunately his stud career was cut short when he contracted thrombosis, resulting in paralysis of his hind quarters and it was necessary to destroy him on 4th June 1917. He was only eleven years old.

When Bayardo was at the height of his fame Alfred Watson asked Alfred Cox how he came to name the horse. The following was sent by way of explanation, the original is reproduced in the endpapers of this book:-

"Bayardo was the famous steed of Rinaldo the Brave, who was one of Charlemagne's Paladins and a cousin of Orlando. He was originally found by Malagigi the Wizard in a cave guarded by a dragon which the wizard slew and handed over to Amadis de Gaul. Bayardo's leap near Sleaford consists of 3 stones 30 yards apart. It is said that Rinaldo was riding on his favourite steed when the demon of the place sprang up behind him, but the animal in terror took three tremendous leaps and unhorsed the fiend. Bayardo was of a bay colour and was a wonder animal. After Rinaldo's death he escaped and could never be caught again though many attempts were made to do so and afterwards it was considered lucky to see the horse. He is supposed to be still alive and the rumour goes that he has been seen on several occasions at various parts of the country, and that some of the braves of the inhabitants have combined together to catch him but so far have failed; also it is reported that a 'demon' horseman rides him now with whom Bayardo seems quite happy"

Here is a summary of his racing record.

Year	distance	race	course	placing	race rating	winnings £
Two years old						
1908	5 f	New Stakes	Ascot	1st	114+	1,817 10s
	5 f	National Breeders Produce Stakes	Sandown	1st	122+	4,357
	6 f	Richmond Stakes	Goodwood	1st	120++	652
	$5\frac{1}{2}$ f	Buckenham (Post Produce) Stakes	Newmarket	1st	82++	1,500
	5 f	Rous Memorial Stakes	Newmarket	1st	100++	730
	6 f	Middle Park Plate	Newmarket	1st	119	2,505
	7 f	Dewhurst Plate	Newmarket	1st	131+	1,477
Three years old						
1909	1 m	Two Thousand Guineas	Newmarket	4th	116	
	$1\frac{1}{2}$ m	Derby Stakes	Epsom	5th	114+	
	1m 5f	Prince of Wales Stakes	Ascot	1st	122+	2,150
	$1\frac{1}{4}$ m	Sandringham Foal Stakes	Sandown Park	1st	138+	1,724
	$1\frac{1}{4}$ m	Eclipse Stakes	Sandown Park	1st	136++	8,870
	$1\frac{1}{4}$ m	Duchess of York Plate	Hurst Park	1st	131++	979
	$1\frac{3}{4}$ m	St. Leger Stakes	Doncaster	1st	130++	6,450
	$1\frac{1}{2}$ m	Doncaster Stakes	Doncaster	1st	130++	475
	$1\frac{1}{4}$ m	Champion Stakes	Newmarket	1st	136+	900
	$1\frac{3}{4}$ m	Lowther Stakes	Newmarket	1st	133++	470
	$1\frac{1}{4}$ m	Sandown Foal Stakes	Sandown Park	1st	119++	1,724
	$1\frac{1}{4}$ m	Limekiln Stakes	Newmarket	1st	132++	425
	$1\frac{1}{2}$ m	Liverpool St. Leger	Liverpool	1st	112++	630
Four years old						
1910	11/2 m	Newmarket Bienial Stakes	Newmarket	1st	127++	573 10s
	$1\frac{1}{2}$ m	Chester Vase	Chester	1st	127+	1,595
	$2\frac{1}{2}$ m	Gold Cup	Ascot	1st	140+	3,700
	$1\frac{1}{2}$ m	Dullingham Plate	Newmarket	1st	134++	830
	$2\frac{1}{2}$ m	Goodwood Cup	Goodwood	2nd	132	

Total winning prize money £44,534
(£2,404,836)

CHAPTER 15

Galicia & Bay Ronald

Bayardo's dam Galicia is rightly considered one of the most famous brood mares in the Stud Book. In addition to producing two outstanding horses in Bayardo and Lemberg her four winners won forty two races worth £88,209 (£3,087,315). She was foaled in 1898, by Galopin out of Isoletta, who was by Isonomy. Her sire was 25 and at the end of his stud career when she was conceived. He was however, champion sire for the third and last time in 1898. Isonomy had been a fine racehorse, if not a great one then very close who won the Ascot Gold Cup twice, and a great sire who was responsible for two Triple Crown winners in Common and Isinglass, a distinction he was later to share with Bayardo.

Galicia traced back in direct female line to another famous mare in Blink Bonny. In 1857 she became only the second filly to win both the Derby and the Oaks. Blink Bonny's victory in the Derby was a close affair with the first seven home covered by a length and a half. However, two days later she disposed of 12 fillies by eight lengths in the Oaks. In total she won 14 races including the Gimcrack, Lancashire Oaks and Park Hill Stakes, in addition she probably should have won the St Leger for which she was an odds-on favourite. However, at the behest of a bookmaker her jockey "pulled" her and she finished only fourth.

Blink Bonny was a daughter of Queen Mary also one of the most influential and prolific broodmares in thoroughbred history. At her death in 1872 at the age of 29 she had produced twenty foals of which two died early and one was by a half-bred stallion. Queen Mary had been given away early in her stud career, only to be hastily retrieved after Blink Bonny's success. Queen Mary's son Bonnie Scotland became champion sire in North America in 1880 and 1882, while her many daughters became ancestors of such important sires as Black Toney, Hampton and Tristan.

Blink Bonny died aged only eight but her three foals were all useful. Her first foal Borealis, a filly by the St Leger winner Newminster, won the Dee Stakes and Liverpool St Leger among other races and finished fourth behind Lord Clifden in the St Leger. She visited the 2000 Guineas and St Leger winner and leading sire Stockwell twice in successive years and produced two colts Blair Athol and Breadalbane. Both were good racehorses and successful sires with Blair Athol winning the Derby and St Leger and Breadalbane winning the Prince of Wales' Stakes at Ascot.

Blink Bonny's female line rested on the exploits of her only daughter Borealis. It was through Borealis's daughter Blue Light, a filly by Rataplan foaled in 1870, that the link with Galicia continues. Rataplan, a tough stayer who won 42 of his 72 races including the Ascot Gold Vase and the Doncaster Cup, was a full brother to Stockwell. Blue Light was therefore a very close relative of the aforementioned Blair Athol and Breadalbane.

As a broodmare Blue Light's best offspring was Lady Muncaster, who won eight races including the Gimcrack Stakes as a juvenile, and it is with Lady Muncaster that the trail to Bayardo begins when Alfred Cox purchased her at the end of her racing career. She visited Isonomy in 1890 and produced a filly Isoletta who would earn her claim to fame as the dam of Galicia. Lady Muncaster in addition to foaling Isoletta produced a colt the following year by Springfield named Speedwell and he won the 1894 Middle Park Plate.

Galicia's dam Isoletta did not race, but she has an interesting pedigree, featuring some influential broodmares. She was 3x4x3 to the full brothers Stockwell and Rataplan, both by The Baron out of Pocahontas. She was a moderate racehorse, and a roarer, but became one of the most influential broodmares of the 19th Century as her 15 foals numbered Stockwell mentioned above who was champion sire seven times; Rataplan, also mentioned above and an excellent sire; and King Tom, twice champion sire. The Baron was a son of Birdcatcher and with the latter's son Oxford and daughter Miss Agnes also appearing in Isoletta's pedigree it meant that she was 4x5x6x5x5 to Birdcatcher. Just for good measure Birdcatcher's full brother Faugh-A-Ballagh also appeared in Isoletta's 5th generation. Birdcatcher was a chestnut with his coat flecked with grey hairs, a characteristic he inherited from his sire Sir Hercules. These so called "Birdcatcher Ticks" are still seen today and it is of interest to wonder how many thoroughbreds inherited these from Isoletta with her five strains of Birdcatcher.

Another important mare to be duplicated in Isoletta's pedigree was Banter, who appeared three times in her 6th generation, twice via her son Touchstone and once via her daughter Jocose, who was the dam of Macaroni. Banter was the daughter of the mare Boadicea, who would earn fame as the ancestress of the great race-mare Pretty Polly. In addition it is interesting that Isoletta was by Isonomy out of a mare by Muncaster, and these two stallions respectively sired the sire and maternal grandsire of Pretty Polly.

Isoletta retired to the paddocks in 1895 and produced winners with her first two foals. In addition to Galicia Isoletta also foaled a daughter in 1903 by Florizel II a son of St Simon named Chere Reine who became an excellent broodmare. She produced two good stayers in Aleppo, winner of successive Jockey Gold Cups, plus the Chester and Ascot Gold Cups and Queens Square who won the Goodwood and Jockey Club

Cups. She also produced Telephus who won the Dewhurst Plate. After foaling Chere Reine, her seventh foal, Isoletta was purchased by the then relatively unknown Italian owner-trainer and breeder Federico Tesio for 470 Guineas (£33,088) in 1903. Joining his stud at Dormello she produced two good winners in Angelica Kauffman and Arnoldo Di Cambio before her death in 1908.

Galicia achieved little on the racecourse winning only one race. However, she was probably a better racehorse than was evident and can be considered unlucky. After a promising third on debut in the Kempton Park Two-Year-Old Plate, when she had the following years Derby winner Volodyovski – always known as "Bottle o' Whisky" or Voly – behind her, she won her second race: the Ascot Biennial Stakes. In her next race, the Exeter Stakes, at Newmarket, according to her jockey Mornington Cannon she was winning easily when she faltered. She had split a pastern. It was said that she was never the same mare afterwards.

As a three year old she ran five times, unplaced in the 1000 Guineas, Oaks and Coronation Stakes, then fourth in the Triennial Produce Stakes. In her final race The Derby Cup, a handicap, it was reported that "she stopped as if she has been shot" and was retired.

Galicia was covered by Eager in both 1902 and 1903. The first covering produced no foal, but the second did, a colt named Eastern. He was a good looking bay colt although he had apparently inherited from Eager small feet and weak fetlocks, which were thought to cause him discomfort on firm ground. At two he was backward until late in the season. It was September before trainer Alec Taylor could get him on to the track. He raced four times, winning once. At three he won just once from fourteen starts. He was second six times and third on three occasions. He was sold at the December sales for 400 guineas (£25,000) and sent to Belgium.

In 1904 Galicia visited Isinglass, a Triple Crown Winner and a great racehorse, and, although a success at stud, he sired nothing comparable to himself. This resulted in a bay colt named Carpathian. Both Isinglass and Isoletta were by Isonomy which meant that Carpathian was inbred 2x3 Isonomy. He showed enough promise for his owner to enter him for all the top juvenile races. Unfortunately, he met with an accident and never raced.

Galicia's next covering in 1905 was to Bay Ronald. It would be an exaggeration to say this would have been everyone's choice. In any event this was the last chance to use the services of Bay Ronald for he was to be sold for £5,000 (£320,000) and exported to France later that year. It may well have been that this mating would not be the choice of many, however, this did result in a bay or brown colt which his owner was to name Bayardo.

In 1906 Galicia visited Cyllene. This was considered a much better mating. Cyllene was a top class racehorse and in 1906 a promising stallion who was to prove outstanding. He sired four Derby winners and was champion sire twice. He was exported to Argentina where he was also champion sire. The result of this mating was a bay colt named Lemberg. He was a tall, leggy two year old who matured into a handsome colt, and it has to be admitted a better looking horse than his half-brother. As a juvenile he won six of his seven races and, like Bayardo, the Middle Park and Dewhurst, a double not achieved again until Diesis in 1982. He may have been unlucky not be unbeaten as he was coughing before his only defeat. At three he won seven of his ten races, including the Derby, St. James' Palace, Eclipse (dead-heat), Jockey Club Stakes and Champion Stakes. He was second in the 2000 Guineas and failed to stay in the St. Leger. At four he won four of seven races including the Coronation Stakes and Doncaster Cup and was second in the Eclipse and Princess of Wales's Stakes and Jockey Club Cup. In all he won seventeen of his twenty four races (including one dead heat). As a sire he was a considerable success being champion in 1922.

Although Galicia lived to the age of 25 she had only another five live foals. None were of the calibre of Bayardo or Lemberg. Silesia, a daughter of Spearmint, was considered a very good looking filly, however, she did not race at two and remained a maiden. She did better as a broodmare producing My Dear who won eight races including the Oaks (on disqualification) and the Champion Stakes. In addition Kwang-Su won the Newmarket Stakes and was second in the 2000 Guineas and the Derby.

Galicia had however, earned her place in history and her record as a brood-mare is as shown below.

Bayardo's sire Bay Ronald was foaled in 1893. He was a bay colt by Hampton out of Black Duchess who was by Galliard. Black Duchess was also the dam of the famous mare Black Cherry. He was markedly over at the knee, which may have been the reason he failed to reach his reserve

1903	barren to Eager	
1904	colt by Eager	Eastern
1905	bay colt by Isinglass	Carpathian
1906	bay colt by Bay Ronald	Bayardo
1907	bay colt by Cyllene	Lemberg
1908	Slipped twins to Isinglass	
1909	bay filly by Spearmint	Silesia
1910	barren to Mistle Thrush	
1911	Twins ch f dead	
	bay filly by Radium	Zia
1912	bay colt by Radium	Radames
1913	bay colt by Cicero	Kwang-Su
1914	barren thereafter	

of 500 guineas (£31,900) when sent to the sales as a yearling. He was sold subsequently for £500 in a private sale.

Bay Ronald was not the most robust of individuals and this was the cause of problems in training him. He failed to win in five outings at two. However, he contested the Windsor Castle, The Lavant and Middle Park Plate and finally the Dewhurst Plate. He kept the best company as a juvenile but lacked the speed to make an impression.

At three he started in the Newmarket Stakes where he finished fourth. He was then unplaced behind Persimmon in the Derby. After this he ran moderately to finish third of four in the Ascot Derby Stakes and reappeared at the same meeting to finish unplaced in the Hardwick Stakes.

At this stage Bay Ronald had kept the best company but was still a maiden after nine starts. Finally when receiving weight from all his opponents he won the Lowther Stakes convincingly. However, his starting price of 8-1 does not indicate that he was expected to win. Two weeks later he added the Limekiln Stakes this time at 10-1. He was less impressive and, as can be seen from his starting price, not really fancied. In his final race that year he was made favourite for the Free Handicap and finished unplaced.

At aged four, on his seasonal debut, Bay Ronald was beaten half a length when second in the City and Suburban Handicap. His next appearance was at Ascot when he comfortably won the Hardwicke Stakes at odds of 11-10. In the Eclipse Stakes he ran well but, not surprisingly, could not cope with Persimmon and Velasquez and he finished third. The policy of keeping him in the best company was maintained for the rest of the year and he was beaten but not disgraced in the Champion Stakes. He was however disappointing in the Cambridgeshire and Liverpool Autumn Cup.

At five he won the City and Suburban Handicap in good style with the previous year's One Thousand Guineas winner behind him. Bay Ronald was a real Epsom horse and he won the Epsom Cup easily after which he was trained for the Ascot Gold Cup. There were grounds for believing that the trip would not be a problem as his sire Hampton had won 19 races including 11 over two miles and above, plus one over hurdles. However, the severe preparation required for the race had an adverse effect on a horse with a moderate constitution. He was unplaced in the Ascot Gold Cup and was reported to have finished distressed. The trip proved to be some way in excess of his stamina. In addition, the hard ground added to his problems. His owner considered that he was never the same horse again. Nonetheless he was out again the following day where he was second in the Hardwicke Stakes. This seems extraordinary. Never considered a very robust type he finished distressed after a race over two and a half miles, yet he was considered well enough to run in a mile and a half race the following day and finish second! Clearly what was considered "not very robust" would qualify as tough today! Bay Ronald had three more unsuccessful outings in the autumn: the Champion, Lowther and Jockey Club Stakes, all at Newmarket. Only in the last did he run badly.

Bay Ronald retired to stud in 1899 having won only five of his twenty six starts in four seasons. He may have had a delicate constitution, but he still managed four rigorous seasons racing was not fortunate enough to contest an easy race and he retired sound. It has never been claimed that Bay Ronald was a top class horse and his record would appear to be a fair reflexion of his ability. He retired to stud for a fee of 25 Guineas (£1,460) which increased by 1905 to 75 guineas (4,400). The writer Alfred Watson described him in maturity as "a beautiful and most bloodlike stallion, with a very perfect head and neck". Unfortunately opportunities at stud were not plentiful and by the time Galicia was sent to him in 1905 he was not considered a great success. However, he was sold for £5,000 (£270,000) to go to France where he died unexpectedly two years later.

Bay Ronald's place in history is, however, secure and in the final analysis he can be considered a success. He was responsible for Bayardo who sired Gainsborough who in turn sired Hyperion and Solario. He also sired Rondeau who was the dam of the outstanding sire Teddy and Dark Ronald, who before being exported to Germany where he was immensely successful, sired Son-in-Law and Dark Legend.

CHAPTER 16

Alec Taylor

Born Alexander Taylor on 15th March 1862 he was the second son of the formidable Alec Taylor senior and the grandson of Tom Taylor. Tom Taylor was for many years the private trainer to Lord Chesterfield at Bretby Park near Burton-on-Trent. He then moved to Newmarket where he trained for the Duke of Grafton, Lord Glasgow, Mr W S Stirling Crawfurd and others. Alec Taylor senior, known as "Grim old Alec", was an independent man given to strong language who showed little or no deference to anyone. He was taciturn by nature in addition he was surly and ungracious to any but his few close friends and owners to whom he was utterly loyal. When congratulated by the Earl of Chesterfield on training the winner of a big race, far from showing any pleasure, he replied dourly "Good horses make good trainers my Lord". Taylor senior won each of the classics twice and the 1000 Guineas four times, but was probably best known for his training of stayers. He started training in 1848 at Fyfield near Marlborough in Wiltshire and remained there until 1870 when he moved to nearby Manton. With its beautiful courtyard, clock tower and attractive creeper-clad house Manton was one of the most imposing and beautiful stables in Britain.

Alec Taylor's move to Manton came at the invitation of Stirling Crawfurd, who was later to become the second husband of Caroline, Duchess of Montrose. He invited Taylor to help establish a new training centre. He chose Taylor because, in Crawfurd's words he was, "Guaranteed to speak his mind without wasting words on small talk, was a wonderful stableman and utterly honest". Between them they created Manton and produced one of the finest training centres in the kingdom. Before 1870 almost 200 acres had been acquired, gallops laid out, cottages built, a stud farm created and the main training block consisting of stables and the trainer's house completed. The principal buildings formed a square three sides of which were the stables and the fourth side the trainer's house, a large gabled red brick mansion. Above the stables were the lad's dormitories and living quarters, so planned that none of the window looked outwards. At night when the massive stable doors were shut it was impossible to have any communication with the outside world. Immediately behind the stables was a deep valley sunk between two high ridges of the Downs which afforded the opportunity for trying horses in privacy. This usually prevented any details of trial gallops being known by the ubiquitous touts. This seems incredible even by the secretive standards of the day, even more so when it is borne in mind that Manton, at that time, was not particularly a gambling stable. The cost of establishing Manton was enormous, but it was money well spent. Alec Taylor rapidly gained the reputation of being one of the outstanding trainers in the country. In addition to providing a premier racing stable Manton also provided Taylor with the privacy he craved.

Taylor senior was especially feared in the back-end handicaps where he was particularly skilful. However, if he fancied backing one of his horses it would not have been via a commission agent as he would have nothing to do with them and never employed one. When he wanted to back a horse he would approach the Hon. George Lambton with a cheque for a £100 (£7,000) asking him to place it on a horse. When Lambton replied that he was not clever at obtaining the best price Taylor would simply ask him to do the best he could.

Probably the most famous owner during Alec senior's time was the above mentioned Caroline Duchess of Montrose. To describe her as simply formidable is to be guilty of a gross understatement. Women were not permitted to register their own colours so the Duchess raced under the nom de course of "Mr Manton", but was commonly known as "Carrie Red". Married to the Duke when she was just seventeen, racing was the principal interest in her life. Tall and upright, she had a fine figure and a stately bearing and was described in her youth as "The most perfect type of English beauty", however, she was a volatile women who liked her own way; blessed with a soft endearing voice she could be sweet and charming one moment, but if matters did not go her way she could become ferocious, with a booming voice, the next. Not above using strong language when she was roused, and, if the mood took her, she was apt to be cruel, cutting and vindictive. As if this was not enough she was also the worst type of owner: she interfered at every opportunity, bet heavily and indiscriminatingly, was a bad loser and was quick to blame all around her, apart from the horse, for any perceived misfortune. As a result the services of trainers and jockeys were seldom retained for long and she seems to have adopted something of a "revolving door" policy.

While when young she was merely something of a hoyden however, when older there were occasions when she really must have seemed like a maenad! Formidable in all walks of life she once stormed out of her own private Church, built in honour of her first husband, during a service. The celebrant had been praying for fine weather in order to help the harvest when one of her horses, due to run in the St Leger, needed soft ground! The Duchess who was the Church's patron with power of nomination immediately dismissed the unfortunate cleric from his living. However, knowing her well this threat was not taken too seriously and sure enough upon returning to better humour she was later prevailed upon to reinstate him. She referred to one handicapper, a mild and amiable man but not one blessed with his looks, as "the man who murdered his mother". She married three times, the final time to a man aged 24 which made him over 40 years her junior. In later years she must have presented a formidable picture with her masculine "horsy" clothes, her face adorned unsparingly with paint and her hair dyed that particular shade of gold that scorns any attempt to deceive.

Despite her volatile disposition she was nonetheless extremely knowledgeable on both form and breeding. There was however, one famous occasion when she berated her jockey, Harry Huxtable, for not coming on at the distance and winning the race. He replied, with, it has to be said, some courage, "I am sorry, Your Grace, but I should have had to come along without the horse".

Alec senior managed her by standing up to her and simply ignoring her wilder instructions. It was said that he was the only man she was afraid of. She once asked him what he thought were the chief dangers to one of her horses in a race. His reply, not very shocking by today's standards but considered strong language at the time, was "Damned to Hell if I know Your Grace"! That she stayed with him is enough of an indication of his own ferocity and training skills. Despite all of these rather tiresome traits, "Old Six Mile Bottom" as she was also sometimes known, was essentially good natured and despite everything was much missed after her death in 1894. With longevity individuals like the Duchess seem to take on the status of a "national treasure" and at the time of her death she was not disliked by everyone and had even become a figure of affection in the racing fraternity.

Alec Taylor senior had always harboured a secret ambition to teach his son Alec all he knew in order that he might become a successful trainer, preferably a private one to a rich owner. However, when Alec Taylor senior died in 1894 he had two surviving sons: Tom, by his first wife, and Alec junior by his second. The, by now, very considerable Manton property was left to the two of them to maintain as a training and farming facility. However, Alec senior favoured young Alec as being potentially the better of the two brothers to take over the stable. He had taught him all he knew and worded his will to ensure that if the partnership foundered, as he must have suspected it would, Alec would be in sole charge. At the time of his death in 1894 Alec senior trained for Lady Meux, Duke of Beaufort, Mr J N Astley, Mr W Clavering, Mr Joicy and Mr Hamar Bass. When Alec junior and Tom began their partnership the only owners were Messrs Astley and Bass and this pair departed within two years. They were replaced by Capt. W Faber and Mr G F Johnson. The former left and was replaced by Messrs Washington Singer, Gaston and Stacey. This hardly suggested that the yard was progressing and indeed it was not. The partnership was not very successful as the brothers were often at loggerheads with each other, although they did have some success and won the Ascot Gold Cup and Jockey Club Stakes with Love Wisely. Matters were not helped when Tom stood trial over the death of an apprentice he had physically beaten. He was acquitted but his reputation was ruined. Sadly the truth was that Tom, who was ten years older than Alec, was a sick man and he retired in 1902 and died two years later. Alec assumed complete control on Tom's retirement in 1902 and from this time the great days returned to Manton.

Alec Taylor had learnt much from his father and had greatly respected him for his knowledge and judgement, especially his stable craft. However, Alec senior had been very hard on his horses. According to reports the yearlings were galloped a couple of miles before Christmas just to see if they had any racing merit! Presumably this also established whether or not they had stamina, good bone and an iron constitution as well! When he "tried" Teddington prior to his winning the 1851 Derby the horse performed so well over the twelve furlong trial course that Alec senior could not believe it was true and assumed he was mistaken. "Well, let us try him again in the morning" said Alec senior. The following morning he was just as impressive thus removing all doubt about his chances at Epsom. However, equally possibly galloping Teddington twice over the full Derby trip twice in two days might just leave the Derby on the Manton trial grounds! That it did not is ample evidence that Teddington must have been a tough customer.

Alec junior did not hold with this view and he treated horses as the youngsters they were until the age of three. He did not spoil them and gave them plenty of work, but he never forced them. He believed that the racecourse, rather than the gallops, was the place to test juveniles: he often ran two unraced and untried juveniles in the same race and it was by no means unknown for the longer priced horse to prevail. It is significant that although he won many races, his juvenile successes, were disproportionately few. In the circumstances it can be readily appreciated how precocious Bayardo was as a two-year-old that he won seven races.

Taylor began training on his own with just three owners: Messrs Bass (later Sir William and son of Hamar), Garton (later Sir Richard) and Singer. Significantly though Taylor secured the horses of Alfred Cox in 1904 to commence what would turn out to be his most successful association. Up until 1910 Taylor trained for the same half a dozen or so owners. Gradually he was able to attract some of the great owner-breeders so that by the end of the Great War he could be considered most fortunate in his patrons. This is not to say that his good luck was not down to his considerable merit. Owner-breeders were very common in those days but are almost extinct today. By the time peace was declared Taylor was training or had trained for Lady James Douglas, Lord Astor, Sir William Bass, Mr Somerville Tattersall, Mr W M Cazalet and of course Alfred Cox. With the conspicuous exception of the latter, all these owners had in common the means and disposition to allow Taylor to exercise his main characteristic which was inexhaustible patience. He disliked heavy gambling owners and apart from Mr Washington Singer, the only one he tolerated was Alfred Cox. Even then there were some big rows when one of his horses was beaten. One other owner Taylor seems to have had problems with was Reid Walker, Lord Wavertree's brother, who was probably the only person who thought Alec Taylor could not train horses. He thought they were "too big" and removed them in order to give them some "proper work" as he put it. Following a period during which it would appear they were galloped to near exhaustion the unfortunate beasts were returned to Manton with all their ribs prominent.

It is worth considering the status of race-horse trainers throughout the nineteenth century and up until after the Great War. The majority were considered little more than grooms capable only of conditioning a horse and getting it fit. For example *Ruffs Guide to the Turf,* although first published in 1842 did not show the name of the successful trainer after each race in its results section until 1896. *Ruffs* listed trainers in a section titled "Names and addresses of Trainers with a list of their employers". *Ruffs* did not publish a list of winning trainers until its 1897 edition. The *Racing Calendar* was worse. It did not publish the name of the winning trainer in its results section until 1932! The results for Ascot of that year were the first races where the trainer was named and given any credit. There was no list of winning trainers covering the season though! *The Bloodstock Breeders Review* was first published in 1912 and had a detailed statistical section. However, it contained no reference to trainers until 1921 when a simple, short list of the top dozen were given. *The Review* could argue that as it dealt with bloodstock issues detailed trainers statistics were outside its ambit. This all seems to confirm that the trainer was considered of lesser importance than the owner and jockey. Only the top half a dozen or so trainers seemed to be held in any regard.

Alec Taylor's skill and patience was never tested more than when he took over the training of Sceptre. She was sent to him as a four-year-old in very poor condition, little more than skin and bone, after she had been bought by Sir William Bass for £25,000 (£3,800,000). Taylor wrote to her former trainer Robert Sievier asking how she should be trained. His horror can be readily imagined when Sievier wired back with typical candour "Treat her like a selling plater". In fairness to Sievier, whose predominant characteristics were not sensitivity and tact, he was probably simply trying to indicate that she needed plenty of work. He could however, have passed on this advice in a less brutal manner. Under Taylor's assiduous care, she was put on a regimen which saw her restricted to light work and allowed to drink two gallons of milk a day.

During this period she regained her strength and condition sufficiently to win the Hardwicke Stakes.

Sceptre then took part in what is generally accepted as the greatest renewal of the Eclipse Stakes, when Derby winner Ard Patrick, after a pulsating duel from a furlong out, won by a neck from Sceptre, with Triple Crown winner Rock Sand in third. Taylor, ever the perfectionist, always believed she would have won if he had been training her longer. Her condition was not yet quite to his liking. George Lambton certainly believed Sceptre was the best horse in the race observing that after the race she blew much harder than horses trained by Alec Taylor would do normally, indicating that she was not in peak condition. It should however, be recorded that Ard Patrick's trainer Sam Darling always believed that he was better than Sceptre and that she was fit for the Eclipse. *A Century of Champions* rated Ard Patrick 137 and Sceptre 135 which seems about right, although a couple of pounds less than Sceptre deserves in this writer's view. However, either way that would mean that in a race provided both horses were at their peak then Sceptre would win because she would be receiving the sex allowance. She later beat Rock Sand in the Jockey Club Stakes, giving him seven pounds more than weight-for-age and sex allowance, by four lengths.

Sceptre won three other races including the Champion Stakes. It seems scarcely believable now but Sir William Bass asked Sievier to assist Taylor in training Sceptre after the Eclipse. It was fortunate that Taylor had by that time been able to improve her condition sufficiently for her to endure the punishing work schedule Sievier subjected her to when he was set loose at Manton. Alec Taylor accepted this with good grace but it can only be imagined what he thought of this. In fairness to Sievier when Sceptre was subjected to some particularly tough work on one occasion prior to the Jockey Club Stakes she blew so hard afterwards that one onlooker doubted she would be fit enough. Sievier however was confident and following similar work the next day she was clearer in her wind.

Sceptre really must have been the most amazing filly. Her victory in the Duke of York Handicap at Kempton almost defies belief. She was thought to be lame on the morning of the race and although this was not the case racing plates could not be fitted. It transpired that on occasions when she walked she displayed symptoms of lameness resembling stringhalt, although she is not recorded as suffering from this condition. Stringhalt which causes jerking of the hock joint is a nervous involuntary condition where the leg jerks up and then comes down sharply on to the ground. Instead of racing plates she ran in exceptionally soft ground in heavy working shoes. Taylor had been understandably worried and anxious. In the straight she was boxed in and was left with an incredible amount of ground to make up. Otto Madden, already nervous about riding her, had been given only one instruction. "You'll be all right if you don't get shut in". Yet here he was shut in not once but three times as he attempted to extract her. It was only in the last stride that she prevailed by a head from Happy Slave who was receiving forty pounds.

Sceptre was unlucky in many respects. Her owner and breeder the Duke of Westminster died and it was necessary to disperse his bloodstock. The sale took place at Newmarket in the summer of 1900 and Sceptre, was brought by Robert Sievier for 10,000 guineas (£672,000), a record for a yearling by 4,000 guineas. Sievier always claimed he would have gone higher as he was determined to get her. Had the Duke not died she would have been trained by the great John Porter and, in all probability, never have been beaten. All may yet have been well for, although now owned by Sievier, she would have been trained by Charles Morton had he not left in the autumn of 1901 to train for Mr J B Joel. Following this Sievier, to whom it would never have occurred that such a venture might fail, decided to train his horses himself.

Had Morton trained Sceptre, she would not have been subjected to the rigorous early season training schedule required to get her ready for an audacious, if lunatic, attempt to win the Lincoln handicap as a three-year-old. Sceptre's training at this stage had been unusual by any standards and as a result of some strange circumstances she had been over-trained at one stage, given the equivalent of four races in as many days on the gallops, yet not race-fit when the Lincoln was run. That she was able to finish second despite not being given the best of rides speaks volumes for her.

Morton would have given her a classic preparation and although Sceptre needed plenty of work, she was inclined to be thick-winded; he would not have over-trained her as early as March. An attempt to win the Lincoln can scarcely be regarded as an ideal preparation for the Guineas and Sievier might easily have ruined the career of a great filly. Remarkably she still won both the 2000 and 1000 Guineas. She later won the Oaks and St Leger and was unlucky not to win the Derby. That she was trained by Sievier is one of the tragedies of the turf. It is a testament to her remarkable toughness, disposition and wonderful durability that she raced twenty five times over four seasons. She was inclined to be less placid when in strong work and, as if aware that he was responsible for her abuse, vented her resentment on Sievier when he entered her box. In the circumstances she can hardly be blamed. One wonders again what further heights Sceptre might have reached had she been more fortunate in her owner and trainer as a three-year-old.

Despite his erratic, eccentric and boorish behaviour Sievier was not a fool and he understood horses and had an affinity with them. Unfortunately he often ran them when he needed money from a successful bet rather than when it best suited the horse. It is not in the least fanciful to imagine that she could have been, not just the best race mare ever, but the best racehorse of either gender. Advocates of Pretty Polly, would dispute this view, but they would surely have to concede that, whereas Pretty Polly was properly and considerately trained, Sceptre was subjected to almost criminal abuse from Sievier. As it is, her place in history is secure as it is almost certain no filly will ever again win four of the five English classics.

Alec Taylor was leading trainer for the first time in 1907 having won 39 races worth £25,793 (£1,650,752). In 1909 he was champion again with a total almost double that, of £47,165 (£3,018,560). By 1910 he had almost doubled his 1907 figure with £48,544 (£3,106,816) from 47 winners. In second place with less than half that was the Hon. George Lambton with £24,765. In 1914 he improved on this with £57,722 (£3,694.120). These were enormous sums in those days. The highest of these figures was not exceeded again until 1925 when Taylor himself did so with £56,638 (£1,982,330). Large as these sums were it should be remembered that John Porter had won 39 races in 1899 worth £56,113 (£3,591,232). It is also worth bearing in mind that the levels of prize money decreased after 1914.

During this period Taylor trained some outstanding horses. In addition to Sceptre, Bayardo, Gay Crusader, Gainsborough and Bayuda, he trained Lemberg to be second in the 2000 Guineas before winning the Derby; and he trained Rosedrop, who won the Oaks before becoming the dam of Gainsborough. In all, he trained the winners of twenty one classic races. Strangely it is possible that Taylor did not consider Bayardo to be the best horse he ever trained. Indeed, he was possibly not even second! He felt that he never realized the true potential of Gay Crusader and was bitterly disappointed when he broke down and could not be trained as a four-year-old. However, he later changed his mind and insisted that Picaroon was the best.

Picaroon was owned and bred by Mr Alexander Robb Cox, who was the younger brother of Alfred Cox, and who had inherited his brother's bloodstock interests on his death. Picaroon, who was foaled in 1922, was a brown colt by Beppo out of Ciceronnetta, who was by Cicero, out of Silesia, a half sister to Bayardo. Taylor said of him, "As a yearling he was not a particularly attractive animal, being somewhat small and mean in appearance, but I have seldom known a horse to make more improvement after he was broken in. He grew and developed in every way in a remarkable manner. He always had a beautiful action, which improved as he grew stronger, and ultimately it was as near perfection as possible".

Picaroon was dogged by misfortune as a juvenile and, as it turned out, all his life. Before he had raced he was lame behind after a gallop; he recovered, only for the same thing to happen again. Taylor's habitual patience ensured he recovered enough to win on his debut at Goodwood.

He missed his next intended race because of coughing but won his other races the Imperial Produce Stakes, impressively, and the Middle Park Stakes. He defeated the following years 2000 Guineas and Derby winner Manna on both occasions and St. Leger winner Solario in the Middle Park. He was rated second in the juvenile handicap, a pound behind Saucy Sue who was also trained at Manton.

Picaroon's classic season began well with a win in the Craven Stakes at Newmarket. However, he missed both the first two classics. He was lame in his near hind leg just prior to the Guineas. He was suffering from sceptic lymphangitis, which was accompanied by a high temperature. The effect was to strip him of all condition. He was forced to miss all his engagements until the autumn. This was a severe test of Taylor's patience and skill. It was not until early August that Taylor was able to contemplate a race and it was now a question of whether the colt could be readied for the St. Leger. He eventually appeared in a Plate at York at the end of August and, although backed down to odds-on, he was comfortably beaten, having not really taken the eye in the paddock. The St. Leger was a fortnight later. He finished fourth, well beaten by a combination of lack of condition and the distance.

Taylor by now had Picaroon somewhere close to his best condition and he won twice in four days, at Newbury in a plate, and then in a stakes race at Newmarket. A fortnight later he beat Pharos, who had finished second in the Derby and was now a five-year-old, in a match for the Champion Stakes. It was a thrilling race and, although they were the only runners, both jockeys set off at a brisk gallop and at the finish Picaroon had prevailed by half a length. He finished the year with an easy win in a stakes race at Newmarket. He was to remain in training as a four year old with much to look forward to. However, it was not to be. He had begun to suffer from arthritis, and this became so bad he had to be destroyed the following May. He was rated 135 by *A Century of Champions*.

Picaroons career has been dealt with in some detail because of Alec Taylor's insistence to the end that he was the best horse he had ever trained. Taylor's standards were always of the highest and, when all the horses he has trained are considered, his view indicates that, with just a little less ill fortune and a sprinkling of good, Picaroon could have been a high-class Classic winner and possibly he may even have lifted the Triple Crown. However, it is strange that Taylor could possibly have considered both Gay Crusader and Picaroon to be superior to Bayardo: most observers would feel that Bayardo was the best of the three, notwithstanding that Gay Crusader won the Triple Crown.

It is possible that Taylor had a slightly jaundiced view of Bayardo and felt he had done as much with him as had been possible. Apart from the Guineas and the Derby, when both he and Bayardo were not blessed with fortune, there was not much more he could have done. In addition some of his comments made with regard to Bayardo suggest that he admired him for his ability but, possibly because he could be difficult, wayward and had mood changes, he did not have the same affection for him that he felt for both Gay Crusader and Picaroon. Taylor spoke about both in glowing terms, particularly concerning their actions and physique, in a fashion he never employed about Bayardo, who, although he improved as he matured, has never been described by anyone as an outstanding physical example of a thoroughbred. With regard to both Gay Crusader and Picaroon there must have been a sense of unfinished business. Although Gay Crusader won the Triple Crown, Taylor felt that the best of him had yet to be seen and that there was more to come at the age four until, after a wonderful trial gallop, he broke down before his four-year-old had season started. With Picaroon, of course, he must have felt he never really had him as he would have wanted.

In such circumstances, even the most balanced judgment can be swayed. In some ways this is analogous with the position of a talented child who shows promise but dies early: he is mourned for what might have been and no matter what another sibling may achieve, they are considered unable to reach the heights forecast for their lost contemporary. It might seem impertinent to question Taylor's judgment with regard to his preference for Gay Crusader and Picaroon over Bayardo. However, it would have been interesting to ask Taylor to make a choice if offered any one of the three after their juvenile seasons. The answer has to be Bayardo simply because, whatever unfulfilled promise lay untapped in the other two, Bayardo would have been, based on his achievements at the age of two, the most likely of the trio to win the Triple Crown. Gay Crusader achieved much less as a juvenile than either Bayardo or Picaroon winning just one race. Bayardo had won seven races and had been undefeated. Picaroon was unbeaten in three races and it is conceded possibly beat better horses than did Bayardo. However, few would argue that Picaroon was a better juvenile than Bayardo. It is said that horses are rarely judged without prejudice and, in short, the accusation, if that is not too strong a word, is that Taylor simply liked Gay Crusader and Picaroon more than he did Bayardo and was guilty of such prejudice. When assessing race-horses many different aspects must be considered including soundness and in that area at least Bayardo was unquestionably the best of the three. He completed three years on the track and retired relatively sound, which was something that proved beyond Gay Crusader or Picaroon.

During his career, Taylor never trained more than 46 horses in any one season. Those were the days when a trainer knew each and every one of his charges, indeed every limb of each, at all stages of their career from breaking through to retirement. Taylor, like most trainers of his era, would have hated training 150-plus horses, as he would not have been able to train each horse. He would have been appalled at the idea of yearlings appearing at his stables broken at another yard by individuals he had never met. He never trained for more than 13 owners at any one time, and often for as few as six or seven; trying to keep in excess of twenty separate owners happy would have been considered a nightmare.

Taylor's relationship with Alfred Cox is something of a mystery. It seems clear judging from the profile of his other owners that he preferred the traditional owner breeder, preferably ones who did not gamble heavily. The only owner who did not fit this profile was Cox. Did Taylor continue to train for him, despite rows over beaten horses, simply because Cox supplied him with good horses? It can only be supposition, but Taylor in all probability decided to adopt a pragmatic view with regard to Cox and to accept that the price for training his horses was his demanding disposition and his lack of consideration and courtesy. It is worth remembering that Taylor trained Bayardo and Lemberg for Cox relatively early in his training career and could have been said to have made his reputation. To have declined to train Cox's horses due to any personal antipathy would have cost him his best owner both then and in the future. It would have resulted in him not training Gay Crusader and probably Picaroon amongst others. It does, however, stretch the imagination to breaking point to believe that Taylor had much respect for many of Cox's views particularly with regard to horse welfare, or that he would ever have sought to spend any time in Cox's company, beyond that which was required professionally. Taylor would have believed that Cox's determination to run Bayardo in the 2000 Guineas threw away his unbeaten record and may have cost him his entire three-year old career. Similarly he was against holding the trial for Gay Crusader over the full Gold Cup trip as a four-year- old which resulted in him breaking down, never to race again. Both these vital decisions were taken by Cox against all Taylor's instincts that in the long run what is best for the horse should always take precedence over any personal feelings or ambition.

Taylor's relationship with Danny Maher would seem to have been fairly harmonious. Apart from their open disagreement with regard to Maher's riding of Bayardo they enjoyed many triumphs together and there is little evidence that Taylor was unhappy to have Maher riding horses from the stable. Taylor would also have appreciated one of Maher's principal virtues: loyalty. After Maher's retirement in 1913, Taylor was left without the services of a top jockey and, although Steve Donoghue had ridden Gay Crusader and My Dear and, was at that time the rising star, he was noted for trying to get the ride on the best mounts, irrespective of who owned or trained them, something Taylor would have abhorred. He would also have been wary of Donoghue's somewhat confused and, at times, unhappy private life.

It should not be assumed that Alec Taylor, although a bachelor and a sober-living man who enjoyed the simple things in life, did not enjoy the company of his fellow man. He found time for Society and his friends particularly Somerville Tattersall and the trainer Robert Sherwood. Bob Sherwood was a friend from Taylor's youth and he stayed with him for Newmarket meetings. They were contrasting characters: Sherwood with his love of the good things in life and Taylor with his love for simplicity. It is true to say that, despite never being short of money, Taylor's lifestyle bordered on the austere. He would rather walk, even if it meant carrying a suitcase, than take a taxi. He travelled second-class on trains unless he was in company of other trainers and owners. He rarely left Manton other than to attend a race meeting, or the sales, and he never took a holiday. However, he had a genuine love of the racehorse and a fine appreciation of whatever was good. There was nothing cheap or tawdry about him. He possessed a dignity born of self restraint and, something perhaps more important in his time than today, inherent good taste. He had a quiet softly spoken voice and a quiet manner. It was his way of building confidence. However, although he left nobody in doubt about who was master, he was never known to lose his temper. He was a strict disciplinarian with his staff and, like his father, he loathed touts. On one occasion shortly after he took control at Manton he heard that touts intended to witness a gallop from the adjoining spinney. Taylor arranged a shoot and had beaters go through the woods. The touts were flushed out and returned to Marlborough feeling very sorry for themselves! He was once described when sitting on a horse as like "an equestrian statue". He was not without a grim sense of humour. He once observed to Somerville Tattersall of the auctioneering firm: "You are the only people who get something out of a bad horse".

Alec Taylor was characterised by his beautiful dress, unhurried manner and kind polite ways. His dress did not however extend to his attire on the gallops. Sidney Galtrey described him thus one morning as he set out for the days work:-

"I shall never forget his appearance and how it flattened out any ideas that trainers were swell fellows in immaculately cut breeches and leggings. He had on the old-fashioned cloth leggings, cut wide, so that they spread over the boot-tops. They descended from unfashionably cut breeches. Really they were shut off by the famous old Melton blue coat which he wore. Once it had a velvet collar. You could see that it was a faithful old friend that had never let him down and which it would break his heart to discard for ever. Some years later, when I was on a visit to him, he was still getting the last thread or two out of it".

It was said that when dressed at Manton for work with horses he could be taken for a gentleman farmer, which in some ways he was as he had once owned 2,000 acres. However, when dressed for the races he could equally be taken for a bank manager, which again, with his excellent head for figures, was not far wrong.

Taylor never married and his modest needs were catered for by his spinster sister Jane. When asked why he had not married he replied "I've got plenty to do without worrying about women". Sidney Galtrey described their home at Manton thus, "Inside there was the unmistakable smell of old furniture, carpets and heavy curtains. It was the home of two contented people, worldly and unpretentious". An alternative view of life at Manton might be that it was oppressively gloomy. The inside was rendered sombre as a result of allowing various types of outside foliage to grow unrestrained by the windows. In addition as Taylor had not introduced electricity and lighting was therefore provided by old-fashioned paraffin lamps.

Although caring little for the luxuries wealth could bring, Taylor managed his financial affairs shrewdly. Realizing how much property had increased after the Great War he decided to sell Manton and in September 1919 it was offered for sale by auction. Shortly after the announcement Joseph Watson bought Manton and the Clatford Park estate privately. A condition included the proviso that Taylor could continue to train there. Over the years Manton had expanded to 5,000 acres and was by now an expansive property. Watson was a northern businessman whose fortune came from soap and oil cake. He was raised to the peerage in 1922 and took the title Lord Manton. However, he died after suffering a heart attack in the hunting field that same year and only after a period of five years and much protracted negotiation did Manton pass to a great friend of Taylor's (and one of his owners) Somerville Tattersall in partnership with Major Gerald Deane.

Alec Taylor's health had been a cause for concern for some time and the new owners in a gesture entirely lacking in any sentimentality and possibly sensitivity, asked Taylor to retire. This was not what he had in mind and was a blow as he had always assumed he would die at Manton. In the event Taylor retired at the end of the 1927 season after which he handed over to his assistant, Joseph Lawson, who had been with Taylor for thirty years, having joined him as a sixteen-year-old. Over the next twenty years Joe Lawson continued the success at Manton, winning 11 classics. He later won the Derby in 1954, after, unwillingly, leaving Manton, with Never Say Die, who provided a first Derby winner for Lester Piggott.

Classic wins

2000 Guineas :	Kennymore	1914
	Gay Crusader	1917
	Gainsborough	1918
	Craig an Eran	1921
1,000 Guineas:	Saucy Sue	1925
Derby:	Lemberg	1910
	Gay Crusader	1917
	Gainsborough	1918
Oaks:	Rosedrop	1910
	Sunny Jane	1917
	My Dear	1918
	Bayuda	1919
	Love in Idleness	1921
	Pogrom	1922
	Saucy Sue	1925
	Short Story	1926
St. Leger:	Challacombe	1905
	Bayardo	1909
	Gay Crusader	1917
	Gainsborough	1918
	Book Law	1927

At his retirement, Taylor had trained 928 winners (1,003 if those prior to 1902 are included) in Britain for a total value of £801,530 (£27,252,020) (£839,070 (£28,528,380) if prize money prior to 1902 is included) plus Grand Prix de Paris. He had been leading trainer in terms of winners 12 times, a twentieth century record, including every year from 1917 to 1923. He had won 21 classics and every big race with the exception of the Cambridgeshire. He had earned the sobriquet (which will probably remain his forever) of "The Wizard of Manton" by which he was popularly known. He was truly a great trainer who personified the old adage that "in racing, the only time you do not need to be patient is when you need to be very patient". Despite some old school trainers feeling that he kept his horses in cotton wool his methods stood the test of time and in all circumstances his view was that the horse's welfare should always have priority. He was rated the fifth greatest trainer of the twentieth century in *A Century of Champions*.

When Taylor retired, he went to live at the Grange Thorpe near Egham where he died on 28th January 1943. He was a very rich man on his death and in his will, made a month before he left a net estate worth £593,098 (£19,572,234). His will left many bequests as befits his generous nature, £10,000 (£330,000) to Joseph Lawson, £500 (£16,500) to the Marlborough saddler and £2,000 (£66,000) to his doctor. His paintings by Alfred Munnings, Lynwood Palmer and others - which were insured for only £1,200 (£40,000)! - were left in trust to his sister and on her death to the

Stewards of the Jockey Club. He bequeathed £20,000 (£660,000) to the
Royal Veterinary College and the same amount to the Royal Air Force
Benevolent Fund and the residue to four other charities. There can be
very few individuals connected with racing who have acquired and, more
importantly, kept such a fortune and yet it was said that he rarely if ever
had a bet.

Training Record

Races	won	Value £
1902	12	2,305
1903	33	18,731.50
1904	27	7,236
1905	38	14,216
1906	39	27,355.50
1907	39	25,953+
1908	29	25,254.50
1909	47	47,165+
1910	47	48,544+
1911	20	15,546
1912	20	7,794
1913	25	14,621
1914	39	51,722.50+
1915	9	3,173
1916	16	8,858
1917	25	17,930+
1918	32	36,674+
1919	39	34,207+
1920	47	35,907+
1921	51	48,298+
1922	56	52,084.50+
1923	46	49,292+
1924	55	47,473
1925	51	56,638+
1926	39	49,623
1927	47	55,199
	928	801,530.50

+ Leading trainer

CHAPTER 17

Mr Fairie

Alfred William Cox was born in 1857 and was fortunate to be able to live life in his own way in a style and fashion which many dream of, but few ever achieve. His life story was of a somewhat legendary nature and would not have been considered credible if presented as a work of fiction. On the whole Cox's life was blessed with considerable fortune in all but one crucial respect: he was afflicted with a condition which blighted his life, something which will be covered later. Born the second son of Alexander Robb Cox of Hafod, Elwy, Denbighshire, a Liverpool jute merchant, he was destined, at least by his family, for a career in the Army. However, at Malvern his concentration was directed more towards games and pastimes rather than study and he failed to pass his examination.

His failure to progress in any way with his education, and his rather too advanced interest in matters of the turf, resulted in his father, very probably in despair, sending him to Australia with £100 (£4,700) plus an allowance in order that he might learn the art of sheep farming. This was in either 1879 or 1880 when Cox was aged 22 or 23. Within five years Cox was a wealthy man. Various stories have been told with regard to the way in which he acquired his fortune which all relates to the Broken Hill Silver mine. The authentic story has only recently been established and romantic as this was the legends that have grown around the manner of Cox attaining his wealth are even more fantastic. The most circumstantial version is one given by "Milroy" in the *Sydney Mail* and the most recent and authentic given in the recently published *Masters of Manton* and supplied by an archivist of the Broken Hill Propriety Company. Those interested in Cox's involvement can find a detailed history in that book. In précis Cox landed in Australia with an introduction to Sir Thomas Elder who owned several stations about 200 miles north of Melbourne.

Characteristically Cox soon involved himself in local horse-racing activities until word reached his father and his allowance and inheritance was threatened. Cox obtained a job as a jackeroo (the name for British hands on outback stations) and met and came to know Mr George McCulloch of Mount Gipps one of the founders of the Broken Hill mine. Cox, not surprisingly, became swept up in to frenzy that any prospecting generates and he asked McCulloch to sell him one of the 14 shares. McCulloch asked £200 (£10,500) for a share that had cost him £35. Cox

175

offered £100 (£5,250) and after this was refused £120 (£6,290) which was also declined. Cox ever the gambler challenged McCulloch to a game of cards to decide matters. If Cox won the share would cost £120 if he lost £200. It was eventually decided that they should play a game of euchre - an American card game, a variant of poker, played with the 32 highest cards in the pack. It was decided to play the best of three and although Cox lost the first game he won the next two. The new agreement was drawn up and among the signatories was "A W Cox station hand". Cox sold some of his holdings quickly and would have sold more if the price had not been considered too high. Within six years each of the original fourteen shares was worth £1,260,000 (£70,000,000). That he was unable to sell more of his shares was an element of good luck which Cox never forgot and it lodged deep in his psyche. Cox was now wealthy beyond the needs of most and he returned to England to the life of a sybarite.

Cox wasted little time in commencing his new life on the turf. During the following winter he hunted in Cheshire and met John Wallace who had horses trained by Jimmy Ryan at Newmarket. In 1887 he registered the nom de course "Mr Fairie", a name under which he raced for almost his entire career as an owner. The Jockey Club permitted individuals to race under assumed names at that time. It is not known why he chose "Mr Fairie" and after his death none of his friends or family could offer any explanation.

At the December sales he purchased the five-year-old Isobar for 810 guineas (£43,700) from Lord Bradford. Isobar had finished second to Melton in the St Leger but he was no longer the force he had been. However he provided Cox - and his colours of "White orange sleeves and cap" which were to become famous - with his first winner. The race was a seller after which he allowed him to be bought for 500 guineas (£26,500). This was not great business and at this time Cox was buying horses, sometimes paying good money, but with only moderate returns. As an example he paid 2,100 guineas (£113,200) for Son and Heir - a colt by Ayrshire - but he proved very modest winning only a £150 (£8,000) stakes race. He also finished first in an apprentice race but was disqualified.

Meanwhile Cox was forming a breeding stud. His stud farm comprised twelve of the Jockey Club paddocks, at Southfields on the Hamilton Road in Newmarket, which he leased. The paddocks were very small: only about three or four acres each. As paddocks, their size would have made them unsuitable in the opinion of many horsemen at that time who thought that horses could only be reared in paddocks which gave them plenty of room to gallop. Cox was to prove that this theory was not infallible. His bloodstock advisors who bought mares for him did so with great discrimination. In 1889 he acquired privately a young mare called Agave by Springfield with a colt foal by Galopin at foot. He became Galeopsis who won three races as a two-year-old, however, he was gelded in an effort to correct his un-cooperative nature; but, more importantly, Agave produced Galeottia, sister to Galeopsis, winner of the One Thousand Guineas in 1895 and granddam of Gay Crusader and Manilardo. Even more important though was the purchase in 1888 for £1,600 (£78,000) of Lady Muncaster. She was the dam of Isoletta who in turn was the dam of Galicia.

Alfred Cox could be considered fortunate in his career as an owner/breeder. He or his advisors had a reasonably simple philosophy which was get plenty of Galopin into the pedigree. A similar policy was adopted with Isonomy and he enjoyed similar good fortune when this produced the Derby winner Lemberg. Nonetheless, whether by luck or good judgment, Cox, with this policy, was ultimately successful. A good example of his excellent fortune occurred in 1894 when Cox was seeking a foal to run in the paddocks with another foal for which he harboured great hopes. Ryan's wife Rosa obliged by selling him a colt called Eager who was considered unlikely ever to amount to much. As luck would have it, Cox's foal disappointed but Eager developed into a top-class sprinter winning the Portland Plate at Doncaster as a four-year-old, then the following year he carried 9 stone 7 lbs to win the Wokingham Stakes at Ascot and then the July Cup at Newmarket.

Alfred Cox's horses were trained by Ryan until 1903. For a year after that they were in the care of Major Charles Beatty but Cox moved them again in 1904 to Manton to be trained by Alec Taylor. It was from that time that Cox's great days on the turf began. However, prior to this there is a strong suspicion that Cox's management of the Jockey Club paddocks left something to be desired. The paddocks had been reduced to such a state that his employees were unhappy with the conditions and had reported the matter to the Jockey Club. It seems there was a possibility that his tenancy was on the verge of termination when the stud produced first Bayardo and then Lemberg at which point all criticism ceased. It should be made clear that this cannot be verified with certainty but, assuming this to be true, it is not clear how producing two top-class horses improved the condition of the paddocks. If they were unsatisfactory, then producing two good horses in them was a result of good mating and nature and nothing to do with the state of the paddocks, which would have retarded rather than advanced their progress. It must be presumed that they remained unsatisfactory but as two good horses had been bred there the case for terminating Cox's tenancy was considered to have been weakened.

Alfred Cox did not enter the world of the turf as a way of advancing his social status. He was a brusque, self-willed and uncompromising individual who despised all social graces and had no objection at all to being unpopular. During this period when class distinction in England was still at its most prominent, Cox would have been unconcerned by such matters, committed frequent solecisms and cared not one jot that he would have been thought something of a *parvenu* by his so-called betters. He was considered by most people in racing to be unapproachable and, with the single exception of Steve Donoghue (and the usual hangers on that any successful individual in the world of racing inevitably attracts,) it seems he had few close friends and he never married. There would have been little point in prospective society mothers, looking for a suitable match for their daughters, considering Cox as an eligible bachelor. His money would have been his only attraction as a husband for their daughters and there is no evidence that he would have given such girls a second glance and enough to believe he may not even have noticed them.

In London Cox earned a reputation as an exceptional judge of Havana cigars and old brandy. It was the ready consumption of these that contributed to his poor health and accelerated his death. However, when not under the influence of the fine brandy, he could be an agreeable companion, although it is also true to say that there seem to have been only a few instances, with the exception of Donoghue, of Cox having much warmth, kindness, humour or generosity. As he had few close friends and was not inclined to spend time socialising in the fashion of the times, it is not clear who it was that may have enjoyed his company, particularly those fine cigars and excellent brandy! He did have a circle of intimate friends but these would seem to be mainly racing acquaintances and then only the sort seeking information for betting purposes. The writer Alfred Watson spoke of Cox in warm terms and claimed a close friendship with him. However, when Watson, in 1910, was planning to write about Cox in the Badminton magazine he thought it would be prudent not to ask him for any help and not even mention it to him! Cox hated to be the subject of discussion and Watson feared that he might take offence at the idea of such an article and would ask that it should not be written! It is possible that Watson need not have worried as five years later Cox commissioned him to write a book about Galicia to be published privately, something he would hardly have done if he had not had trust in Watson.

On the racecourse Cox could be seen, often sadly the worse for the effects of alcohol, strutting around, clad in a frock coat, silk hat upon his head and with his trousers pressed at the side in the manner favoured by King Edward VII. He generally wore a gardenia in his buttonhole and was usually accompanied by the inevitable long cigar between his fingers.

Cox had a home in Newmarket, Warren Cottage on the Severals which he had brought from Captain Machell, and when racing at Headquarters he would sometimes drive to the races in a carriage and pair. It was not unknown for him to remain in his carriage at the races and have his runners brought to him for inspection before and after the race. He displayed little emotion after even the biggest win often looking almost disinterested and, as befits a good poker player, wearing an inscrutable expression. There was, however, at least one exception, when Bayardo won the Ascot Gold Cup and his joy and relief was clear for all to see. He could be brutally rude on occasions. In 1913 after his colt Aleppo had finished second in the Goodwood Cup he was being pestered by individuals keen to buy the horse as a stallion prospect. Cox was not it would seem in the best of tempers and was described as "like a dream walking". He brushed aside the enquiry of a "very important individual" and retorted "I've not made up my mind yet to sell him or (pause) have him gelded".

His trainer Alec Taylor, as a person the antithesis of Cox, seems to have understood him and managed him better than most, although, as will be seen, Cox always seemed to have his way on all matters and on at least two occasions this was to the serious detriment of the horses concerned. He insisted that Bayardo run in the Two Thousand Guineas when not ready, which threw away his unbeaten record and he instructed Taylor to arrange a trial for Gay Crusader as a four-year-old over the full Cup distance. This was unnecessary as he had demonstrated that he stayed the distance of the Ascot Cup in any case. Gay Crusader worked brilliantly, but broke down and never raced again. Cox liked his horses to race where engaged and in the instances of both Bayardo and Lemberg they ran with remarkable frequency, twenty five times and twenty four respectively. He was difficult and uncooperative as regards his horses in training with Taylor and often refused to allow any of them to be tried or worked in company with the horses of any other owner. This caused difficulties in deciding which unexposed horses should be run in which race. It was not uncommon for Taylor to run two or three unraced horses in one race and to win with the least fancied in the betting. It also made difficulties in deciding which horses to run in big races. Cox would also not allow his horses to be shown to anyone without his express permission. He had difficulties with his previous trainers and there is one story of an incident with a previous trainer which may be apocryphal but does have an authentic feel to it. Lord Howard de Walden found Cox one day chasing the head man at the stables armed with a Long Tom – a large horse-whip. "I suppose you've come here for the same purpose as me" Cox said to his Lordship. He then resumed the chase! He was a big gambler, certainly before Taylor trained his horses, and in all probability on a similar scale afterwards at least for a while. It would seem that Cox was not a successful gambler and eventually stopped altogether. He would remark to Alec Taylor when one of his horses was the probable winner "If this had been in my betting days I should have had a couple of thousand (£128,000) on it".

Steve Donoghue liked Cox and described him as a man of decided views and a remarkable personality. Donoghue was a kindly man and this seems like diplomatic language. Eventually even he was forced too add that he also thought him capricious, very critical, rather exacting and perhaps not always impartial. On the credit side he also says Cox was kind and treated him with cordial friendliness and that he had a great affection for him.

In his autobiography *Just My Story* Donoghue describes how "He (Cox) often came to see me at my rooms in London sometimes quite unexpectedly. I would arrive back after racing and occasionally get quite a shock, my housekeeper telling me that Mr Cox had been waiting upstairs for an hour. I would run upstairs, distressed to think he had been kept waiting, as his health was always rather delicate, and there he would be, peacefully asleep, in a big arm-chair facing the picture he had given me of his horse Gay Crusader. "Ah Donoghue" he would say on awakening, "there you are; I just dropped off after having a look at the old horse. I like your picture of him better than mine". And we would have great chats about his horses and his plans for them". However, not all jockeys were treated as well. On one occasion in the paddock a jockey unwisely suggested that his mount, owned by Cox, did not have much chance. Cox's response was to poke the unfortunate jockey in the diaphragm with his stick then tell him to return to the weighing room and take off his colours! Notwithstanding this and his capricious nature, he was considered a good sportsman and it has not been possible to find any reference to contradict this view.

His first classic success was with Galeottia, a daughter of Galopin, in the 1000 Guineas of 1895. It was to be fourteen years before his next success when Bayardo won the St. Leger. Lemberg, who was a half brother to Bayardo, won the Derby the following year. His other classic successes were with his Triple Crown winner Gay Crusader and Oaks winner My Dear. It is perhaps no coincidence that these two were bred on very similar lines. My Dear was by Beppo out of Bayardo's half sister Silesia, while Gay Crusader was bred on almost the reverse cross, being by Bayardo out of a daughter of Beppo. This combination was to be found in two other top-class horses trained by Alec Taylor and owned by the Cox family, namely Aleppo and Picaroon. Aleppo won the Ascot Gold Cup in 1914 and was by Beppo out of Chere Reine who was a half sister to Bayardo's dam Galicia.

Cox generally enjoyed good fortune with his breeding policies. However, he had an opportunity to establish a record that would almost certainly never have been equalled. Cox bred Gay Crusader who won the Triple Crown. However, for a period he owned Rosedrop who became the dam of Gainsborough who also won the Triple Crown, doing so the year after Gay Crusader. Simon Harrison had bought both Rosedrop and her dam Rosaline in December 1907 for 900 guineas (£60,480) and then subsequently offered Rosedrop for sale with other yearlings. Harrison tried to persuade Cox to bid for her but the latter declined to do so as he disliked her flaxen mane and tail. However, the filly went to Manton anyway after Sir William Bass secured her with a bid for 700 guineas (£47,040), and, it was for him that she won the Oaks. When Sir William sold his stud in May 1911, Cox, by now one assumes prepared to overlook Rosedrop's mane and tail as she was a classic winner, paid 4,500 guineas (£302,400) for the filly. Then, as a four-year-old, he ran her twice, but without success. She was sent to Bayardo the following year but was barren, after which Cox sold her privately to Lady James Douglas. Had Cox held on to Rosedrop, it is entirely possible that he could have bred Gainsborough and been responsible for breeding and owning two Triple Crown winners in consecutive years.

Alfred Cox was a great admirer of Danny Maher. In 1910 he was particularly keen to obtain his services for Bayardo and Lemberg. He was unable to secure first claim and had to settle for a second one at an annual cost of £2,000 (£128,000). Cox was convinced that not having Maher on board Lemberg in the 2000 Guineas cost him the race and equally that a poor ride by Maher on the same horse cost him the St Leger! In addition Cox was unimpressed by his ride on Bayardo in the Goodwood Cup. After Maher's ride on Lemberg in the St. Leger, Cox's arrangement with him was terminated. Ironically, Cox probably had little to complain about in the St. Leger as Lemberg was outstayed. Despite this Maher rode many winners for Cox and won far more races that he should not have done compared to those lost that he should have won.

For all that Cox could be a demanding and, on occasions, a disagreeable man, he was strangely sentimental with regard to his horses and he became somewhat over-attached to them. This was demonstrated by his unwillingness to sell all but a few of them, despite some very tempting offers. It may have been that he was attached to his horses or, if a more cynical view is taken, it may have been that he did not want to risk them turning out better under someone else's ownership! He would have been conscious that he had tried hard to sell his shares in the Broken Hill mine probably thinking they were not worth much. Had he succeeded he would of course not have been a wealthy man. He was very involved with the decisions with regard to how his mares were mated and also how the resultant produce performed on the gallops as well as the racecourses.

Cox had always raced under the nom de course of "Mr Fairie". However in 1917 he decided to race under his own name. He had raced during 1892 under the name "A W Cox" but during every other year he had raced as "Mr Fairie. The reason he raced as "Mr Fairie" was certainly not to hide his identity as he was invariably referred to as, amongst other things, "Fairie Cox". Why he raced under an assumed name and why he decided to drop it is unknown. It would seem that the matter must remain as a mystery and be considered just one more aspect of his idiosyncratic nature.

While at Newmarket for the Craven meeting of 1919, Cox was seized with illness and he consequently returned to London. It was soon realized that there was no hope of recovery and he died on Sunday 4th May. It was stated earlier that his life had been blessed with good fortune in all aspects except one. His health had never been good and there is no doubt that he was an alcoholic. His addiction blighted his life and only a marvellous constitution helped him to withstand his inner demons for so long. Cox was said to be heavily inebriated on more than one occasion in public resulting in his behaviour being either embarrassing, boorish or both. However, with the realisation that he was ill and not always able to control his behaviour it is perhaps more understandable and it is therefore possible to view him and his eccentricities a little more charitably.

Cox never married and although this fact, and his tendency to coxcombry, would lend itself to the assumption that he was homosexual by inclination there is no evidence or suggestion that he was a pederast. When taken ill Cox had attended Headquarters to see Manilardo, a brother to Gay Crusader, run. He won the Wood Ditton Stakes easily and proved to be Cox's last winner. Cox's life had never straightforward and, somehow, it is not a surprise to learn that he had had a premonition that he would die during 1919.

From 1888 until his death, Cox won 183 races for a value of £186,009 (£11,900,000). He was leading owner and breeder in 1909, 1910 and 1917. As an owner-breeder Cox can be considered an outstanding contributor to the breed. After the initial years he relied entirely on the produce of his own small band of brood mares. He was rated 60th out of 100 makers of the twentieth century in *A Century of Champions*.

Alfred Cox was 62 when he died and his racing interests and considerable wealth were inherited by his brother, Alexander Robb Cox who maintained both the racing and breeding operations. In addition,

The field assembles at the start of the St Leger. Bayardo is on the extrame left

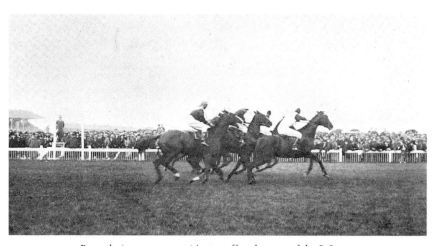

Bayardo (nearest camera) jumps off at the start of the St Leger

Two views of the finish. From both angles Maher can be clearly seen standing up in his irons as Bayardo waltzes home

The Royal Box at Doncaster. Edward VII watches his last St Leger

Bayardo is led in after the St Leger

Just two days later Bayardo canters home in the Doncaster Stakes

Bayardo – judging by his coat this picture was taken in the spring!

Bayardo as a three-year-old with Danny Maher up

The Birdcage at Newmarket

The Rowley Mile Stands in Bayardo's time

Bayardo in uncooperative mood before the Limekiln Stakes

He clearly had no idea the easiest of tasks was before him!

Bayardo as a three-year-old. The look of eagles?

notwithstanding some generous offers for Gay Crusader and others he continued Alfred Cox's determined policy of not selling his horses.

Alfred Cox generously bequeathed £5,000(£105,000) to Alec Taylor, although it would be stretching matters to say that he was in need of money, £2,000(£42,000) to his stud groom and £500(£10,500) to Joseph Lawson, one time head lad and eventually successor to Taylor at Manton.

Cox's Classic successes		
2000 Guineas:	Gay Crusader	1917
1000 Guineas:	Galeottia	1895
Derby:	Lemberg	1910
	Gay Crusader	1917
Oaks:	My Dear	1918
St. Leger:	Bayardo	1909
	Gay Crusader	1917

CHAPTER 18

Danny Maher

Daniel Aloysius Maher was born of Irish parents on 29th October 1881 in Hartford, Connecticut. He weighed only 4 stones 9 pounds when he began riding at the age of 14. Three years later at the age of 17 in 1898 he was champion jockey in North America. Maher was nurtured by the remarkable William C Daly a native of County Cork who emigrated from Ireland to America when he was aged seven. Daly lost a leg while working in a stone quarry, then worked as a bartender until he could buy a horse. He began with trotters before moving on to training thorough-breds and then to training jockeys. Known as "Father Bill", Daly was strict and eccentric but, in addition to Maher, he was also responsible for several other top jockeys.

Maher had his first winner on Phoebus, his second mount. In 1898 he headed the list of American jockeys and was champion with 167 wins. It was a meteoric rise. All went well in his career until the summer of 1900 when his riding of a horse was called into question. He was exonerated, however, he felt his character had been damaged and he made the decision to come to England. This was characteristic of Maher, who was very protective of his good name. This was again demonstrated in England when in 1911 his riding of a horse called Sallust was called into question by the stewards at Leicester. He was again exonerated, but even so he felt that he had been subjected to an injustice and he refused to ride at Leicester again. In his short riding career in North America, Maher rode the winners of the Champagne and Tremont Stakes plus the Gazelle, Brooklyn, Toboggan, Metropolitan, Carter and Ladies Handicaps.

About this time racing in America was undergoing a fundamental change and particularly with regard to jockeyship. Two jockeys, "Snapper" Garrison and Tod Sloan were largely responsible for the change in style to short stirrups and the adoption of the forward seat. In addition, racetrack surfaces were scraped, combed and rolled, the turns graded and speed promoted as opposed to stamina as previously. North America had staged four-mile races until about 1880. There was considerable anti-gambling sentiment in America at the turn of the century driven mainly by puritans and racing was restricted. Several owners and trainers brought their horses to England, along with some jockeys, to try their luck.

Not everybody from America had British racing's best interests at heart. Unfortunately, the straightforward and honest were accompanied by some very undesirable adherents. Their principal aim seemed to be to separate the betting ring from its assets by means of doping horses to win. They were singularly successful in their aims and some spectacular betting coups left the bookmakers reeling. Whilst many felt little sympathy for a body of men whose livelihood depended on punters losing, it was obvious that betting on horses, for those outside the American tent, was a forlorn pastime as they had little chance of winning. George Lambton observed to the American trainer John Huggins "I suppose there are many rogues and thieves racing in America". Huggins replied "There is not one, they have all come over here."

Maher came to England with several other jockeys and transformed riding in this country. Maher initially came over in the autumn of 1900 principally to ride the horses of Mr Pierre Lorillard – whose place in history is secure as the owner of the first American-bred horse to win the Derby, Iroquois in 1881 – and he first rode in England at the Manchester September meeting in 1900. His first two mounts were favourites and he won on both. By the end of the season he had ridden 27 winners at a high percentage of twenty one. Four of the American jockeys, Maher, Tod Sloan and Lester and Johnny Rieff had strike rates of over twenty percent. At Ascot that year sixteen of the twenty eight races had been won by American jockeys.

It is no exaggeration to say the effect of the arrival in England of American jockeys was seismic. It was not just that American jockeys rode much shorter than their English counterparts. In addition they rode with a forward seat, as against an upright one, which made better use of the horse's centre of gravity. However, the main difference was the way they rode races. Until this time races in England, except sprints, were slowly run with jockeys holding up their mounts until the last possible moment, with a victory by a short head considered an act of artistry. The pace of races could be very slow. On one occasion the starter at Winchester claims to have beaten the whole field home on his hack in one race, so slow was the pace with all the jockeys holding up their mounts. American jockeys believed they could win the race much earlier by going to the front some way out, challenging their rivals to try to catch them. English jockeys felt that they had more control over their mounts in a finish. The problem seemed to be that they were unable to catch the horses ridden by American jockeys and thereby engage them in any sort of finish! Immediately after the start of a race while the English jockeys were taking a "pull" the American jockeys were rousting their mounts along and establishing leads which were impossible to reduce and as a result the English jockeys were made to look foolish.

American jockeys ride against the clock as this is the way horses are trained and consequently are wonderful judges of pace. A good American work-rider can gallop a horse, for example, four furlongs in 48.2 seconds, not 47.3 or 49.1. English trainers preferred to train one horse against another so English jockeys had not been made to develop the same awareness of times and of speed. Faced with rivals who were armed with superior tactical acumen as well as a more effective riding style, the English jockeys were thus left with a stark choice: pull up their leathers or get out of racing. Mornington Cannon a great horseman of the old school declined to adapt and drifted out of racing. Although it is true to say that Cannon was known to be indifferent to riding and he lacked the passion for winning possessed by Fred Archer for example. It was said that Cannon preferred to go boating or watch cricket than ride in races. It would be wrong to claim that the American style was supreme. Eventually a mixture of the two became the norm. However, the Jockey Club became sufficiently alarmed about opportunities for native jockeys and in response the apprentice allowance was adopted to encourage them.

Pierre Lorillard died in 1901 and Maher established his reputation on two horses belonging to Sir James Miller: Aida in the 1000 Guineas and Rock Sand in the Derby and St Leger of 1903. Rock Sand also won the 2000 Guineas but Maher missed out on his chance of the Triple Crown as he rode Flotsam in the Guineas where he finished second. Flotsam was owned by Sir Daniel Cooper and there is a story that Sir James and Sir Daniel tossed a coin for Maher's services in the Guineas. As matters turned out the coin fell the wrong way for Maher. Nevertheless, as he had ridden Skyscraper to finish third in both the 1000 Guineas and the Oaks it meant that Maher had been placed in all five Classics of 1903.

Maher soon adapted his riding to English courses. His pronounced style developed for the fast level tracks of America was unsuited to English courses with their undulations. He discovered that it was impossible to get horses balanced again if they changed their legs or rolled about. "His seat became a perfect mixture of the old and the new" said George Lambton. "His patience was wonderful and nothing would induce him to ride a horse hard unless he had him going as he wanted". From this period onwards, British jockeyship would never be the same, although American Jockeys, with the exception of Maher, had left England within ten years of arriving. Even so, they had left their mark.

In retrospect it can be seen that British racing was all the better for the American jockeys influence. Most would agree that it was better that races were now run more often at a true gallop rather than a gentle canter followed by a sprint. Not everyone saw matters this way. One owner of long standing declared that "the American seat has entirely destroyed true horsemanship, because although it wins races it is entirely trick riding and smacks more of the circus than the racecourse". Another experienced horseman wrote about twenty years after "the American invasion", "We have many jockeys nowadays, but few horsemen". He considered that although the forward seat was better in distributing weight on a horse, it was bad because it meant an increased use of the whip, which caused horses to swerve, bump and cross more than was the case before.

Viewing matters in hindsight, it can safely be said that both these opinions were wrong. Few would disagree that the most important thing is that a race represents a true indication of which horse is best over the distance of the race. Therefore it follows that a true pace will ensure that outcome more often than a crawl. In other words the horse is far more important than the jockey, and seeing a thoroughbred outrunning his peers in a truly run race is of greater consequence, and, indeed, of greater visual enjoyment, than seeing a jockey display nerve and timing to get his mount up on the line in a race run at little more than a hack canter until the distance pole.

The great trainer John Porter whose career spanned both the old style and the new had no doubt that the new style was superior. He wrote, with reference to Tod Sloan, "From the long stirrup and the long rein we passed to the other extreme – the short stirrup and the short rein. Here again we found a genius, who not only set a new fashion in riding races but showed us a new way in running them. Instead of the slow, muddling way of waiting, we had races run as they should be. In this Sloan showed his superiority by his knowledge of pace. He did not ride from pillar to post, as others were apt to do, but at a pace that would give his horse a chance to carry him to the end of the race." Tod Sloan, who did not suffer from self doubt or any bouts of modesty, agreed with Porter's lofty estimation of his abilities and declared when writing about his riding of Caiman to beat Flying Fox in the Middle Park Plate that "There was such a hopeless ignorance of pace among the majority of those riding in the race that I suppose I was able to kid them."

The first horse-race to be filmed is probably the 1896 Derby won by the Prince of Wales's Persimmon who beat St Frusquin, the odds-on favourite, by a neck after a pulsating duel. However, the initial impression of the film is one of mild amusement at the jockeys' almost comical upright riding seat. There is a photograph taken as the horses are about to round Tattenham Corner and without exception every jockey is either upright or slightly leaning backwards. Within ten years almost every jockey had pulled up his stirrups and adopted a forward seat. Modern jockeys look much neater in the saddle than their nineteenth century counterparts and it inconceivable that anyone could argue that a modern jockey would not out-ride one from the Victorian age using a style from that period. By nineteen twenty four the transformation had been completed for some time and a picture of Sansovino leading the Derby field round Tattenham Corner clearly shows every rider with higher stirrups and a forward seat.

The clock certainly indicates that British racing benefited from the American jockeys innovations. From 1900 until the Great War races were run in much quicker times, although times for sprint races did not change all that much. Even so races under a mile were still run about two seconds faster than during the period from 1887 until 1900. Races between a mile and a mile and a half were about four and a half seconds faster and races of two miles and upwards an incredible ten to twelve seconds faster.

English owners were beginning to fight shy of American riders most of which had crossed the channel to Paris in order to continue their more nefarious practices this time on the French! Maher, despite his promising beginning, did not acquire instant fame. His breakthrough had come with Rock Sand and in the next three years he rode two more Derby winners. Firstly on Cicero (possibly a little fortunately as Jardy, who was probably a better horse, was coughing just before the race) in 1905, and the following year with the unlucky Spearmint who developed leg trouble and raced only once more after his Derby success. Interestingly, Spearmint, who was a comfortable winner from a better than average field, would not have run if the filly Flair, who was considered better, had not gone wrong shortly after winning the One Thousand Guineas, which she had done with considerable ease. Of the three Maher considered Spearmint the best, but that he was inferior to Bayardo.

One of the few setbacks in Maher's career at this time occurred during the summer of 1903 when he met with a serious accident while driving his car near Lingfield. The base of his skull was fractured and he was kept out of the saddle for a number of weeks. One view suggested that he was not so good afterwards, although events would not have supported his view. By this time Maher had become very popular with the racing public, who idolised him. He was honest, straightforward, brilliant and personable and, unlike his compatriot riders who had lived a high old life, Maher lived quietly in his rooms in Newmarket and was invariably known simply as "Danny".

Maher won his only Oaks on Keystone II in 1906 and was at his brilliant best in plotting the downfall of the great Pretty Polly in the Ascot Gold Cup of that year. He believed that she was vulnerable at the extreme distance of the Cup in a truly run race. He had conceived the idea after riding Pretty Polly to her only defeat, at that stage of her career, in Longchamp. A stable companion set a strong pace for a mile and a half and in a pulsating finish Bachelor's Button held the great mare by a length, although it is true to say that Pretty Polly was said not to be herself that day. In the event, on this occasion, the outcome of this example of his brilliance was more likely to have brought opprobrium rather than praise as of course Pretty Polly was a national heroine who won twenty two of her twenty four races.

In addition to the incident mentioned earlier at Leicester, the only other occasion that Maher was potentially in trouble occurred during the York August meeting in 1906. Maher had finished second in the Gimcrack and was accused by the owner of a beaten horse of foul riding, something which then, as at any other time, was the most serious offence of which a jockey could found guilty. The local stewards held an enquiry and "cautioned Maher to be more careful in future". The owner, unhappy at this, requested the Jockey Club to look further into the matter. However, they endorsed the view of the local stewards. Nonetheless this experience would not have been forgotten by Maher.

Over the next eight years Maher cemented his reputation as a top rider, probably none better. Only Frank Wootton approached him in merit and he was not a stylist in Maher's mould. The trainer Jack Jarvis observed that Wootton was very effective, but to compare him with Danny Maher was like comparing a Model-T Ford with a Rolls Royce. Jarvis noted that both got you there in the end but one got a far better ride with the Rolls!

Maher and Wootton did not, by all accounts, have any great affection for each other and fought out some legendary finishes. Theodore Felstead described them as "always at daggers drawn". The Hon. George Lambton felt that this rivalry was more Maher's fault than Wootton's, due in some degree to Maher's quick temper. Notwithstanding this, in a conversation with Lambton, Wootton said he thought Maher was a marvel, especially at Newmarket, York and Ascot. On one occasion when Maher produced what was considered by some observers a masterful ride on Minoru to win the Free Handicap at Newmarket in 1909, the King was sufficiently impressed to visit the weighing-room to shake his hand, although Minoru's trainer, Richard Marsh, was not so enthusiastic. This was the only occasion when Maher won in the Royal colours and it was an ambition realised.

Maher had always thought that he might like to ride over hurdles and in December 1908 he gratified this whim by riding at Kempton Park under National Hunt rules. Strange as it may seem, although he had ridden almost a thousand winners on the flat, under National Hunt rules he was able to claim a 5 lb allowance. His mount, Dafila, started as the favourite and won. Maher was content with that and never felt the desire to repeat the experience.

Sadly, even at this stage he was inclined to be consumptive although this did not seem to prevent him from riding a strong finish when required. On many occasions he was rendered speechless after such an effort for want of breath. During this period his popularity with the racing public continued and his demeanour remained as always, pleasant and well-mannered. In addition to his classic success, Maher won many big races for the wealthiest owners, particularly Lord Rosebery for whom he was first jockey. He was champion for the first time in 1908, the year he began his partnership with Bayardo. About this time Maher bought Cropwell Hall, Cropwell Butler, near Nottingham from where he hunted for several seasons.

By 1910 Maher could have asked for any amount as a retainer, but refused to exploit this situation to the fullest advantage. Alfred Cox was particularly concerned to secure his services to ride Bayardo, by now a four year old with the Ascot Gold Cup as his target, and Lemberg, who had the Triple Crown in sight. Cox made a generous offer. However, Maher had a genuine affection for Lord Rosebery and indicated to his Lordship that provided his retaining fee could be raised to somewhere near Cox's offer, he would continue to ride for him. Lord Rosebery increased his retainer to £4,000 (£256,000) and Cox had to be happy with a second retainer for which he paid £2,000 (£128,000), while Leopold de Rothschild also paid £2,000 for third claim. He also rode frequently for Lord Derby. As an example of the reasons why owners would pay such a lucrative retainer for his services, Maher's riding of the brilliant but temperamental Neil Gow in the 1910 Two Thousand Guineas, where they beat Lemberg by a short head, would be as good as any. Alfred Cox was not alone in his belief that had Maher been on Lemberg the result would have been reversed.

Maher continued to win big races up to the Great War. In addition to his wins on Bayardo, in 1910 he rode Lemberg to a fourth Derby success. Two years later he won another Two Thousand Guineas on Sweeper in 1912. His retainer with Alfred Cox was, however, terminated in the same year that it was arranged. Although details of their relationship are scarce, it is not really surprising that they failed to see eye to eye. Maher was stubborn and determined, while Cox was no less stubborn and demanding! Cox considered that Maher had ridden an ill-judged race on Lemberg in the St Leger. Maher had appeared to give Lemberg too much to do to behind Swynford, who was an outstanding horse in his own right, and then found that he could not be caught. Hindsight suggested that Maher was not altogether at fault, as Lemberg was subsequently shown to be a non- stayer. In addition Swynford was the better horse as he proved the following year. However, as Cox would still have been smarting form the debacle on Bayardo in the Goodwood Cup this may have been the last straw.

Maher could probably have won another Derby in 1913 but he would not break his retainer for Lord Rosebery, even with his Lordship's permission. He was offered £2,000 (£128,000) to ride the ill-fated Craganour, but refused as Lord Rosebery had Prue, who had no chance, in the race. Craganour has claims, it has to be said stronger than those of Bayardo, to being the unluckiest horse in the histories of both the 2000 Guineas and Derby. A brilliant two-year-old winning five of his six races, he was beaten a head in the Guineas when, although most observers thought he had won, crucially one of those was not the judge. Craganour raced under the stands rail and the other prominent horses were on the far side. It seems that the judge gave his assistant the numbers of the first three to finish on the far side to put up in the results board. His assistant asked where he would place Craganour and the judge was reputed to have replied that he had not seen Craganour. Upon being told that the colt had been racing prominently on the near side and had passed the post with the winner, the judge placed him second. He was the favourite in the Derby and after a desperate battle won by a short head in a bruising finish. The stewards objected and called for an inquiry, which they sustained and Craganour, amidst considerable controversy, was disqualified. He never raced again and was sold to Argentina where he was a great success as a sire.

It is entirely possible that with any luck in the Guineas, and, had Maher been on board for that race and the Derby, Craganour would have won both races legitimately. In those circumstances he would then have been at short odds for the St Leger. It is not stretching matters much further to say that he could so easily have been a Triple Crown winner and would of course have stood as a stallion in England. He was a success at stud in Argentina and so although it can only be conjecture, these unfortunate events may have resulted in a serious loss to British bloodstock.

In the spring of 1913 Maher became a naturalised British subject with Lord Rosebery being one of his guarantors. In the same year he married Dorothy Fraser, who was described as having some connection with the stage. This was a euphemism as she was an actress and the darling of the Lyceum. Lord Rosebery was one of the witnesses at their union. Maher was champion again during the 1913 season, but the years of wasting and the debilitating effects of his tubercular condition, which was not helped by heavy smoking, forced him to retire at the end of the year. His last winner was Declaration in a Liverpool seller.

During the winter of 1913-14 Maher went to South Africa as a guest of Sir Abe Bailey in the hope that the dry, warm climate might improve his condition. In 1915 he returned to England keen to ride again and although he returned bronzed from the sun and looking in excellent shape, his doctor, probably realising that he was not as well as he looked, was against the idea. However, Maher persisted, even sleeping in a tent on the lawn of his home in the hope that the fresh air might help. The inescapable thought remains that the damp night air, in probability, did not. In September at Newmarket he had the mount on Mr J B Joel's Sun Yat, who, although burdened with 10 stone 1 lb in a plate race, was considered a good thing. His mount was made 6 to 5 favourite of the eleven-horse field and as he cantered past the post the public gave him a

rousing cheer. It only remained for Sun Yat to win. Alas he faded badly
away and finished sixth. There was general disappointment as it was felt
that this was probably his last mount and so it proved.

Although Maher was back at Newmarket in 1916 for the Cambridgeshire watching the racing from a motor car his health did not improve
and he succumbed to the effects of consumption in a London nursing
home on 9th November 1916. The funeral arrangements were made by
Lord Rosebery who accompanied the coffin to the graveside at Paddington
Cemetery, Mill Hill London. A wreath from Lord Rosebery bore the
inscription "From his faithful friend". Bob Sievier sent one saying
"Weighed in old boy, farewell". Similar tributes came from Lord Derby
and Prince Leopold of Battenberg. There was also one from "His
sorrowing Mother and Sisters in USA".

In his will Maher left everything to his wife. However, the gross
amount was only £5,933 (379,712) which was a surprise in view of the
sums he had earned. It seems he lost considerable sums due to the collapse
of some American investments.

After maturity Maher could never ride below eight stone. He was a
polished horseman, and a clever jockey. In addition he was a supreme
stylist and a strong finisher. He had the gift of beautiful hands, a good
judgement of pace (well nearly always) and immense patience. His
method with doubtful stayers was to nurse them until the last possible
moment before calling on one supreme effort on the post. It was said that
when Maher had plenty up his sleeve he rode with his elbows out,
conversely when he had nothing left his elbows were tucked in and he
was motionless!

The trainer Jack Jarvis and jockey Freddie Fox were amongst many
who considered him the best jockey they ever saw. Jarvis had a simple
way of deciding who the best jockey was: the one who wins the most
races that he was not entitled to win. In his view that was Maher. George
Lambton considered him supreme as a jockey and horseman for the
period Maher was riding. Meyrick Good of *The Sporting Life* considered
him the "aristocrat" of all the jockeys he had known. "He was the most
stylish finisher" said Good. "I have seen him ride races that almost made
your hair stand on end". The jockey Fred Rickaby thought that at his
best Maher was superior to Tod Sloan. Interestingly Fox seemed to
believe that Maher's style, with his tendency to hold his mounts up until
the very last moment, did not suit Bayardo. It has to be said that there
was more than enough evidence by the end to support Fox's view! He
thought Maher got into some dreadful tangles when riding Bayardo.
Notwithstanding this Maher was a great jockey with probably only
Gordon Richards, Lester Piggott and possibly Steve Donoghue, superior.
He was rated third in *A Century of Champions*.

Maher's character was one of contrasts. He possessed a blend of intelligence and charm to earn the friendship and affection of Lord Rosebery and many others. Lord Rosebery invited him to cruise on his yacht and to stay at Dalmeny his Scottish country seat. However, he had a quick temper, was easily flattered and, like some of his fellow American riders, he was on intimate terms with some disreputable individuals. Notwithstanding this, it should also be made clear that, unlike his fellow compatriot jockeys, Maher was considered incorruptible, a belief which further enhanced his popularity.

Maher's first winner in Britain was Paiute at Manchester in September 1900. In his riding career of twenty years Maher had 6,781 mounts and rode 1771 winners for a winning percentage of 26.1. Of those winners 1,421 were in Britain. He also won on his only mount over hurdles. In 1955 he was one of the original inductees into the American Racing Hall of Fame.

Classic successes

2000 Guineas:	Neil Gow	1910
	Sweeper II	1912
1000 Guineas:	Aida	1901
Derby:	Rock Sand	1903
	Cicero	1905
	Spearmint	1906
Oaks:	Keystone II	1906
St. Leger:	Rock Sand	1903
	Bayardo	1909

Riding record in England

	Mounts	Wins	Percentage
1900	128	27	21.09
1901	418	94	22.48
1902	451	106	23.50
1903	298	56	18.79
1904	462	115	24.89
1905	411	101	24.57
1906	353	103	29.17
1907	424	114	26.88
1908	491	139	28.30 +
1909	423	116	27.42
1910	460	127	27.00
1911	436	99	22.70
1912	443	109	24.60
1913	425	115	27.12 +
1915	1	—	—
	5624	1421	25.26

+ First in the list of leading riders.

CHAPTER 19

Gay Crusader

Gay Crusader was a bay colt foaled on the 2nd April 1914 and bred by Alfred Cox. He was out of Gay Laura who was by Beppo, a first foal and from Bayardo's third crop. Gay Crusader was inbred 4x3x6x3 to Galopin and it is interesting to note that his maternal grandsire Beppo was a son of a mare by St Frusquin who was also the maternal grandsire of Gainsborough. Therefore Bayardo's two Triple Crown winners were bred on very similar lines.

Gay Crusader was not a very impressive yearling when he went into training and was described as "small and mean looking" as a two year old, leggy and "rather common in appearance, plain about the neck and quarters". The change began in the spring of his juvenile year and he improved sufficiently to be later on in the year considered as having "a fine racing action and a courageous spirit".

Early in his juvenile year Gay Crusader was working well and "won" a trial at Manton. Unfortunately, soon afterwards he developed sore shins and he was on the easy list until the autumn. He was again working well and "won" another trial after which he made his debut on the Rowley Mile at Newmarket. It was at that venue or on the July course that, due to the Great War, he was to race his entire career. He was disappointing, finishing down the field, but he obviously benefited from the experience as a fortnight later he won the Criterion Stakes over six furlongs.

From two to three years of age, he improved considerably. It was said that no horse at Manton had ever become so transformed in both appearance and ability. In place of the unattractive yearling Gay Crusader had grown, in the manner of the ugly duckling, into a beautiful looking horse. He was a sleek extremely handsome racing machine, commanding of stature and possessing a wonderful perfect action. In addition he loved racing and had a calm and kindly disposition which made him an easy and pleasant horse to deal with. In short a model racehorse. How many owners and trainers dream of having such an animal in their yard!

Gay Crusader had one race before the 2000 Guineas finishing second, when short of peak fitness and not fancied, in the Column Produce Stakes. This performance did no more than confirm his well being but it was not a bad performance to concede 11 pounds to a decent horse over an inadequate trip. However, his jockey Steve Donoghue was not impressed by him prior to the Guineas and his confidence was not high that he could beat his stable companion Magpie. Alec Taylor was not sure which of the two was in the best form because Gay Crusader and Magpie were in different ownerships and, of course, Alfred Cox would not allow them to be tried together.

Between his seasonal debut and the 2000 Guineas Gay Crusader had a formal trial at Manton over a mile. He was opposed by Telephus, who had won the Dewhurst the previous year, and Gay Crusader "won" the trial by two lengths. This should have put Gay Crusader nearly straight for the first classic. However, Donoghue thought he looked light and leggy in the paddock and this simply increased his apprehension as he thought that Magpie was, at that time, at least his equal. Donoghue, who always gave considerable thought to how races may be run, decided that Gay Crusader would need all his celebrated cunning to prevail. This was how he saw the race:-

"There were about fourteen runners in the race for the Guineas and we jumped off to a good start and in the dip Magpie and Gay Crusader singled themselves out and we drew right away from the others and ran home locked together. Straight as a die we raced side by side and Magpie was going every bit as well as Gay Crusader. I knew well that if Otto (Madden) could give his mount one reminder with the whip, the horse (Magpie), though running lazily as was his nature, would gamely respond. So without touching Magpie I kept Gay Crusader so close to him on the whip hand that Otto could not use his whip to inspire his horse to pull out that little bit which he certainly had in reserve. I knew he must be a little rusty from his long absence from the saddle and this gave me just the shade of advantage as he could not get his whip over to his left hand quite quickly enough and I had won the race on Gay Crusader by a head!"

Donoghue thought he was lucky to beat Magpie on the day and the two horses never met again as Magpie, who was found to be affected in his wind, was sold to go abroad. Certainly Gay Crusader was the beneficiary of a splendid tactical ride, as, at the line, he had held on only by a head. Donoghue may well have been right to say that Gay Crusader was fortunate to win. It is difficult to be certain as the photo of the finish is not conclusive. Either way that was to prove the best chance any horse had for the rest of the year to defeat him.

Sadly the state of the World and Britain's position in it by 1917 was far from sanguine. The Great War was still raging and opposition to racing was considerable. It was a sombre outlook. Casualties were on an appalling scale and the battle of the Somme during the summer of 1916 had resulted in deaths and injuries of a vast, scarcely believable magnitude. This meant the true horror of the war, which many had thought would be over in months but was now of over two years duration, could no longer be concealed and the whole task of fighting the war seemed increasingly Sisyphean. The position with regard to shipping was causing particularly anxiety, they were being lost at a rate of one hundred a month, and the end of the War had seemed a long way off. A question in the House of Commons, on the propriety of feeding oats to racehorses in this time of crisis, resulted in the Government banning all racing after the First Spring meeting at Newmarket and racing ceased on Friday 4th May. The Jockey Club and the Bloodstock Breeders Association fought the decision and eventually won a concession that racing could continue on a limited scale and it was resumed at Newmarket on Tuesday 17th July.

Racing may have been banned, but racehorses still had to be fed and exercised. Under the new restrictions brought in on 11th May horses in training were allowed seven pounds of oats a day. This would be just over a third of the amount they would normally have. This was increased to fifteen pounds from 4th July. Exactly what state of fitness Gay Crusader was in on this restricted diet - he had been described as a horse in need of plenty of sustenance – has not been recorded. However, he was a clean winded type and did not take too much getting fit.

Following a satisfactory trial at Manton, Gay Crusader again beat Telephus, this time by three and a half lengths, he started to thrive and by Derby Day he had reached his peak. He impressed many in the paddock beforehand and Steve Donoghue thought he was a "horse and a half". It can only be imagined that he had been eating some other poor horse's rations!

The New Derby of 1917 eventually took place on 31st July the latest date ever that the great classic race, in any guise, had been run. There was no Magpie in opposition as he had been sold and exported to Australia, where he was to win both the Melbourne and Caulfield Stakes and then prove to be a most successful sire. It may have been the end of July but the weather was appalling. Rain had fallen continuously for forty eight hours prior to the race, although it had cleared by the scheduled off time. There was very little transport and the majority of the modest crowd had to walk from Newmarket station and arrived at the course wet through and somewhat weary. Gay Crusader, based now at Newmarket where Alec Taylor had rented stables, took the eye in the paddock, looked trained to the minute and it was declared that he had improved considerably since the Guineas. He was in heavy demand in the ring and started as the 7/4 favourite. Gay Crusader won easily by four lengths, despite Donoghue encountering problems when he tried to come through on the rails, being twice baulked and losing several lengths in the process.

The first two classics had been won and it looked certain that Gay Crusader would complete the Triple Crown by winning the St Leger. However, Doncaster had refused in 1915 to allow a substitute St. Leger to be staged elsewhere. Therefore Newmarket held the wartime substitute renewals as the September Stakes, without Doncaster's blessing. Despite there being thirty entries for the race only two horses opposed Gay Crusader who started at 11-2 on and won easily Donoghue pulling up before the line. So Gay Crusader had won the Triple Crown. Well possibly. In some eyes he never will be because all his races had been at Newmarket. As if this was Gay Crusader's fault! He had proved the best horse of his generation over three different distances and was entitled the status of Triple Crown winner.

By now Gay Crusader was considered unbeatable and little in the way of opposition could be mustered against him. He finished the season winning the Newmarket Gold Cup, a war time substitute for the Ascot Gold Cup over two and a half miles at odds of 8-100, the Champion Stakes at 9-100, the Lowther Stakes at 1-25 and the Limekiln Stakes at 15-100. Unfortunately only a total of seven horses opposed him in those four races all of which were won with considerable ease. He had won seven of his eight races as a three year old.

Gay Crusader was kept in training at four with a second Gold Cup as his objective. He had done well over the winter and was in prime condition and Alec Taylor did not consider it necessary to subject him to any trial, formal or otherwise. However, Alfred Cox was always a man to have his way and he brought Steve Donoghue down to Manton for a gallop, over the full Gold Cup trip, which amounted to a trial. Never had Gay Crusader worked more brilliantly. Owner, trainer and jockey were delighted. In the words of Alec Taylor "he went like a steam engine" He pulled up well and walked home sound. However, by the evening the worst was known. A routine visit to his stable revealed that he was lame. On inspection it was discovered that he had sprained a tendon in his foreleg. It seems that Donoghue may have pulled him up to quickly after the gallop. He would not be able to race again.

Race Record all races at Newmarket

Year	Distance	Race	Placing	Win Prize money
1916	51/2f	Clearwell Stakes	—	
	6f	Criterion Stakes	1st	1066
1917	8f	Column Produce Stakes	2nd	
	8f	2000 Guineas	1st	3950
	12f	New Derby Stakes	1st	2050
	14f	September Stakes	1st	1625
	20f	Newmarket Gold Cup	1st	850
	10f	Champion Stakes	1st	950
	14f	Lowther Stakes	1st	470
	10f	Limekiln Stakes	1st	285
				11,246

Gay Crusader had stood out among three year olds. Alec Taylor was not alone in considering that he was so far ahead of his contemporaries that his true ability was never established. For years he was unable to decide who was better, Bayardo or Gay Crusader. In the end he felt it was Gay Crusader because as Taylor put it "he was equally brilliant at five furlongs or two miles; in fact I really don't know how good he was. It was just a disaster that I was not able to train him as a four year old". Steve Donoghue always maintained he was the best horse he ever rode. This was because although he was the finest stayer he ever rode, after a two mile gallop he could pull out the speed of a five furlong sprinter. It is impossible to have a higher recommendation. It should also be borne in mind that all his races were at Newmarket. It says much for his enthusiasm that he was as willing in his last race as in his first. In *A Century of Champions* he was rated 138.

CHAPTER 20

Gainsborough

Gainsborough was a foaled on 24th January 1915 and was out of the Oaks winner Rosedrop by St. Frusquin. He was from Bayardo's fourth crop and was bred by Lady James Douglas who at this time was a wealthy widow in her sixties. Lady James had bought a property near Newbury and founded the Harwood Stud there. One of her early purchases was the mare Rosedrop who was visiting Bayardo for the third year running when she gave birth to a colt. It was Lady James's practice to sell most of her yearlings and the colt was to be sent to the Newmarket sales. Prior to this she asked Alec Taylor if he would visit her stud and take a look at the yearling. Taylor had trained both the sire and dam and she considered that his opinion would be valuable. Lady James explained her policy and that the colt would be one of the contingent for the sales and asked Taylor how much of a reserve to put on the colt.

Taylor thought the colt rather long in the pasterns and somewhat heavy looking about the shoulders. He was altogether a stuffy sort of young thoroughbred. Notwithstanding this, he liked him and thought he had potential. Taylor suggested a reserve of 2,000 guineas (£73,500), which was a high figure for a war-time sale and with the immediate future of racing in doubt. However, Lady James agreed with this and he was duly dispatched to the sales.

The colt should have been bought to race in America. Mr John Stanford of New York instructed Mr W F Smith, one of Newmarket's leading vets to bid for the colt up to £2,000 (£70,000). After inspecting the colt his opinion was that his frame was too heavy for his legs and that he would not stand training. Smith did not therefore bid and he cabled Stanford with his reasons and advising him that the colt had gone through the ring unsold at 1,800 guineas (£69,300). Stanford was not pleased with his agent and cabled instructions to offer 2,000 guineas for him. However, by now Lady James had increased the reserve to 2,500 guineas (£96,250). The lower offer was made and refused upon which Stanford offered 2,300 guineas. This too was refused and, as Lady James observed, every one had had a chance of buying the colt, but would not pay her price. She decided to keep the yearling and race him herself.

The unnamed colt was therefore sent to be trained by Colledge Leader in Newmarket. Leader shortly afterwards went into the army and, after more offers had been made and refused "I would not take 4,000 guineas for him now", a resolute and determined Lady James proclaimed, he went to Alec Taylor at Manton. He was now given the name Gainsborough. It is often assumed he was named after the famous portrait painter. No, it would seem not! Lady James, who liked colts to have manly names, was struggling to think of an appropriate name and eventually gave up the task and instead picked up a railway timetable, turning page after page. She reached Gainsborough and said" That will do, it sounds well and has a good masculine ring about it".

Naming a racehorse is something that attracts much comment, not all of it favourable. For many years the Jockey Club permitted juveniles to race without names and only required that the horse be named when it had turned three. It is not clear why this was allowed. However, one reason was the shortage of suitable names and it was considered wasteful to use up a good name if the horse turned out to be moderate, or worse still, useless. It was possible to wait until the youngster had demonstrated some ability and then name it appropriately. It is said that no good horse is ever given a bad name. This is largely true however, it is only necessary to look at some of the names of horses in training, some in England but particularly in America, for ammunition to support the view that many individuals can't be trusted with this responsibility. Some of these include well bred sorts and blue-bloods that cost considerable sums at the sales.

It is also true to say that many bad horses have excellent names. Some prominent people in history have been fortunate and Nijinsky and Nureyev are probably the best examples, of having good horses named after them and the best character from fiction was undoubtedly Brigadier Gerard. Others have not been so fortunate. At least thoroughbred racing is largely spared the grotesque interference of corporate naming in order to advertise. Show jumping had no such qualms. Who can forget Harvey Smith competing on that fine horse whose name was changed in order that it could compete under the egregious title of Sanyo Music Centre.

Some of the names given to the progeny of Bayardo have shown a dreadful lack of imagination and most seem to start with Bay. It is gratifying that all of his colts that won over £2,000 in prize money were given good names. In particular the colt that he bequeathed to racing, and was to make such a huge impact on the breed, was given such a fine name as Gainsborough.

In other spheres naming has not always been such a great success. In gentler times there was a once prominent titled Lady who took no interest in horticulture but was always rather proud that a garden flower had been specifically named after her. One day she idly opened a gardening book and glanced at the entry for the flower concerned. She was horrified to read that, in the writer's view, for the best results, she was "better up against a wall than in a conventional bed"! She was said not to feel quite the same level of pride from then on! It does seem a pity that Lady James did not have Thomas Gainsborough in mind when she named her horse.

Gainsborough, the horse that is, was not a big juvenile and no more than promising when he made his debut on the Rowley Mile at Newmarket. Due to the War he raced only at headquarters either on the Rowley Mile or the July course. He was beaten in his first two starts but finished the season by impressively winning the Autumn Stakes over six furlongs. The style of his win must have pleased because, as a result, it drew yet more offers for him. Lady James grew so tired of turning down offers she suggested a sign be erected in his paddock reading "Gainsborough is not for sale at any price". Joking apart, it would have been a disaster for the future of British Bloodstock had he been sold abroad. *The Bloodstock Breeders Review* stated, long pasterns notwithstanding, that they had seldom seen a better looking two year old.

During the winter Gainsborough improved significantly. He did not grow but he fined down and now had great quality. He was a medium sized, extremely powerful colt, very muscular with a short strong back good bone and excellent limbs. He stood 15.3 hands. He resembled his sire Bayardo, more perhaps than Gay Crusader who was more light-framed. He was blessed with a flawless action, although not considered quite the equal of Gay Crusader in this respect. In addition he had a wonderful temperament. He was described as a Christian of a horse, sensible, placid and kind. He took after his sire in another way in that, although to a lesser extent than Bayardo, he also banged his chin on his manger.

The weather in the early part of 1918 was cold and inclement. Alec Taylor surprisingly did not run Gainsborough in one of the accepted classic trials. He felt he needed sharpening up and instead he reappeared in a five furlong sprint. The weather was miserable, cold and wet. In addition the going was heavy. He created an unfavourable impression on the paddock judges whose verdict was the he was "nowhere near ready". Not surprisingly he was unplaced having never troubled the leaders but the outing sharpened him up nicely for his attempt at the 2000 Guineas.

Gainsborough was given a trial over a mile between his seasonal debut and the Guineas which satisfied Alec Taylor that he was ready. The weather had improved considerably by this time and Gainsborough had put on condition as, like his sire, he thrived in the warmer weather. Two Thousand Guineas day was dull with a searching northerly wind. The going was however, perfect. He looked very fit and impressed those same paddock judges who had decried him on his seasonal debut. He was considered to be easily the best of the field on looks and won comfortably. It was an average 2000 Guineas at best, although, of course, he was an above average winner. Lady James Douglas therefore created history as the first woman to win a classic race with a horse carrying her own colours. She was warmly applauded as she stood beside Gainsborough in the unsaddling enclosure. The picture she presented brought this description from Roger Mortimer; "Lady James appears as a short, erect and stoutly-built figure attired in a coat and skirt of severe cut, spats, a bow tie and a hat more practical than alluring. She conveys a strong impression of a woman of independent and determined character".

Gainsborough continued to please Alec Taylor and he did not consider it necessary to give him either a race or a trial prior to the Derby. He would be an automatic favourite for the race. However, as the race drew near rumours and opposition grew and other contenders including the filly Zinovia and King John were supported. However, on the day Alec Taylor produced Gainsborough looking a picture of health and he was backed down to odds on by the off. He was always travelling well and moved smoothly through to take the lead and had only to be shown the whip to win comfortably. Lady James was warmly applauded as she proudly led her winner into the unsaddling enclosure, creating more history as the first woman to win the Derby in her own colours. It was not a vintage Derby and Gainsborough was easily the best.

Gainsborough demonstrated his stamina by defeating two older opponents to win the Newmarket Gold Cup, the war time substitute for the Ascot Gold Cup, before completing the "Triple Crown" by winning the September Stakes, the War-time substitute for the St Leger, in a canter from four opponents, two of which came from his own stable. Sadly Gainsborough emulated Bayardo by losing his last race. Like his sire's last race it should have been a formality. The mile and three quarters Jockey Club Stakes for which Gainsborough started at 11-2 on looked easy enough but he was beaten by his stable companion Prince Chimay whom he had defeated with considerable ease in the St Leger. There had been coughing at Manton which may have played its part and a whip cracked at the start may have upset him and Joe Childs had been unable to settle him. There was a suspicion that his jockey was outsmarted by Otto Madden who got first run. On this depressingly low note

Racing record all at Newmarket.

Year	Distance	Race	Placing	Win Prize money
1917	5f	Thurlow Plate	4th	
	5f	Ramsey Plate	3rd	
	6f	Autumn Stakes	1st	670
1918	5f	Severals Stakes	—	427
	8f	2000 Guineas	1st	5100
	12f	New Derby	1st	4000
	16f	Newmarket Gold Cup	1st	960
	14f	September Stakes	1st	3350
	14f	Jockey Club Stakes	2nd	
				14,507

Gainsborough's career drew to a close. He was rated 137 in *A Century of Champions*.

Gainsborough was not kept in training as a four year old, but for some unknown reason did not immediately commence stud duties either. He had won five of his nine races and is regarded as a great horse and his record does not quite do full justice to his ability.

CHAPTER 21

Greatness – with some observations on modern racing

"Never use a superlative" the late Joe Estes, long-time editor of *The Blood-Horse* once said to one of his junior reporters. "Nothing you run into on this kind of beat ever justifies a superlative". Estes had a scholar's dislike of superlatives for undoubtedly in many instances a sounder, more rational appreciation of events is to be arrived at by avoiding them and certainly discretion resides in limiting their use. This is how *Timeform* began their essay on Nijinsky in the 1970 *Racehorses* annual. The point is that in Nijinsky's case it was now time to use superlatives in describing a truly great horse.

Bayardo was a great horse. That is beyond dispute. But what made him a great horse? What are the minimum qualifications for such an accolade? Ask that question and the answer will vary vastly according to whom it is asked. Joe Estes warning is rarely heeded nowadays and a number of horses in recent years that won a few big races in good style were championed as "great horses" sometimes by individuals in the media who should know better. Frequently a trainer, owner or jockey will refer to a good horse as a "great horse". Such comments devalue words to a level where they have little meaning. So many horses have been called "great" in recent years that when a genuine great appeared in 2009 – Sea The Stars – the media were slow to acknowledge his status. This may have been partly because his trainer John Oxx, although one of the best ten trainers of the last fifty years, is allergic to hyperbole in any circumstances and always chooses his words with care.

"There is no objective test for greatness in a racehorse. Appreciation of a performance depends on the impact it makes on the individual critic, but there are certain indefinable critical standards formed by experience which can be accepted as reliable, even though they are subjective." This quote from *Timeform's Racehorses* annual for 1965 is taken from their essay on Sea Bird who is generally acknowledged as the best horse to race in Europe since the Second World War. It concisely encapsulates the difficulty concerning the subject of greatness while at the same time making it clear how with the requisite knowledge and experience any horse can be assessed for qualification as a great racehorse.

To illustrate the difference between a top-class horse and a great one it may be useful to compare two horses that raced in recent years: Oiuja

Board and Zarkava. Oiuja Board was an exceptionally brave, genuine and in every way an admirable race-mare who won seven Group One races and gave immense pleasure to everyone, not least because she was never certain to win. However, she was beaten twelve times and if matched against Zarkava, assuming both participants were at their peak, she would have stood little chance and would on all known form probably have been beaten about 3-4 lengths. However, because she raced until the age of five she will be remembered with greater affection by many racing enthusiasts than Zarkava who will be recalled principally for her brilliance over a relatively brief period.

Racing enthusiasts will remember Giant's Causeway some years ago popularly known as the "Iron horse" and frequently described as "great". He was not. He was brave, genuine and had a tremendous will to win. His never-say-die attitude rightly earned him the admiration and affection of the race-going public. However he was out-speeded on two occasions and was below the standard required to be described as great. He would have stood no chance against a horse of the calibre of Sea The Stars over any distance.

Switching continents a similar comparison can be made with Curlin, the mighty Curlin as some pundits in North America dubbed him. He has been feted as a great horse yet if he were to oppose Secretariat over any distance at the wire Secretariat would be anything up to about six to eight, possibly even ten, lengths in front. Again this is simply the difference between a top class racehorse and a genuine great. Oiuja Board, Giants Causeway and Curlin, although fine and admirable race-horses, were top-class but not great.

To digress for a moment and ask a question: was Secretariat really that much better than Curlin? North America's speed-figure guru Andy Beyer has allocated a best speed figure of 119 to Curlin which is excellent. However, when asked what figure he gave to Secretariat for his phenomenal thirty one length winning effort, in an unbelievable time of two minutes twenty four seconds flat, when winning the twelve furlong Belmont Stakes, he said that 139 was the figure he arrived at.

A Beyer speed figure is about 10 -14 pounds less than a typical *Timeform* figure. *Timeform* rated Curlin 134, *A Century of Champions* rated Secretariat 144. However, there is considerable evidence that his rating should be between 147 and 151 which would make him the highest rated thoroughbred anywhere in the world since the beginning of the Twentieth Century and therefore the best racehorse of the period. It is a discussion for another day but it is worth considering that great as Secretariat was as a dirt runner there are horseman in North America who swear that on the evidence of his work and two wins on turf he was equally as good on either surface. If Secretariat is considered an extreme example then be assured any of the following great horses that raced in

North America, Citation, Native Dancer, Seattle Slew, Affirmed, Spectacular Bid, Cigar or – a recent example - Ghostzapper would all have beaten Curlin comfortably.

Many observers are convinced that racehorses that achieve greatness have an indefinable aura about them and, although it may be imagination, the horses concerned seem perfectly aware of this. For evidence it is only necessary to look at archive film of the great North American horse Man o' War. He was an equine who was never in doubt about his own status and his head, even at an advanced age, was always held high as if he was looking down on the rest of the world. The Triple Crown Winners Secretariat and Affirmed were both conscious of their special appeal and enjoyed the attention they were given. Both would stop if they heard a camera shutter and look in its direction and pose. On one occasion when close to the end of his life Secretariat was being led and had his head down looking almost dejected. A visitor's camera clicked and immediately his head shot up and he was ready with a pose more in keeping with his status. As stated earlier greatness is difficult to define, but as someone once said "greatness is like pornography, hard to describe, but one knows it when one sees it".

It might be as well to establish some parameters for any horse to be considered great. Here are some criteria which perhaps most critics can agree with.

1. Undoubted superiority at age two, three and preferably four.
2. Ability to show dominance at a variety of distances.
3. Able to beat older horses as a three year old and three year olds as a four year old.
4. Able to overcome difficulties and still prevail.
5. Ability to act on any going
6. Able to act on a variety of courses.
7. Have the necessary temperament to show their best form in big races.
8. Reproduce a top level of form regularly and over a period of time.
9. To lose very few of the races they competed in.

Others may wish to add to these. One possible addition to the above might be the ability to beat inferiors when conceding weight. It is excluded because great horses have not been asked to concede weight in stakes and handicap races for many years. There would not be any kudos today in winning the Cambridgeshire or the Cesarewitch when conceding weight. Bayardo gave considerable weight and a beating to his opponents on two occasions. However, by the time Bayardo was racing although some horses just below the very top level were still running in the most valuable handicaps this was in decline and not so prevalent as during the nineteenth century. It is hard to credit today but Isonomy, a dual Ascot Gold Cup winner and certainly one of the best twenty horses to race in the nineteenth century missed the Derby and the St Leger in order to execute a successful betting coup in the Cambridgeshire!

Looking at the European horses since 1900 which could be argued as at least outstanding, if not great, none of them were able to fully meet all of these conditions. However, as it is greatness under discussion and not perfection it is unlikely that any horse will fulfil all criteria. Some would say that number one in the list of requirements is unfair to late developing types in that they were not mature enough to dominate as juveniles. This is true. However, few horses with a claim to greatness showed nothing at all as two-year-olds, but certainly not dominating as a two-year-old would not exclude any horse from being considered great. For example Shergar won only a conditions race and was beaten on the only occasion that he raced in Pattern company as a juvenile. Dancing Brave won only a maiden and a conditions stakes as a juvenile and even Sea Bird was beaten as a two-year-old.

Some may argue that number two is also unfair. Is it not possible to have a great sprinter, stayer or specialist miler? Of course it is. But true greatness of the towering sort rarely seen involves overcoming difficulties of different kinds. Brigadier Gerard was a great miler, almost certainly the greatest in racing's history, who could perform as well over ten furlongs but would have had the speed to compete successfully at the top level over 6/7 furlongs. His tremendous will to win did not lessen in adversity as he displayed in soft ground which he hated. In these conditions he refused to give in and battled on grimly to win the St James's Palace Stakes and also to a lesser extent his first Champion Stakes win. His greatness, which he initially established in the 2000 Guineas, was reinforced when he stretched every sinew and drained his reserves of raw courage and mental strength to win a Group 1 race over twelve furlongs a distance at which he was neither bred for or would normally be physically able to stay at the top level. Such was his level of courage and determination that there is little doubt that had Brigadier Gerard been asked to race over two miles plus he would not have surrendered until he had collapsed from exhaustion.

How close does Bayardo get? Of the nine he qualifies under one, two, three, five, six, eight and nine and he partly qualifies under four and seven.

1. He was champion at two three and four and was indisputably superior to all contemporaries.
2. He won races that today form part of the pattern, at the following distances: 5, 6, 7, 10, 12, 14 and 20 furlongs.

3. He beat older horses in the Eclipse, Champion and Lowther Stakes as a three year old and three year olds as a four year old in the Chester Vase, Ascot Gold Cup and Dullingham Plate.

4. It is not easy to argue that he always overcame difficulties and prevailed. He met interference on two occasions, was twice asked for very nearly the impossible and once raced when under the weather and a little below his best. He was beaten three times. Firstly in the Two Thousand Guineas, convincingly, although short of peak condition. In the Derby when badly hampered, a handicap which was impossible to surmount and finally in the Goodwood Cup partly as a result of Danny Maher's knuckle-headed ride. On the credit side he won the Middle Park Stakes as a juvenile when not at his best and he overcame Maher's overconfident ride to win the Chester Vase as a four year old.

5. He won on all types of going. However, he was undoubtedly better when there was give in the ground due to him suffering from sensitive feet.

6. He won on eight different courses.

7. His temperament was ultimately beyond reproach, although undoubtedly it was under question for all his classic year and until he won the Ascot Gold Cup.

8. He won twenty two races including fifteen in succession. He maintained his form as a two year old from June until October and as a three year old from the time he regained his form at Ascot until almost the middle of November. As a four year old his form was consistent from the middle of April until the end of July.

9. He was beaten only three times.

Where does Bayardo rank against other great horses of the twentieth century? It can only be conjecture. Comparisons between horses that raced in different eras are invidious, would be the mantra of mature sober judges. They are probably right! After all, any horse can only beat those put against them at the time asked and under the conditions prevailing. Even the greatest horses, if asked to race at a different time and in conditions totally against them, might be made to look very ordinary.

It has been suggested that the thoroughbred has not improved significantly from about Bayardo's time. *A Century of Champions* makes the point that after 200 years of selective breeding the thoroughbred by 1900 was virtually beyond improvement. Many years ago Peter Burrell, director of the National Stud, had asserted that the thoroughbred had reached the highest level attainable before the Great War and that further improvement was unlikely. That may or may not be true but comparisons from the beginning of the Twentieth Century are possible due to the pace of races becoming more uniform. Better course management and advances in turf technology mean that race-horses today compete on better surfaces than a century ago but there is no evidence that they are genetically better. Comparing modern thoroughbreds with those earlier than 1900 is difficult due to the false pace that almost all races, apart from sprints, were run at prior to the "American invasion". It is therefore not unreasonable to make some comparisons with Twentieth Century horses and unlike many other pastimes it does no harm to anybody!

Comparing racehorses from different eras in the Twentieth Century has already been done. In *A Century of Champions* John Randall and Tony Morris produced ratings for all the top horses that raced in that period. They used *Timeform's* ageless and peerless method of calculation which enables enthusiasts and scholars alike to compare horses that raced anything up to sixty years apart. Now thanks to Messrs Morris and Randall it is possible to compare horses separated by over one hundred years. One argument against comparing horses from different eras is propounded by those who say that training, feeding and general horse husbandry have improved since 1900 and therefore using that logic horses must be better and faster today. How can this be certain? Methods may be different – for example all weather training surfaces usually mean few race-horses today race when unfit - but feeding and general care? How arrogant of such people to assume without ever experiencing training methods from one hundred years ago to assume that modern ones are automatically better. They point out that all sports have progressed so why not racing. Certainly sports concerning man alone have improved but horse racing is largely about horses with man's contribution secondary to the animal's talent. It is stating the obvious but while moderate training can ruin a horse even the best trainers can't make an average horse into a champion.

Race times offer some support to the theory that race horses have not improved over the last century. For example the first sub two minute thirty five second Derby was recorded by Spion Kop in 1920. This is a faster time than achieved by many Derby winners in the last forty years. In case anyone thinks that was just a freakish performance Captain Cuttle beat Spion Kop's record two years later and this in turn was beaten in 1927 by Call Boy and equalled the following year by Felstead. A fast time in itself should not be taken as proof of anything apart from the probability that the race concerned took place on fast going and was run at a true pace. However, a number of times taken together can be taken as reasonable evidence that a modern Derby winner is no better than his counterpart of one hundred years ago. It is worth repeating that if individuals of the experience and knowledge of Peter Burrell and Tony Morris consider that the thoroughbred was beyond improvement one hundred years ago this author is not disposed to disagree.

Listed below are the best thirty six colts all rated 138 and up, using the *Timeform* scale, since the beginning of the Twentieth Century. Not all of them are great. However, about a dozen or so definitely are and certainly no truly great horse since 1900 has been omitted. The ratings are *Timeform* from 1948 to 2010 and from *A Century of Champions* from 1900 until 1947. The ratings are as a two-year old, three-year old and where appropriate as a four-year old. Only one horse capable of earning a rating of 138 or above raced as a five year old, the age at which a thoroughbred is fully mature, and that was Daylami. In the cases of Sceptre, Bayardo, Swynford, Coronach and Colorado at ages three and four and Hurry On, Fairway, Bahram, Blue Peter, Sun Chariot, Dante, Roberto and Nashwan as three-year olds these ratings are the writer's. The ratings for Pinza, Ribot, Nijinsky and Troy as three-year-olds are from *A Century of Champions* and not *Timeform*. All other ratings are *Timeform* or *A Century of Champions* from the years stated. The next set of figures relate to the spread of distances in furlongs over which each horse won and the number of wins to races.

Most racing students and enthusiasts understand both the strengths and weakness of ratings. However, if this is not clear it should be understood that any of the horses listed below are capable of beating any of the others. All that is required is that the distance, going and fitness of the horse concerned be at the optimum and another horse to be in some way disadvantaged by the same. In addition the pace of any race will have some bearing on the rating given to the winner. In a truly-run race the best horse will probably enjoy full advantage if it is ridden properly. However, in a slowly run race or one with a moderate early pace the best horse, however much it is superior, may only win narrowly. Only two of the horses listed below, who raced a minimum of ten times, were unbeaten. This demonstrates the old adage that if you race a horse often enough, sooner or later, it will be beaten. The unbeaten horses concerned are Italian bred, Ribot and Nearco who both won many races in their native land which were not much more than public workouts.

Ratings sometimes fall short in there capacity to reflect a horse's superiority when it wins "easily", "with plenty in hand" or "in a canter". In addition any horse that remains unbeaten is hard to rate accurately. However, it is also worth remembering that a horse winning any race at the top level in a very comfortable manner often has less in hand than it appears and would not have won by much more if ridden out. In some instances that follow a horse may have been given two or three pounds for winning easily but rarely more.

Horses marked with* are those that are generally considered to be great horses. Ratings marked + indicate that there is evidence to suggest the horse may have been capable of a higher rating.

Sea Bird*	129	145			7-12	7/8
Brigadier Gerard*	132	141	144		5-12	17/18
Ribot*	?	133	143		5-15	16/16
Bayardo*	131	140	142		5-20	22/25
Hyperion*	120	142	134		5-14	9/13
Tudor Minstrel*	133	142			5-8	8/10
Abernant*	133	136	142		5-7	14/17
Mill Reef*	133	141	141		5-12	12/14
Pharis	--	141+			12-15	3/3
Hurry On*	--	140+			8-20	6/6
Bahram*	127	140+			5-14	9/9
Vaguely Noble*	132	140			7-12	6/9
Nijinsky*	131	140			6-14	11/13
Shergar*	122	140			8-12	6/8
Dancing Brave*	110	140			8-12	8/10
Dubai Millennium*	108	132	140		8-10	9/10
Sea The Stars*	109	140			7-12	8/9
Windsor Lad*	110?	136	139		6-14	10/13
Brantome*	?	139	?		5-20	12/14
Epinard	?	139	?		5-8	12/20
Pappa Fourway	114	139			5-6	12/15
Reference Point	132	139			8-14	7/10
Generous	115	139			5-12	6/11
Swynford	?	132	138		10-14	8/12
Gay Crusader*	?	138+			6-20	8/10
Fairway*	124	134	138		5-18	12/15
Sardanapale	?	138			6-15	11/16
Coronach	126	138	138		5-14	10/14
Colorado	119	136	138		5-12	9/16
Nearco*	?	138+			5-15	14/14
Blue Peter*	122	138+			8-12	4/6
Dante*	130	138+			5-12	8/9
Pinza*	129	138			7-12	5/7
Alleged*	112	137	138		7-12	9/10
Roberto	127	138	131		6-12	7/14
Troy	122	138			7-12	8/11
Nashwan	106	138			7-12	6/7
Daylami	112	124	126	138	8-12	11/21

The best fillies are as follows, note that six of these raced when aged five:-

Pretty Polly*	130	137	137	129	5-18	22/24
Sun Chariot*	114	137+			5-14	8/9
Allez France*	126	132	136	132	8-12	13/21
Sceptre*	110	136	136	130	6-14	13/24
Dahlia	?	132	135	128	5-13	15/47
Coronation	118	135	132		5-12	6/13
Pebbles	114	124	135		6-12	8/15
Petite Etoile*	120	134	134	131	5-12	14/19
All Along	?	129	134	125	8-13	9/21
Godiva	118	134			5-12	6/8
Zarkava*	117	133+			8-12	7/7
Goldikova	101+	129	133	133	8-9	13/19**

**As at 15/08/10

It will be seen that the best fillies are about five or six pounds inferior to the colts. There are some who question why fillies and mares receive an allowance when racing against colts and geldings. This is an excellent example of why. The weight allowance gives them a better chance of competing on approximately level terms. It is sometimes said by uninitiated pundits "she gets a useful 3/5 pounds". No she does not. She gets a sex allowance which is more than simply useful in the vast majority of cases it is essential.

It will be seen that since Generous in 1991 only Dubai Millennium, Daylami and Sea The Stars have been good enough to be rated 138 or above. Dubai Millennium was a great horse but only as a four year old. He is the only European horse to have produced great performances over both dirt and turf in the renewals of the Dubai World Cup and the Prince of Wales Stakes of 2000. The sight of him making the running comfortably, using his ground devouring stride that enabled him to travel within himself, while his opponents were under pressure to stay in touch, will stay in the memory of all who saw him on those two occasions. Pharis is not indicated as a great horse. However, he may well have been but as he raced only three times it is hard to say how good he really was. Daylami is an excellent example of allowing a good horse to reach full maturity before retiring him. Daylami was a very good top-class racehorse who came close to greatness at age five when he was mature.

This raises a pertinent question: what has racing been deprived of by the decision to retire so many horses prematurely? How many horses would have improved again after age three and four if allowed the opportunity? A top horse being retired prematurely, when perfectly sound, is bad enough but to have connections claiming complacently that the horse concerned has "nothing left to prove" is particularly hard to stomach. Prematurely retiring top racehorses is a peculiarly European practice only recently adopted by North America. There are numerous examples during the last century of outstanding entire horses racing at least twenty times in North America and for three seasons, sometimes more. However, in Europe, Bayardo who raced for three years and twenty five times is the exception. Why is this? It seems that with some notable exceptions and particularly in the last forty years since the inception of the pattern, connections can't wait to win a couple of Group One races, announce that their horse "has nothing left to prove" and lead them to the covering shed. This is, of course, complete nonsense as the horse concerned has not proved that it is superior to the next generation. In some cases the horse concerned has not even proved it is the best in his own generation. This is of course what scares connections most. The possibility that their horse might not be as good as they would like breeders to believe. Absurdly, the horse in question, although bred to be a racehorse, has become too valuable to race. If it was not so sad for racing it would be laughable.

Do owners of potential stallions really think that a horse that has raced half a dozen times, or sometimes even less, will be considered better than he is just because he has avoided defeat, mainly because he has been lamentably under-tested on the racecourse? But what harm is done by being beaten? If a horse is well-bred then his chances at stud will not be affected as long as the horse concerned sees out his career and remains sound. In those circumstances he has then gained something: the horse will have been fully tested over different distances and surfaces. The stallion owner can then claim that their horse is not only a top class, well-bred horse, but in addition, has raced for three years at the top level, been fully tested and has stayed sound. Now that really IS something to put on a stallions CV! The fact that he was beaten on occasions will not matter in these circumstances.

Conversely, if the horse is not sound, this is also important to breeders who can then take the decision not to patronise any such stallion with an unsound mare. It is, perhaps, stating the obvious to say that this should be a major consideration for everyone with the welfare of thoroughbred racing in mind as it is crucial to the future well-being of the breed. It may be that the thoroughbred reached perfection over 100 years ago, and, that the purpose of racing is no longer to improve the breed, but continual breeding using unsound stock will quickly weaken it over the next century until keeping the majority of racehorses sound for any period may well prove almost impossible.

Apologies for the diversion and to return to the subject: since Generous in 1991, Daylami in 1999, Dubai Millennium in 2000 and Sea The Stars in 2009 the following have come closest to a rating of 138 - Mark of Esteem, Peintre Celebre and Montjeu all rated 137. Hellissio, Sahkee and Hawk Wing all rated 136. Of the above only Mark of Esteem was retired prematurely. It is sad that keeping Peintre Celebre and Hellissio in training did not work out but it certainly did for the other three, all of whom were beaten on occasions but not to the detriment of their reputations. It is hard to imagine any breeder planning a possible mating for his mare being put off any of them because they were beaten occasionally.

Although these things are often a matter of opinion, most independent observers would agree that the twenty-five colts indicated were great horses. Of these eleven raced at age four but none at age five. Fairway, owned by that great sportsman, racing benefactor and quite rightly *A Century of Champions* "Man of the Twentieth Century" the 17th Earl of Derby, would have raced at age five but for injury. As would Mill Reef, who was owned by a similarly great sportsman in Paul Mellon, but for his dreadful gallops injury that almost cost him his life. Of the nine

retired prematurely two, Hurry On and Gay Crusader, were both retired
during the Great War although both would have raced at age four but
for injury in the case of Gay Crusader although why Hurry On did not
race is not clear; six raced after the Second World War, since which time,
with the exception of a small handful of owners who put racing first,
horses of outstanding ability, and plenty with less, are retired as quickly
as possible to maximise stud value or in reality to avoid any possible
damage to his reputation.

Bahram, was owned and bred by the Aga Khan III who never
subscribed to the view that a racehorse was for racing. He was a
commercial breeder and notorious for prematurely retiring and selling
his horses, rather than fully testing them on the racecourse. Worse still
he then sold many of them to America thus depriving British breeders the
use of them. These included the Derby winners Blenheim, Bahram,
Mahmoud, and Tulyar; selling these classic winners, not surprisingly,
caused resentment amongst British breeders. The sale of Nasrullah was
equally unfortunate as, although not a classic winner and the possessor
of an erratic disposition to accompany his considerable talent, he became
an outstanding stallion. It is impossible to calculate the harm caused to
British bloodstock breeding by the sales of these horses.

The only other horses retired prematurely between the Wars were
Nearco a great horse whose only blot on a flawless record, apologies for
the oxymoron, was that he did not race in England. It was a considerable
disappointment that he did not contest and win the Ascot Gold Cup as a
four-year-old. The other was Blue Peter who is discussed in detail later
on. All of the eight great horses retired at age three since the Second
World War, were, as far as it is possible to ascertain, retired sound and
still had much to contribute to racing. It is conceded that Nijinsky,
although physically sound, may possibly have been difficult to train,
from a mental standpoint, at aged four.

It will be seen that Zarkava, although noted as a great horse, has not
been rated by *Timeform* as highly as she might. This is because although
unbeaten she was retired prematurely. It will be seen that only the
brilliant Sun Chariot of all the great fillies was retired at aged three. This
was due to a combination of temperament and the War. Sun Chariot's
merit will be discussed later. There is no such excuse, at least as far as a
War is concerned, in the case of Zarkava who, it was assumed retired
sound. It is conceded that Zarkava could be a handful and it is possible
that her temperament may not have stood another years training. She
had plenty to prove, contrary to the ridiculous claims of connections that
she did not, by showing at age four that she could beat the best three year
olds. In particular had she stayed in training she could have met Sea The
Stars on the racecourse. It is a sad comment on racing that instead she
will only meet him in the covering shed. The resultant foal will create

plenty of interest but if it can win a couple of races at Group 1 level the chances of it racing beyond its three-year-old season, on past evidence at any rate, are about equal to those of a domestic dog preparing its owners breakfast.

These examples are bad enough but surely the nadir was reached when Holy Roman Emperor was retired after his JUVENILE year and did not even race as a three-year-old! It was sad that George Washington was virtually impotent, the reason given for Holy Roman Emperor's retirement, but it still left an unpleasant taste that the 2000 Guineas of 2007 was missing the previous years two best juveniles. Teofilo was injured but Holy Roman Emperor was, as far as was known, fit and well. Whatever, racing was the loser again.

Zarkava racing against Sea The Stars! Now that really would have been a spectacle to savour! It would negate all the "initiatives" from racing's seemingly directionless hierarchy who, possibly in desperation, hire at considerable cost "consultants" those over-paid, rather self-important types who prepare endless reports about how "re-branding" racing will make it more "attractive" to the young. If that sounds a shade harsh then the reader has clearly not heard of that ghastly exercise in irrelevance called "Racing for Change" in which, amongst other things, a race-goer is described as a race-day customer. Good grief! The flat racing season is said by RFC to need a "narrative". What on earth do they think it already has? One of the lessons taught to all individuals learning about flat racing by their mentors is to understand the pattern and rhythm of the season from the Lincoln to the November Handicap and everything in between.

At the time of writing the idea seems to be that the flat-racing year must lead up to a number of "championships" of different sorts for practically everyone involved in the sport. Rubbish! All that flat-racing needs is to regularly stage racing between the best horses and make sure the public know when the meetings – sorry they are all "festivals" now – are to take place. All Group 1 races open to four-year-olds and up should be a million pounds guaranteed with huge bonuses – possibly as much as five million - for winning five races at that level in any one season or a consolation two million bonus for winning four.

One way might be to group races together for example any four-year-old and up winning the Prince of Wales Stakes, the Eclipse and the Champion Stakes all over ten furlongs or perhaps the Queen Anne, the Sussex and the QE II all over a mile could qualify for a bonus. In this way a colt winning three or more Group 1 races could cover one season's stallion earnings or very close. Available money must be invested at the top in order to attract new race-goers to the premier meetings and races. Racings rulers should concentrate funding on excellence at all levels at the expense of mediocrity which should be allowed to find its own level with funding only for integrity services. Moderate racing could possibly be paid for by the bookmaker's as it they who seem most keen that plenty of it should be staged. Whatever the outcome of some costly and unnecessary tinkering by RFC one thing is certain. Unless the public can be induced to find the spectacle of one thoroughbred outrunning others interesting and exciting then no amount of phoney "championships", "pop" concerts or any other entertainment will persuade more individuals to follow this most wonderful sport.

To return to Zarkava and her *Timeform* rating of 133, this reflects the comfortable manner of most of her wins. Also to an extent the, by Group One standards, average opposition she beat in the "Arc", where by *Timeform's* ratings she did not need to be at her best to prevail, despite giving them a substantial lead. There is little doubt in the minds of many independent observers that Zarkava was a great filly and racing is very much the poorer for the decision, for which connections were fortunate not to have attracted far more opprobrium than they did, to retire her. Racing in Europe can ill afford to lose racehorses of her quality.

By contrast in North America Zenyatta a five year old mare and competing for the fourteenth time in the 2009 Breeders Cup completed her unbeaten career by winning the Breeders Cup Classic. The enthusiastic scenes that greeted her win will stay in the memory and encourage more people to go racing. She was then retired only for connections to change their minds and decide to race her as a six-year-old! This wonderful news only makes it all the sadder that top owners in Europe are so feeble and chicken-hearted. Credit is due to Wertheimer et Frere owners of the wonderful Goldikova for keeping her in training as a five-year-old when she really did not have anything left to prove after her win in the Breeders Cup last year. They can only have done it because they love seeing their filly perform something shared by all lovers of thoroughbreds. How admirable is that? It is possible to hear mutterings from some who would say an owner has the right to do exactly what he likes with his horses and should not have to put up with the sort of impertinence propagated here. The answer to that is simple: don't owners owe any responsibility to the sport that provides the opportunities for them to gain fame and recognition for their horses and indeed improve their value?

It is a simple enough formula: get the best horses to race each other and against different generations. It would seem to be a forlorn hope as far as Britain and Europe is concerned and, of course, depressingly, the best three-year-old horse to have raced in Europe for at least twenty years – Sea The Stars – was retired after his three-year-old season. Persuading all the parties: racing's rulers, owner's, trainers, racecourses, breeders and, of course, bookmakers to agree on anything is the Holy Grail which eludes all worthy attempts. It would be easier to bottle smoke or gift-wrap a ferret.

The effect of this ghastly infighting is that the sport is burdened by far too much moderate racing from which only the bookmakers profit. It simply dilutes and devalues the sport while those in control make little or no attempt to promote quality competition, beyond sprinting that is, which seems an obsession at present. But above all they fail to elevate in public awareness the principal players of racing which are of course the horses!

CHAPTER 22

Bayardo's place in history

Attempting to compare horses over a period of one hundred years plus presents many problems. It was stated earlier that any outstanding horse from any period would be able to beat any other if the circumstances were in its favour. However, if it is the case that the thoroughbred has not improved genetically since the beginning of the Twentieth Century then by using certain standard criteria and with reference to the leading observers of each period it should be possible to discuss the various merits of different horses. It is not of course possible to be definitive even about modern horses and no claim is made with regard to the validity of one view against another.

The best horses from 1900 until the Great War were Sceptre, Pretty Polly, Ard Patrick, Spearmint, The Tetrarch, Swynford and Prince Palatine. Stedfast won 21 races but benefited from three walkovers and Lemberg - Bayardo's half-brother - won 17 of his 24 races. However, in terms of ability both would be behind Bayardo. These are the only horses that could be compared to Bayardo during this period. It may seem strange that the two Triple Crown winners of this time, Diamond Jubilee and Rock Sand have been excluded. However, the former was temperamental, a contender for one of the centuries biggest understatements, and beaten in as many as ten of his sixteen races, and the latter, although the winner of sixteen of his twenty races, was exposed as below the very top by Sceptre. In addition the four races he lost were crucial to his reputation.

The Tetrarch, who only raced as a juvenile, was of course superior as a two year old to Bayardo and, more than likely, any other juvenile in the history of the sport as well. He was an astonishing youngster, unbeaten in seven races. Six were won with conspicuous ease. However, in the National Breeders Produce Stakes at Sandown he only just got up on the line to win by a neck. Because of poor visibility the start could not be seen from the grandstand and there was universal disappointment at his apparently below par performance. However, The Tetrarch had been bumped twice and left at the start, in addition Steve Donoghue had been unable to balance him quickly and at half-way his chance seemed forlorn. It is difficult to imagine just how brilliant his speed was for him to get up and win giving the second 17 pounds. Donoghue informed trainer "Atty" Persse that he had won comfortably at the finish.

Unfortunately he was injured and never ran after his juvenile career. Just how far a horse with his brilliant speed could have stayed as a three year old is, therefore, open to speculation. Persse certainly never accepted that he would have been a non-stayer although Donoghue thought he would not have stayed because he liked to make the running from the start and was averse to settling. There is every indication that he would have stayed twelve furlongs on breeding. There was stamina on both sides of his pedigree. His sire was an out and out stayer, his dam stayed eleven furlongs and his dam sire was responsible for winners over twelve furlongs. Persse was of the view that the horse was a freak and that he would never have been beaten over any distance having both the breeding and conformation of a stayer. On the gallops he went ten furlongs at a "really good gallop" and comfortably gave between one and two stone to two good horses one that had won the Irish Derby. On another occasion against two good horses over twelve furlongs but only at a three parts gallop he was not extended or indicating that his stamina was running out. The question has to be asked: with his breeding how did he manage to sire three St Leger winners in five years if he was a non-stayer? His versatility as a sire was demonstrated when he sired the brilliantly fast Mumtaz Mahal. Unfortunately he was a shy breeder and a poor foal-getter and sterile after about ten years at stud. Incidentally, like Bayardo he had a habit of standing still and gazing into the distance something he did in the paddock at Goodwood once. One thing is without dispute, had The Tetrarch been able to reproduce, when three years old, the level of his juvenile form over 8-12 furlongs, then any discussion about the leading horse of the Twentieth Century would be irrelevant.

Sceptre and Pretty Polly would both have provided stiff opposition at any age and over any distance. Sceptre was beaten as a two year old but was probably superior at a mile. But Bayardo was probably better over 12 furlongs plus and would not have been beaten had they met in the Ascot Gold Cup. Pretty Polly was Bayardo's equal as a juvenile winning nine times including some top races. She may even have beaten him as she would have received a sex allowance. As a three year old she won the fillies' Triple Crown and would have provided stern opposition in the St Leger. As an older horse she was beaten only once in the Ascot Gold Cup when she was a five year old. Bayardo would probably have been better than Pretty Polly over the Cup distance. However, in fairness to Pretty Polly, it is possible she was not at her best in the Gold Cup and did not benefit from a very inspired ride. Conversely her conqueror was given an inspired ride by Danny Maher. It is undoubtedly true that both Sceptre and Pretty Polly would have been very hard to beat with the sex allowance.

Ard Patrick was an outstanding horse and close to greatness. He twice beat Sceptre against only one defeat, however, few would not consider

Sceptre the superior horse, although not by much. They are both rated 137 but that would mean that Sceptre would usually win with her sex allowance. Ard Patrick was not outstanding as a juvenile but was as a three and four year old. However, he would not have beaten Bayardo in either the St Leger or Ascot Gold Cup. Spearmint was once considered by Danny Maher to be the best horse he rode. However, Bayardo supplanted him. Swynford did not win as a juvenile and would not have beaten Bayardo over staying trips. Prince Palatine like Bayardo won as a juvenile and won the Ascot Gold Cup twice, but was inconsistent and inferior to him in all respects.

During the years of the Great War the only horses that came near to Bayardo were two of his sons Gay Crusader and Gainsborough plus the gigantic Hurry On. Comparing Bayardo with Hurry On is very difficult. Hurry On, who stood at 16.3, could not be trained as a juvenile, but at three he raced six times was never beaten and indeed never seriously challenged. He had not been entered for the substitute Derby but he did win the substitute St Leger. He was kept in training as a four-year-old but did not race and can be considered unlucky to be racing during the Great War as he did not really have the opportunity to show just how good he was. His conformation polarised opinion amongst judges with some considering him ugly whilst others thought him an outstanding looking horse. His trainer, the great Fred Darling, said he was the best horse he ever trained or was ever likely to train. That should be good enough for anyone.

The best horses between the wars and up to 1946 were Coronach, Colorado, Brantome, Hyperion, Bahram, Fairway, Windsor Lad, Sun Chariot, Blue Peter and Dante. Pharis raced only three times and it is hard to know how good he was, beyond of course, the probability that he was very good. Of those mentioned Bahram, Sun Chariot, Blue Peter and Dante did not race at four, so their claims, with the exception of Blue Peter, rest on unbeaten records at two (like Bayardo) and outstanding performances at three. However, Bahram, Sun Chariot, and Dante never met older horses.

Was Bayardo better than Bahram? It is impossible to know just how great Bahram was. His trainer Frank Butters said "Not even I knew how good he was". Bahram raced only nine times, was never seriously tested and retired with his true ability a closely guarded secret possibly known only by the horse himself and his maker. He was a placid indolent sort well proportioned and of considerable quality. He easily won all his five races as a juvenile including the National Breeders Produce Stakes and the Middle Park. At three he won the Triple Crown and the St James's Palace Stakes. At no stage in winning these races was he particularly impressive but also he was never asked for any appreciable effort. What was remarkable about him was that his trainer could produce such a lazy horse fit and well without any preparatory races in his classic year. The Newmarket touts were convinced he had not done enough work to win the Two Thousand Guineas and he stared second favourite. Had he been kept in training at age four and entered for the Ascot Gold Cup one of the great races of the century would have been in prospect. In the event a filly, Quashed, beat the American Triple-Crown winner Omaha by a short head in an exciting race. However, how much more thrilling would it have been to have had two Triple-Crown winners from either side of the Atlantic in the same race? This is yet another example of racing missing out because an owner, in this instance a fabulously wealthy individual, would not put the interests of the sport before profit. Assessing Bahram is almost impossible and any rating is largely guesswork.

Blue Peter was beaten in both his races as a juvenile and, although obviously smart – he was second in the Middle Park Stakes and rated second in the Free Handicap - gave no indication of greatness. At three he was unbeaten winning the Blue Riband Trial Stakes, 2000 Guineas, Derby and Eclipse where he beat older horses. In the Eclipse, once he had been roused from his indolence, he could not be pulled up until he had reached the starting gate where the race had started. Sadly he was denied the chance of securing the Triple Crown by the outbreak of War causing the St Leger, of which he was the likely winner, to be cancelled. In addition, but for the war, he would probably have raced at four. He can be considered a great horse but just how great will never be known. Blue Peter was a big, rangy colt, who stood just over 16 hands, in the same mould as his sire Fairway, although more robust in appearance, and had not reached his peak at the time of his last race. He produced an astonishing piece of work in a trial over fourteen furlongs, shortly before the St Leger was due to be run, where he sprinted clear and which suggested he could have won the Manchester November Handicap as a three-year-old with a weight of eleven stone. His rating of 138 possibly understates his ability and winning the St Leger and Ascot Gold Cup would have justified a higher figure. Blue Peter shares with Call Boy, and of course Bahram, the dubious honour of being the best horses between the wars whose true ability will never be known. No sport other than Thoroughbred Horseracing suffers so much from the agony of unfulfilled talent either by the fates or from deliberate acts of sabotage.

It is interesting that Peter Willett in his standard work *An Introduction to the Thoroughbred*, when discussing horses that had both brilliant speed and stamina, uses Bahram and Hyperion as examples. He draws attention to the fact that both won over five furlongs at two and had the stamina to win the St Leger over 14 plus furlongs at three. Yet Willett ignores Bayardo, both in this context and any other, there is no mention of him anywhere in the book, yet he was champion juvenile, won over five furlongs and was considered by *A Century of Champions* to be a better juvenile than either Bahram or Hyperion. In addition he had the stamina to win the St Leger at three and the Ascot Gold Cup over two and a half miles at four, something that Bahram, who had been prematurely retired, and Hyperion failed to achieve. Again Bayardo's failure in the Derby seems to have counted against him. Hyperion's merits against Bayardo are discussed shortly.

Brantome was champion juvenile and undefeated in four races, one over five furlongs, two over six and one over a mile. He was probably equal to Bayardo as a juvenile. At three he was champion again and unbeaten in five starts over distances ranging from a mile to fifteen furlongs. His wins included the French 2000 Guineas and Prix de l'Arc de Triomphe. He was forced to miss the French Derby due to coughing which necessitated his absence from the racecourse for all of June, July and August. At four he continued his triumphant way by winning his first two races including the Prix du Cadran over two and a half miles by fifteen lengths. What followed was dreadfully unfortunate. He was about to run in the Prix du Dangu at Chantilly when he broke loose on the way to the course and injured himself galloping round the town. He was given medication in preparation for the Ascot Gold Cup in which he was sensationally beaten into fourth place. Lack of stamina and the effects of the anti-tetanus injection were given as excuses. In the autumn he won the Prix d'Orange in preparation for the 'Arc but he was beaten into fifth place after which he was retired. In the final analysis Bayardo can be considered marginally superior. However, like Bayardo, Brantome's supporters can lament their bad luck that their colt lost his unbeaten record. Had he not suffered coughing as a three year old he would probably have won the French Derby and but for his escapade at Chantilly he would have been fighting fit for the Ascot Gold Cup. He was a great horse definitely a "crack" and not far behind the very best in the twentieth century. Physically he was no more than medium-sized but well-balanced and deep through the girth with a short back. One observer noted that he had the straightest hocks he had ever seen, something that is clear from his portraits. Brantome is covered in some detail as his career has some parallels with Bayardo's in that he was acknowledged as a great horse but with a little better fortune may have achieved more.

Hyperion was a great race-horse who stood at just over 15.1 hands when in training. He really was a wonderful horse: a veritable *multum in parvo*! Hyperion was exceptionally small and weak as a foal and there was a possibility that he would be destroyed as being potentially useless. However, he grew stronger and never lacked power and bodily he was medium sized. It was the shortness of his cannon bones that made him appear small. Hyperion has a record at two three and four to compare with Bayardo and like him he had a good juvenile record winning three of his five starts. But he would not have been as good a juvenile as

Bayardo and he was not champion two-year old. At three Hyperion was better than Bayardo but not by much. He won all four of his races against eleven of thirteen by Bayardo, however, he did win the Derby and the St Leger. Hyperion was an outstanding Derby winner but is credited by a judge, who must have been looking the wrong way at the time, as winning by only four lengths. The photographs of the finish suggest it more like seven or eight! At four Bayardo was better winning four out of five against two from four. Importantly Bayardo won the Ascot Gold Cup which Hyperion, possibly because of some less than competent training, did not. Coincidentally, Hyperion's last race ended in a surprising defeat conceding considerable weight, just like Bayardo.

Fairway, like Bayardo was champion at two three and four. At two he won three of his four races. At three he won four of five suffering his only defeat in the Derby, in which he was most unfortunate. The day was a fiasco and Fairway was mobbed by an excited crowd and lost all chance before the race was run. He won the St Leger but like Bayardo Fairway was an unlucky horse: he was the warm favourite for the Two Thousand Guineas but had a mouth ulcer on the eve of the race and unable to run. It is not unreasonable to say that with a little better fortune he may have been a Triple Crown Winner. At four he won five from six against Bayardo's four from five. The main difference was Bayardo's Gold Cup win and Fairway's only defeat in the Eclipse Stakes at odds of 2-5. Fairway was to have raced at age five with the Gold Cup as his objective but suffered an injury in the spring. Had he won the Gold Cup (his inferior stable companion won on his absence) then Fairway would have matched Bayardo for versatility.

Windsor Lad was a modest juvenile winning one from three. However, at three he won five from six including the Derby and St. Leger. His only defeat came against older horses in the Eclipse, a race Bayardo won at three. At four, Windsor Lad remained unbeaten and confirmed himself a great horse winning four races including the Coronation Cup and Eclipse in which race he was at a considerable disadvantage by having to make his own running. He was Champion older horse.

One horse mentioned earlier but not granted status amongst the elite is Call Boy. From racings point of view it was most unfortunate that his owner died shortly after his Derby win and all his engagements cancelled. He had been a top juvenile winning the Middle Park Stakes. However, as he was by Hurry On he was always likely to be better as a three year old. He was beaten a short head in the Guineas before winning the Newmarket Stakes. He made almost all the running in the Derby and, as he was a big strong sort, as befits a son of Hurry On, his best days should have been ahead of him. Instead he was retired to stud where he was almost sterile. Call Boy certainly had the potential for greatness.

Two horses foaled in the same year who with better luck may have had claims to greatness were Coronach and Colorado. Both raced for three seasons both won classics and each looked better than the other at different times. As juveniles both won good races but Colorado's form tailed off badly and Coronach was beaten in the Middle Park Stakes in a three-runner race in which he was the 1-7 favourite. As three-year-olds Colorado won the Two Thousand Guineas beating Coronach who was the 5/4 favourite but was beaten in the Derby by Coronach who went on to win the St Leger as the odds-on favourite and gave every indication that he was outstanding. Colorado did not race after Ascot. As four-year-olds both looked potentially great. Coronach continued his triumphant progress with impressive wins in the Coronation Cup and Hardwicke Stakes. Colorado started the year moderately but he won the Newbury Summer Cup impressively before slamming Coronach in the Princess of Wales's Stakes and then equally convincingly he beat him again in the Eclipse. Unfortunately Coronach had gone in his wind and did not race again while Colorado ended his career losing at odds-on in the Champion Stakes. Both had the potential to be great but neither was consistent and there remains the suspicion that neither was in peak form at the same time and they are impossible to split them in terms of ability. At their very peak both came close to greatness and, although inferior to Bayardo, both would have troubled him if producing their best.

The best two-year-old between the wars was possibly Colombo. He was a tremendous colt as a juvenile winning all his seven races including the National Breeders Produce and the Imperial Produce Stakes. He was significantly better than any other juvenile of his year and at least the equal of Bayardo. At three he won the Craven Stakes before comfortably winning the Two Thousand Guineas at odds of 2-7 the shortest price since 1896. There will always be controversy about his Derby. Would he have won with Steve Donoghue on board? Donoghue knew both the horse, who he had ridden when he was a juvenile, and Epsom better than Colombo's jockey Rae Johnstone. It is also fair to say that Donoghue knew Epsom better than any other jockey as well! In the event Johnstone did not shine in the race getting boxed in and snatching up his mount which meant he was too far back at Tattenham Corner and then coming wide. Once free Colombo heroically made up most of the lost ground but was beaten just over a length. It is hard to imagine Donoghue making a similar mistake. He claimed afterwards that if he had been on board Colombo he would have won "on the bit". Colombo was dogged by misfortune and after defeat at Ascot, when possibly not himself but again given too much to do by Johnstone, he was injured whilst preparing for the St Leger and retired. Colombo was probably a great horse and may have proved to be so if fate had been kinder.

If Colombo was not the best juvenile between the wars then it was Tetratema although Bahram may well have been the best two-year-old but he is hard to assess accurately as he was not really tested. Tetratema won all five of his races at two including the National Breeders Produce and the Imperial Produce Stakes and the Middle Park Stakes, although the opposition was not strong and he was long odds-on for all four races after his debut. At three he was surprisingly beaten in the Greenham Stakes before winning the Two Thousand Guineas. He failed to stay in the Derby and Eclipse Stakes but became an outstanding sprinter. He would have troubled Bayardo as a juvenile but not thereafter.

The best filly during this period was Sun Chariot. Although truly great, at least the equal of both Sceptre and Pretty Polly, on occasions when her temperament got the better of her, the most polite thing that can be said about her was that she was a cow. She could be impossible to handle and at different times she broke various bones of three different stable-lads. To say she could be uncooperative on occasions is to be guilty of a gross understatement and in addition she disliked going right-handed. She won eight of her nine races but threw away her unbeaten record by refusing to take hold of her bit in a minor race, although the soft ground may have been against her. She won all four of her races as a juvenile including the Queen Mary and Middle Park Stakes, the latter in a facile manner. At three she won four of her five races including the fillies Triple Crown. In the St Leger she beat the Derby winner Watling Street. *Raceform* states that Sun Chariot took the lead "on the bit" before winning "easily". Some observers thought she made a hack of him.

There were though two sides to her, King George VI, to whom she was leased, visited Beckhampton to watch her work prior to the Oaks. She refused to start for some time and then galloped off into a ploughed field whereupon she sank to her knees and roared like a bull. She was mulish before the Oaks, held that year because of the war on the July course at Newmarket, and spoiled three starts. When the gate went up she ran across the course and ruined her chance giving the rest of the field almost a furlong start. Gordon Richards, who was having a poor run, despaired. However, Sun Chariot, her competitive instincts roused, began to make up the ground and, despite running wide at the bend, incredibly passed all the runners and was pulling herself up before the line. Her Oaks performance was the most remarkable in the history of the race as the filly that finished second, Afterthought, later that year beat colts in the Jockey Club Cup.

Sun Chariot's rating of 137 can only be an educated guess and she could, at her best, have made a mockery of any figure. There is sufficient evidence to believe that there is no horse, of either gender, in the Twentieth Century that she could not have beaten. Her jockey Gordon Richards thought she was the best horse he ever rode. When it is remembered that he rode Tudor Minstrel the magnitude of that complement can be readily understood. Sun Chariot was only medium sized but beautifully made, rangy and with considerable power behind the saddle. If she had a conformation fault it was that she was a little too straight in front. In assessing racehorses she is a loose cannon and almost impossible to rate accurately.

Looking at the best horses from 1946, in terms of speed Bayardo would not have beaten Tudor Minstrel at any distance between 5 and 8 furlongs and it is probably true to say no horse ever foaled could, with the exception of The Tetrarch as a juvenile. However, he would have done at any distance from 10 to 20. It would have been interesting to see if Tudor Minstrel could have lasted nine furlongs against Bayardo, as he would definitely not have lasted ten, if they could have met as three year olds. In some ways this is almost the most fascinating race for the imagination. Tudor Minstrel would have made the running striding clear at the sort of lung-bursting pace that no three-year-old horse could ever have matched. After a mile Bayardo would have been anything up to ten lengths behind and would have had a furlong to catch Tudor Minstrel who would be gradually slowing down as his stamina leaked away. Bayardo's chances would have been considerably enhanced if he could have had company as he chased Tudor Minstrel.

In *A Century of Champions* Tudor Minstrel is given the accolade of the best horse of the Twentieth Century to be beaten in the Derby removing this unofficial title that Bayardo had held for nearly forty years. However, Bayardo's claim to this title is stronger than Tudor Minstrel's. Tudor Minstrel was probably the best horse ever foaled at any distance from five to eight furlongs. However, he was about ten pounds below his best at ten furlongs and about fifteen below at twelve. Therefore he was someway below the best horses of the Century at any distance beyond ten furlongs. Bayardo had few superiors at twelve furlongs and considering all the Derby winners of the Century only Sea Bird and Hyperion were rated as high or higher.

At middle distances, the best horses in the years after the War were Pinza, Ribot, Crepello and Sea Bird. None of them, except possibly Ribot, would have had the speed to have beaten Bayardo as juveniles and only Ribot raced at four. Bayardo would have needed to be at his best to beat any of them at age three. He would not have beaten the mighty Sea Bird at 12 furlongs, however, bearing in mind that Sea Bird was not an outstanding juvenile, he would probably have done at between 5 and 8 and 16 to 20. It would have been interesting at 10 or 14, particularly if Sea Bird had been allowed to race at four. Crepello was probably a great horse but he was not able to prove it. He would have been a Triple Crown winner but for injury prior to the St Leger and in all he raced only five times.

If races at distances from 16 to 20 furlongs are considered it is not unreasonable to claim that Bayardo was the best of those asked to race over these distances. In saying this it must be remembered that his trainer Alec Taylor considered Gay Crusader, a son of Bayardo, to be the greatest horse he had trained. This lofty status was shared by jockey Steve Donoghue, who considered him the best horse he rode. However, he was considerably inferior to Bayardo as a juvenile and, due to breaking down, could not be trained for the Ascot Gold Cup as a four year old. Gay Crusader won a very weak renewal aged three, which was run at Newmarket as a substitute race during the Great War. It is only fair to point out that Alec Taylor did also claim subsequently that the ill-fated Picaroon, whose grand-dam Silesia was a half sister to Bayardo, was the best!

In addition to Sea Bird during the sixties Vaguely Noble and Sir Ivor were the outstanding horses. Vaguely Noble would not have had the speed to beat Bayardo as a juvenile, although it would have been close if they had met over a mile. Sir Ivor would not have had the speed to beat Bayardo as a juvenile or the stamina to beat him over any distance beyond twelve furlongs. During the same period Royal Palace came close to winning the Triple Crown. Although he won nine of his eleven races and beat Sir Ivor in the Eclipse he has never been good enough to be considered a great horse. If a minor injury had not prevented him competing in the St Leger, a race he would probably have won, then he may have been more highly regarded.

A debate with regard to his merits against Brigadier Gerard and Mill Reef, both of whom, like Bayardo, raced for 3 seasons, would be lively. Both at almost any other time in history would each have been champion at 2, 3 & 4. However, while a race between the three of them at any distance between 5 & 12 furlongs would have been as the author and writer Roger Mortimer liked to say "worth walking a mile in tight boots to see" it would surely have been no contest at any distance from 14 to 20. Brigadier Gerard has strong claims to being the greatest European horse of the Twentieth Century and was almost the perfect racehorse. He is the only horse of the Twentieth Century to have opposed and beaten comfortably another horse, Mill Reef, rated 140 or higher.

Bayardo's merits in comparison with Nijinsky's make for a fascinating debate. Physically they were the antithesis of each other and Nijinsky would have towered over Bayardo had they been able to stand next to each other. They were of equal merit as juveniles and three year olds. Nijinsky probably has the claim at a mile with Bayardo superior at beyond twelve furlongs. However, it is almost impossible to separate them at 10-12 furlongs. It is true to say that although as a three year old Bayardo raced thirteen times as against Nijinsky's eight, the later was tested more in his classic season. What however is surely beyond dispute is that Nijinsky could not have returned at four to win the Ascot Gold Cup, even assuming his connections would have wanted too, which of course they did not! On a lighter note the image of Bayardo meeting Nijinsky in a match for a mythical Champion Stakes would be entertaining by any standards. Nijinsky, edgy, on his toes, sweating, about to explode and making it clear he had had enough and would rather be somewhere else and Bayardo refusing to canter to the start!

In recent years the best horses have been Alleged, Shergar, Dancing Brave, Generous, Dubai Millennium, Montjeu and Sea The Stars. All, except Dubai Millennium who was an 8-10 furlong horse, would have given Bayardo one hell of a race over 10-12 furlongs at three and he would not have been certain to beat any of them. None, with the possible exception of Montjeu, could have beaten him in the St. Leger or Ascot Gold Cup. Montjeu, had his temperament permitted, would have made an outstanding Cup horse as unlike the others he was bred to stay. However, he like the others would have stood no chance against Bayardo's speed in their juvenile season and they would not have beaten him at distances beyond twelve furlongs. Goodness knows if Bayardo could have given Dubai Millennium a race in the Dubai World Cup or Montjeu any trouble in the King George!

Vincent O'Brien trained two horses in the early 1980's that were close to greatness in Golden Fleece and El Gran Senor. Golden Fleece is a particularly difficult horse to rate he won all his four races including the Derby and was never really tested. However, he did not race after the Derby because of illness and injury and it will never be known what heights he may have achieved. He was probably a great horse, close in ability to his sire Nijinsky, but he was an unlucky horse and was denied the chance to prove it. El Gran Senor was an outstanding horse as good as any, apart from Brigadier Gerard, at a mile and very good at twelve furlongs. He was also unlucky suffering a foot ailment which prevented him racing after the Irish Derby. If he had been allowed the opportunity to race over ten furlongs there is little doubt he would have shown himself to be a great horse. Only over a mile would El Gran Senor have been able to beat Bayardo and Golden Fleece could have beaten Bayardo over twelve furlongs. Neither would have beaten Bayardo over twelve furlongs plus.

Bayardo against Sea The Stars! Clearly Bayardo would be superior as a juvenile. However, Sea The Stars would have beaten Bayardo in both the Guineas and the Derby simply because he was at or near to his optimum and Bayardo was not. Only by the time of the Eclipse would they have met when both would have been at there best. Race conditions were very different. In 1909 the ground was soft – which suited Bayardo but would not have suited Sea The Stars - and in 2009 it was fast which was the other way around! It is safe to say that neither could have beaten the other in their respective races in the prevailing conditions. There lies the problem in comparing them. Sea The Stars would not have been allowed to race when the ground was soft and they could only have met on fast ground which would have been to Bayardo's disadvantage. It is not certain but probably Sea The Stars could not have beaten Bayardo in the Ascot Gold Cup on any surface.

Comparisons certainly are difficult and of course one is no nearer solving any issues after making them than before. However, the crux of this debate is a possible claim by Bayardo to be the most versatile of all the horses, generally regarded as great, who raced in the twentieth century. Advocates of Hyperion have a good case in that he won over 5 furlongs at two and, but for some incompetent, or if one is inclined to be charitable, not very assiduous training, would probably have won the Ascot Gold Cup at 4. The great Ribot won from 5 to 15 furlongs and was of course never beaten. Had he been entered for the 1956 Ascot Gold Cup, he would have started at very short odds. None of runners that year would have been within a stone and a half of him. Ribot would have won too, and in all probability raced the entire trip without coming off the bridle!

Bayardo was certainly the best winner of the Ascot Gold Cup since the beginning of the Twentieth Century and his performance would almost certainly have won any renewal since that time. Few if any other Cup winners were good enough to be champion juvenile and be unbeaten in seven races. His win in the Ascot Gold Cup was his greatest performance and one which he dispelled forever the theory that he was in any way dishonest or needed to be held up until the last possible moment. The Ascot Gold Cup was the principal target and of supreme importance for top older horses until the Second World War. Even before the War the race had been subjected to ignorant criticism by some who should have known better. The furore when the connections of Windsor Lad declined to take on Brantome in the 1935 Gold Cup, showed clearly enough that the race was losing its allure to some. After the War its importance diminished and became a race for established stayers only. It has been supplanted entirely in the last 40/45 years by The King George VI & Queen Elizabeth II Stakes, as the principal mid season middle distance objective. Even the "King George" is now losing its' allure and few three year olds are now directed at it, connections preferring ten furlong contests or waiting for the "Arc".

In the final analysis if a series of races were held in elysian fields at ages two, three and four between the best horses since the start of the twentieth century that raced for at least three seasons over five, six and seven furlongs at two, a mile, ten, twelve and fourteen furlongs at three and twelve, sixteen and twenty furlongs at four the winner of most races, on all known evidence, could only come from the following six horses;

Pretty Polly, Sceptre, Brantome, Hyperion, Nearco, Ribot and Bayardo. Brigadier Gerard and Mill Reef could also compete but neither would have stood much chance in the races beyond, in the Brigadier's case ten and Mill Reef's twelve, furlongs. It is not claimed that Bayardo would win most of the races simply that he would have as good a chance as any.

CHAPTER 23

Conclusion

Racing history is full of stories of bad luck and what might have been. However, to do full justice to Bayardo it is a tenable claim that he can be considered unfortunate ever to have been beaten. The statement that "Bayardo was head and shoulders above all opposition at age two, three and four" would attract a *consensus gentium* among those who saw him race. It is frustrating that Bayardo was ever beaten as he was able to demonstrate that he was considerably superior to the five horses that ever finished in front of him. However, the fact that they did can't be simply ignored.

Bayardo won 22 races. If considering only those horses that raced since the beginning of the Twentieth Century that could be considered either great or close to greatness, Pretty Polly alone can equal this figure. The following all won ten or more races:-

The following could also be considered outstanding if not great, but as sprinters only. Diomedes won 17 and Right Boy 16. Abernant, who certainly was great, won 14, but as he never won beyond 7 furlongs (and only once over that distance at odds of 1/25), he is in a class of his own as the greatest sprinter of all time. However, Tudor Minstrel would have

Bayardo 22	Mill Reef 12,
Pretty Polly 22	Fairway 12
Brigadier Gerard 17	Brantome 12
Lemberg 17	Tantieme 12
Marsyas 17	Pappa Fourway 12
Ribot 16	Halling 12
Rock Sand 16	Pearl Cap 11
Prestige 16	Nijinsky 11
Dahlia 15	Prince Palatine 11
Tenerani 15	Sardanapale 11
Pharos 14	Le Moss 11
Nearco 14	Daylami 11
Abernant 14	Montjeu 11
Petite Etoile 14	Coronach 10
Ardross 14	Windsor Lad 10
Sceptre 13	Sayani 10
Tetratema 13	Chanteur 10
Allez France 13	Tanerko 10
Moorestyle 13	Sagaro 10
Park Top 13	Indian Skimmer 10
Goldikova 13	Swain 10

provided stern opposition over sprint distances, but he was not a Champion sprinter simply because he never raced over sprint distances as a three year old. Tetratema won 13 and did win the 2000 Guineas, but lacked stamina and was a great sprinter. Pappa Fourway won 12, but was also a sprinter. The Tetrarch has a claim to be the best two-year old of the twentieth century.

At the other extreme Marsyas won 17 but he was an out and out stayer, albeit a very fine one. Similarly the wonderful and genuine Brown Jack won 18 races on the flat, plus five over hurdles, and raced for eight seasons. But he was well below the standard required to be considered a great horse. Sagaro with 10, Le Moss 11 and Ardross 14 were a trio of outstanding Ascot Gold Cup winners, but none would have been effective at less than twelve furlongs and they were only able to dominate at distances of two miles and above. The remarkably durable and genuine Yeats raced for seven seasons and won 15 races including four Ascot Gold Cups and a Group One race over twelve furlongs. However, longevity is not an automatic qualification for greatness and he was inferior to the trio of Sagaro, Le Moss and Ardross as a stayer. Indeed if *Timeform* are correct for a period of at least two years he was not even the best stayer in his own stable! Septimus was rated higher and had the form to beat Yeats but he was never asked to race against him. This was not the fault of Yeats who could only beat those horses put against him. It was simply that the staying division is weak and he beat some moderate horses, by Group One standards, and below those beaten by Sagaro and Le Moss in a total of five Gold Cups between them. For example both had to beat Buckskin who was rated higher by *Timeform* than Yeats. Le Moss also had to beat Ardross. In turn, Ardross's short-head second in the Arc de Triomphe was better than anything Yeats achieved.

The very game and tough Diadem is not overlooked. She won 24 (including three walk-over's) of her 39 races and never gave less than everything. Although she won the 1000 Guineas and was second in the New Oaks, she was really a sprinter and was unable to dominate over a variety of distances.

From this impressive list of all time top horses it can be seen that winning more than ten races at the top level is not easy. How much harder then is it to dominate for three seasons and win 22 races over distances from five furlongs to two and a half miles? Cynics may point out that not all of his races were very competitive. This is true. When any horse establishes considerable superiority over his contemporaries, opposition tends to drain away. Of the 15 races he won at aged three and four, in seven stakes and plate races he beat a total of 16 opponents at odds of 2/11, 1/7, 9/100, 7/100, 1/33, 1/66 & 9/100. At least two of his wins were in races that might as well have been walkovers. This does, however, still demonstrate remarkable durability, particularly when it is considered that he ran a total of eighteen races during this period, thirteen at aged three, and the last seven he won in sixty four days! Of course not all the races of those great horses mentioned in comparison were particularly well contested, with plenty winning uncompetitive races at long odds on.

The lack of suitable opposition for great horses has always been a problem. In North America, just after the Great War, the immortal Man o' War won 20 of his 21 starts. As a three year old he won all of his eleven races. In the last ten he beat a total of 25 horses. Many considered the three year olds he raced against to be ordinary. This does not make him any less great. Connections of possible opponents were frightened to take him on and those that did were beaten either easily or very easily! Even when the previous years Triple Crown winner (although it was not called the Triple Crown at that time), Sir Barton, took him on in a match race, Man o' War won comfortably. The only occasion he was shown the whip was to beat a very good horse called John P Grier when Man o' War was giving 18 pounds and after a stirring battle the great horse simply ground him down. Next time they met Man o' War comfortably galloped John P Grier legless and the unfortunate horse was eased when he had given everything in defeat. On another occasion he carried 9 stone 10 pounds to victory. As none of his contemporise could extend him he had only the clock to beat. In six races he broke track or national records and on another occasion he equalled one. Incredible when it is considered that he was galloping on his own most of the time with his jockey holding him under a tight reign with instructions not to let Man o' War have his head for fear that he may injure himself!

When Bayardo was foaled he had unlimited potential. He was described when moving as being capable of easily maintaining his position in a race or gallop whatever the pace, distance or opposition. Of his 22 wins one was described as a common canter, eleven as a canter (including the Eclipse and Ascot Gold Cup) five as easily (including the National Breeders Produce Stakes and St. Leger and one other race when hampered) and one cleverly, (Champion stakes).

Therefore in eighteen of his twenty two wins he was not considered to have fully extended himself by contemporary observers. In most of his races, where there was worthwhile opposition, he simply kept pace with them and then when asked he out-speeded them usually settling the issue "in a matter of strides". Races are seldom won today in a canter, races at the top level even less so. However, if anyone is in any doubt about how this appears, they have only to look at recordings of either Nijinsky or Montjeu in the "King George" renewals of 1970 and 2000 respectively, Shergar in the Irish Derby in 1981 when he travelled the entire mile and a half under Lester Piggott's iron hand-lock as connections had been apprehensive about the firm ground, or Ardross in the 1981 Ascot Gold

Cup. Even when allowance is made for the over use of the word canter in describing wins by observers in Bayardo's time, it is still an impressive record. It is difficult at this distance to be sure but if pressed the feeling persists that the single horse it would be best to avoid of all the Twentieth Centuries champions it would be Sun Chariot who demonstrated in the Oaks that her capacity for brilliance was almost limitless.

Nature, however, decreed that Bayardo would be born with fleshy, sensitive feet, a condition which turned out to be laminitis, and meant that throughout his career he often did not have conditions to suit him. It is also fair to say that once the 1909 season was underway there was enough rain to ease the ground on many occasions. Alec Taylor was at pains to make Danny Maher understand that he was to be ridden tenderly whenever the ground was too hard. It is notable that on the eight occasions he had give in the ground Bayardo won either in a canter or easily. There were, of course, no watering systems in those days to ease the ground. To compound this the winter prior to his classic season was exceptionally cold and dry. Had he been just a little more fortunate, and the weather normal, the gallops at Manton would not have been so hard and if the temperature not quite so bitterly cold he might have thrived, as he did in the spring of the following year. As it was, even with the elements conspiring against him, all might have been well, had he been injured on some ice. Without that accident he would not have been held up in his work and might have been fitter earlier. Had Alec Taylor had his way and Bayardo been scratched from the 2000 Guineas he may have been in better shape for the Derby. If only if only if only …

Again at stud he was less than fortunate. His freshman season was 1914. Once war was declared his opportunities at stud were necessarily reduced and of course racing was restricted. He died in 1917 at which time his true potential was unrealised. Afterwards with two Triple Crown winners the full impact of his early loss, already regretful, was understood. It was, in fact, a serious blow for British bloodstock. As it was he sired a horse almost as good as himself in Gay Crusader and also Gainsborough, not far behind in ability and outstanding as a sire, who in turn was responsible for Hyperion, whose influence on British and world bloodstock breeding in the twentieth century was immense and probably without equal.

Bayardo sired two of the three Triple Crown winners during the Great War. It is not unusual for some to claim that these should not count as equal in status with other Triple Crown and classic winners. The matter was discussed by Roger Mortimer some years later as follows;

"There were three Triple Crown winners during the war years –
Pommern, Gay Crusader and Gainsborough. Their statuses as such, and their achievements, have sometimes been subject to sharp

devaluation on the grounds that competition was far less intense than usual owing to wartime restrictions on racing. Furthermore, it is said that since all wartime classic races were run at Newmarket, wartime classic contenders did not have to cope with the differing conditions existing at Epsom and Doncaster. The fact remains, though, that the wartime Triple Crown winners proved themselves beyond argument the best of their respective generations and they would in all probability have exercised a similar superiority under peace time conditions".

Sir Charles Leicester writing in his standard work on breeding had no doubt that they were all worthy Triple Crown Winners and that each were easily the best of their respective generations. Incredibly it is possible that there was an even better horse during the War years than any of the three Triple Crown winners in the unbeaten and untested Hurry On. He was considerably superior to all opposition during 1916 but had not been entered for the Derby. He won the substitute St Leger.

The jockey Steve Donoghue had no doubt as to the merit of two of these Triple Crown winners. He always maintained that Gay Crusader was the best horse he ever rode and Pommern the next. Although it is true to say he did not reaffirm the status of Pommern in his later autobiography. Donoghue did not ride against Bayardo and does not offer any opinion as to his merit.

Without wishing to labour the point even peace-time Triple Crown winners did not always face tough opposition. Bahram was a great horse. However, he was largely untested in just four races by the relatively weak three year olds of 1935. He did not race against older horses at all and was retired prematurely. This was not his fault and quite rightly his reputation is unimpaired. Yet similarly sympathetic standards of judgement have not applied to the three war-time Triple Crown winners simply because they only raced at Newmarket and were unable to demonstrate versatility to accompany their superiority.

Was Bayardo a great sire? On balance it has to be said that he fell short. He sired only seven crops. Had he not died prematurely he would have had the opportunity to advance his claim. Bayardo was not fortunate at stud but it could have been worse. There were a significant number of small minded anti-racing bigots that took the opportunity that War provided to vent their unpleasantly prejudicial spleens against the sport. They secured a Government decision that racing should be banned after the Guineas meeting in 1917 until after hostilities had ceased. Had that decision not been reversed then instead of having two Triple Crown winners to his credit Bayardo would have had just one Two Thousand Guineas winner. It would have been interesting to see what he may have achieved as a peacetime stallion after the war when restrictions had been lifted. As it was he sired two Triple Crown winners, one of whom

Gainsborough sired Hyperion. For that alone his place in history is secure.

The more one considers Bayardo's life, both on the racecourse and at stud, the more it becomes clear that perhaps with just a little more good, and a little less ill fortune, he could have been even greater in both spheres than he was. He certainly deserves more recognition. For years before each Royal Ascot various previews look back over the history of the meeting. It is a vain search for any reference to a horse that won three years in succession and was almost certainly the best winner of its showcase race.

It is certain that no horse since the beginning of the twentieth century has been able to display high class brilliant speed as a juvenile and equally high class stamina as a four year old. It is also true that no stallion can lay claim to two Triple Crown winners and be the grand sire of such a great racehorse and stallion as Hyperion. However one considers the life of Bayardo it has to be conceded that along with his brilliance he was eccentric by any standards. Despite this it has never been suggested that he was anything other than honest when racing. He deserves a more prominent position in racing's history and to be remembered as more than a brilliant but quirky, moody and temperamental horse that was beaten at odds on in the Two Thousand Guineas and was the best horse of the Twentieth Century not to win the Derby.

APPENDICES

The Pedigree of Bayardo

BAYARDO [B. C., foaled January 31, 1906].					
Bay Ronald (B. 1893).	Hampton (B. 1872).	Lord Clifden (B. 1860).	Newminster (B. 1848).	Touchstone.
				Beeswing.
			The Slave (B. 1852).	Melbourne.
				Volley.
		Lady Langden (Br. 1868).	Kettledrum (Ch. 1858).	Rataplan.
				Hybla.
			Haricot (Br. 1847).	Lanercost.
				Queen Mary.
	Black Duchess (Bl. 1886).	Galliard (Br. 1880).	Galopin (B. 1872).	Vedette.
				Flying Duchess.
			Mavis (Ch. 1874).	Macaroni.
				Merlette.
		Black Corrie (Bl. or Br. '79).	Sterling (B. 1868).	Oxford.
				Whisper.
			Dau. of (B. 1861).	Wild Dayrell.
				Lady Lurewell.
Galicia (B. or Br. 1898).	Galopin (B. 1872).	Vedette (Br. 1854).	Voltigeur (Br. 1847).	Voltaire.
				Martha Lynn.
			Mrs. Ridgway (B. 1849).	Birdcatcher.
				Nan Darrell.
		Flying Duchess (B. 1853).	Flying Dutchman (Br. 1846).	Bay Middleton.
				Barbelle.
			Merope (B. 1841).	Voltaire.
				Velocipede's dam.
	Isoletta (B. or Br. 1891).	Isonomy (B. 1875).	Sterling (B. 1868).	Oxford.
				Whisper.
			Isola Bella (Ch. 1868).	Stockwell.
				Isoline.
		Lady Muncaster (Ch. 1884).	Muncaster (Ch. 1877).	Doncaster.
				Windermere.
			Blue Light (Ch. 1870).	Rataplan.
				Borealis.

APPENDIX 1

Bayardo at Stud

By the time he went to stud in 1911 Bayardo was considered a handsome horse, standing just under 16 hands. His picture certainly shows a more distinguished horse in full maturity than when racing. He stood at Manton under the management of Alec Taylor for a fee of 300 guineas (£19,200), and nominations were eagerly sort after.

His first crop was of modest size and contained just one winner, but fortunately she was very decent. She was named Good and Gay and was a daughter of the outstanding broodmare Popinjay who was also a useful racehorse, although she only raced as a juvenile. She won a stakes race and was placed at both Ascot and in the Cheveley Park Stakes. Good and Gay was the first of eight winners she produced, including two more by Bayardo namely Lord Basil and Pompadour. Good and Gay won the Bessborough Stakes at Ascot and the Buckenham Stakes at Newmarket. However, fine prospect as she was, Good and Gay was Bayardo's only winner in his freshman season in 1914.

Interestingly the mare Popinjay developed a fruitful relationship with Bayardo and his sire Bay Ronald. In addition to Good and Gay and her full siblings mentioned above, Popinjay's foals by Bayardo's son Gay Crusader were Crossbow, winner of the Newmarket Stakes, Newmarket St Leger and Royal Hunt Cup; and the mare Gay Bird. Since Popinjay shared the same sire, St Frusquin, as Gainsborough's dam Rosedrop they were all bred on similar lines to that Classic winner.

Gay Bird became the matriarch of a successful family that included the influential stallion Clarion (inbred 3x3 Gay Crusader) and Intermezzo II, winner of the Austrian Derby, Hungarian St Leger and a successful sire in Hungary. His dam was inbred 3x4 Bayardo via Gainsborough and Gay Bird, and he himself 2x4 Gay Crusader. Furthermore when crossed with Dark Ronald, a stallion like Bayardo by Bay Ronald and inbred to the mare Queen Mary, Popinjay produced Magpie, Champion Sire in Australia in 1928/29, along with Popingaol, a mare who foaled Epsom Oaks winner Pogrom when mated with Bayardo's half-brother Lemberg. Another daughter of Popingaol named Splendid Jay won the Yorkshire Oaks and was sired by Bayardo's half-brother Kwang Su whose sire Cicero shared the same grand dam as Popinjay.

It is possible that this affinity could be attributed to the fact that Bayardo's third dam Lady Muncaster had a very similar pedigree pattern to Popinjay's dam Chelandry. If their pedigree's are compared it will be seen that Lady Muncaster's sire Muncaster, with strains of Doncaster, Macaroni and Miss Agnes close up, mirrored that of Chelandry's grand sire Ormonde, while Lady Muncaster's dam Blue Light, being by Rataplan out of a daughter of Blink Bonny, was a very close relative to Blair Athol (by Rataplan's full brother Stockwell out of Blink Bonny), the sire of Chelandry's grand dam Paraffin.

Bayardo's offspring fared slightly better on the racecourse in 1915, when as a result of the Great War, racing was restricted. Again both his winners were juveniles, Ali Bey winning three of his seven races and finishing second in three others and Bay D'Or winning a minor event. Good and Gay raced only once, unplaced, and did not race again.

After two racing seasons it was undeniable that Bayardo had made a moderate start to his stallion career. Winners would need to be more plentiful, and at a higher level, if he was to justify his stud fee and cement his position as a major stallion. Fortunately, 1916 saw Bayardo reach 11th position in the list of leading sires with ten winners of eleven races worth £4,082 (142,870). More importantly it heralded the appearance on the racecourse of a top horse of the calibre that was expected for one of his standing. Gay Crusader began modestly with no sign of the triumphs to follow. He won his second start and, with Sir Dighton who dead-heated for the Craven Stakes, also winning, there were signs that better times were ahead.

In 1917 Gay Crusader carried all before him winning the Triple Crown. Almost single-handed he ensured that Bayardo would be champion sire for the first time. However, among the six winners representing him that year was a juvenile who would eventually have the most profound effect on thoroughbred breeding for the rest of the century. He was Gainsborough. Sadly in this pivotal year of Bayardo's stud career and aged only eleven he suffered a thrombosis resulting in paralysis in his hindquarters and it was necessary to destroy him on 4th June 1917.

Bayardo was champion again in 1918 for the second and final time with Gainsborough following Gay Crusader and also winning the Triple Crown. As in the previous two years there was a juvenile who would win a classic the following year. This was Bayardo's daughter Bayuda won the Cheveley Park Stakes.

1919 saw a return to a fuller racing programme and Bayardo's standard bearer was Bayuda. She won the Oaks, back at its proper home of Epsom, and became his third classic winner carrying the same colours as Gainsborough. Bayardo was deprived of the opportunity of siring the Derby winner for the third year in succession when Alfred Cox died. His colt Manilardo had finished third in his only juvenile appearance before winning the Wood Ditton Stakes by four lengths. Alec Taylor considered him to have had an excellent chance in the Epsom classic but all his engagements had been cancelled on Cox's death. This was to be Bayardo's most successful year numerically and he finished 14th in the list of winning sires.

1920 would be the last season that Bayardo would be represented by a full crop of horses on the racecourse. He finished eighth in the list of leading sires and his offspring captured several important races: Allenby won the Newmarket Stakes and St James's Palace Stakes; Braishfield the Sussex Stakes and Great Yorkshire Stakes; Manilardo the Coronation Stakes; and the juvenile filly Pompadour the Imperial Produce Stakes.

Pompadour won the Nassau Stakes in 1921 and Braishfield the Churchill Stakes. A four year old Palomides won four races and, although he was to win no major races, he eventually became Bayardo's fourth biggest earners on the racetrack. He recorded a total of fifteen wins and in 1926 he became Bayardo's final winner.

Offspring of Bayardo with winnings over £2,000

Colts	Races won	Value in £
Gainsborough	5	14,080
Gay Crusader	8	11,246
Allenby	3	5,813
Palomides	15	4,033
Manilardo	4	3,297
Braishfield	3	2,735
Bantry	9.5	2,658
Ali Bey	5	2,645
Fillies	Races won	Value in £
Bayuda	2	6,275
Good And Gay	2	3,632
Pompadour	3	3,129
Rothesay Bay	4	2,232

Winners sired by Bayardo in Great Britain and Ireland

1914	Dam	Dam Sire	Races Won	Value in £
Good And Gay	Popinjay	St Frusquin	2	3,632
TOTAL			2	3,632

1915	Dam	Dam Sire	Races Won	Value in £
Ali Bey	Mowsali	Flying Fox	3	1,818
Bay D'Or	Dame D'Or	Bend Or	1	186
TOTAL			4	2,004

1916 (11th)	Dam	Dam Sire	Races Won	Value in £
Ali Bey			2	827
Bay D'Or			1	100
Bayard	Elizabeth M	Watercress	0.5	118
Bayberry	Catalpa	Sundridge	1	195
Bayodee	Cheshire Cat	Tarporley	1	176
Blackadder	Ajanita	Ajax	2	894
Cranford	Wise Joan	John O'Gaunt	1	197
Gay Crusader	Gay Laura	Beppo	1	1,066
Helenora	Helvia	Cicero	1	262
Sir Dighton	Princesse de Galles	Gallinule	0.5	247.50
TOTAL			11	4,082.50

1917 (1st)	Dam	Dam Sire	Races Won	Value in £
Bapaume	Scabieuse	Isinglass	1	256
Bay D'Or			3	694
Gainsborough	Rosedrop	St Frusquin	1	670
Gambardo	La Roche	St Simon	1	100
Gay Crusader			7	10,180
Hampshire Lily	Lily of the Valley	Martagon	1	169
Inversnaid	Inheritance	Isinglass	1	268
TOTAL			15	12,337

1918 (1st)	Dam	Dam Sire	Races Won	Value in £
Bayuda	Jessica	Eager	1	1,325
Evan	Evadne	Sidus	1	265
Gainsborough			4	13,410
Glenbay	Glamourie	The Victory	1	100
Lord Basil	Popinjay	St Frusquin	1	550
TOTAL			8	15,650

1919 (14th)	Dam	Dam Sire	Races Won	Value in £
Allenby	Tagalie	Cyllene	1	877
Baal-Gad	Jubilee	Diamond Jubilee	1	175
Bapaume			1	100
Bayodee			1	100
Bayuda			1	4,950
Daybreak	Golden Dawn	Raeburn	3	332
Lady Bayardo	Veldt	Pietermaritzburg	1	227
Manilardo	Gay Laura	Beppo	2	577
Peach Blossom	Cornfield	Isinglass	1	100
Pesaro	Persepolis	Persimmon	1	176
Rothesay Bay	Anchora	Love Wisely	4	2,232
Tussock Grass	Bunch Grass	Sainfoin	1	264
TOTAL			18	10,114

1920 (8th)	Dam	Dam Sire	Races Won	Value in £
Allenby			2	4,936
Bacton Lad	Cyanin	Cyllene	0.5	126
Bantry	Ulster Queen	Cicero	2	731
Barribel	Queensland	Desmond	1	836
Border Don	Loch Doon	Bread Knife	2	491
Braishfield	Beaune	St Frusquin	2	1,635
Evan			2	382
Manilardo			2	2,720
Manton	Jane Grey II	Le Sancy	1	904
Pompadour	Popinjay	St Frusquin	2	1,989
Royal Bay	Signorina	Saphir	1	184
TOTAL			17.5	14,934

1921	Dam	Dam Sire	Races Won	Value in £
Baal-Gad			2	756
Bacton Lad			1	100
Bantry			3.5	1,112
Braishfield			1	1,100
Palomides	Paloma	Cyllene	4	959
Pompadour			1	1,140
Queen Wasp	Mother in Law	Matchmaker	2	846
TOTAL			14.5	6,013

1922	Dam	Dam Sire	Races Won	Value in £
Bantry			4	815
Palomides			3	704
TOTAL			7	1,519

1923	Dam	Dam Sire	Races Won	Value in £
Palomides			2	1,113
TOTAL			2	1,113

1924	Dam	Dam Sire	Races Won	Value in £
Palomides			2	483
TOTAL			2	483

1925	Dam	Dam Sire	Races Won	Value in £
Palomides			3	625
TOTAL			3	625

1926	Dam	Dam Sire	Races Won	Value in £
Palomides			1	147
TOTAL			1	147

Summary
Individual Winners in England & Ireland - 39
Total Races Won in England & Ireland - 105
Value in £ - £72,653.50
14 fillies winning 22 races worth £18,632
25 colts winning 83 races £54,021.50
16 two-year-old winners of 21 races worth £14,926
The average winning distance of his progeny was 9.35 furlongs.

When he first went to stud the king was among the owners who sent mares to Bayardo. One of these was Loch Doon, a tough mare who won six of her twenty-five races over three years. She had already produced two winners and the result of her union with Bayardo was a bay colt named Border Don which was "generally admired". His trainer Richard Marsh said that he "looked like racing and showed all his sire's quality". He was sufficiently well thought of to be entered in twenty six races as a juvenile. Unfortunately, he did not thrive and only appeared in October, after he had been gelded. He proved a disappointment and did not win until the age of five when he won two selling handicaps. Alfred Cox had few foals by his own horse. One mare, Bona Dea, a once raced maiden, produced a filly named Ferrara who, although entered for some top races, never ran.

1913 saw Bayardo's first yearlings offered for sale at public auction and four passed through the sales ring. On the morning of 3rd July, at Newmarket, the first of this quartet came under the hammer. A bay son out of the mare Lady Raeburn, a once raced maiden, but the producer of three winners and the producer of two more in future, was sold to Mr A E Barton for 810 guineas (£29,800). He raced under the name of Bayardino but failed to gain even a place in six races.

As summer drifted into autumn the yearling sales circuit moved on to Doncaster where three colts by Bayardo were included in the catalogue. A son out of The Broom, an unraced mare who was to produce two winners, made 450 guineas (£16,540) and was named, with a stunning lack of imagination, Broomardo, but he never raced in England. Next a son out of Royal Marriage, another once raced mare that was to produce three winners, made 1,500 guineas (£55,100); he was named Arkroyal but he never made it to the racecourse. Finally, a son of Alicia fetched the most at 3,700 guineas (£136,000) when sold to Lord Lonsdale. Named Alfana he must have been difficult to keep sound as he raced only five times in four seasons.

At the Newmarket December sales one of his sons was the most expensive of the entire sale being knocked down to Mr H G Morris for 3,100 guineas (£114,000). His dam, Cheshire Cat, had won three of her four races, and although a maiden mare at this time, she was to go on and produce seven winners. This colt was named Bayodee and won two races worth £276 (£9,700), some way below his purchase price.

In 1914 four yearlings, three colts and a filly, by Bayardo were sold realising an average of 1,392 guineas (£51,200). Bay D'Or, a son out of Dame D'Or made 3,000 guineas (£110,200). Dame D'Or failed to win any of her six races but proved to be a great success at stud. She had already produced four winners and was to produce two more including Bay D'Or who won five races. Bay D'Or was to prove the best horse by Bayardo ever sold at public auction. Although his five wins realized only £980 (36,000), against his purchase price of over three times that amount, he did become a stallion. His portrait suggests he had some resemblance to his sire and he had certainly inherited Bayardo's knees! It is difficult to be certain but it could well be that Bay D'Or was the only son sold at public auction, apart from those that were pin-hooked, that the buyer ever made a profit on. There is one other possibility which will be referred to later. Another son out of Elizabeth M made 1000 guineas (36,700) and Capt. Homfray must have endured many a sleepless night thinking of a suitable name for his colt and eventually came up with the mind numbingly boring appellation, Bayard. Sons of Bayardo were not often named with much imagination: *bis repetita placent!* Elizabeth M won four times and bred six winners including Bayard whose sole win was a dead-heat in a moderate handicap. A son out of Evadne made 700 guineas (25,700) and named Evan he won three races. A daughter out of Star of the Sea made 870 guineas (32,000) and was named Starlight Bay. This is a lovely name, displays some imagination and has the virtue of not starting with bay! Star of the Sea was tried in the best company but was never even placed but produced four winners at stud. However, none were by Bayardo. Starlight Bay was unplaced from two starts but did later produce a winner by Long Set.

Bayardo was being given every chance but was not proving to be an instant success. Alfred Cox reduced his fee to 200 guineas (7,350) as a concession to the problems breeders were suffering as a result of the Great War. The fourth and fifth seasons of a stallions' career can, in any event, be particularly difficult ones. The offspring of a stallion soon go out of fashion at the yearling sales as their novelty value begins to lose its attraction. Unless a stallion has enjoyed some marked success with his first two crops then interest will quickly wane.

In 1915 a combination of the Great War and Bayardo's disappointing performance as a stallion resulted in the three yearlings offered for sale realizing much less than previously. These were one colt and two fillies and, although all three sold, none of them ever won. However, one of the fillies, Bayora, went on to produce six winners. Oh dear some of his fillies were not named with much flair either!

In 1916 eight yearlings were sold at public auction: five colts and three fillies. However, they could only muster one win between them. One colt, Wigstone, he was not the winner, sold for 510 guineas (18,750), and did stand as a stallion in Canada. It is possible that he is the only other son of Bayardo, after Bay D'Or, sold at public auction, whose buyer made a profit on him. Wigstone's dam, Blue Tit, achieved little on the racetrack but produced seven winners at stud but none by Bayardo.

The 1917 sales for Bayardo's stock were viewed in a slightly more positive manner due to Gay Crusader's exploits. In addition as a result of his recent death there would be less opportunity to buy his progeny in future. There were high hopes for his yearlings and this proved to be the case. All five of his yearlings fetched over 1000 guineas. The top price paid was 2,700 guineas (99,200) for a colt Wayardo. Substituting a W for B does makes a change of some sort! This represented a good profit for the seller as he had brought him as a foal for only 700 guineas (£24,500). Unfortunately he never won a race.

With the end of the Great War in sight and Gainsborough advertising Bayardo's stock by winning the Triple Crown, the 1918 yearling sales held up well. Four of the seven yearlings sold each fetched over 1,200 guineas (£43,200). The most expensive filly sold for 1,250 guineas (£45,000), later named Peach Blossom, she was a daughter out of Cornfield. Peach Blossom won only one race but produced four winners at stud.

The sales of 1919 saw the final crop of Bayardo's yearlings and they produced his best ever sale. Four yearlings each fetched over 1100 guineas with the top lot being a colt, later named Katerfelto, reaching 4,100 guineas (£151,000). He must have had some temperament issues as he was gelded after his only juvenile race. He never won. The second highest was a filly, later named, Despina, who realized 3,500 guineas (£128,600). She raced only at two but from six outing she could not even manage a place. However, she did produce three winners at stud. Katerfelto is the most expensive colt by Bayardo ever brought at public auction and Despina the most expensive filly.

There is no escaping the fact that the racing records of Bayardo's progeny sold at public auction were dire. Of the 35 yearlings brought just 8 managed to win a race and none managed to recover their purchase price in prize money. With the exception of Bay D'Or, who had some success as a stallion, none of his colts made much impact.

Bayardo works under Alec Taylor's watchful eye

Easing down. Now to get him back in his stable!

The stands at Sandown

Alfred Cox with Capt. Weyland and Peter Gilpin before the Sandown Foal Stakes

Bayardo easily wins the Sandown Foal Stakes

Bayardo in the unsaddling enclosure after his win

The Ascot grandstand in Bayardo's time

The Ascot paddock in Bayardo's time

Women have never been more beautifully dressed than in Edwardian times. A view of the paddock at Ascot

The Ascot Gold Cup

A pensive Danny Maher before the Ascot Gold Cup

Bayardo drops Maher before the Ascot Gold Cup

Bayardo produces an astonishing turn of foot and leads the field at Swinley Bottom

Bayardo is on the bridle as he passes the post to win the Ascot Gold Cup

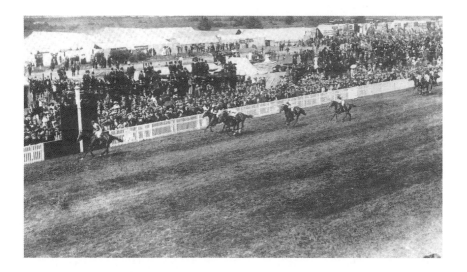

Alfred Cox leads in Bayardo after the Ascot Gold Cup

Bayardo concludes the greatest day of his life as he had begun so many;
by refusing to enter his box!

Foals by Bayardo sold at public auction

1912

Foal	Dam	Price (guineas)	Subsequent Career
Bay Marie (b f)	Queen's Marie	2,500	Failed to win

N.B. Purchased as part of the sale of the mare, who was in foal to Bayardo

1913

Foal	Dam	Price (guineas)	Subsequent Career
Bayodee (b c)	Cheshire Cat	3,100	Won 2 races worth £276

1915

Foal	Dam	Price (guineas)	Subsequent Career
Glenbay (b f)	Glamourie	410	Won 1 race worth £100
Lady Bayardo (b f)	Veldt	250	Failed to win

1916

Foal	Dam	Price (guineas)	Subsequent Career
Wayardo (b c)	Birdswing	700	Failed to win

N.B. Purchased as part of a sale of the mare

1918

Foal	Dam	Price (guineas)	Subsequent Career
Granite (b c)	Cyanin	1,600	Failed to win

Yearlings by Bayardo sold at public auction

1913 Average 1,615 guineas; Median 1,155 guineas

Yearling	Dam	Price (guineas)	Subsequent Career
Alfana (b c)	Alicia	3,700	Failed to win
Arkroyal b c)	Royal Marriage	1,500	Failed to win
Bayardino (b c)	Lady Raeburn	810	Failed to win
Broomardo (b c)	The Broom	450	Failed to win

1914 Average 1,392 guineas; Median 935 guineas

Yearling	Dam	Price (guineas)	Subsequent Career
Bay D'Or (b c)	Dame D'Or	3,000	Won 5 races worth £980. Stallion
Bayard (b c)	Elizabeth M	1,000	Won 0.5 races worth £118
Starlight Bay (b f)	Star of the Sea	870	Failed to win
Evan (b c)	Evadne	700	Won 3 races worth £647

1915 Average 340 guineas; Median 300 guineas

Yearling	Dam	Price (guineas)	Subsequent Career
Bayonne (b f)	Alicia	510	Failed to win
Bayora (b f)	Honora	300	Failed to win
Rotterdam (b c)	Chaffaway	210	Failed to win

1916 Average 472 guineas; Median 450 guineas

Yearling	Dam	Price (guineas)	Subsequent Career
Old Drury (b c)	Mistress Nell	850	Failed to win
- (b f)	Glenbloom	560	Failed to win
Wigstone (b c)	Blue Tit	510	Failed to win
Cattewater (b c)	Cattish	500	Failed to win
Glenbay (b c)	Glamourie	400	Won 1 race worth £100
- (b c)	Retort	400	Failed to win
Bayling (b f)	Startling	360	Failed to win
Guerdon (b f)	Loyal Cheer	200	Failed to win

1917 Average 1,620 guineas; Median 1,600 guineas

Yearling	Dam	Price (guineas)	Subsequent Career
Wayardo (b c)	Birdswing	2,700	Failed to win
Bradamante (b f)	Ena	1,650	Failed to win
Daybreak (b c)	Golden Dawn	1,600	Won 3 races worth £336
Tussock-Grass (b f)	Bunch Grass	1,100	Won 1 race worth £264
Elsie (b f)	Seccotine	1,050	Failed to win

1918 Average 1,406 guineas; Median 1,250 guineas

Yearling	Dam	Price (guineas)	Subsequent Career
Rinaldo (b c)	Killising	3,100	Failed to win
Bacton Lad (b c)	Cyanin	2,000	Won 1.5 races worth £226
Tantallon (b c)	Alnmouth	1,800	Failed to win. Stallion
Peach Blossom (b f)	Cornfield	1,250	Won 1 race worth £100
Bayena (b f)	Queen Helena	720	Failed to win
Inlet (b f)	Queenlet	700	Failed to win
Bayamo (b f)	Conciliation	270	Failed to win

1919 Average 2,612 guineas; Median 2,625 guineas

Yearling	Dam	Price (guineas)	Subsequent Career
Katerfelto (b c)	Lilydale	4,100	Failed to win
Despina (b f)	Hippolyte	3,500	Failed to win
Rhodope (b f)	Temple Bell	1,750	Failed to win
Philosophy (b f)	Lady Burghley	1,100	Failed to win

Two-year-olds by Bayardo purchased at public auction

1916			
2-Y-O	Dam	Price (guineas)	Subsequent Career
- (b rig)	White May	160	Failed to win

1918			
2-Y-O	Dam	Price (guineas)	Subsequent Career
Gambardia (b f)	Game Hen	500	Failed to win

Three-Year-olds by Bayardo sold at public auction

1916			
3-Y-O	Dam	Price (guineas)	Subsequent Career
Chevalier Bayard (b c)	Ormeda	85	Failed to win

1918			
2-Y-O	Dam	Price (guineas)	Subsequent Career
Royal Bay (b c)	Signorina	46	Won 1 race worth £184

When analysing the pedigrees of Bayardo's major winners one name stands out above all others, that of St. Frusquin. Bred by Leopold de Rothschild and foaled in 1893 he won eight races. At two he won a plate race, the Sandringham Gold Cup, the Chesterfield Stakes, the Middle Park Plate, (beating the Derby winner Persimmon) and the Dewhurst Plate. His only defeat came in the Imperial Produce Stakes when he finished second. At three he won the Column Produce Stakes, 2000 Guineas, the Princess of Wales's Stakes and the Eclipse. His only defeat was in the Derby (2nd by a neck to Persimmon). Sadly whilst training for the St Leger he was injured and never raced again. If he was not a great horse then he was very close. He was a great success as a stallion heading the list of sires in 1903 and 1907.

Bayardo had just ten offspring from mares carrying a strain of St Frusquin. These were Baydrop, Braishfield, Gainsborough, Gay Crusader, Good and Gay, La Tosca, Lord Basil, Manilardo, Pompadour and Rosa Bonheur. Of these six won important races. Was there an affinity? Well possibly; Bayardo was inbred 4x2 Galopin and 5x5x5 to full brothers Rataplan and Stockwell, while St Frusquin's sire St Simon was by Galopin out of a mare by King Tom, the latter a half brother to Rataplan and Stockwell.

Bayardo's inbreeding to the Derby winner, and three times leading sire Galopin, does seem to be of importance, with reinforcement of this inbreeding in the dams of his major winners. For example, Braishfield's dam was 3x3 Galopin; the dam of Gay Crusader and Manilardo had Galopin 5x3; while Rothesay Bay's third dam Ayrsmoss was 3x2 Galopin and being by a son of Hampton out of a full sister to Galliard was bred on very similar lines to Bayardo's sire Bay Ronald, who was by Hampton out of a Galliard mare. A very similar sort of pattern was present in Craven Stakes winner Sir Dighton, whose grand-dam was by Persimmon, a horse by Galopin's son St Simon out of a mare by Hampton. Other major winners possessing a strain of Galopin in their dam were Gainsborough, Good and Gay, Pompadour and Samic. The latter is especially interesting as this French-bred son of the Perth mare Philanoe won the Prix Penelope. His dam was 3x2 to Galopin's son Galliard, and his grand-dam Philae was a close relative to Bayardo's dam Galicia. Galicia was by Galopin out of a mare by Isonomy who traced back to Blink Bonny, while Philae was by a son of Galopin out of a mare by Isonomy who traced back to a mare by Blink Bonny's son Blair Athol. Furthermore Samic's maternal grand-sire Perth had a cross of Galliard and Lord Clifden, the reverse of Bayardo's sire Bay Ronald.

Sterling and his son Isonomy are other names that appear in Bayardo's better offspring. Bayardo was inbred 4x4 Sterling once via Isonomy, who was a great horse by any standards, who stood at only 15.2 hands. He was also a great sire being responsible for two Triple Crown winners in Isinglass and Common. Bayardo's son Allenby was out of a mare 3x4 Isonomy and he also features in the dams of Samic and Sir Dighton. Finally, many of the above strains were brought together in the pedigree of Bayardo's Oaks winner Bayuda. Her dam Jessica boasted a pedigree very similar to Bayardo's grand-dam Isoletta, courtesy of strains of Sterling, Muncaster and Blink Bonny's son Breadalbane.

With just two main stallion sons in Gay Crusader and Gainsborough, inbreeding to Bayardo was not a common occurrence. However, it is behind three European Classic winners in Galcador, Museum and Skoiter, as the table on the next page illustrates.

Winners of Major Races with a Duplication of Bayardo within their First Four Generations

Horse	Inbreeding	Major Races Won
Museum (1932)	3x3	1935 Irish 2000 Guineas (8f.)1935 Irish Derby (12f.)1935 Ebor Handicap (14f.)1935 Irish St Leger (14f.)
Don Pedro (1942)	3x4	1945 C B Fisher Plate (12f.)
El Hawa (1945)	3x4	1947 Rous Memorial Stakes (6f.)
Flexton (1944)	3x4	1947 Greenham Stakes (7f.)
Lake Placid (1945)	3x4	1948 King George V Handicap (12f.)1948 Great Yorkshire Handicap (14f.)1950 Manchester Cup Handicap (12f.)
Skoiter (1936)	3x4	1939 Irish St Leger (14f.)
Intermezzo II (1944)	3x4x5	1947 Austrian Derby (12f.)1947 Hungarian St Leger (14f.)
Desplante (1944)	4x3	1948 Clasico Chacabuco (15f.)
Bounteous (1958)	4x4Also 5x5 Lemberg, a half brother to Bayardo	1960 Dewhurst Stakes (7f.)1962 Grand Prix de Deauville (13.5f.)1962 Prix Kergorlay (15f.)
Damnos (1945)	4x4	1947 Prix D'Arenberg (5f.)1948 Prix de Meautry (6f.)1948 Prix du Petit Couvert (5f.)1948 Prix Quincey (8f.)
Flanc (1939)	4x4	1942 Hungarian 2000 Guineas (8f.)
Galcador (1947)	4x4	1950 Prix Daphnis (9f.)1950 Epsom Derby (12f.)
Greek Warrior (1942)	4x4	1945 Interborough Handicap (6f.)
Herbarz (1953)	4x4	1956 Nagroda Pryzchowku (11f.)
Kiyofuji (1948)	4x4	1951 Yushun Himba (12f.)1952 Kawasaki Kinen (13f.)
Nishi Tap (1945)	4x4	1950 Kyoto Kinen (Spring) (15f.)
Phoibos (1945)	4x4	1948 Linlithgow Stakes (8f.)1948 Caulfield Guineas (8f.)1948 C B Fisher Plate (12f.)
Poprad (1943)	4x4	1946 Polish St Leger (14f.)
Portobello (1936)	4x4	1938 Clearwell Stakes (5f.)1938 Windsor Castle Stakes (5f.)1939 July Cup (6f.)1939 Nunthorpe Stakes (5f.)
Rear Admiral (1945)	4x4	1948 Free Handicap (7f.)
Sierra Nevada (1952)	4x4	1955 Blue Riband Trial Stakes (8.5f.)
Hi Jinx (1955)	6x4x4	1960 Melbourne Cup (16f.)

Bayardo combined with his half-brother Lemberg in the pedigrees of

Djelfa	(Prix D'Arenberg, French 1000 Guineas),
Early School	(unbeaten in 3 starts including the Coventry Stakes),
Finis	(Yorkshire Cup and Ascot Gold Cup),
Hametus	(Imperial Stakes and Dewhurst Stakes),
Hippius	(Champion Stakes in consecutive years)
Reading II	(AJC Derby and St Leger, Victoria Derby and St Leger),
Rockefella	(successful sire), Sweet Abbess (Woodcote Stakes),
Tai Yang	(unbeaten in two starts including Jockey Club Stakes).

Also of interest was the mare Deva, who was by Bayardo's son Gainsborough out of the Lemberg mare Lake Van. On the racetrack Deva won only one race. However, when retired to the paddocks she produced four winners and her descendants included the following;

Cestra	(Lancashire Oaks)
Double Cream	(Lincoln Handicap)
French Beige	(Queen's Vase, Newmarket St Leger, Doncaster Cup Jockey Club Cup)
French Cream	(Lancashire Oaks and Irish Oaks),
Ludovich	(Group 3 Furstenburg-Rennen and Group 3 Spreti-Rennen)
Rowston	(Lingfield Derby Trial).
Manor	

Double Cream is of special interest as he had a pedigree bristling with strains of Bayardo. As well as the aforementioned Deva, he was by a son of Clarion 3x3 to Bayardo's son Gay Crusader. Gay Crusader also appeared in the pedigree of Double Cream's dam , while Double Cream's maternal grand-sire King of the Tudor was 5x5 Bayardo via his son Gainsborough and daughter Bayberry.

In summation, while it could not be claimed that Bayardo was a great sire he was certainly not a failure. He was unlucky on two important counts. The Great War began when he had been at stud for only three years and his first foals were juveniles and his early death after he had sired only seven crops. Nonetheless for siring Gainsborough alone his place in history is secure. Gainsborough, although not as good a racehorse as his sire, was a truly great sire himself and he ensured that Bayardo's line would continue strongly through his son Hyperion.

Hyperion became the most successful British-bred sire of the Twentieth Century. Although less than 15.2 hands, he was so small and weak as a yearling that there was talk of putting him down, Hyperion proved to be a great racehorse winning nine of his thirteen races including the New Stakes, Dewhurst Stakes, Derby and St Leger. Had he been properly trained he would almost certainly have won the Gold Cup as a four year old as well. Great racehorse that he was he proved to be an even greater sire. He was champion sire six times, 1940, 1941, 1942, 1945, 1946 and 1954, and second on three other occasions. His progeny came in all shapes and sizes and many bore little resemblance to their sire. However, he sired seven classic winners from his first eight crops and his offspring won eleven classics in seven years. In addition he was a great sire of sires and this has ensured that the name of Bayardo still features in the pedigrees of stallions standing in Britain today. The following nine stallions standing in 2010 all trace back to Bayardo:-

Cadeaux Genereux, Young Ern, Mind Games, Superior Premium, Tomba, Bahamian Bounty, Pastoral Pursuits, Babodana and Major Cadeaux.

```
Bayardo
  Gainsborough
    Hyperion
      Owen Tudor
        Tudor Minstrel
          Will Somers
            Balidar
              Young Generation
                CADEAUX GENEREUX
                  MAJOR CADEAUX
                  BAHAMIAN BOUNTY
                    PASTORAL PURSUITS
                    BABODANA
      Aristophanes
        Forli
          Thatch
            Thatching
              ' Puissance
                MIND GAMES
          Formidable
            Efisio
              YOUNG ERN
              TOMBA
          Forzando
            SUPERIOR PREMIUM
```

It is interesting that a sire-line that was originally the source of middle distance classic performers has evolved over time to become one of sprinter/milers. The chances of Tomba, Mind Games, Superior Premium, Young Ern or Babodana producing anything worthy of standing at stud are not very likely. Therefore the survival of Bayardo's sire line probably rests with Cadeaux Genereux, Bahamian Bounty and Pastoral Pursuits that is unless Major Cadeaux, against expectations it has to be said, produces a top performer. Fortunately Bahamian Bounty has produced plenty of good performers and Cadeaux Genereux could still produce another one so there is a strong likelihood that the line will continue for some time to come.

Gay Crusader at Stud

Gay Crusader was retired to stand at Manton House Stud in 1919 at a fee of 400 Guineas (14,700) which was to remain unchanged throughout his entire stud career. When peacetime racing was resumed Mr J B Joel offered £100,000 (£3,500,000) for him. But Alfred Cox's brother, who had inherited his interests on his death, was unwilling to sell. The very best mares were sent to Gay Crusader but it is no exaggeration to say that he was a bitter disappointment. The 14 crops he sired resulted in 310 winners of races worth £139,353 (£4,877,000) in England and Ireland, with the stamina index of his progeny being 8.33 furlongs.

Gay Crusader finished in the top twenty in the leading sire lists in 1924, 1925, 1926, 1927, 1930 and 1931 with a best place of 6th in 1926. However, considering the support he enjoyed this was well below

The best horses sired by Gay Crusader were:-
Algonguin, (St George Stakes)
Bright Knight, (Boscawen Stakes, Moulton Stakes, North Derby, Gratwicke Stakes, March Stakes, 2nd 2000 Guineas),
Caissot, (Prince of Wales's Stakes, Liverpool St Leger, Newmarket St Leger),
Cap-A-Pie, (won 14 races including the Ebor),
Criss Cross, (Waterford Stakes)
Cross Bow, (Newmarket Stakes, Newmarket St Leger, Royal Hunt Cup),
Daimyo, (Churchill Stakes, Great Yorkshire Handicap),
Fianna, (Great Surrey Foal Plate)
Gay Angela, (Buckingham Stakes)
Gay Camp, (Newmarket October Handicap)
Guiscard, (Queens's Prize Handicap)
Hot Night, (2nd in the Derby),
Hurstwood, (Newmarket Stakes, Hardwicke Stakes),
Inglesant, (Sussex Stakes),
Isfandiar, (Great Yorkshire Handicap)
Kincardine, (Column Produce stakes, St James's Palace Stakes),
Kings Oven, (won 10 races including Newbury Summer Cup),
Legatee, (Bendigo Stakes)
Medieval Knight, (Coventry Stakes, Middle Park Stakes, Lingfield Derby Trial, Jersey Stakes),
Saracen, (November Handicap)
Sir Kenneth, (Union Jack Stakes)
Taj Kasra, (Windsor Castle Stakes)
Troubadour, (Newbury Autumn Cup)
Templestowe, (Seven races value £2,945, including the Yorkshire Cup)
Wings Of Love, (Granville Stakes)

expectations and there was a feeling that his offspring lacked resolution. They gradually acquired a bad reputation amongst trainers and his popularity steadily waned and the quality of mares began to decline. He did not manage to sire a single English or Irish classic winner although he did manage seven places.

In addition to his disappointing record as a sire he was also a poor sire of sires. He had eight sons at stud in England and Ireland: Knight of the Leopard, Royal Crusader, St. George and Tournament II, Hot Night, Hurstwood, King's Oven and Legatee, however, only the latter four achieved anything of note. However, his son Gay Lothario, who won only two minor races in England, was a success in Australia, and Kincardine did well in New Zealand. Gay Crusader was also a disappointing broodmare sire, he finished in the top 20 only twice with a second place in 1940, however, it would be through his daughters that Gay Crusader would exert some influence on the breed. Loika was dam of the great Djebel, Indolence was the dam of Prince Rose who sired Prince Chevalier, Prince Bio and Princequillo and Gay Camp was the dam of El Greco. One of his daughters, Gay Bird, became the matriarch of a successful family. These included the stallion Clarion (inbred 3x3 Gay Crusader) and Intermezzo, a successful sire in Hungary.

Winners sired by Gay Crusader in Great Britain and Ireland

Year	Winners	Races Won	Value in £
1922	1 (1)	1 (1)	168 (168)
1923	9 (4)	13.5 (7.5)	6,591 (5,584)
1924 (12th)	13 (4)	22.5 (8)	10,494.50 (2,256)
1925 (8th)	19 (3)	30 (3)	16,693.50 (1,273)
1926 (6th)	18 (4)	30 (4)	20,157.50 (1,532)
1927 (9th)	14 (5)	30.5 (6.5)	16,368 (2,505)
1928	12	15	8,910
1929	9	17	5,937
1930 (18th)	18 (3)	29 (3)	9,106 (1,009)
1931 (20th)	17 (4)	22 (4.5)	9,188.25 (2,021)
1932	12 (7)	23 (9)	8,058 (3,065)
1933 (9th)	14 (6)	23.5 (11.5)	14,715 (7,729)
1934	10 (1)	17 (1)	4,894.25 (146.50)
1935	11 (2)	17.5 (1.5)	3,750.50 (245)
1936	8	10	2,972
1937	4	6.5	1,036
1938	1	2	314
Total		310 (60.5)	139,353.75 (27,533.50)

N.B. Figures in brackets refer to two-year-olds
Summary
81 colts won 247 races worth £121,967.00
42 fillies won 63 races worth £17,386.75

Sadly, Gay Crusader, who had not always been the most agreeable and tractable horse at stud, became more irascible and extremely bad-tempered as he grew older. In the end only his lad could be trusted with him. His lack of good temper was not helped by his becoming almost blind by the end and he was destroyed at Manton stud in September 1932.

Winners produced by daughters of Gay Crusader in Great Britain and Ireland

Year	Winners	Races Won	Value in £
1928	3	4	573
1929	4	6	3,280
1930	6	9	1,805
1931	3	4	575
1932	8	9	1,246
1933	14	15	3,580.50
1934	10	12	2,912
1935	14	18	4,307
1936	17	20.5	4,162.50
1937	15	22	5,944.50
1938	19	31	7,743
1939 (15th)	21	32.5	8,175
1940 (2nd)	8	10	7,026
1941	2	2	151
1942	2	6	704
1943	3	4	827
1944	2	2	281
1945	4	12	3,096
1946	4	7.5	2,685
1947	6	14	8.325
1948	5	8	2,178.25
1949	4	8	4,274.25
1950	3	4	755
1951	2	6	1,367
1952	1	3	1,211.75
1953	2	4	1,093.75
1954	1	2	787.25
Total		275.5	79,065.75

APPENDIX III

Gainsborough at Stud

Gainsborough retired to Manton House Stud in 1920 at a fee of 400 Guineas (£14,700). He soon established himself as a solid success. His second crop contained his first Classic winner Solario. He won the St Leger in 1925 and the following year he won the Coronation Cup and Ascot Gold Cup. This ensured that Gainsborough reached 4th position on the list of leading sires in 1925 and over the next decade he built up a consistent record rarely being out of the top four. He sired his second classic winner in 1930 when Singapore captured the St Leger, and in addition, he also won the Doncaster Cup the following year.

Gainsborough was not a prolific sire of two year olds winners, but in 1931 his son Orwell, racing that season unnamed as Golden Hair colt, won five major juvenile events. His successes in the Chesham Stakes, National Breeders Produce Stakes, Champagne Stakes, Middle Park Stakes and Imperial Produce Stakes, helping Gainsborough to become that years leading sire of juveniles. Also in 1931 Goyescas won the Champion Stakes and was also second in the 2000 Guineas helping Gainsborough to finish second in the list of winning sires.

Solario and Orwell have interesting similarities in their pedigrees. Solario's dam was by Sundridge out of a mare by Ayrshire, who had a cross of Hampton and Galopin. Orwell's dam was by Sundridge's son Golden Sun out of a mare bred on a Galopin/Hampton cross. Furthermore Orwell traced back in female line to the mare Queen Mary, who was also the ancestress of Gainsborough's sire Bayardo.

1932 proved to be a significant year; Orwell won the 2,000 Guineas and Gainsborough became the leading sire for the first time. It also saw the debut of Gainsborough's greatest son, a horse that would seal his reputation as a great sire, Hyperion. He won the New Stakes and Dewhurst Stakes and aged three the Chester Vase, Derby, Prince of Wales's Stakes and St Leger. His four year old career was a slight anticlimax. However his exploits at three helped secure Gainsborough his second and final sire's title. All this was but a prelude to Hyperion becoming the one of the most important stallions of the Twentieth Century. He was the son of a mare by Chaucer and once again the recurring pattern of breeding is seen for Chaucer was by Galopin's son St Simon out of a mare by Tristan, who was a great grandson of that same mare Queen Mary.

By 1938 Gainsborough was only covering a few mares, and his fee was reduced to 198 Guineas (£6,650). He remained at Lady James's Harwood Stud and after her death in 1941, at the age of eighty seven, the stud was bought by Herbert Blagrave. However, it was sold on condition that Gainsborough would remain there for the rest of his life. He died on the 5th June 1945 at the age of thirty and was buried at Harwood. His name was to live on as the name of the stud was changed to Gainsborough just prior to Sheikh Maktoum Al Maktoum's purchase of it in 1981.

In total he sired the winners of 474 races worth £340,144 (£11,560,000) with an average winning distance of 10.29 furlongs. He also sired the

---

Gainsborough's best progeny were as follows:-

Hyperion	(9 wins including Derby & St Leger)
Solario	(6 wins St Leger, Coronation Cup & Ascot Gold Cup)
Orwell	(8 wins 2000 Guineas, Middle Park Stakes, Champagne Stakes and National Breeders Produce Stakes).
Singapore	(3 wins St Leger and Doncaster Cup)
Goyescas	(8 wins Champion Stakes, Prix Edmond Blanc and Hardwicke Stakes).
Grace Dalrymple	(3 wins Dewhurst Stakes)
Pinxit	(4 wins King Edward VII Stakes).
Star of England	(One win Yorkshire Oaks)
Winterhalter	(7 wins Coronation Cup)
Gainsborough Lass	(5 wins Coronation Stakes)
Silvana	(Italian Oaks)
Tournesol	(6 wins Princess of Wales's Stakes)
JR Smith	(Hardwicke Stakes)
Gainly	(2 wins Park Hill Stakes)
Costaki Pasha	(9 wins Middle Park Stakes, Cork and Orrery and Chesham Stakes)
Emborough	(3 wins Manchester Cup and Liverpool Autumn Cup)
High Art	(Ascot Gold Vase)
La Gaiete	(Molecomb Stakes)
Mon Tresor	(Prix Daru)
Vermillion Pencil	(Chester Vase, Manchester Cup and Queen Alexandra Stakes)
Painter's Song	(5 wins Waterford Testimonial Stakes)
Raymond	(Princess of Wales's Stakes and Cambridgeshire)
Bobsleigh	(3 Wins Richmond Stakes and Newmarket Stakes)
Artist's Proof	(8 wins Rous Memorial Stakes and March Stakes Waterford Stakes)
Rothesay Bay	(4 Wins Great Yorkshire Handicap)
Moti Begum	(Ham Produce Stakes)
The Blue Boy	(Criterion Stakes)
Artist Glow	(Durban Gold Cup)
Blue Lake	(Criterion Stakes)
Rameses the Second	(3 wins Liverpool St Leger)

winners 81 National Hunt races. In addition he sired the winners of over 200 races abroad. Curiously on the racetrack Gainsborough's fillies were considerably inferior to his colts in terms of ability and colts accounted for 83% of his total earnings as a stallion. However, when retired to the paddocks as mares they were not found wanting and he became champion brood-mare sire in 1931. This was largely due to Cameronian, who was a son of Una Cameron, who won the 2000 Guineas, Derby, St James's Palace Stakes and Champion Stakes. Cameronian was bred on almost the reverse cross to Hyperion, being by Pharos, a horse bred on the reverse Cyllene/Chaucer cross to Hyperion's dam Selene. A second Derby winner followed for Gainsborough as a brood-mare sire in 1936 courtesy of Mahmoud, who was by Blenheim.

Gainsborough soon made an impact as a sire of sires. In Britain and Ireland his major stallion sons were Hyperion, Bobsleigh, Orwell, Singapore and Solario who all sired European Classic winners.

There is no doubt that Gainsborough was a great sire, even if he was eclipsed by his own son Hyperion, who was of course his greatest legacy. It is worth remembering that Hyperion's great rival for the title of the

Winners sired by Gainsborough in Great Britain and Ireland

Year	Winners	Races Won	Value in £
1923	3 (3)	5.5 (5.5)	2,491.50 (2,491.50)
1924	11 (6)	18 (9)	8,902 (4,305)
1925 (4th)	16 (4)	30 (6.5)	27,809.50 (2,208.50)
1926 (4th)	17 (2)	30 (5)	24,979.75 (859.75)
1927 (4th)	19 (2)	35 (2)	22,390 (314)
1928 (6th)	19(7)	35 (12)	22,374 (14,052)
1929 (8th)	15(4)	28 (6)	16,178 (3,281)
1930 (3rd)	28 (6)	39.5 (6.5)	37,903.75 (4,112.50)
1931 (2nd)	27 (3)	38.5 (7)	34,336 (19,410)
1932 (1st)	24(7)	33.5 (8.5)	34,759.50 (12,394)
1933 (1st)	17 (1)	32 (2)	38,138.50 (362)
1934 (3rd)	22 (4)	35.5 (4)	20,253.50 (4,383.50)
1935 (15th)	14 (1)	16 (1)	9,802.25 (186)
1936 (12th)	14 (3)	18 (5)	11,331.50 (5,268.50)
1937 (8th)	14 (2)	21 (2)	13,368 (2,510.25)
1938	12	20	5,193.50
1939	13 (2)	17.5 (2)	5,318.75 (696.75)
1940	3	6	1,340.25
1941	3	5	1,227.50
1942	3	3	478.75
1943	4 (2)	4 (2)	1,192 (549)
1944	1	3	345.50
Total		474 (86)	340,144 (77,809.25)

N.B. Figures in brackets refer to two-year-olds
Summary
110 colts won 365 races worth £282,988.75
67 fillies won 109 races worth £57,155.25

most influential sire of the Twentieth Century, Northern Dancer, was line bred 4x5 to Gainsborough.

Being the sire of Bobsleigh, Emborough, Hyperion, Singapore, Solario and Taj Ud Din, and maternal grandsire of Cameronian and Mahmoud, then inbreeding to Gainsborough was always going to be popular. There were a number of examples of really close inbreeding producing important winners as the tables below illustrate.

Major winners with a duplication of Gainsborough within their first four generations include Above Suspicion (St. James's Palace Stakes,

Winners produced by daughters of Gainsborough in Great Britain and Ireland

Year	Winners	Races Won	Value in £
1928	1	3	3,310
1929	3	6	5,267
1930	3	5	2,346
1931 (1st)	5	9	30,988
1932	8	12	3,486.50
1933	7	17	5,872
1934	11	15	3,517
1935 (6th)	14	20	17,061.25
1936 (5th)	26	41	24,732.75
1937 (12th)	24	34.5	13,899.25
1938 (17th)	29	40	10,596
1939	14	22	4,124
1940 (7th)	10	15	4,524
1941 (11th)	7	15	4,974.75
1942 (10th)	12	20	4,824.50
1943	10	11	2,175
1944 (20th)	12	13	2,953.75
1945 (16th)	20	25	6,151.50
1946 (15th)	18	31	11,334
1947 (16th)	27	36	13,970.75
1948 (3rd)	22	37.5	29,680.75
1949 (3rd)	17	28.5	34,166.25
1950	10	11.5	4,966
1951	9	15	10,298.25
1952	8	16	6,257.75
1953	11	20.5	9,065.75
1954	6	7	2,900.25
1955	2	4	1,263.50
1956	4	7	4,656.75
1957	1	1	207
1958	1	1	338
1959	1	1	392
1960	1	1	202
1961	2	3	2,186
1962	2	3	5,146
1963	1	2	6,145
Total		549.5	293,979.25

Gordon Stakes), Ballymoss (Irish Derby, English St. Leger, Coronation Cup, Eclipse Stakes, King George VI & Queen Elizabeth Stakes, Prix de L'Arc de Triomphe), Determine (Kentucky Derby), Gallant Man (Belmont Stakes), Happy Laughter (1000 Guineas, Coronation Stakes, Falmouth Stakes, Nassau Stakes), Major Portion (Middle Park Stakes, St James's Palace Stakes, Sussex Stakes, Queen Elizabeth II Stakes), Petite Etoile (1000 Guineas, Oaks, Sussex Stakes, Champion Stakes, Coronation Cup twice), Rockavon (2000 Guineas), Royal Challenger (Middle Park Stakes), Royal Highway (Irish St. Leger), Shandon Belle (Irish 1000 Guineas), Sherluck (Belmont Stakes), Talgo (Irish Derby), Tudor Melody (Chesham Stakes and important sire) and Twilight Alley (Ascot Gold Cup).

Horse	Inbreeding	Major Races Won
White Heather (1944)	2x3	1949 Queen's Prize Handicap (16f.)
Antar (1948)	3x3	1952 El Ensayo (12f.)
Filgaro (1944)	3x3	1947 Ascot Vale Stakes (6f.)
Gainsboro Girl (1950)	3x3	1954 Delaware Handicap (10f.)
Midontrial (1952)	3x3	1955 Desmond Stakes (8f.)
Moondust (1952)	3x3	1949 Craven Stakes (8f.)1949 Diomed Stakes (12f.)
Sunny Boy (1944)	3x3	1947 Prix Reiset (15f.)
Wild Child (1944)	3x3	1947 Nassau Stakes (10f.)

APPENDIX IV

Sons as Stallions

It is an inescapable fact that only a minority of stallions can be classified as really successful, and even fewer succeed as a sire of sires. With just seven crops Bayardo never really had a chance to prove himself, but apart from Gainsborough, and to a lesser extent Gay Crusader, his sons made little impact as stallions in Europe, although they had more success overseas.

ALI BEY (1913 b c Bayardo – Mowsali by Flying Fox)			
Year	Form	Winning Distances	Value in £
1915	0122112	5f, 5f, 5.5f	1818.00
1916	02211	6f, 6f	827.00

Owned and bred by the Duke of Westminster Ali Bey was inbred to Galopin as he was by Bayardo (4x2 Galopin) out of a mare by Flying Fox (3x2 Galopin). A most consistent performer, Ali Bey finished out of the first two only twice in a twelve race career. After finishing unplaced in a five furlongs maiden at Newbury on his debut, he was then long odds on, and justified this faith, by winning a plate race over five furlongs at Chester. Just two days later he returned to Chester to finish a neck second in the five furlongs Ormonde Stakes, and was later beaten by the same distance when runner-up at Newmarket over six furlongs. He returned to winning ways by scoring in a five furlongs event at Newmarket, before emulating his sire by winning the valuable five and a half furlongs Buckenham (Post Produce) Stakes. Back in action the following day he concluded his juvenile campaign with a neck second in the five furlongs Hopeful Stakes. He was allotted 8st 3lbs in the Free Handicap eleven pounds below the top weight. His rating would have been about 116.

As a three-year-old Ali Bey made his reappearance in the 2000 Guineas but finished unplaced. He returned to the same track to finish runner-up in a seven furlongs handicap carrying 7st.5lbs., and was then second again at the same venue over a mile. His three-year-old career ended on a high note with two victories in handicap company at Newmarket over six furlongs, firstly carrying 8st.3lbs. and then in a more valuable race shouldering 8st.4lbs. His rating as a three year old would have been about the same as his juvenile one of 116.

These five victories earned his owner £2,645, (£92,500) and following a brief spell racing in India, Ali Bey returned to Europe in 1919 to stand in France as a stallion. He sired the mare Source who became the fourth dam of Pikotazo and Mandilon. Winner of the Derby Mexicano, Gran Premio Nacional and Jockey Club Mexicano in his native Mexico, Pikotazo also scored in one of the most important races in the Caribbean, Puerto Rico's Clasico El Caribe, in 1980. Meanwhile, his half brother Mandilon gained victory in the Futurity Mexicano. Another descendant of Source, named Fire Alarm, won the Berkeley Handicap in America.

Winners produced by daughters of Ali Bey in Great Britain and Ireland

Year	Winners	Races Won	Value in £
1933	1	1	103.00
Total		1	103.00

ALLENBY (1917 b c Bayardo – Tagalie by Cyllene)

Year	Form	Winning Distances	Value in £
1919	31	5f	877.00
1920	210130	10f, 8f	4936.00

In 1912 Mr. Walter Raphael's home-bred filly Tagalie, a daughter of Cyllene, bought off the unusual double of 1000 Guineas and Derby and in the process had the distinction of being the only grey filly to win the Derby. When retired to the paddocks one of her four winners was Bayardo's son Allenby, who also raced in Mr. Raphael's colours of dark blue, scarlet hooped sleeves and cap. Allenby's half brother Tag Rag proved to be a good sprinter and sired an even better one in Tagend who won the King's Stand Stakes, three renewals of the Nunthorpe Stakes and back-to-back runnings of the Portland Handicap. On the racetrack Allenby won 3 races worth £5,813 (£203,500), making his debut as a juvenile in April at the Newmarket Craven meeting when he finished third. Made joint favourite for a stakes race on the same course at the Second Spring meeting he recorded his first success, scoring by four lengths, but that was the last to be seen of him for the year. He got cast in his box and damaged a hock so badly that he was unfit until the autumn. Even then he was kept to light work at Newmarket to give him every chance of a full recovery. Allenby was allotted 7st 12 lbs in the Free Handicap twenty three pounds below the top-rated horse the outstanding Tetratema. His rating as a juvenile would be 110.

At three he began with a half a length second to Tetratema in the 2000 Guineas. This represented a tremendous improvement on his juvenile form. Allenby went down bravely by half a length after a spirited duel and at one point he seemed to be getting the better of the exchanges. Allenby then lined-up for the important Newmarket Stakes the best trial for the Derby after the 2000 Guineas. He started joint-favourite and won comfortably in a fast time. The day was marred for Mr. Raphael by the death of Tagalie during the morning foaling to Tracery. Victory in the ten furlongs Newmarket Stakes resulted in Allenby becoming second favourite at 9-2 for the Derby behind Tetratema. However, at Epsom he broke a blood vessel and was pulled up having not taken the eye in the paddock prior to the race. He recovered in time to appear at Ascot where he won the St James's Palace Stakes by three lengths, but may have been lucky as the favourite Sarchedon whipped round at the start and was left. However, it created a good enough impression for him to start co-favourite for the Eclipse Stakes with Tetratema and the previous year's winner Buchan. Allenby put up a sound effort to finish third to Buchan. He was then rested and prepared for the St Leger where he concluded his career by finishing unplaced. His rating as a three year old was about 128.

Allenby was retired to Heath Lodge in Newmarket, where an advertisement stated that he would cover ten mares at 98 sovereigns (£3,400) each with the condition that he would not cover any maiden mares. Physically he was a good-topped colt with muscular quarters. Unfortunately he was also described as having straight forelegs something he inherited from his dam. He was not a conspicuous success and by 1925 he was standing at Loughbrown Stud at The Curragh in Ireland at a fee of 48 sovereigns (£1,700). In total he sired the winners of 91 races worth £14,116.50 (£494,000) in Great Britain and Ireland with an average winning distance of 9.43 furlongs, before his death in 1934. He also sired the winners of 11 hurdle races and 3 steeplechases worth £1,214 (£42,500).

Allenby best offspring was the 1930 Irish 1000 Guineas winner and Irish Oaks fourth Star of Egypt. He also sired Tel-Asur, placed third in the Lincoln Handicap and fourth in the Victoria Cup, before being exported to India, where he won the King Emperor's Cup. Another son of Allenby named Irish Lancer sired the New Zealand Cup winner Royal Lancer, and furthered his influence in the antipodes at stud for his daughters' descendants included Eiffel Tower (Wellington Cup), Epigram (G3 Launceston Cup), Fair Chance (Easter Handicap, Wellington Cup), Great Sensation (Wellington Cup), Kaidahom (G3 N E Manion Cup), Lady Dahar (G3 New Zealand St. Leger), Piping Lane (Melbourne Cup), Simple As That (G3 Victoria Handicap), Summer Haze (G1 Manawatu Sires Produce Stakes) and Tawbeau (G2 Hawkes Bay Cup).

In his role as a broodmare sire Allenby produced the dam of Lafcadio, winner of both Grand Premio del Jockey Club and St Leger Italiano in 1939.

The winner of 4 races the Allenby mare Telegraphic Address founded a successful family that included Brief Star (Ayr Gold Cup) and the latter's daughter Asterina (G3 Seaton Delaval Stakes), Corral's Bond (Dutch Derby), First View (National Produce Stakes, Anglesey Stakes), Mystic Chantry (G2 Western Australian Oaks) and Stella Grande (G2 Tulloch Stakes). Brief Star had a pedigree packed with Bayardo, for her sire Sammy Davis was inbred 6x6x6 to him, and her dam Solar Telegram had him 5x5x5.

Another Allenby mare worthy of mention is Eastern Light. Her granddaughter Maria Zell, by Beresford and thus 3x3 Bayardo, became the ancestress of Legal Eagle (G2 Richmond Stakes) and Ryu Forel (Kobe Shimbun Hai, Tenno Sho Autumn, Takarazuka Kinen, Naruo Kinen, Arima Kinen, Kyoto Kinen Spring).

Legal Eagle and Ryu Forel became the maternal grandsires of Zucchero (Lincoln Handicap) and Raiba Foot (Keio Hai Autumn Handicap) respectively, while another grandson of Maria Zell named Hard Win sired the dam of Jet Berge (Keisei Hai Sansai Stakes). Finally, Allenby's daughter Mother's Chicken became the fifth dam of G3 Elwick Stakes winner How's Moon Ray, whose third dam Devon River was 4x4 Bayardo.

Winners sired by Allenby in Great Britain and Ireland

Year	Winners	Races Won	Value in £
1926	1 (1)	2 (2)	990.00 (990.00)
1927-1928	0	0	0
1929	3 (3)	5 (5)	829.25 (829.25)
1930	11 (7)	22 (9)	3,453.50 (1,377.50)
1931	11 (3)	14 (5)	2,032.00 (1,028.50)
1932	12 (1)	16 (2)	2,544.00 (293.00)
1933	5 (1)	7 (1)	852.00 (44.00)
1934	2	7	1,452.00
1935	4 (2)	7 (5)	437.00 (251.00)
1936	4	7	928.75
1937	2	3	432.00
1938	1	1	166.00
Total		91 (29)	14,116.50 (4,813.25)

N.B. Figures in brackets refer to two-year-olds

Winners produced by daughters of Allenby in Great Britain and Ireland

Year	Winners	Races Won	Value in £
1932	1	1	775.00
1933	1	1	146.50
1934	1	2	166.00
1935	3	3	749.25
1936	5	4.5	407.25
1937	6	11	1,617.00
1938	4	8	1,142.00
1939	4	5	701.00
1940	2	2	85.00
1941	1	2	164.00
1942	1	1	83.00
1943	2	5	910.50
1944	0	0	0
1945	1	1	74.00
1946	1	3	705.50
Total		49.5	7,726.00

BAAL-GAD (1916 b c Bayardo – Jubilee by Diamond Jubilee)

Year	Form	Winning Distances	Value in £
1918	300		
1919	0232010200	8f	175.00
1920	032300300		
1921	031100	17f, 17f	756.00
1922	0000000		

He may not have been Bayardo's best offspring, but there were not many tougher than Baal-Gad, a son of the good racemare Jubilee, whose victories included the Park Hill Stakes. Jubilee's sire Diamond Jubilee and maternal grandsire Isinglass were both Triple Crown winners, and Baal-Gad possessed a tight-knit pedigree for Jubilee was bred on very similar lines to Bayardo himself, both having that same cross of Galopin, Hampton and Isonomy.

Baal-Gad raced over five seasons winning three of his thirty-five starts for total prize money of £931 (£32,600) in the process. He was a consistent sort and rarely received much mercy from the handicapper. His first win came on his ninth start when, starting an odds on favourite, he scored in a Kempton Park maiden over mile. At four he was placed in good handicaps at Chester (twelve furlongs carrying 8st.9lb.), Hurst Park (thirteen furlongs carrying 7st.8lb.), Gatwick (twelve furlongs carrying 9st.) and Hurst Park (two miles carrying 7st.5lb.). Then sold by Alfred Cox's brother, who had taken over his racing interests following his brothers death, to Joseph Watson, Baal-Gad began 1921 with an unplaced effort in a twelve furlongs handicap at Epsom carrying 8st.13lb, before a third at Ascot in a handicap over the same distance shouldering 7st.12lb.

It appeared he was still in the grip of the handicapper, but stepped up to two miles one furlong he then reeled off successive victories in handicaps at Sandown, in the first scoring by five lengths under second top weight of 8st.1lb., and then under top weight of 8st.9lb. They were to be his last victories, and once again in the grip of an unsympathetic handicapper finished unplaced in all his remaining races. Sold to Mr.W.Swire before the start of the 1922 season, he was retired sound at the end of that year, and stood as a stallion in England, but had little chance to prove himself before being exported to Brazil in 1924. Rating him is not easy as a juvenile he would have earned a figure of about 105 but nothing he achieved after that would have justified anything much higher.

Winners sired by Baal-Gad in Great Britain and Ireland			
Year	Winners	Races Won	Value in £
1928	1	2	304.00
1929	0	0	0
1930	1	3	420.00
1931	1	2	244.00
1932	1	1	117.00
Total		8	1,085.00

BAY D'OR (1913 b c Bayardo - Dame D'Or by Bend Or)			
Year	Form	Winning Distances	Value in £
1915	210	5f	186.00
1916	0010	6f	100.00
1917	31110	10f, 10f, 8f	694.00
1918	32		0.00

A 3,000 guineas (£105,000) purchase as a yearling, Bay D'Or raced for 4 seasons winning 5 minor races worth £980 (£32,000). He raced un-named as a juvenile and was beaten by a short head on his juvenile debut at Newmarket over five furlongs, he was an odds-on favourite to lose his maiden tag at Windsor over the same distance next time out, and duly obliged. His juvenile season concluded with him finishing unplaced over six furlongs at Newmarket. He did not earn a figure in the Free Handicap and his rating would have been about 95.

Bay D'Or was evidently not considered classic material and all his four races at aged three were in handicaps. He was unplaced in valuable handicaps at Lingfield and Windsor over seven and eight furlongs respectively with burdens of 8st.0lbs. and 8st.11lbs. Bay D'Or then justified favouritism to land a modest six furlongs handicap at Lingfield carrying 8st.1lb., before finishing the season unplaced in the valuable one mile Gatwick Cup under 8st.0lbs. His rating would have been a little higher than his juvenile one possibly about 110.

Bay D'Or again raced only in handicaps as a four-year-old. Beginning by finishing third in the six furlongs Bretby Handicap at Newmarket carrying just 7st.3lbs, this proved to be the prelude to a hat trick of wins at the same course; a moderate handicap over ten furlongs as favourite carrying 8st.3lbs., a similar event over ten furlongs shouldering 8st.8lbs., and a mile event of similar value with a burden of 8st.3lbs. These victories earned him a place in the Cambridgeshire Handicap for which he was allocated second top weight of 8st.3lbs. behind Phalaris. However, this was to prove too much and he finished unplaced behind the lightly weighted three-year-old Brown Prince. Nonetheless he had improved and could now be rated about 120.

Possibly due to his high rating as a five-year-old Bay D'Or was switched to stakes races. Although he raced only twice, both at Newmarket, he finished placed both times, firstly third in the ten furlongs March Stakes, and then second in the Burwell Plate over twelve furlongs. On the evidence of these two races his rating would have stayed at 120.

Retired at the end of 1918 he took up stud duties as a stallion at Wyld Court Stud, Newbury. From 1919 when his fee was £48 (£1,700) it dropped £23, (£800) before moving to Ballinahown Stud, County Cork, Ireland. Bay D'Or died in 1938 and sired the winners of 96.5 races worth £15,888.75 (£560,000) in Great Britain and Ireland with an average winning distance of 7.07 furlongs, in addition to the winners of 6 hurdle races and 11.5 steeplechases worth £1,945.50 (£68,000).

Bay D'Or's daughter Golden Lullaby became the dam of Control (by Embargo) a horse best known as the sire of National Hunt performers including Aintree Grand National runner-up Carrickbeg. Control also sired the mare Red Tape, granddam of St. Leger third and Ormonde Stakes winner David Jack, another horse who did well as a National Hunt sire, his offspring including Davy Lad (Cheltenham Gold Cup Chase), Dramatist (Cathcart Chase at Cheltenham Festival) and Salkeld (Scottish Grand National Chase), as well as the granddam of Denman (Cheltenham Gold Cup Steeplechase). Control's half sister Berceuse (by The Panther) made a name for herself as the granddam of South African Oaks heroine Westerford.

Another top steeplechaser with Bay D'Or in his pedigree was Gay Spartan (Sun Alliance Novice Chase and King George VI Chase); his third dam Lady Rushmount being by Bay D'Or, and his dam Copper Lace 4x4 Bayardo. We have already seen the affinity between Bayardo and his sire Bay Ronald with the mare Popinjay. Here we find another example of this affinity, as Gay Spartan's maternal grandsire Copernicus was by Bayardo's grandson Solario, with his granddam Popingaol being by Bay Ronald out of the aforementioned Popinjay.

Returning to the flat, two daughters of Bay D'Or's of interest are Bar One, who became the fourth dam of Honinha (G2 Premio Outono – Brazilian 2000 Guineas) and Red Dame, the third dam of Yokozuna (Kyoto Kinen Spring).

Winners sired by Bay D'Or in Great Britain and Ireland

Year	Winners	Races Won	Value in £
1922	3 (3)	5 (5)	953.00 (953.00)
1923	6 (2)	9 (4)	1,961.00 (729.00)
1924	4 (4)	7 (7)	1,925.00 (1,925.00)
1925	4 (1)	6 (1)	1,561.00 (194.00)
1926	3 (1)	5 (1)	1,061.00 (192.00)
1927	2	3	744.00
1928	5 (2)	11 (6)	1,552.50 (625.50)
1929	2	4.5	454.50
1930	4 (1)	11 (1)	1,724.00 (171.00)
1931	4	5	853.00
1932	0	0	0
1933	1 (1)	2 (2)	294.50 (294.50)
1934	1	2	166.00
1935	3 (2)	4 (3)	508.50 (312.50)
1936	2	3	305.25
1937	2	2	88.00
1938	2	6	593.00
1939	3	4	406.50
1940	2	3	411.00
1941	1	1	168.00
1942	1	2	85.00
1943	1	1	74.00
Total		96.5 (30)	15,888.75 (5,396.50)

N.B. Figures in brackets refer to two-year-olds

Winners produced by daughters of Bay D'Or in Great Britain and Ireland

Year	Winners	Races Won	Value in £
1927	1	2	370.00
1928-1930	0	0	0
1931	1	2	281.00
1932	0	0	0
1933	1	1	182.00
1934	1	2	255.00
1935	3	6	684.00
1936	2	4	630.00
1937	1	2	367.00
1938	1	3	667.00
1939	3	3	338.00
1940	2	4	591.00
1941	1	1	83.00
1942	1	1	369.00
1943	0	0	0
1944	1	1	74.00
1945-1954	0	0	0
1955	1	1	296.00
Total		33	5,187.00

BAYDROP (1918 b c Bayardo – Rosedrop by St. Frusquin)

Year	Form	Winning Distances	Value in £
1921	0		

The differences that can occur between full brothers in the genetic game of chance are perhaps never better illustrated than by Baydrop. A full brother to Gainsborough, he raced just once, starting at an unfancied 10-1 shot and finishing unplaced in the valuable North Derby at Newcastle over twelve furlongs as a three year old. Baydrop's illustrious pedigree earned him a place as a stallion at Stanton Stud, Shifnal, England in 1922, where he stood for just 19 guineas (£670). In a long career before his death in 1941 he sired the winners of 35.5 races worth £4,718.50 (£165,000) in Great Britain and Ireland with an average winning distance of 9.73 furlongs, as well as the winners of 11 hurdle races and 10 steeplechases worth £1,933 (£67,700).

Purchased as a two-year-old for just 70 guineas (£2,700) at the 1927 Newmarket December Sales the Baydrop filly Nirvana was exported to Argentine, where she became the granddam of Gualicho. He proved to be a very useful performer in Brazil by winning back-to-back runnings of the Grande Premio Brasil, Gran Premio Sao Paulo and Grand Premio Derby Sul Americano in 1952 and 1953.

Nirvana was also the ancestress of Loretta, winner of the 1949 Gran Premio Marciano de Aguiar Moreira, and the latter's son Lohengrin brought more prestige to the family by winning the Gran Premio Salgado Filho in 1959 and 1961.

A particularly interesting racehorse with Baydrop in his pedigree was Kiyofuji, winner of the Yushun Himba and Kawasaki Kinen in Japan. Not only was he a grandson of the Baydrop mare Golden Dart, but also his sire Kumohata was by Gainsborough's son Tournesol, making Kiyofuji 3x3 to the full brothers Gainsborough and Baydrop. Kiyofuji's half brother Tosa Homare (by Tsukitomo) was also a useful performer in Japan, taking the Nakayama Kinen Spring.

Baydrop also proved influential in the National Hunt sphere, via his daughters Ash Drop, Bayfly and Fenora, especially at the Cheltenham National Hunt Festival. Solfen (dam Fenora) and Young Ash Leaf (granddam Ash Drop) both won the Stayers Hurdle, while Snow Drop (fourth dam Fenora) took the Triumph Hurdle and Mr Midland (granddam Bayfly) scored in the National Hunt Chase. Solfen became one of the few horses to win twice at the same Cheltenham Festival when adding the Sun Alliance Chase. Finally Young Ash Leaf, who incidentally was 5x3 Gainsborough/Baydrop, proved a good chaser too, winning the 1971 Scottish Grand National.

Winners sired by Bay Drop in Great Britain and Ireland

Year	Winners	Races Won	Value in £
1925	1 (1)	1 (1)	177.50 (177.50)
1926	0	0	0
1927	2	2.5	607.00
1928	2 (2)	3 (3)	482.00 (482.00)
1929	2 (1)	3 (1)	872.00 (196.00)
1930	4 (1)	5 (1)	758.50 (284.00)
1931	1 (1)	4 (4)	772.00 (772.00)
1932-1935	0	0	0
1936	1	1	44.00
1937	3 (1)	4 (2)	381.00 (290.00)
1938	3	7	320.50
1939	2	3	132.00
1940	1	1	83.00
1941-44	0	0	0
1945	1	1	89.00
Total		35.5 (12)	4,718.50 (2,201.50)

N.B. Figures in brackets refer to two-year-olds

Winners produced by daughters of Bay Drop in Great Britain and Ireland			
Year	Winners	Races Won	Value in £
1933	1	1	191.00
1934	2	2	208.50
1935	1	1	117.00
1936	1	1	100.00
1937	1	1	166.00
1938-1949	0	0	0
1950	2	2	288.00
1951	1	1	287.00
1952	0	0	0
1953	1	1	100.00
1954	0	0	0
1955	1	1	100.00
Total		11	1,557.50

BRAISHFIELD (1917 b c Bayardo – Beaune by St. Frusquin)			
Year	Form	Winning Distances	Value in £
1919	23		
1920	020001143	8f, 12f	1635.00
1921	00123	16f	1100.00

Bred by Lady James Douglas, the owner-breeder of Gainsborough, it is perhaps no surprise to see that Braishfield was bred on very similar lines to her Triple Crown hero, and not solely because both were by Bayardo out of mares by St. Frusquin. In addition Braishfield's granddam Burgonet was by Morion with a granddam by Musket, this being the reverse pattern to that found in Gainsborough's granddam Rosaline who was by Musket's son Trenton with a granddam by Rosicrucian, the latter a full brother to none other than Morion's dam Chaplet. Originally named 8th Division and racing under that name as a juvenile, Braishfield proved to be a late developer on the racetrack, racing just twice as a juvenile. After a second in the Clearwell Stakes over five and a half furlongs at Newmarket, he followed up with a third in the equally valuable Moulton Stakes over five furlongs. These performances would entitle him to a rating of about 100.

As a three-year-old and still racing under the name of 8th Division he was unplaced in Newbury's one mile Greenham Stakes on his seasonal debut before filling the runner-up spot in the ten furlongs Prince of Wales' Stakes at Kempton, although he was beaten 20 lengths by Torelore. He was then unplaced in the one mile Royal Standard Stakes at Manchester, and fared no better when again unplaced in Ascot's Prince of Wales' Stakes over thirteen furlongs. He was then sold by Lady James to Mr. G. H. Deane and his name changed from 8th Division to the much more suitable Braishfield. He was bought to make the pace for Buchan in the Eclipse Stakes and, not surprisingly, after setting a brisk pace he finished unplaced. However he broke his maiden next time, taking the one mile Sussex Stakes at Goodwood, after which a half share was bought by Mr. E. S. Tattersall, and carrying his colours he followed up by winning the twelve furlongs Great Yorkshire Stakes at York. His season concluded with two placed efforts at the St. Leger meeting, first finishing fourth in the St.Leger itself, and then third in the Doncaster Cup over two miles two furlongs. His rating would have been about 120.

He returned to the track at four with unplaced efforts in the valuable twelve furlongs Manchester Cup, where he carried 7st.10lb., and equally valuable Newbury Summer Cup Handicap over twelve furlongs with a burden of 8st.1lb. Royal Ascot's Churchill Stakes over two miles was the scene of his next race and final victory, and he followed this up by a five lengths second to Craig An Eran in the Eclipse Stakes, with a daughter of Bayardo named Pompadour back in third. Braishfield showed his versatility by stepping back up in distance in his final start, when as favourite he finished third in the Goodwood Cup over two miles five furlongs. His considerably improved form would entitle him to a rating of 122. He retired at the end of the season and was sold at the Doncaster sales for 520 guineas (£14,500).

Retired to stud at Wisdom Stud, Wetherby, England in 1922 at just 18 guineas (£630), his fee did increase to 48 sovereigns (£1,700) in 1928 and 1929 following some early juvenile winners, but then returned to its former level. In all he sired the winners of 27.5 races worth £4,614.75 (£162,000) in Great Britain and Ireland, while one hurdle race and 7 steeplechases were also won by his offspring. Given that Braishfield was a late developer himself, it is odd to note that 13 of his 14 individual winners won races as two-year-olds, and if fact only three of his individual winners scored at age three or more.

Braishfield's owes his existence in current pedigrees to his daughter Curlecue via her granddaughter Dorrie Wyn, whose sire Emborough was by Gainsborough, thus ensuring Dorrie Wyn was 3x4 Bayardo. Dorrie Wyn's descendants included the full brothers by Scenic named Count Scenario (G3 Grafton Cup) and Dashing Scene (G3 Kingston Town Stakes) plus Bynsaab and her daughter Surfside Lady, who both won the Western Australia Champion Fillies Stakes.

Another descendant of Dorrie Wyn who really brought this family to the fore in recent years was Cap D'Antibes, a good sprinter/miler in Australia, where she won the G1 Flight Stakes, Newmarket Handicap, Invitation Stakes and Lightning Stakes. It is interesting to note the build-up of Bayardo in her pedigree for she was by Better Boy (4x4 Gay Crusader/Gainsborough) out of the mare Tereus (5x5x5 Gainsborough plus Braishfield). Cap D'Antibes spent some of her stud career in America where her foals included a daughter of Nureyev named Breath Taking, who racing in France won the G3 Prix Eclipse and G3 Prix de Meautry. Breath Taking's foals included two Group race winners, namely Borodislew (G3 Prix de la Porte Maillot, G2 Chula Vista Handicap, G2 Hawthorne Handicap) and Breath Of Love (G3 Premio Chiusura). Borodislew further enhanced the family fortunes when she retired to the paddocks, for her sons Canadian Frontier and Seeking Slew won the G3 Bold Ruler Handicap and G3 Kent Breeders Cup Handicap respectively.

Winners sired by Braishfield in Great Britain and Ireland

Year	Winners	Races Won	Value in £
1926	2 (2)	3 (3)	924.00 (924.00)
1927	4 (4)	6 (6)	1,621.00 (1,621.00)
1928	4 (3)	4.5 (3.5)	939.50 (547.50)
1929	3 (2)	3 (2.5)	490.50 (392.50)
1930	1 (1)	1 (1)	103.00 (103.00)
1931	1 (1)	1 (1)	146.00 (146.00)
1932-1935	0	0	0
1936	1	2	86.00
1937	1	3	119.75
1938	1	2	95.00
1939	1	2	90.00
Total		27.5 (17)	4,614.75 (3,734.00)

N.B. Figures in brackets refer to two-year-olds

Winners produced by daughters of Braishfield in Great Britain and Ireland

Year	Winners	Races Won	Value in £
1932	1	1	292.00
1933	1	1	166.00
1934	4	5.5	831.00
1935	7	12.5	2,183.00
1936	2	2	239.00
1937	1	1	192.00
1938	1	1	292.00
1939-1944	0	0	0
1945	1	1	181.00
1946	1	3	582.50
1947	1	1	138.00
Total		29	5,096.50

GLENDOE (1917 b c Bayardo - Maid Of The Mist by Cyllene)

Year	Form	Winning Distances	Value in £
1919	0		
1920	00		

Glendoe was a son of Maid of the Mist, herself a daughter of the wonderful filly Sceptre, who won four of the five English Classics. Glendoe finished unplaced in Newmarket's Chesterfield Stakes over five furlongs on his sole juvenile outing. At three he fared no better being unplaced in both a valuable stakes race at Manchester over a mile, and then the Liverpool St Leger over twelve furlongs. Glendoe certainly did not live up to his heritage for his siblings included two English Classic winners in Craig An Eran, winner of the 2000 Guineas, Eclipse and St James's Palace Stakes, and Sunny Jane who took the Oaks at Epsom, while another half sister named Hamoaze produced the top-class colts Buchan, Saltash and St. Germans.

Presumably this earned him a place at stud as a stallion, but he did little in the role siring the winners of 4 races worth just £674 (£24,000) in Great Britain and Ireland, together with the winners of 5 hurdle races worth £320 (£11,200).

Winners sired by Glendoe in Great Britain and Ireland

Year	Winners	Races Won	Value in £
1925	1 (1)	1 (1)	144.00 (144.00)
1926	0	0	0
1927	2 (1)	2 (1)	294.00 (194.00)
1928	0	0	0
1929	1	1	236.00
Total		4 (2)	674.00 (338.00)

LORD BASIL (1916 br c Bayardo – Popinjay by St. Frusquin)

Year	Form	Winning Distances	Value in £
1918	14	5.5f	550.00
1919	03		

Lord Basil was another example of Bayardo being crossed with Lord Astor's Popinjay family, being a full brother to Good and Gay and Pompadour. Things looked promising for him when we won the Buckenham (Post Produce) Stakes at Newmarket over five and a half furlongs at Newmarket on his debut, and followed this up with a fourth to Stefan The Great in the Middle Park Stakes over six furlongs. Despite this effort Lord Basil was omitted from the Free Handicap, possibly by mistake, for which he would probably have been allocated about 8 st. He can be rated 112 on these two efforts.

The following season he was fifth in the 2000 Guineas, before finishing third in the Newmarket Stakes at odds of 4-11. This was disappointing as he had "won" a trial at Manton just before the 2000 Guineas beating Manilardo and Buchan, the latter going on to finish runner-up in the classic. Lord Basil had been 5-1 for the Derby before the Newmarket Stakes but his attitude before the race had not impressed: swishing his tail and looking uninterested. He was withdrawn from the Derby the day before the race and a few weeks later sold for export to Argentina. There would seem to be little doubt that his temperament was the deciding factor in his sale. His performances in these two races would give him a rating of 112, the same as his two-year-old figure.

Notwithstanding this he was reasonably successfully as a stallion in Argentina, siring Zarpazo II, winner of the 1926 Clasico Chacabuco, 1927 Gran Premio Miguel A Martinez de Hoz and 1927 Gran Premio Jose Pedro Ramirez. His highest placing was a 10th in the list of Argentine winning sires in 1928.

Lord Basil was also the maternal grandsire of Black Arrow (Gran Premio Montevideo, Gran Premio Polla de Potrancas, Gran Premio Selleccion), Desplante (Clasico Chacabuco) and Don Bingo (Suburban Handicap). Desplante was by Hyperion's son Selim Hassan, and thus inbred 4x3 Bayardo. Don Bingo was to become the horse that ensured Lord Basil's place in modern pedigrees for he sired the mare Ablamucha who became the granddam of Nodouble, winner of 13 of his 42 starts including the Arkansas Derby, Hawthorne Gold Cup – twice, Santa Anita Handicap, Californian Stakes, Brooklyn Handicap and Metropolitan Handicap. Retired to stand as a stallion at Three Chimneys Farm, Kentucky, Nodouble sired numerous winners and was the Champion Sire in America in 1981. Nodouble traced back in direct male line to Gainsborough, so was in fact 6x6 Bayardo.

Perhaps the daughter of Lord Basil that was responsible for the most prolific family was Magia, via her daughter, the aforementioned Black Arrow. This family included Barons Pit (G3 Norfolk Stakes, G2 Diadem Stakes), Bedouine (Gran Premio Eliseo Ramirez), Bienandante (G2 Gran Premio Ciudad La Plata, G3 Clasico Benito Lynch), Blackie (Gran Premio Seleccion, Gran Premio Polla de Potrancas, Gran Premio de Honor), Black Out (Gran Premio Polla de Potrillos, Clasico Miguel Cane), Bordonero (G3 Clasico Velocidad, G3 Clasico Santiago Lawrie, G3 Clasico Gay Hermit), Ground Control (Acorn Stakes), Prendase (Clasico Simon Bolivar), Senegal (Clasico Simon Bolivar – twice), Straight Ahead (Gran Derby Columbiano), Tello (Gran Premio Jockey Club) and Trail City (G2 Arlington Classic). Of the above Black Out proved to be a reasonably successful sire in South America, finishing 9th on the leading Argentine sires list in 1951 and 1955, in the process siring the Gran Premio Polla de Potrancas heroine Chapineta, and the dam of Peruvian Derby winner Tabasco.

Another successful stallion to trace his ancestry to a Lord Basil mare was Gran Premio Jockey Club winner Guatan, his granddam being the Lord Basil mare Partida Falsa. Guatan gained a top 10 place in the

Argentine Sire lists four times between 1953 and 1960, including a third place in 1957, as well as finishing runner-up on the broodmare sire list in 1976 and 1977. Indeed, Guatan and Black Out were to form a fruitful partnership for mares bred on this cross became either the dam or granddam of Kalcura (G3 Clasico Omega, G3 Clasico Mexico), Kascura (G1 Gran Premio Jorge de Atucha, G2 Clasico Carlos Casares, G3 Clasico Omega, G3 Clasico Eudoro J Balsa), Manzanera (G1 Gran Premio Polla de Potrancas, G3 Clasico Omega, G3 Clasico Eudoro J Balsa), Melodien (G1 Gran Premio Jorge de Atucha), Mia (G1 Gran Premio Seleccion, G1 Gran Premio Polla de Potrancas), Nebraska (G2 Clasico Ocurrencia), Serxens (G1 Gran Premio Nacional) and Wings Of Jove (G1 Matron Stakes, G2 Astaria Stakes).

Finally, a pair of daughters of Lord Basil to merit attention were Caperucita Roja, whose grandson Copete captured the Gran Premio Raul Y Raul E Chevalier; and Legendaria, the third dam of Gran Premio Ignacio E Ignacio F Correas winner Rama Caida.

MANILARDO (1916 b c Bayardo – Gay Laura by Beppo)			
Year	Form	Winning Distances	Value in £
1918	3		
1919	112	8f, 12f	577.00
1920	21012	12f, 12f	2720.00
1921	00000		

A full brother to Gay Crusader, bred and originally owned by Alfred Cox who thought so highly of Manilardo as a yearling that he was convinced he would turn out to be the best son of Bayardo. He raced only once at age two finishing third over five and a half furlongs in the Boscawen Stakes at Newmarket in October behind a decent sort in Polygnotus. This performance would be worth a rating of about 109.

At three, in 1919, the first season after the Great War ended, Manilardo raced only three times winning twice. After winning the Wood Ditton Stakes, in good style by four lengths on his three-year-old debut, his owner Alfred Cox died, and consequently all his engagements were cancelled. This was unfortunate as he had run well in a trial at Manton finishing second but in front of Buchan who went on to finish second in the 2000 Guineas. Manilardo's ownership passed to Cox's brother and he was off the track until the last day of October when he won a modest plate. The year was completed by being easily beaten in a match for a plate in the final meeting at Manchester. He is hard to rate on these performances and it is probably safe to give him a figure of 116.

At four he was able to realise his talent to the full. He began with a second place in the Jubilee Handicap at Kempton, carrying 8st.3lb., the race was run in heavy going after a very wet and miserable day. This was a prelude to victory in the Coronation Cup at Epsom. In the former race he was beaten by Tangiers to whom he was conceding eight pounds. However, in the Coronation Cup Manilardo was the even money favourite as he was now receiving ten pounds which represented a turn-round at the weights of eighteen pounds. He would have been odds-on but for the very firm ground which many assumed would not suit Manilardo. He won in a time which equalled the course record set by Spion Kop the previous day. Interestingly the Great Jubilee Handicap was worth £2,500 (£62,000) to the winner and the Coronation Cup £1,890 (£47,250). After disappointing as favourite for Newmarket's Princess of Wales Stakes he took the Dullingham Plate at the same venue. He finished the year with a fine second under joint top weight of 9st. in the Ebor Handicap at York, where he was beaten only three-quarters of a length conceding the winner Iron Hand 30 pounds. Manilardo beat into third place the previous years St Leger winner Keysoe conceding her four pounds. This year marked the peak of Manilardo's career and he can be rated 130. In addition he was described as now filled out physically and showing a good outline whereas previously he had not presented an attractive appearance.

As a five year old he failed to win in five races, unable to obtain a place in the Jubilee Handicap (8st.12lb.), the Coronation Cup, the Royal Hunt Cup (9st.1lb.), a valuable twelve furlongs handicap at Newmarket, in which he carried 9st.10lb., and finally the Cambridgeshire. In the latter he shouldered third top weight of 8st.7lb. He was clearly not as good as the previous year, and could not be rated more than 120. Good horse that Manilardo his overall form suggested that he just below the top level. In total he notched up 4 wins worth £3,297 (£115,400).

He was retired to Hamilton Stud, Newmarket at a fee of £24 (£840) in 1922, standing alongside Bayardo's half brothers Lemberg and Kwang-Su. He had little chance to prove himself, being found dead in his box in August 1927, but still sired the winners of 23 races worth £5,062 (£177,000) in Great Britain and Ireland with an average winning distance of 8.06 furlongs, together with the winners of 2 hurdle races and 5 steeplechases worth £806 (£28,200).

Bayardo with Danny Maher up and Alec Taylor

Gay Crusader

Gainsborough

Bayardo – probably taken at Manton Stud

The ill-fated Picaroon

Bayardo at stud

Bayardo

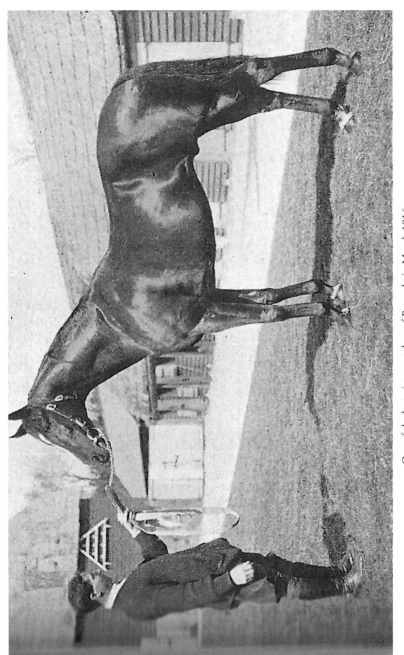

One of the last pictures taken of Bayardo in March 1916

Winners sired by Manilardo in Great Britain and Ireland

Year	Winners	Races Won	Value in £
1925	1 (1)	1 (1)	192.00 (192.00)
1926	1	1	192.00
1927	3 (1)	4 (2)	1,256.00 (957.00)
1928	2 (1)	3 (2)	510.00 (343.00)
1929	1	1	138.00
1930	2	4	1,043.00
1931	2	3	497.00
1932	2	2	591.00
1933	1	2	411.00
1934	0	0	0
1935	0	0	0
1936	1	2	232.00
Total		23 (5)	5,062.00 (1,492.00)

N.B. Figures in brackets refer to two-year-olds

Winners produced by daughters of Manilardo in Great Britain and Ireland

Year	Winners	Races Won	Value in £
1940	1	1	167.00
Total		1	167.00

MANTON (1917 b c Bayardo - Jane Grey II by Le Sancy)

Year	Form	Winning Distances	Value in £
1919	00		
1920	02130	11f	904.00
1921	000000		
1922	00300		

Another son of Bayardo bred by Lady James Douglas, Manton won only one of his eighteen starts. However, as he was named after his famous stable and as he was entered in as many as seventeen early-closing juvenile races including all the most valuable ones it can be assumed that he was considered to be a top prospect. He raced just twice as a two-year-old starting unfancied and finishing unplaced both times at Newmarket in the Prendergast Stakes over five furlongs, and the seven furlongs Dewhurst Stakes, both valuable two-year-old events. On the strength of these two races he can be rated about 100.

At three Manton began at Newmarket running unplaced in the one mile Craven Stakes, before he was stepped up to twelve furlongs to finish runner-up in Chester's Dee Stakes. He broke his maiden at Liverpool in the eleven furlongs St. George Stakes, and finished his second campaign with a third in the St. Leger, one place ahead of his paternal half brother

Braishfield, before an unplaced effort in Newbury's valuable twelve furlongs Autumn Cup under joint top weight of 8st.8lb. This was a good season and he can be rated 120.

At four he continued to compete in good class events, but did not gain a place in his six starts, beginning by finishing unplaced in Kempton's Prince of Wales' Stakes over ten furlongs. Following a lengthily break he returned in the autumn but fared no better in the Great Yorkshire Handicap, Newbury Autumn Cup, Newbury Autumn Handicap, Derby Cup and Manchester November Handicap. He seemed to deteriorate as the season progressed and by the end he could not be rated more than 110.

Kept in training at five in 1922 he registered just one place from his five starts, when gaining third place in a two miles handicap at Windsor carrying 8st.1lb. His rating would have been no better than the previous year 110.

Manton went through the ring at the 1922 Newmarket December Sales. He was sold for 1,250 guineas (£43,750) to take up stud duties in Poland, where he stood as a stallion from 1923 with success. He sired Wagram, winner of the 1931 Polish 2000 Guineas, and became maternal grandsire of Polish Classic winners Jeremi (Polish 2000 Guineas, Polish Derby, Polish St Leger) and Pasjans (Polish 2000 Guineas). Pasjan's later sired the 1947 Polish Derby winner Gniew, while Pasjan's full brother Skarb became a successful stallion too, siring Branza (Polish 1000 Guineas), Czarnogora (Polish Oaks), Solali (Polish Derby and St. Leger), Solanka (Polish Oaks), and Solnica (Polish 1000 Guineas) in addition to becoming maternal grandsire of Czada (Polish 1000 Guineas) and Tarnawa (Polish 1000 Guineas and 2000 Guineas). Another interesting son of Skarb was Herbarz, winner of 1956 Nagroda Przychowku, for his granddam High Force was by Gainsborough, making Herbatz inbred 4x4 Bayardo.

Manton's daughter Hulanka proved to be a prolific source of Polish Classic winners for her descendants numbered Polish 1000 Guineas winners Narbona and Nevada; Polish Oaks heroines Nancy, Novara and Nursja; Polish Derby scorer Neman, plus a Polish St Leger winner in Nimrod. In addition Narbona and Ner won one of Poland's most important juvenile events, the Nagroda Produce Stakes, while Neman also scored in the Austrian Derby, and another descendant Nager took the Slovak St. Leger. Both Nevada and Nimrod were sons of another Polish Derby winner in Demon Club, and it is worth noting that the latter's third dam Duma II was a daughter of the aforementioned stallion Jeremi, whose dam was also by Manton.

Four other daughters of Manton who merit a mention are Miss Mistinguett, the ancestress of Miss Victory (Nagroda Produce Stakes) and the latter's son Mister Tory (Polish Derby); Grangarda, the third dam of Russian

Oaks winner Plomba; Arrow whose descendant Lanos took the Polish 2000 Guineas; and the oddly named Mokka B W the ancestress of Russian Derby winner Eten and Polish St. Leger scorer Wolarz.

PARSIFAL (1915 br c Bayardo- Prim Nun by Persimmon)			
Year	Form	Winning Distances	Value in £
1917	2		
1918	40		

A half brother to the successful sprinter and stallion Friar Marcus, Parsifal failed to win himself, although was second on his only juvenile start, the five and a half furlongs Clearwell Stakes at Newmarket. For this effort he can be rated 104.

The following year his career was restricted to just a couple more outings, fourth to Benevente in Newmarket's Craven Stakes and unplaced in a six furlongs sweepstakes at the same venue. Neither of these performances would have improved his juvenile rating of 104.

Parsifal was bred on similar lines to two very speedy horses in Beresford and Lady Abbess, both being by Friar Marcus out of Bayardo mares. He originally stood as a King's Premium stallion for Bedfordshire, Huntingdonshire, Leicestershire, Northamptonshire and Rutland. Founded in 1886, this was a scheme whereby premiums were awarded annually, via a grant from the Treasury, to thoroughbred stallions so they might travel around the rural districts to encourage farmers to use those stallions to breed horses likely to make good hunters or Army remounts. There was an annual show every February of the thoroughbred stallions at the Agricultural Hall, Islington, London, when they were judged, with premiums being awarded to stallions of suitable quality and confirmation.

Parsifal was later sold for 300 guineas (£10,500) at the 1922 Newmarket December Sales, when he was one of a number of lots purchased for export to Poland, a country where the horse population had been ravaged by the First World War, with a reported 165,000 animals lost during the conflict. In Poland he stood as a stallion with limited success, siring the mare Walkirja who became the granddam of Polish St Leger winner Poprad. Poprad's sire Gainslaw was out of a daughter of Gainsborough, ensuring that Poprad was 4x4 Bayardo.

SIR DIGHTON (1913 b c Bayardo – Princesse De Galles by Gallinule)			
Year	Form	Winning Distances	Value in £
1915	330		
1916	1000	8f	247.50
1917	03		

Sir Dighton was a son of Princesse De Galles, a filly bred by King Edward VII, who proved herself one of the best juveniles of 1908, when her four victories from six starts included the Chesterfield Stakes, New Ham Stakes and Boscawen Stakes. She showed she had lost none of her ability when runner-up to Electra in the 1000 Guineas, and became a strong fancy for the Oaks. However on arrival at Epsom she was found to be in season but a still ran a creditable race to finish second to Perola. She made up for this defeat by winning Royal Ascot's Coronation Stakes, but was then defeated by Electra in the Park Hill Stakes.

Sir Dighton raced three times as a juvenile, beginning with third places in both the Exeter Stakes over six furlongs, beaten just over a length, and the Buckenham (Post Produce) Stakes over half a furlong shorter. It should be added that he was last of three beaten six lengths. He finished his first season running unplaced in the seven furlongs Dewhurst Plate. He can be rated about 100 for these efforts.

His only victory came on his three-year-old bow, when dead heating in a mile maiden at Newmarket, and this earned him a place in the 2000 Guineas, although he never troubled the judge. Further unplaced efforts at Newmarket followed in a couple of one mile handicaps under 8st.6lb and 6st.2lb, respectively. None of these efforts would have improved his juvenile rating of 100.

At four he raced twice in handicaps without success. Firstly he was unplaced in a six furlongs Newmarket event under 7st.6lb, before returning to the same track to carry 8st.5lb and finish third. His rating would remain about 100.

Sir Dighton was then exported to stand as a stallion in Australia in 1918, where he was reasonably successful. His offspring included Princess Dighton (AJC Gimcrack Stakes), Royal Dighton (Sydney Tattersalls Cup), Royal Smile (Brisbane Cup), and Wallun (Doomben 10000), while he became the maternal grandsire of Esmeroic (WATC Karrakatta Plate), Sir Chrystopher (AJC Doncaster Handicap, AJC All Aged Stakes) and Skyro (WATC Sires Produce Stakes).

Sir Dighton's daughter Dympna founded a family that included Harbor Charade (G3 Keisei Hai), Harbor Hikari (Meguro Kinen Spring) and Harbor Young (Mainichi Okan). These Japanese winners were all daughters or granddaughters of the mare Minato Belle Anne, who was sired by Gay Crusader's grandson Gay Lad, making Minato Belle Anne 4x5 Bayardo.

A further daughter of Sir Dighton, named Pet Girl was the ancestress of Make Mine Magic (G2 Grand Prix Stakes, G2 Sir Byrne Hart Stakes and G3 Doomben Summer Stakes) and Australian stallion Vain Prince.

Melhero was another stallion to stand in Australia who descended from a Sir Dighton mare, with his granddam being Sir Dighton's daughter Esme Dighton. Melhero kept his name to the fore as the maternal grandsire of the Australian Oaks winner Jane Hero, and she in turn was the dam of Lord Dudley, winner of the G1 Blue Diamond Stakes and G1 Australian Cup before carving out a successful career as a stallion. The pedigree of Jane Hero is worthy of further study, beginning with her dam Golden Jane who is yet another example with Bayardo combining successfully with the Popinjay family. As well as Golden Jane's sire Melhero having Bayardo via Sir Dighton, Melhero's maternal grandsire Heroic was a son of Popinjay's half sister Chersonese. Furthermore Golden Jane's also has the stallion Magpie, who was by Bayardo's sire Bay Ronald out of Popinjay. Moving forward a generation to Jane Hero, we find she was by Persian Book, a stallion 4x5 Bayardo. Just to complete the story, another daughter of Golden Jane named Regal Jane was by Persian Lyric (5x6x5x6 Bayardo), and her grandson Royal Domination took the G3 Birthday Cup.

TANTALLON (1917 b c Bayardo – Alnmouth by Gallinule)			
Year	Form	Winning Distances	Value in £
1920	032		
1921	00		

Purchased as a yearling for 1,800 guineas (£63,000), Tantallon was a half brother to the 1920 Richmond Stakes winner Sunblaze. His granddam Queen Fairy had been another speedy juvenile, taking the 1898 Gimcrack Stakes. Unraced as a juvenile, Tantallon began with an unplaced effort in a ten furlongs plate at Newmarket. He then dropped back to five furlongs to finish third in Ascot's Granville Stakes, before filling the runner-up spot in a one mile plate at Brighton. His form is not easy to evaluate be he can probably be rated about 105

Kept in training at four, he fared no better, being unplaced in two welter handicaps at Windsor over six furlongs under 9st.9lb, and at Newbury over a furlong further carrying 8st.13lb. It has not been possible to allocate a rating based on these two runs.

Although Tantallon failed to win a race, he stood in England as a stallion, however he only sired a single winner of 4 races worth £625.00 (£21,900) in Great Britain and Ireland.

Winners sired by Tantallon in Great Britain and Ireland			
Year	Winners	Races Won	Value in £
1929	1	1	192.00
1930	1	2	333.00
1931	1	1	100.00
Total		4	625.00

THE ACE (1918 br c Bayardo – Usaa by Knight Of Malta)

Year	Form	Winning Distances	Value in £
1920	00		

The Ace made his debut in Epsom's Woodcote Stakes over six furlongs along with another colt named Humorist. Here their paths diverged, for Humorist went on to win and returned to Epsom a year later to take the Derby, while The Ace finished unplaced and again failed to trouble the judge in his only other start, Royal Ascot's Chesham Stakes, over five furlongs. It has not been possible to allocate any sort of rating.

The Ace was a half brother to the 1920 Hardwick Stakes winner Black Gauntlet. He was inbred 5x3x3 Galopin as well as being 2x3 to the very similarly bred pair Bay Ronald and Panzerschiff; both being bred on a Lord Clifden, Rataplan and Vedette cross. He was exported to New Zealand to stand as a stallion in 1921 siring the full siblings, Fast Passage, winner of the New Zealand Cup and CJC Winter Cup, and Waterline who took the VRC All Aged Stakes, Rawson Stakes, Underwood Stakes and C M Lloyd Stakes. Waterline's victory in the 1931 C M Lloyd Stakes came at the expense of the legendary New Zealand-bred champion Phar Lap, who he beat by a neck receiving 21 pounds. Phar Lap had come into the race on a winning streak of 14, and it was one of just three defeats inflicted on him his final 35 starts. Waterline later finished third to Phar Lap, at level weights, in the Memsie Stakes. Both Fast Passage and Waterline were inbred 4x4 to the mare Pilgrimage via her sons Knight Of Malta and Pilgrim's Progress, and this same mare Pilgrimage also appeared 3x4 in Selene, the dam of Bayardo's grandson Hyperion.

The Ace's most influential daughter was almost certainly Miss Ridicule, for her descendants included Alberton Star (G2 Taranaki Classic, G3 Ellerslie Eclipse Stakes), Alcopop (G2 Herbert Power H) Arrabeea (G3 Thoroughbred Club Stakes, G3 Doomben Classic), Count Chivas (G3 Victoria St. Leger, G2 Sandown Cup, G1 South Australian Derby, G1 Sydney Cup), Dan Baroness (G3 Moonee Valley Champagne Stakes), Hi Jinx (Melbourne Cup), John's Hope (Blue Diamond Stakes, Golden Slipper Stakes), Lady Alberton (G3 Ellerslie Eclipse Stakes), Pride Of Rancho (G1 VRC Sires Produce Stakes, G2 Sir Byrne Hart Stakes) and Sir Alberton (G2 Wellington Guineas) and Te Akau Rose (G2 Matamata Breeders S). John's Hope went on the become a reasonably successful sire in Australia, siring Group 1 winners Gold Hope and Grey Receiver, while another descendant of Miss Ridicule named Somebody II sired Faneuil Lass, who won the G3 Railbird Stakes and G3 Princess Stakes in America before producing G3 Los Angeles Handicap victor Sam Who. Before leaving Miss Ridicule it is worth taking a look at the pedigree of the aforementioned Melbourne Cup winner Hi Jinx. He was sired by Pride Of Kildare, a stallion inbred 4x2 Gainsborough, thus making Hi Jinx 6x4x4 Bayardo.

The above-mentioned Fast Passage became the granddam of Conclusion, who victories included the New Zealand Cup and Wellington Cup, and later as a stallion sired the dam of Caulfield Stakes winner Hamua. Conclusion's pedigree merits closer scrutiny for his sire Finis, a leading stayer and winner of both Ascot Gold Cup and Yorkshire Cup, was inbred 4x2 to Bayardo and his full brother Lemberg.

Meanwhile Fast Passage's full sister Sailor's Love founded a family that included King's Fair (Newmarket Handicap), Le L'Argent (G3 A Gleam Handicap), Sounds Like Fun (G3 Queen Elizabeth Handicap, G3 Waikato Gold Cup, G2 Great Northern Oaks, G3 Rotorua Challenge Plate, G2 Te Rapa International Stakes) and Wandering (G2 British Columbia Derby).

Other daughters of The Ace to leave their mark included Babel, the ancestress of Flotilla (G2 Alister Clark Stakes, G2 Warwick Stakes, G1 Castlemaine Handicap, G1 Australian Guineas, G1 Queensland Sires Produce Stakes, G1 Chipping Norton Stakes), Gretel (G1 AJC Sires {Produce Stakes) and Proud Knight (successful sire in Australia); Lone Flier, whose descendants number the full brothers Arwon (G1 Melbourne Cup) and Flash Guy (Sandown Cup); Nora Lee, the ancestress of Ansin (Wellington Cup), Be Careful (G3 Bagot Handicap, G3 N.E. Mannion Cup, G2 T.S. Carlyon Cup) and Sports Ruler (G3 Brisbane Turf Club Cup); and Scotch Wit, who numbered Gypsy Babe (G3 Eulogy Stakes and Philco (G2 New Zealand Thoroughbred Breeders Stakes) amongst her descendants.

Finally, the stallion Sir Galloway, a son of The Ace's daughter Green Cloth, can be found in the pedigree of Allez Bijou (G2 Sandown Cup, G2 Dalgety Handicap, G1 Rawson Stakes), De Montfort (G3 Easter Classic, G3 Horlicks Challenge Stakes, G3 Dunedin Gold Cup), King Johny (G3 Manawatu Classic), Prince Majestic (G1 Spring Champion Stakes, G1 AJC Queen Elizabeth Stakes, G3 Tattersalls Club Cup, G2 P.J. O'Shea Stakes, G1 H.E. Tancred Stakes), Princess Mellay (New Zealand Oaks), Ranger (G3 Easter Classic), The Bandette (G2 Quick-Eze Stakes, G3 Harlow Butler Handicap) and Yarra Bay (G3 Canterbury Cup).

WIGSTONE (1915 b c Bayardo – Blue Tit by Wildfowler)

Year	Form	Winning Distances	Value in £
1917	00		

A 510 guineas (£17,900) yearling, Wigstone was a son of the successful broodmare Blue Tit, and a half brother to a host of good performers including Blue Dun (Railway Stakes, November Handicap), British Sailor (Great Yorkshire Stakes), Teresina (Great Yorkshire Stakes, Goodwood Cup and Jockey Club Cup) and Westward Ho (Great Yorkshire Stakes). Westward Ho fetched a European record price when sold as a yearling in 1919 for 11,500 guineas, (£402,500) a record that was beaten the following year by Blue Tit's next foal named Blue Ensign. Wigstone never reached those heights and after finishing unplaced in a five furlongs plate at Newmarket, he returned to the same track to run second in a maiden selling plate over the same distance. Claimed by Mr De Freitas after the race he was subsequently retuned to his original owner, before being exported to Canada, where he later took up stud duties. His son Sullivan Trail and grandson Gold Trail also stood as stallions in North America. Wigstone's daughter Linaloa became the dam Victoria M, who took second place in the 1941 Alberta Derby, before producing Victor Stream, winner of the 1946 Calgary Juvenile Stakes.

Daughters as Broodmares

With just seven crops to represent him Bayardo was never going to have the number of mares to make a real impact as a broodmare sire. Volume 25 of the General Stud Book that contains the foalings for the years 1921-1924 records 47 Bayardo mares, while Sunstar had 107, Spearmint 104 and Polymelus 78.

Nevertheless, the classic victories of Good and Gay's daughter Saucy Sue, heroine of the 1925 English 1000 Guineas and Oaks, ensured Bayardo was the leading broodmare sire of that year. That season Saucy Sue also took the Coronation Stakes at Royal Ascot, and other offspring of Bayardo mares including Alexandrian, Brodick Bay, Jessel and Beresford made it a year to remember. Beresford would later make his name as a good sire of sprinters.

Winners in Great Britain and Ireland by year produced by Bayardo mares

1920	Races Won	Value in £
Bayonne (by Diadumenos – Bayazid)	3	1,214
Far South (by Farman – Haygun)	1	297
Henley (by Junior – Helenora)	1	258
The Villager (by Rossendale - Cranford)	3	623
TOTAL	8	2,392

1921	Races Won	Value in £
Baytoi (by Achtoi – Bay Marie)	1	178
Floria (by Neil Gow – La Tosca)	1	168
Longship Light (by Long Set – Starlight Bay)	1	198
W.A.A.C (by Swynford – Good and Gay)	1	415
TOTAL	4	959

1922	Races Won	Value in £
Baytoi (by Achtoi – Bay Marie)	1	213
Bold and Bad (by Swynford – Good and Gay)	1	890
Jason (by Sunder – Jessin)	2	892
The Villager (by Rossendale – Cranford)	3	1,835
TOTAL	7	3,830

1923 (17th)	Races Won	Value in £
Beresford (by Friar Marcus – Bayberry)	5	5,050
Bold and Bad (by Swynford – Good and Gay)	3	3,120
Heliaster (by Sunstar – Helenora)	2	1,270
Jason (by Sunder – Jessin)	2	492
Pride of Inglewood (by Happy Warrior – Bayora)	3	550
Tuscar Rock (by Sunstar – Tussock Grass)	1	461
TOTAL	16	10,943

1924	Races Won	Value in £
Bustle Up (by Hurry On – Cranford)	1	220
Heliaster (by Sunstar – Helenora)	1	830
John Wallop (by John O' Gaunt – Hampshire Lily)	1	100
Pride of Inglewood (by Happy Warrior – Bayora)	0.5	68.50
Sandblast (by Hurry On – Herne Bay)	1	337
Saucy Sue (by Swynford - Good and Gay)	3	3,129
Spindrift (by Chaucer – Rothesay Bay)	4	1,707
Unnamed filly (by Theo Bold – Lady Bayardo)	1	261
TOTAL	12.5	6,652.50

1925 (1st)	Races Won	Value in £
Alexandrian (by Sunstar – Hypatia)	1	2,000
Atreas (by Pelops – Despina)	1	166
Bayford (by Swynford – Bayora)	1	838
Bay Friar (by Friar Marcus – Bay Marie)	4	659
Beresford (by Friar Marcus – Bayberry)	1	723
Brodick Bay (by Swynford – Rothesay Bay)	1	840
Bustle Up (by Hurry On – Cranford)	1	187
Costermonger (by Blank – Harriet)	1	142
Cross Fox (by Grey Fox II – Bay Lady)	1	192
Hawk's Castle (by Hapsburg – Bayberry)	1	128
Jessel (by Polymelus – Jessin)	2	1,242
Lotus Flower (by Golden Sun – Peach Blossom)	2	176
Pride of Inglewood (by Happy Warrior – Bayora)	2	383
Redeem (by Silvern – Rosa Bonheur II)	1	142
Saucy Sue (by Swynford - Good and Gay)	5	22,155
St Jerome (by Friar Marcus – Philosophy)	1	692
Swift and Sure (by Swynford – Good and Gay)	1	1,190
Unnamed filly (by Glanmerin – Lady Bayardo)	2	316
TOTAL	29	32,171

1926 (16th)	Races Won	Value in £
Atreas (by Pelops – Despina)	1	125
Bay Friar (by Friar Marcus – Bay Marie)	1	884
Bayford (by Swynford – Bayora)	1	720
Bloodhound (by Brigand – Spirit of Bay)	1	185
Costermonger (by Blank – Harriet)	3	609
Glen Rosa (by Swynford – Rothesay Bay)	2	1,200
Hera (by Sky-Rocket - Helenora)	2	2,010
Jessel (by Polymelus – Jessin)	1	417
Nuthatch (by Star and Garter – Inversnaid)	2	386
Poet (by Chaucer – Pompadour)	1	138
Pride of Inglewood (by Happy Warrior – Bayora)	1	194
Rhonia (by Stefan The Great – Rhodope)	4	1,625
Sandblast (by Hurry On – Herne Bay)	2	461
Sand Hill (by Prince Galahad – Bayberry)	1	198
St Jerome (by Friar Marcus – Philosophy)	1	840
Swift and Sure (by Swynford – Good and Gay)	1.5	2,050
TOTAL	25.5	12,042

1927	Races Won	Value in £
Atreas (by Pelops – Despina)	1	100
Bay Friar (by Friar Marcus – Bay Marie)	1	364
Blue Boy (by Blue Ensign – Herne Bay)	1	138
Bracknell House (by Star And Garter – Inversnaid)	1	178
Calcaria (by Planet – Lady Bayardo)	1	266
Despo (by Syndrian – Despina)	1	358
Golden Bay (by Golden Myth – Bayazid)	1	167
Hera (by Sky-Rocket – Helenora)	1	211
Janus (by Soranus – Jessin)	1	1,072
Philammon (by Sunstar –Hypatia)	1	287
Poet (by Chaucer – Pompadour)	1	392
Pretty Swift (by Swynford – Pompadour)	1	138
Sandblast (by Hurry On – Herne Bay)	1	422
St Jerome (by Friar Marcus – Philosophy)	1	265
TOTAL	14	4,358

1928 (13th)	Races Won	Value in £
Bracknell Home (by Star And Garter – Inversnaid)	1	117
Bright Glen (by Silvern- Inversnaid)	2	582
Carl Rosa (by Orpheus – Rosa Bonheur II)	2	238
Corks (by Somme Kiss – Elsie)	1	183
Eudaemon (by Thunderer – Hypatia)	1	875.50
Hera (by Sky-Rocket – Helenora)	1	1655
Janus (by Soranus – Jessin)	1	865
Lamlash (by Swynford – Rothesay Bay)	4	1,024
Lorel (by Brigand – Spirit Of Bay)	1	144
Lyre (by Orpheus – Peach Blossom)	1	162
Meadow Lark (by Orpheus – Peach Blossom)	2	386
Nestorian (by Archaic – Placentia)	1	163
Old Dromore (by Devizes – Helenora)	2	385
Pladda (by Phalaris – Rothesay Bay)	2	812
Rose Of Athens (by Rock Flint – Rhodope)	1	176
St Jerome (by Friar Marcus – Philosophy)	4	2,094
Thunder Squall (by Noblesse Oblige – Bayamo)	4	980
TOTAL	31	10,841.50

1929 (17th)	Races Won	Value in £
Adne (by Bachelor's Double – Despina)	1	100
Bay Friar (by Friar Marcus – Bay Marie)	2	708
Byron (by Beppo – Cranford)	1	197
Cragadour (by Craig An Eran – Pompadour)	1	945
Despo (by Syndrian – Despina)	1	142
Lady Abbess (by Friar Marcus – Bay Lady)	5	5,102
Pladda (by Phalaris – Rothesay Bay)	2	444
Poet (by Chaucer – Pompadour)	1	197
Rose Of Athens (by Rock Flint – Rhodope)	2	372
Snoops (by Pelops – Haygun)	3	513
St Jerome (by Friar Marcus – Philosophy)	1	323
Whitsbury (by Swynford – Bayora)	2	326
TOTAL	22	9,369

1930	Races Won	Value in £
Adne (by Bachelor's Double – Despina)	1	178
Bachelora (by Bachelor's Double – Bayora)	1	128
Botany Bay (by Phalaris – Rothesay Bay)	4	1,265
Dombey (by Captain Cuttle – Bay Maiden)	1	107
Nestorian (by Archaic – Placentia)	2	387
Old Dromore (by Devizes – Helenora)	2	329
Polo (by Poltava – Lady Bayardo)	2	255
Thunder Squall (by Noblesse Oblige – Bayamo)	3	733
Whitsbury (by Swynford – Bayora)	1	191
TOTAL	17	3,573

1931	Races Won	Value in £
Blisk (by Somme Kiss – Bay Lady)	1	166
Bute (by Phalaris – Rothesay Bay)	2	487
Cospatrick (by Tetratema – Rhodope)	1	540
Double Bay (by Bachelor's Double – Bayora)	1	146
Mowgli (by Asterus – La Belle Alliance)	1	245
Nestorian (by Archaic – Placentia)	2	217
Polo (by Poltava – Lady Bayardo)	2	442
Pompier (by Hurry On – Pompadour)	1	900
Quick Rise (by Hurry On – Pompadour)	1	166
Thunder Squall (by Noblesse Oblige – Bayamo)	2	340
Whitsbury (by Swynford – Bayora)	1	100
TOTAL	15	3,749

1932	Races Won	Value in £
Bayonet (by Verdun – Bayuda)	1	182
Blisk (by Somme Kiss – Bay Lady)	1	142
California (by Colorado – Rothesay Bay)	1	187
Pompier (by Hurry On – Pompadour)	2	1,538
Thunder Squall (by Noblesse Oblige – Bayamo)	1	347
TOTAL	6	2,396

1933	Races Won	Value in £
Alruna Maid (by Apelle – Hypatia)	1	177
Bay Monk (by Friar Marcus – Bay Lady)	1	346
Nestorian (by Archaic – Placentia)	2	259
TOTAL	4	782

1934	Races Won	Value in £
Bay Monk (by Friar Marcus – Bay Lady)	2	412.50
Curraghmore (by Friar Marcus – Bayberry)	1	166
TOTAL	3	578.50

1935	Races Won	Value in £
Bideford Bay (by Baytown – Bay Lady)	2	1,408
Caddle Combe (by Cadum – Spirit of Bay)	2	228
Curraghmore (by Friar Marcus – Bayberry)	3	736
Glum Jess (by Glommen – Jessin)	2	125
Miss Honor (by Mr Jinks – Bayora)	3	390
TOTAL	12	2,887

1936	Races Won	Value in £
Bayport (by Polyphontes – Bayamo)	1	103
Bideford Bay (by Baytown – Bay Lady)	1	244
Petrograd (by Stefan The Great – Rhodope)	1	127
Stormpetal (by Cyclonic – Peach Blossom)	1	166
TOTAL	4	640

1937	Races Won	Value in £
Curraghmore (by Friar Marcus – Bayberry)	1	167
TOTAL	1	167

Summary
Individual Winners in Great Britain and Ireland - 90
Total Races Won in Great Britain and Ireland - 231
Value in £ - 108,330.50 (3,792,000)

The following are the daughters of Bayardo who had most influence on the breed via their descendants.

BAYBERRY (1913 b f Bayardo – Catalpa by Sundridge)

A half sister to the useful juvenile Bambusa, Bayberry was a daughter of the Sundridge mare Catalpa. She was unplaced on her only appearance as a juvenile in a maiden. At three she won one of her four races: a modest plate at Newmarket. She failed to win any of her six races as a four year old and was only placed once: second in a plate but beaten six lengths.

On retiring to the paddocks she bred 4 winners of 13 races worth £7,168 (£250,880), easily the best of them was Beresford (by Friar Marcus). A 700 guineas (£27,000) yearling purchase, Beresford recorded 5 victories as a juvenile, among them the Newmarket Stud Produce Stakes and Champion Breeders Produce Stakes over five furlongs. As a four year old he took the Royal Handicap at Epsom before finishing runner-up to the leading sprinter Diomedes in Royal Ascot's King's Stand Stakes. Retired to stud in Ireland Beresford became a good sire of sprinters such as Portlaw (Nunthorpe Stakes, Champagne Stakes, Middle Park Stakes and himself a sire of sprinters), Scotia's Glen (Windsor Castle Stakes) and Hyndford Bridge (Prince of Wales Plate), although his first crop did include an Ebor Handicap (14 furlongs) winner in Cat O'Nine Tails and second crop the winner of the Cambridgeshire Handicap (9 furlongs) in Disarmament. The latter carved out a successful career as a stallion in Chile, where he finished runner-up on the winning sires list in 1943 and 1951, and secured the crown of that country's leading broodmare sire of 1958.

One of Portlaw's best offspring was Portobello, a colt who won all his 5 starts as a juvenile by an aggregate of 18¼ lengths, including the Clearwell and Windsor Castle Stakes, to be rated the third best two year old of 1938. The following year he developed into a leading sprinter taking both July Cup and Nunthorpe Stakes. Portobello's dam was by Solario, a St. Leger and Ascot Gold Cup winner, who was by Bayardo's son Gainsborough out of a Sundridge mare, and thus bred on similar lines to Beresford's dam Bayberry. This, of course, meant that Portobello was inbred 4x4 Bayardo. Another horse with inbreeding to Bayardo via Gainsborough and Beresford was the 1948 Free Handicap winner Rear Admiral, who was by Hyperion's son Devonian out of a Beresford mare and thus 4x4 Bayardo.

Another daughter of Bayberry, named Bayleaf (by Knockando) did not record a win but later became the third dam of Stenigot, winner of the Exeter Stakes at Newmarket in 1949 and second in the Chester Vase the following year; and fifth dam of Hokuto Matsushima, who triumphed in the 1981 Kokura Sansai Stakes in Japan.

BAYENA (1917 b f Bayardo – Queen Helena by Laveno)

This daughter of the Laveno mare Queen Helena had a rather cosmopolitan history. Although based in England, her dam Queen Helena was actually owned by the Russian Government Stud. A 720 guineas (£27,700) yearling purchase, and unraced herself, Bayena was exported to Argentine as a three-year-old in 1920 after being covered by Call O' The Wild. Although not an immediate success there her descendants included Baturro (Clasico Maipu, Clasico Palermo), De Los Rios (G1 Triple Crown 1600 in South Africa), Laconique (Gran Premio Polla de Potrillos – Argentine 2000 Guineas), Sandunguera (Cape of Good Hope Paddock Stakes – in South Africa), Stein (G1 Gran Premio Presidente de la Republica – Gavea, G1 Gran Premio Presidente de la Republica – Cidade Jardim - both in Brazil) and Surera (G2 Gran Premio Eliseo Ramirez, G1 Gran Premio Seleccion - Argentine Oaks).

BAY GAL (1916 b f Bayardo – Kilmein by Gallinule)

Bayardo's dam Galicia boasted a cross of Voltigeur and Isonomy, and as these two individuals were found close up in the pedigree of the successful sire Gallinule, it was no surprise to see Bayardo cover a number of Gallinule mares. The result of one of these matings was Bay Gal, a daughter of the Gallinule mare Kilmein. A non-winner, Bay Gal managed just two third places from seven outings and was a moderate racehorse and was sold for 2,100 guineas (£81,000), in foal to Buchan, to French breeder Victor Duret at the 1922 Newmarket December. The resulting foal named Bouche Bee became the ancestress of Bakuba (G3 Prix Caracalla), Belle Shika (Prix Vanteaux, Prix du Moulin, Prix Chloe),

Boucan (Criterium de Maisons-Laffitte), Brisemaille (Prix D'Hedouville) and Mil Foil (G3 Prix Thomas Byron).

BAY LADY (1915 b f Bayardo – Silent Lady)

An unraced daughter of the Cyllene mare Silent Lady, Bay Lady produced 5 winners of 14 races worth £8,012 (£280,400). Lady Abbess (by Friar Marcus), a 4,800 guineas (£184,800) purchase as a yearling, proved to be easily the best of this quintet, scoring five times over five and six furlongs as a juvenile, including the Fulbourne Stakes, Granby Stakes, Moulton Stakes and Woodcote Stakes. In the Hopeful Stakes, she was beaten 1½ lengths by subsequent Epsom Derby winner Blenheim receiving three pounds, and also finished third in the Queen Mary Stakes and National Produce Breeders Stakes. She was bred on very similar lines to the aforementioned good sprinter Beresford, who was also by Friar Marcus out of a Bayardo mare. Originally exported to Argentina in 1920, Bay Lady later returned to England where her daughter Sweet Abbess emulated her mother by winning the Woodcote Stakes, while Lady Abbess's other descendants included Duc De Gueldre (Prix Lupin), Important Reason (G3 Woodlawn Stakes), Loyal Magique (Prix D'Astarte) and Sun Ohi (Tokyo Daishoten).

It was left to Bay Lady's non-winning daughters to further her influence. Her daughter by Hurry On, named Hurry Off, became the granddam of three useful performers in France, namely Chrysler (Prix de L'Esperence), L'Amiral (Prix Hocquart) and Royal Drake (Prix des Reservoirs, Prix de Guiche, March Stakes twice and runner-up in Epsom Derby). Others to descend from Hurry Off included Dancienne (G3 Prix des Chenes, G2 Prix du Conseil de Paris), Lombard (Calcutta Gold Cup – twice), Night Nurse (Champion Hurdle), Speedway (Prix Eugene Adam), Spring Song (Prix de Guiche) and Termienne (G3 Prix Penelope).

Finally Bay Lady's daughter Miramar (by Friar Marcus) produced two contrasting performers in Monasterevan, winner of one of South Africa's most important races the July Handicap, and Kingscraft who took the 1960 Grand Steeplechase de Paris.

BAYORA (1914 b f Bayardo – Honora by Gallinule)

A half sister to Hakim (by Friar Marcus), winner of Royal Ascot's New Stakes, and Lemonora (by Bayardo's half brother Lemberg), who scored in the Champagne Stakes at two and Grand Prix de Paris the following year, Bayora was a daughter of the Gallinule mare Honora. After being purchased for 300 guineas (£11,550) as a yearling, she failed to emulate her siblings on the racetrack, but at stud produced 6 winners of 17.5 races worth £4,034.50 (£141,200). Two of that sextet, namely Bachelora (by Bachelor's Double) and Miss Honor (by Mr Jinks) were to found families that not only included English Classic winners, but also still flourish to this day.

Bachelora, an expensive 7,500 guineas (£288,750) yearling purchase but only the winner of a minor race at three, went on to become the ancestress of Bailonguera (G3 Clasico Marcos Levalle), Batallosa (G1 Gran Premio Saturnino J Unzue, G1 Gran Premio Jorge de Atucha), Beauty Halo (G3 Clasico Manuel J Guirades), Bonaventura (G1 Gran Premio de Honor, G3 Clasico Chile), El Bandido (Arlington Handicap, Canadian International, Jockey Club Cup Handicap), El Hawa (Rous Memorial Stakes), Fantasio (G1 Gran Premio Copa de Oro - twice, G2 Clasico Progreso, G1 Gran Premio Miguel A Martinez de Hoz, G1 Gran Premio Comparacion), Feloniously (Hawthorne Derby), Flexton (Greenham Stakes and sire in Chile), Kachamandi (G1 Premio Alberto Vial Infante, G3 Premio Comparacion, G2 Clasico Carlos Bello Silva), Kandaly (G3 Louisiana Derby), Macho Again (G1 Jim Dandy Stakes), Mowerman (G3 Ajax Stakes, G3 Ipswich Cup), Paloma Infiel (G2 Premio Stud Book de Chile, G1 El Ensayo, G1 Copa de Plata Italo Traverso Pasqualetti, G1 Premio El Derby), Pranke (G1 Gran Premio Polla de Potrillos, G1 Gran Premio 25 de Mayo, G1 Sunset Handicap), Punch (G1 El Ensayo in Chile), Rose Royale (English 1000 Guineas, Prix du Moulin, Champion Stakes) and Tibaldi (G2 Clasico Ensayo, G1 Gran Premio San Isidoro, G2 Gran Premio Miguel A Martinez de Hoz, G2 Clasico Progreso, G2 Clasico Ecuador). Of the above, the full brothers El Hawa and Flexton were both by Hyperion and thus inbred 3x4 to Bayardo.

Miss Honor, a lot cheaper fetching just 800 guineas (£30,800) as yearling, recorded three victories, and her descendants included Artic Envoy (G3 Premio Ellington), Behaviour (G3 Appleton Handicap), Bounteous (Dewhurst Stakes, Prix Kergorlay, Grand Prix de Deauville, runner-up in St. Leger), Caitano (G2 Union Rennen, G1 Gran Premio del Jockey Club, G1 Aral-Pokal, G2 Idee Hansa-Preis, G2 Grosser Preis der Baden Airpark, G2 Bosphorus Cup), El Fabulous (G3 Prix Cleopatre), El Mina (G3 Prix Minerve), St Mawes (G3 Gordon Stakes), On My Honor (California Derby), Steppe Dancer (G3 September Stakes), Tap On Wood (G2 National Stakes, G1 English 2000 Guineas, G3 Park Stakes), Utmost Respect (G3 Chipchase Stakes, G3 Prix de Seine-et-Oise) and Watchyerback (G3 Standish Handicap).

BAYUDA (1916 b f Bayardo – Jessica by Eager)

Bred at the Harwood stud, near Newbury, by Lady James Douglas Bayuda was trained by Alec Taylor. She was out of Jessica, who, although just below the top grade, was one of the fastest three-year-old fillies of her year. Although as a juvenile she made her debut in a selling race Jessica won four of her seven races that year. As a three-year-old she won two of her five races, including one at Ascot, retiring to the paddocks at the end of the season. She was a most successful brood-mare producing nine winners from thirteen live foals. Between them they won a total of thirty-four races.

Bayuda's juvenile career consisted of four races at Newmarket, finishing fourth on her racecourse debut in the valuable Soltykoff Stakes over five and a half furlongs, beaten by Grand Parade who won the Derby the following year. On this same day Gay Crusader won the St Leger substitute the September Stakes. She showed the benefit of this outing by next finishing runner-up in an even more valuable race the Autumn Stakes over six furlongs beaten less than a length by a colt, The Panther, who went on to finish as top juvenile at the end of the season. She certainly did not begin her career in moderate company! She broke her maiden in the Cheveley Park Stakes over six furlongs winning "in a canter" before finishing the season with a third in the six furlongs Free Handicap conceding the winner Gipsy Lad to whom she was conceding 13 lb. Her rating for the year would have been 114.

She began 1919 with a fourth place, as the second favourite at 7-2, behind the favourite and convincing winner Roseway in the 1000 Guineas. Six weeks later at Epsom, despite starting at odds of 100-7, Bayuda won the Oaks decisively by one and a half lengths from her 1000 Guineas conqueror Roseway who had started at odds-on. The turnaround in form was almost certainly accounted for by Bayuda's superior stamina. Bayuda had not been certain to run in the Oaks. Alec Taylor was so unhappy with her work over twelve furlongs at Manton that it was seriously considered not running her. Fortunately she produced a much better performance in a subsequent gallop which put her back on track. Bayuda's final race came in the valuable eleven furlongs St. Georges Stakes at Liverpool, where she finished second, ironically beaten by another Bayardo filly named Rothesay Bay to whom she was conceding twenty-one pounds. Alec Taylor then trained her for the St Leger but an injury shortly before the race made it necessary that she be taken out of training. Her three-year-old rating would have been 123. She was described as a good-looking medium-sized filly.

On the racecourse she may have won the Oaks, but she had a contrasting record when retired to the paddocks and she endured a most unfortunate experience with her very first foal. Mated with Hurry On she produced a filly that created considerable interest in July 1922 at the Newmarket Yearling Sales and she was knocked down for 4000 guineas (154,000) when bought by George Lambton on behalf of the Aga Khan and subsequently named Hajibibi. However, Bayuda suffered internal injuries when producing the foal and she proved difficult subsequently to get in foal, and it was to be 18 years after her classic triumph at Epsom, that her son Bayonet (by Verdun) recorded Bayuda's sole victory as a broodmare when taking a £182 (6,400) event. However, thanks to Hajibibi, Bayuda's dynasty still wields an influence today. Hajibibi first foal Grand Bibi (by Grand Parade) became the granddam of Favorita, who took both Belgian 2000 Guineas and Grand Prix de Bruxelles in 1952.

Another daughter of Hajibibi named Hajiri (by Papyrus) was the ancestress of Vacarme, whose victories included the Paradise Stakes and Jockey Club Cup, and El Canchero who scored in Brazil's Group 1 event the Gran Premio Oswaldo Aranha, but it was to be Hajibibi's daughter Shah Bibi (by Pharos) who proved most influential. Her most important descendant was the Middle Park Stakes winner and important sire Sharpen Up. It is interesting to note that as well as tracing to a Bayardo mare Sharpen Up was inbred 5x3 to Bayardo's grandson Hyperion and also carried a line of Bayardo's half brother Lemberg. Other major winners to descend from Shah Bibi included Back Da Chief (G2 Waikato Gold Cup), Chiming (G3 Yerba Buena Handicap), Elgay (G1 Derby Italiano), Exclusive Halo (G2 Maribyrnong Plate), First Waltz (G1 Prix Morny), Jonjas Chudleigh (Irish Cambridgeshire Handicap), Knight Of Mercy (Wokingham Handicap, Stewards Cup Handicap), Man From Wicklow (G2 W L McKnight Handicap G1 Gulfstream Park Breeders Cup Handicap), Miss Jugah (G3 Mannerism Stakes), Outcrop (Yorkshire Oaks, Park Hill Stakes), Rarotonga Treaty (G1 Premiers Champion Stakes), Syrona (G3 Lingfield Oaks Trial) and Wild Heart Dancing (G3 My Charmer Handicap, G3 Canadian Stakes, G3 Athenia Handicap).

BRADAMANTE (1916 b f Bayardo – Ena by Ian)
Although 1,650 guineas (£63,500) was required to purchase Bradamante as a yearling, the sole claim to fame of this daughter of the Ian mare Ena was as the third dam of Nishi Tap, winner of the 1950 Spring Kyoto Kinen in Japan. Nishi Tap was inbred 4x4 Bayardo as a result of his sire Tokino Chikara being by Gainsborough's son Tournesol.

CORALLE (1914 b f Bayardo – Cosette by Cyllene)
This daughter of the Cyllene mare Cosette was exported to Eastern Europe, where her daughter Cartouche foaled Cagliostro, winner of the Hungarian Derby and St. Leger, and in turn the sire of Kamares (Hungarian 2000 Guineas, Hungarian Derby), Relka (Hungarian Oaks, Hungarian St. Leger) and Flanc (Hungarian 2000 Guineas). The latter descended from the Bayardo mare Rothesay Bay, so was in fact inbred 4x4 Bayardo.

Another Eastern European classic winner to hail from this family was Leu (Romanian Derby), whose dam Colienne was another daughter of Coralle.

DESPINA (1918 b f Bayardo – Hippolyte by Veles)

Despina was a daughter of the Veles mare Hippolyte, and became the most expensive daughter of Bayardo purchased at public auction when changing hands for 3,500 guineas (£134,750) in 1919. However, on the racecourse she could not even manage a place from six juvenile outings. She did better at stud and became the dam of 3 winners of 7 races worth £1,169 (£41,000). Her first foal Atreas (by Pelops) recorded 3 of those victories over 3 seasons, and was then sold for 400 guineas (£15,000) at the 1927 Newmarket October Sales to race in India, where he was an immediate success; his 9 wins in that country including the Calcutta Gold Cup.

GOOD AND GAY (1912 b f Bayardo – Popinjay by St. Frusquin)

Bred by owned by Mr Waldorf Astor (later the 2nd Viscount Astor) Good and Gay was a daughter of the St. Frusquin mare Popinjay and was bred on very similar lines to Gainsborough. She proved in the short term to be Bayardo's most successful broodmare, although her offspring did not leave a lasting legacy. On the racetrack she had the distinction of being the first winner sired by Bayardo when she scored in the five furlongs Bessborough Stakes at Ascot on her debut. She was then beaten in the Chesterfield Stakes at Newmarket, before returning to that venue in the autumn to take the five furlongs Buckenham (Post Produce) Stakes, a race also won by her sire. Her only outing as a three-year-old was an unplaced effort in the Culford Three-year-old handicap at Newmarket in which she carried top-weight of 8st 6lbs.

At stud Good And Gay bred four winners from five foals, namely the headstrong Saucy Sue, whose eight wins included the 1000 Guineas, Oaks and Coronation Stakes; Swift And Sure, winner of the Chester Vase; Ascot Derby and Gordon Stakes winner Bold and Bad; and W.A.A.C. All four were sired by Swynford, which made them close genetic relatives to none other than Hyperion. Good And Gay's first foal Tea Tray (by The Tetrarch) was at one time well regarded by his trainer, but never saw the racecourse. Purchased in January 1921 for 190 guineas (£7,300), his buyer subsequently sold him on for a decent profit to go to New Zealand, where he took up stallion duties. He became a successful sire there, finishing in the top ten leading stallions for 3 seasons between 1930-31 and 1932-33.

Saucy Sue proved to be the leading juvenile filly of 1924, remaining unbeaten with wide margin wins in the Lavant Stakes at Goodwood, and Bretby and Criterion Stakes at Newmarket. She was placed at the head of the Free Handicap with 9st 2lbs and her rating was 126. This ensured she started a hot favourite for the 1000 Guineas at odds of 1/4, and she won as a hot favourite should, hard held by six lengths from Miss Gadabout. It was the same story at Epsom in the Oaks where Miss

Gadabout was disposed of by eight lengths, and after a ten lengths victory at odds of 1/10 in Royal Ascot's Coronation Stakes, and a three lengths stroll in the Nassau Stakes at Goodwood, she was being likened to Pretty Polly. However she began to suffer from cracked heels and she was subsequently not the force she was. In addition it should be borne in mind that good filly as Saucy Sue was she was the best in an ordinary year. She probably failed to stay the fourteen furlongs in the Park Hill Stakes, finishing a well-beaten third to Juldi, a filly she had beaten easily at Goodwood, and then finished third in the Royal Stakes over ten furlongs at Newmarket, before ending her career with victory in the Atalanta Stakes. Her rating as a three-year-old was 131.

Saucy Sue died in 1938, but in that time produced just one winner, namely Truculent, a son of Teddy who showed good form as a three year old, winning the Royal Standard Stakes at Manchester, as well as beating subsequent classic winners Cameronian and Sandwich, when runner-up in the Craven Stakes. At stud he died when only ten, siring the useful performers Merry Mathew and Flag Of Truce, the latter subsequently becoming the maternal grandsire of 2000 Guineas hero Nearula.

After making his racecourse debut in Royal Ascot's Coventry Stakes, where he finished sixth to Colorado after being slowly away, Saucy Sue's year younger full brother Swift And Sure, reversed the form with Colorado on eight pounds better terms, winning the Exeter Stakes at Newmarket with Colorado back in fifth place. He was well beaten in his final two starts as a juvenile, but the following season won the Chester Vase before running fourth to Coronach in the Epsom Derby, and dead-heating for the Duchess Of York Plate. Swift And Sure was exported to America in March 1927 where he sired Eastport (Arkansas Derby), Sir Marlboro (Canadian Championship, King Edward Gold Cup Handicap), Sure Delight (My Dear Stakes) and Swivel (Pimlico Futurity).

HELENORA (1914 b f Bayardo – Helvia by Cicero)

Racing as an un-named filly Helenora won just a modest nursery from five outings as a juvenile and was a daughter of the Cicero mare Helvia. Her career as a broodmare was quite successful for she produced 4 winners of 12 races worth £6,948 (£243,000). The best was probably Hera (by Sky-Rocket), a speedy filly who won the Wokingham Handicap at Royal Ascot, although she left nothing of note as a broodmare.

Helenora's first foal Henley (by Junior) scored once as a juvenile. Her daughter, Hastily (by Hurry On), was sold for 1,100 guineas, (£38,500) in foal to Lancegaye, at the 1930 Newmarket December Sales to American Mr.F.Wallis Armstrong. Hastily foaled a colt the following spring named Cavalcade, and his two wins as a juvenile, including the Hyde Park Stakes, earned him second place on the Experimental Handicap. At three he etched his name in racing history by taking the

Kentucky Derby, and failing by a nose to beat stablemate High Quest in the Preakness Stakes, before returning to the winning trail with victories in American Derby, Detroit Derby and Classic Stakes.

Cavalcade's half sister Hastily Yours became the dam of Alerted (Jerome Handicap, Dixie Handicap, Saratoga Handicap) and the granddam of Prime Action (Prix de Saint-Georges), while Swingin Sway, a descendant of Hastily Your's full sister Rash Hurry, took the G3 Board of Governor's Handicap.

Two other daughters of Helenora worthy of mention are Phacelia (by Phalaris) and Pontresina (by Corcyra). While neither won a race, Phacelia produced the mare La Naine (sired by Ellangowan, who was a son of Bayardo's half brother Lemberg) who became the granddam of Minnetonka (sired by Jubie whose maternal grandsire was Bayardo's son Gainsborough), winner of one of South Africa's most prestigious races the 1955 J&B Metropolitan Handicap, while Pontresina's son Pontet Canet scored in the 1930 Prix Jacques Le Marois

HERNE BAY (1913 b f Bayardo – Pincushion by Oberon)

A daughter of the Oberon mare Pincushion, Herne Bay was a highly inbred mare being 4x4 Galliard, 5x3x3x5 Galopin, 4x4 Isonomy, 5x5x5 Sterling, 5x5x6 Newminster and 6x6 Wild Dayrell. She failed to win but became the dam of 2 winners of 5 races worth £1,358 (£47,500). One of these winners, her daughter Blue Bay (by Blue Ensign) was the ancestress of Alter Ego winner of the G2 Gilbey's Trial Handicap and G2 Durban Merchants Handicap in South Africa; and Dalry whose C.V. boasted a win in the Horris Hill Stakes and second in the Irish 2000 Guineas, and earned him a place as a stallion in Argentine where he sired Group 1 winners Dalry Blu (Gran Premio Saturnino J Unzue), Fabiolo (Gran Premio Polla de Potrancas) and Sendita (Gran Premio Saturnino J Unzue).

HYPATIA (1917 b f Bayardo – Laikipia by Spearmint)

This daughter of the Spearmint mare Laikipia was purchased by Jack Joel and became the dam of 4 winners of 4 races worth £3,339.50 (£116,500). Amongst them was Alexandrian (by Sunstar) who won the valuable Prince of Wales's Stakes at Goodwood on his racecourse debut. Alexandrian was later exported to South Africa where he won two races in 1929 including the important Peninsula Summer Handicap. He was being prepared for a crack at the prestigious Durban July Handicap when he contracted biliary fever and died a fortnight before the race.

INVERSNAID (1915 b f Bayardo – Inheritance by Isinglass)

A mare bred on quite similar lines to Herne Bay, being out of the Isinglass mare Inheritance, and being inbred 4x3 Galliard, 5x3x4 Galopin, 4x3 Isonomy, 5x5x4 Sterling, 4x5 Lord Clifden and 5x6x5 New-minster. She won once as a juvenile and later became the dam of 3 winners of 6 races worth £1,263 (£44,200). Her daughter Inmate (by Manna) produced the 1939 Hungarian 2000 Guineas winner Indolent.

JESSIN (1915 b f Bayardo – Highness by Cyllene)
A half sister to the useful stayer Air Balloon, winner of the Queen's Prize and Queen Alexandra Stakes for the Cox family, as well as runner-up in the Chester Cup, Ascot Stakes and Goodwood Plate, the non-winner Jessin was bred by Alfred Cox and purchased by Mr Solomon "Solly" Joel. She failed to gain even a place in four races as a two and three-year-old. She was another mare inbred to both Galopin (5x3x3) and Isonomy (4x4), and a close relative to Gay Crusader since her dam Highness (by the Ascot Gold Cup winner Cyllene) was a half sister to the dam of Gay Crusader. The 4 winners Jessin produced won 11 races worth £5,105 (£178,600), including Jessel (by Polymelus), winner of the Woodcote Stakes and runner-up to subsequent 2000 Guineas hero Colorado in Royal Ascot's Coventry Stakes. Another with close inbreeding, Jessel was 2x3 Cyllene and 3x4 Hampton.

Jessel's three-quarter sister Joodin (by Polymelus's son Pommern) only fetched 110 guineas when passing through the Newmarket sales ring as a yearling in July 1930, and although she failed to win a race, was the ancestress of Dance Every Dance (G2 Clairwood Golden Slipper, G2 Cape Fillies Guineas), Name The Key (G3 Clairwood Christmas Handicap), Next Edition (G2 Clairwood Golden Slipper), Sarabande (G1 Majorca Handicap) and Sharp Ledge (G3 Henry Eatwell Memorial Handicap) in South Africa.

JOYEUSE (1914 b f Bayardo – Joie De Vivre by Gallinule)
A daughter of the Gallinule mare Joie De Vivre, and a half sister to Alan Breck, a successful sire and winner of both New Stakes and Chesterfield Stakes as a juvenile, Joyeuse was exported to Australia, where she was retired to the paddocks and developed a successful partnership with the stallion Comedy King. Matings between the pair produced colts named Mimetic and Joy King who respectively won the Great Northern Foal Stakes and Royal Stakes, along with two fillies named Joy Bells and Nyamba who were at the head of successful families in Australia

Joy Bells was the ancestress of Duo (Metropolitan Handicap), Jingle Bells (Victoria Oaks), Le Dejeuner (G3 Liverpool City Cup), Master Eclipse (G3 Port Adelaide Cup), Ossie Pak (G3 WATC Prince of Wales Stakes) and Sweet Chime (Victoria Oaks, Caulfield 1000 Guineas, Australian Oaks), while Nyamba's descendants included Belle Tetue (G3

AJC Gimcrack Stakes), Magic Of Money (G1 AJC Galaxy), Prince Frolic (G2 Castlemaine Handicap, G2 Tulloch Stakes, G2 Phar Lap Stakes) and Sormani (G2 Black Opal Stakes).

POMPADOUR (1918 br f Bayardo – Popinjay by St. Frusquin)

A full sister to Good and Gay, out of the St. Frusquin mare Popinjay, was thus another bred on similar lines to Gainsborough. Pompadour was equally good on the racetrack as her full sister and her home reputation must have preceded her onto the racecourse for she made a winning debut in the valuable Imperial Produce Stakes at Kempton in October, starting at odds of 2-5, in a field of four. Just six days later she started favourite for the Bretby Stakes at Newmarket, beating her two opponents. She could be rated about 105 for these efforts.

Pompadour began her three-year-old career with a third in the 1000 Guineas beaten just under two and half lengths by Bettina. She was then unplaced in both Oaks and Coronation Stakes at Ascot. Both were disappointing efforts as she had started third favourite in the former and 6-4 favourite in the latter. However, she did a little better in the Eclipse Stakes finishing third, albeit beaten eight lengths by the winner Craig an Eran. Her only win of the year was then secured in the Nassau Stakes at Goodwood, before ending her career by being unplaced in a handicap at Derby and finishing second in a stakes race at Newmarket. Pompadour's rating as a three-year-old would be about the same as her rating as a juvenile 105 possibly a shade higher.

Pompadour developed into a successful broodmare producing 5 winners of 9 races worth £4,414 (£154,500). The best of thus quintet was probably her third foal Cragadour, a son of the 2000 Guineas winner Craig An Eran. At two Cragadour finished a two lengths runner-up to Mr Jinks on his debut in Royal Ascot's New Stakes. Unfortunately that was to be his only race as a juvenile, as he developed splints on the inside of his near foreleg and had to be pin-fired. He must have been showing good form at home for he started an 11-10 favourite for his racecourse return the following April and justified that faith by winning the Craven Stakes. In the 2000 Guineas Cragadour started second favourite behind his old adversary Mr Jinks, and with the pair drawn on opposite sides of the course they contested a close finish with Mr Jinks prevailing by a head. The pair occupied the same position in the betting five weeks later in the Derby at Epsom, but both disappointed with Cragadour finishing seventh. It had been intended to run Cragadour at Royal Ascot, but these plans were abandoned when during that week Lord Astor sold him to Count John McCormack, a famous tenor singer of the time. Cragadour was moved to Ireland where he was a well- beaten third in the Irish Derby. He never recaptured his sparkle finishing fourth in the Duke Of York Plate, fourth in the Irish St.Leger and unplaced in the Irish

Cambridgeshire. As a four year old Cragadour was moved back to England to be trained by Dick Dawson, but his form was very moderate being unplaced in all four starts. In the autumn a half share in him was sold to Mr.B.J.Hilliard and he was due to take up stallion duties in Ireland, but became blind and was put down.

Pompadour's influence was carried forward to the present by the winning mares Pretty Swift (Swynford) and Quick Rise (by Hurry On), the former becoming the ancestress of Bright Bird (Princess of Wales Stakes), Diamante (Queen Elizabeth II Commemorative Cup), Gold Chest (Urawa Kinen – twice), Session (Victoria Oaks) and Speed King (Keio Hai Autumn Handicap).

Quick Rise's influence continued through Aragen (G2 Silver Shadow Stakes, Queensland Sires Produce Stakes), Arctic Cosmos (G1 English St. Leger), Brockette (G3 Premio Dormello), Castle Royale (G2 Sheepshead Bay Handicap), Censor (Connaught Cup), Deferential (G2 Pago Pago Stakes), Early School (unbeaten in 3 starts including Coventry Stakes), How Should I Know (Queenston Stakes), Judge Angelucci (G2 San Bernardino Handicap, G2 Longacres Mile Handicap, G1 Californian Handicap, G2 Bel Air Handicap, G1 San Antonio Handicap, G2 Mervyn Leroy Handicap), L'Alezane (Shady Well Stakes, G3 Schuylerville Stakes, G2 Alcibaides Stakes, G3 Adirondak Stakes, Selene Stakes), Lil Sister Stich (G3 Monrovia Handicap), Masake (G3 Honeymoon Handicap), Miss Snow Goose (My Dear Stakes), Peace (G2 Cinema Handicap,G3 Premier Handicap, G1 John Henry Handicap), Regent Bird (Kingarvie Stakes), Scottish Halo (G3 Laurel Futurity), Sir Shackleton (G3 West Virginia Derby, G3 Derby Trial Stakes, Richter Scale Handicap), Southern Arrow (Premio Parioli), Speirbhean (Derrinstown Stud 1000 Guineas Trail), Strike Willow (G3 Clasico Loteria Nacional, G3 Clasico General Viamonte), Tennessee Girl (G3 Fantasy Stakes, G3 Centaur Stakes), Teofilo (G1 National Stakes, G2 Futurity Stakes, G1 Dewhurst Stakes), The Cheat (Vigil Handicap), Victorian Prince (G2 Lakeside Handicap, G2 Arlington Park Handicap), War (G2 Coolmore Lexington Handicap, G1 Blue Grass Stakes) and Woolloomooloo (G3 Dance Smartly Handicap).

Another horse to claim Quick Rise as his dam was Double Remove, a horse inbred 3x3 to Lemberg and his half brother Bayardo. Although he did not win a race, Double Remove finished runner-up to subsequent Irish Derby winner Raeburn in the Column Produce Stakes at Newmarket. He was sold for 800 guineas (£28,000) at the 1936 Newmarket December Sales to stand as a stallion in Australia and proved quite successful with his daughter All Love proving to be one of the best two-year-olds of the 1940/41 season. Double Remove was also placed 4th of the list of leading broodmare sires in 1956/57.

RHODOPE (1918 b f Bayardo – Temple Bell by Marco)

A non-winning daughter of the Marco mare Temple Bell, Rhodope was purchased as a yearling for 1,750 guineas (£67,500) and became the dam of 4 winners of 9 races worth £2,840 (£99,500). Her daughter Rhonia (by Stefan The Great) won the Great Sapling Stakes at Sandown as a two-year-old, and later became the fifth dam of the 1973 Indian Derby winner Mansoor.

Another of her winners, Rose Of Athens (by Rock Flint), founded a family that produced Blue Refrain (winner at Royal Ascot for three consecutive years in the Windsor Castle Stakes, G3 Jersey Stakes, G3 Queen Anne Stakes), Creetown (G3 Diadem Stakes), En Avant (G2 South African Fillies Sprint), Galroof (G3 Doomben Classic), Lavella (twice winner of Irish Cambridgeshire), Little Indian (G3 Solario Stakes), Reunion (G3 Nell Gwyn Stakes), Taban (G3 South African Airways Sprint, G1 Computaform Sprint, G2 Concord Stakes – twice, G2 Durban Merchant's Handicap – twice, G2 Chairman's Stakes – twice, G1 Gilbey's Stakes, G1 Mercury Sprint) and Tenga Suerte (G2 Gran Premio Presidente Luiz Oliveira de Barros).

RIGHT WHEEL (1916 br f Bayardo – Wheelabout by Carbine)

Exported to France in 1921, this daughter of the Carbine mare Wheelabout boasted some famous ancestors as both her second and third dams, Wheel of Fortune and Queen Bertha, won the Epsom Oaks. Right Wheel founded a family that included Longpont, winner of the 1968 Prix de Conde, and Herodote who scored in the 1957 Prix la Rochette.

ROSA BONHEUR II (1918 b f Bayardo – Ventura by St. Amant)

Bred by the legendary Italian breeder Federico Tesio this daughter of the St. Amant mare Ventura was a three quarter sister to Rosalba Carriera (by Bayardo's half brother Lemberg), who scored in the Furstenberg-Rennen. Rosa Bonheur II herself was exported to Italy as a foal, returning to England in 1921, where she produced 2 winners of 3 races worth £380 (£13,300), one of whom, Carla Rosa, becoming the ancestress of 1988 Austria Preis winner Love Lady. Rosa Bonheur's granddaughter Miramare founded a very successful family in Poland that included Polish Oaks winners Dalila, Dora, Magenta, Maracana and Marsala; Polish 1000 Guineas heroines Doris Day, Maracana and Marwer, together with Mokosz who claimed the Polish Triple Crown of 2000 Guineas, Derby and St. Leger; plus Polish St. Leger scorer Monaco.

ROTHESAY BAY (1916 b f Bayardo – Anchora by Love Wisely)

A Lord Derby bred half sister to the influential broodmare Scapa Flow (dam of Pharos and Fairway), Rothesay Bay could manage only a fourth in a nursery from six outings as a juvenile. She did much better as a three-year-old winning four of her nine races: a handicap, a Plate, the St Georges Stakes and the Great Yorkshire Handicap (14 furlongs). When retired to the paddocks she bred 8 winners of 22 races worth £7,966 (£278,800). Her first foal Spindrift (by Chaucer) won the Derby Cup (14 furlongs) as a three-year-old, but her only real descendant of note was Don Lorenzo, winner of the 1976 Niagara Handicap (G3) in Canada, who boasted Spindrift as his fifth dam.

Her second foal Brodick Bay (by Swynford) took the Yorkshire Oaks (12 furlongs) at three and was then sold by Lord Derby to Lord Beaverbrook for 1,700 guineas (£65,500). At stud she produced Gimcrack Stakes and Eclipse Stakes winner but stud failure Miracle, and Free Handicap scorer Phaleron Bay. This pair was both bred on similar lines to the successful stallions Fairway and Pharos. Brodick Bay's daughter Flamingo Bay (by Flamingo) later produced the Hungarian 2000 Guineas scorer Flanc (by Cagliostro).

Rothesay Bay's next two foals, Glen Rosa (by Swynford) and Lamlash (by Swynford) won two and four races respectively, and the latter's daughter Canon Belle (by Canon Law founded a successful dynasty in Australia that included 1984 Melbourne Cup winner Black Knight and horses successful at Group 1 level in the antipodes such as Bold Extreme (WATC Railway Stakes), Mr Celebrity (George Main Stakes) and Prince Salieri (Castlemaine Stakes and Underwood Stakes), together with Cate's Mill (G3 Bagot Handicap) and Kiss Me Cait (Victoria Oaks),

Rothesay Bay's next three foals Pladda, Botany Bay and Bute were all winners, and were each sired by Phalaris, making them three quarter relatives to Fairway and Pharos. Pladda's second foal was the late-maturing colt Plassy. Placed fourth in the St. Leger before winning the Jockey Club Stakes, Plassy went on at four to score in the Coronation Cup, and stood as a stallion in France at Haras De Breville, where his best winners were Arcot, Nepenthe and Vandale.

California (by Colorado), Rothesay Bay's final winner, only won a minor race, but her dynasty left a lasting legacy to this day for it includes Alcimedes (twice winner of Kempton Park's Jubilee Handicap, Champion sire in Australia in 1966/67 and 1969/70 and sire of Melbourne Cup winner Silver Knight), Beat Me Daddy (G3 Tremont Stakes), Bloomerace (Swedish Derby), Cooliney Prince (G3 Leopardstown 2000 Guineas Trial), Cutting Wind (Free Handicap), Erimo Marchs (Sapporo Kinen, Mainichi Hai), Filipepi (Greenham Stakes), Golden Eye (G3 Hakodate Kinen, G3 Tokyo Shimbun Hai), Happiness (G1 Thorndon Mile), Hello Gorgeous (G2 Royal Lodge Stakes, G1 William Hill Futurity Stakes, G2 Dante Stakes) Kribensis (Champion Hurdle), Lady Oakley (G3 Distaff Handicap), Millward (G1 VRC Sires Produce Stakes), Nihon Pillow Homare (Spring Kyoto Kinen), Roman Blue (G2 Premio Dormello, G2 Premio Regina Elena), Sabana Perdida (G3 Prix du Pin, G3 Chartwell

Fillies Stakes, G2 Windsor Forest Stakes), St. Clair Ridge (G3 Futurity Stakes) Sirmione (G1 LKS Mackinnon Stakes, G1 Australian Cup), Sugihime (Japanese Oaks), Sunray (G3 New Zealand St. Leger, G3 Rotorua Challenge Plate), Superlative (G2 Flying Childers Stakes, G3 July Stakes and sire of G1 winners Superpower and Kornado), Sweet Revenge (G3 Prix Maurice de Gheest, G1 Prix de L'Abbaye, G1 King's Stand Stakes), Tempest Boy (Royal Hunt Cup), Wolvette (G2 VRC Bloodhorse Breeders Stakes), Young Ida (New Zealand Oaks) and Zip Home (G2 Theo Marks Quality Handicap).

The final daughter of Rothesay Bay to merit attention was her 1932 foal by Kantar named Islay II, who although failing to win a race was the dam of Anglesey (by Wyndham), a winner not only on the flat but also of the prestigious Imperial Cup Hurdle at Sandown Park. Anglesey's full sister Windy Isle became the granddam of Motoichi (Hanshin Daishoten, Spring Kyoto Kinen), while another daughter of Islay II, named Columbia (by Colombo) kept her name to the fore as the ancestress of Armansco (G3 Railway Stakes), Azzurrina (G2 Premio Regina Elena, G3 Premio Legnano, G1 Premio Lydia Tesio), Kris the Brave (G3 Fuji Stakes), Loyal Lady (Woodcote Stakes), Mystery Guest (G1 Gosforth Park Fillies Guineas), Nhlavini (nine time Group winner and successful in the G1 Cape Flying Championship twice), Raffingora (Temple Stakes, King George V Stakes and sire of G1 winners Patsy and Raffindale) and Vielle (G3 Lancashire Oaks, G2 Nassau Stakes).

SAMIC (1918 b f Bayardo – Philanoe by Perth)

Racing in France this daughter of the Perth mare Philanoe captured the Prix Penelope. A closely inbred mare she had Galliard 4x4x3, Galopin 5x3x5x4, Isonomy 4x4, Sterling 5x5x5 and Lord Clifden 4x5. Samic's daughter Diamond Star produced the Prix du Conseil Municipal winner Horatius, and the latter's full sister Astaria later became the granddam of Euridice, who founded a successful family that included Bubble Gum Fellow (G1 Asahi Hai Sansai Stakes, G1 Tenno Sho Autumn, G2 Fuji TV Sho Spring, G1 Naruo Kinen, G2 Mainichi Okan and successful sire), Intimiste (G1 Criterium de Saint-Cloud, G2 Prix Noailles), Love And Bubbles (G3 Prix Chloe), Manic Sunday (G2 Yonsai Himba Tokubetsu), Perfect Cat (G3 William Donald Schaefer Handicap), Prodice (G1 Prix Saint-Alary), Sangue (G3 Prix de Psyche, G2 Yerba Buena Handicap, G1 Vanity Handicap, G2 Beverly Hills Handicap, G1 Yellow Ribbon Stakes, G2 Santa Maria Handicap, G2 Ramona Handicap, G1 Matriarch Stakes, G3 Golden Harvest Handicap, G3 Chula Vista Handicap), Shonan Peintre (G1 Hanshin Juvenile Fillies Stakes) Smokin Beau (Portland Handicap), That's The Plenty (G3 Radio Tampa Hai Nasai Stakes, G1 Kikuka Sho), Tokio Perfect (G3 Crystal Cup) and Urupema (G3 Grande Premio Roger Guedon).

SCUOLA D'ATENE (1917 b f Bayardo – Spring Chicken by Gallinule)

The legendary Italian breeder, owner and trainer Federico Tesio purchased the mare Spring Chicken in foal to Bayardo, and the resultant filly was named Scuola D'Atene. She soon became a half sister to the top-class colt Scopas (by Sunstar), whose major race victories included the Gran Premio Del Jockey Club, Gran Premio Di Milano and Grosser Preis Von Baden and Scopello (by Havresac II), winner of the Gran Criterium and Criterium Nazionale as a juvenile in 1925.

While not attaining the heights of some of Tesio's broodmare band, Scuola D'Atene carved out a reasonable record producing Sanzio (by Papyrus), winner of the Gran Premio Di Milano and Grand International Ostend in 1932, and Simon Memmi who took one of Italy's leading races for juveniles, the Premio Tevere in 1927.

Another daughter of Scuola D'Atene, namely Scuola Genovese (by Galloper Light) became the dam Simone Da Bologna (by Donatello II), who won the Premio Parioli (Italian 2000 Guineas) and granddam of Polish St Leger winner Turysta (by Bellini – Scuola Bolognese). Turysta went on to sire winners several Polish Classic winners, namely Dora (Polish Oaks), Epikur (Polish Derby), Erotyk (Polish Derby), Eskadra (Polish 1000 Guineas), Jagoda (Polish 1000 Guineas) and Nutria (Polish Oaks).

SHOREDITCH (1916 b f Bayardo – Jane Shore by Cupbearer)

A non-winner from just two races Shoreditch was exported to France in 1921 after being covered by Phalaris, Shoreditch was a daughter of the Cupbearer mare Jane Shore, and a half sister to Jean Gow, a mare who also wielded an influence in France as the ancestress of stallions Le Fabuleux, Norseman and Worden II. Shoreditch's descendants included Canotier (Prix Prince Palatine), London Bridge (Premio Chiusura), Rimesault (Criterium de Maisons-Laffitte) and Tour De Londres (Prix Herod, Prix Vanteaux).

SPIRIT OF BAY (1914 b f Bayardo – Cross As 2 Sticks by Mauvezin)

A daughter of the oddly named Mauvezin mare Cross As 2 Sticks, Spirit Of Bay was a three quarter sister to the 1924 Newbury Summer Cup winner Baton Rouge (by Bayardo's half brother Lemberg). Spirit of Bay failed to gain even a place from six outings as a juvenile and one as a three-year-old. Retired to the paddocks she produced 3 winners of 4 races worth £557 (£19,500). Her foal by Galloper Light, named The Ram's Wife, became the dam of Dan Bulger who dead-heated with Midstream (later Champion sire in Australia 3 times) in the 1935 Criterion Stakes to earn a rating just 9 pounds below the leading juvenile of that year Bala Hissar. Over the following two seasons he triumphed in both Cambridgeshire Handicap and Rous Memorial Stakes.

Dan Bulger's half sister Lily B founded a family that produced South African Group 1 winners Hammer Belle (G1 Allan Roberson Fillies Championship) and Signor Amigo (G1 Mercury Sprint – twice, G1 Cape Flying Championship – twice, G1 Gilbey's Stakes, G3 Rupert Ellis Brown Plate).

STARLIGHT BAY (1913 b f Bayardo – Star Of The Sea by Gallinule)

A daughter of the Gallinule mare Star Of The Sea, Starlight Bay fetched 870 guineas (£33,500) as a yearling, but was unplaced on all of her three races one as a juvenile and two as a three-year-old. As a brood-mare she bred just one minor winner of a race worth £198 (£6,950). She was eventually exported to Argentine in 1923, in foal to Abbot's Trace, where her daughter Spanish-Fly (by Silurian) became the ancestress of Morumbi, winner of Argentine's Gran Premio Major Suckow and Rapallo, who scored in Brazil's Gran Premio Ministro de Agricultura and Gran Premio Ipiranga (Brazilian 2000 Guineas).

SWEET BALM (1913 b f Bayardo – Slim Lady by St. Simon)

Sweet Balm raced as an un-named filly as a juvenile and was unplaced in both her races, the only races of her career. As she was the daughter of the St. Simon mare Slim Lady, Sweet Balm was inbred 5x3x3 to Galopin, and possessed a tight-knit pedigree also being 5x3 to the three-quarter brothers Muncaster and Kendal. Her granddam Laodamia had been a decent stayer wining the 1896 Doncaster Cup. In addition to failing to win Sweet Balm also failed to produce any winners but her daughter Curragh Balm founded a reasonably successful family of National Hunt performers that included Assessed, winner of the Arkle Perpetual Novice Chase, and Daring Run. The latter proved to be one of the leading hurdlers in the 1980's winning both Irish Champion Hurdle and Aintree Hurdle in 1981 and 1982, as well as being placed in three Cheltenham National Hunt Festivals – second in the 1980 Supreme Novices Hurdle, third in the 1981 Champion Hurdle and third in the 1984 Stayers Hurdle. Daring Run was by Deep Run, a stallion 5x6x5x6 to Bayardo's son Gay Crusader and Gainsborough. The aforementioned mare Curragh Balm was by Grey Fox II, and with Flying Fox (3x2 Galopin) as the latter's maternal grandsire, Curragh Balm was 6x5x6x4x4 to Galopin.

TUSSOCK-GRASS (1916 b f Bayardo – Bunch Grass by Sainfoin)

A 1,100 guineas (£42,500) yearling purchase, Tussock-Grass earned a second and third placing from three races as a Juvenile and a win and a third on her two outings as a three-year-old. Tussock-Grass was a daughter of the Sainfoin mare Bunch Grass. Her three quarter sister Meadow Grass (by Bayardo's half brother Lemberg) later became the granddam of the prolific Australian winner and successful sire Ajax, while Bunch Grass's own dam Charm scored in the 1891 Yorkshire Oaks.

Tussock-Grass's bred just one winner of a single race worth £461 (£16,000), this being her first foal and 1,600 guineas (£61,500) yearling purchase Tuscar Rock, but that mare would keep the family name to the fore. Tuscar Rock's descendants included Be Cautious (St. Hugh Fillies Stakes, Betsy Ross Stakes, Test Stakes, Black Helen Handicap), Black Rock (Churchill Stakes), Fleeting Spirit (G3 Molecomb Stakes, G2 Flying Childers Stakes, G2 Temple Stakes), Greenore (Great Surrey Foal Plate, Nunthorpe Stakes, Stewards Cup Handicap, Ayr Gold Cup Handicap), Hombre Rapido (G3 Los Angeles Handicap), Husson (G1 Gran Premio Raul Y Raul Chevalier, G1 Gran Premio Gran Criterium, G1 Gran Premio Internacional de Las Americas, G2 Clasico Benito Villaneuva), My Corncrake (Sara Open Sprint Championship), Rockstone (Criterium Nazionale, Premio Emilio Turati, Premio Chiusura), Super Optimista (G2 Clasico General Pueyrredon), The Bean Sidhe (G3 1000 Guineas Trial), Venus Observed (Jubilee Handicap) and Whisky (Czech 1000 Guineas, Czech Oaks, runner-up Czech Derby).

Tussock-Grass was eventually exported to France in 1924, in foal to Sunstar

Other leading progeny

Apart from his progeny that stood as stallions or became broodmares the following two horses are also worthy of mention:-

BANTRY (1917) b c out of Ulster Queen (Cicero).

Bantry owes his inclusion not to the good races he won but to his toughness and resolution. He did not race as a juvenile but then completed five seasons running a total of forty-nine times and winning on ten occasions. He raced in handicaps and sellers and was twice sold out of selling races. Rather sadly as each year passed he went into steady decline and the company he kept correspondingly reduced in quality. He failed to win a race of any sort in his last two racing seasons. At his best he would have earned a rating of about 90.

PALOMIDES (1917) b c out of Paloma (Cyllene)

Palomides was far from being the best of Bayardo's progeny. However, he was amongst the best in providing entertainment and durability. He ran from the age of two until ten – nine seasons – competed in a total of eighty-four races winning fifteen and he finished his racing career as an entire. In addition he was placed many more times and because of this he never enjoyed much relief from the handicapper.

He began his career by racing four times both as a juvenile and as a three-year-old but without success. However, in the next five seasons he raced sixty-six times winning fourteen. He raced in handicaps for most of his career but during the last four or five years he ran in more selling races and exclusively in those races during the last two years. He changed hands on a few occasions but always came back to run up to his best. At his peak he could have been rated about 105 but towards the end of his career he would have been some way below that figure.

Sources

The Sporting Life
The Sporting Chronicle
The Sportsman
The Times
The Daily Mirror
The Illustrated Sporting and Dramatic News
The Diamond Racing Journal
Timeform 1948-2009
Best horses 1942-1947
Raceform 1936 onwards
The Racing Calendar 1900-1932
The Bloodstock Breeders Review 1912-1980
The British Racehorse 1949-1981
Ruffs Guide to the Turf 1900-1986
M'Call's Racing Chronicle 1908-1910
The American Racing Manual 1919-2009

Bibliography

Allison William	– Memories of Men and Horses
Bland Ernest Ed.	– Flat Racing Since 1900
Bowen Edward	– Man o' War
Boyd Eva Jolene	– Native Dancer
Browne T H	– History of the English Turf
Burch Preston M	– Training Thoroughbred Horses
Church Michael	– Eclipse
Church Michael	– Classic Pedigrees
Church Michael	– Champion Sires
Church Michael	– The Derby Stakes
Churchill Jennifer, Reichard Andrew & Rogers Byron	– Great Thoroughbred Stallions of the World
Cooper Page & Treat Roger	– Man o' War
Crofton Ian	– History without the Boring Bits
Darling Sam	– Sam Darling's Reminiscences
Donoghue Steve	– Just My Story
Drape Joe Ed.	– To the Swift
Fletcher J S	– The History of the St Leger Stakes
Felstead S Theodore	– Racing Romance
Fitzgeorge-Parker Tim	– Training the Racehorse
Graham Clive	– Hyperion
Galtrey Sidney	– Memoirs of a Racing Journalist
Harewood the Earl of & Others	– Flat Racing
Harrod-Eagles Cynthia	– The Dream Kingdom
Hewitt Abram	– Sire Lines
Hislop John	– The Brigadier
Hislop John	– Of Horses and Races
Hislop John	– Racing Reflections
Lambton George	– Men and Horses I Have Known
Logan Guy	– The Classic Races of the Turf
Leicester Sir Charles	– Bloodstock Breeding
Lyle R C	– The Aga Khan's Horses
Maloney Alison	– Life After Victoria
Marsh Richard	– A Trainer to Two Kings
Mathieu Paul	– The Masters of Manton
Morris Tony	– Thoroughbred Stallions
Mortimer Roger	– The History of the Derby Stakes
Mortimer Roger	– Twenty Great Horses
Mortimer Roger & Willett Peter	– Great Racehorses of the World

312

Mortimer Roger & Willett Peter	– More Great Racehorses of the World
Mortimer Roger, Onslow Richard, & Willett Peter	– Biographical Encyclopaedia of Flat Racing
Morton Charles	– My Sixty Years of the Turf
Nack William	– Secretariat
O'Gorman Bill	– Racing Horses
Onslow Richard	– The Heath and the Turf
Orchard Vincent	– The Derby Stakes
Petrie Charles	– Scenes of Edwardian Life
Porter John	– John Porter of Kingsclere
Plumptree George	– The Fast Set
Shoop Robert	– Down to the Wire
Tanner Michael & Cranham Gerry	– Great Jockeys of the Flat
Tyrrel John	– Running Racing
Randall John & Morris Tony	– A Century of Champions
Richardson Charles Sir	– The English Turf
Robertson William	– The History of Thoroughbred Racing in America
Seth-Smith Michael & Mortimer Roger	– Derby 200
Stewart Lt. Col PD	– Training the Racehorse
Thompson Laura	– Newmarket
Ulbrich Richard	– The Great Stallion Book
Vamplew Wray	– The Turf
Watson Alfred	– The Racing World and It's Inhabitants
Watson Alfred	– The Turf
Watson Alfred	– Galicia
Welcome John	– Neck or Nothing
Willett Peter	– An Introduction to the Thoroughbred

Index

Bayardo was the famous steed
of Rinaldo the Brave, who was
one of Charlemagne's Paladins &
cousin to Orlando. He was
originally found by Malagigi,
the wizard, in a cave guarded
by a dragon which the wizard
slew & handed him over to
Amadis de Gaul. Bayardo's
leap near Sleaford consists
of 3 stones 30 yards apart. It is
said that Rinaldo was riding
on his favourite steed when the
demon of the place sprang up
behind him; but the animal
in terror took three tremendous